EX LIBRIS
CLAUDE RAINS

SCREEN CLASSICS

Screen Classics is a series of critical biographies, film histories, and analytical studies focusing on neglected filmmakers and important screen artists and subjects, from the era of silent cinema to the golden age of Hollywood to the international generation of today. Books in the Screen Classics series are intended for scholars and general readers alike. The contributing authors are established figures in their respective fields. This series also serves the purpose of advancing scholarship on film personalities and themes with ties to Kentucky.

Series Editor
Patrick McGilligan

Claude Rains

AN ACTOR'S VOICE

DAVID J. SKAL
with **JESSICA RAINS**

THE UNIVERSITY PRESS OF KENTUCKY

Frontmatter illustrations
p. i: Claude Rains's personal bookplate.
p. xii: "Like a lion." Pacific Palisades, California, 1963 (courtesy of Roddy McDowall).

Scholarly publisher for the Commonwealth, serving Bellarmine University, Berea College, Centre College of Kentucky, Eastern Kentucky University, The Filson Historical Society, Georgetown College, Kentucky Historical Society, Kentucky State University, Morehead State University, Murray State University, Northern Kentucky University, Transylvania University, University of Kentucky, University of Louisville, and Western Kentucky University.

Editorial and Sales Offices: The University Press of Kentucky
663 South Limestone Street, Lexington, Kentucky 40508-4008
www.kentuckypress.com

Unless otherwise noted, photos courtesy Jessica Rains.

14 13 12 11 10   5 4 3 2 1

The Library of Congress has cataloged the hardcover edition as follows:

Skal, David J.
  Claude Rains : an actor's voice / David J. Skal with Jessica Rains.
     p. cm. — (Screen classics)
  Includes bibliographical references and index.
  ISBN 978-0-8131-2432-2 (hardcover : alk. paper)
1. Rains, Claude, 1889–1967. 2. Actors—United States—Biography. I. Rains, Jessica. II. Title.
  PN2287.R225S53 2008
  791.4302'8092—dc22
  [B]   2008026317
  ISBN 978-0-8131-9261-1 (pbk. : alk. paper)

This book is printed on acid-free recycled paper meeting the requirements of the American National Standard for Permanence in Paper for Printed Library Materials.

Manufactured in the United States of America.

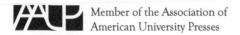
Member of the Association of
American University Presses

For Claude, of course

Contents

Acknowledgments

GRATEFUL ACKNOWLEDGMENT IS DUE to the dozens of institutions and individuals who helped make the idea for this book a reality.

Claude Rains: An Actor's Voice would not exist without the support and assistance of Jessica Rains, who entrusted me with the responsibility of giving narrative shape to her father's life, in the process making available to me all of Rains's surviving papers and visual documents and her own extraordinary and vivid memories. An equal debt is owed to the late Jonathan Root, whose preliminary notes and audiotaped conversations with Rains during the 1960s provided a practical basis for this book.

Thanks to the University of Victoria, Department of Germanic and Slavic Studies, and the Lansdowne Visiting Scholar Program for a residency that made possible this project's completion. In particular, I am indebted to department chair Peter Gölz, acting chair Sehry Yekelchyk, and Dean of Humanities Andrew Rippin. Additional thanks in Victoria are owed to Gregory Burt, Paul and Dagmar Henry, Dave O'Brien, Linda Ulrich, Robert Beaupre, Graydon Guest, Mike Belknap, and the Journey-Men: Steve, John, Tom, Mike, Chris, and Chris.

At the University Press of Kentucky, I owe much to Leila Salisbury, Rick McCormick, and Lin Wirkus; thanks also to Donna Bouvier for her intelligent and perceptive copyediting (not to mention her special interest in all things Rainsian). I am equally grateful to Tom Jones for his uncommonly eagle-eyed proofreading. And what can I say about Jen Huppert's stunning cover design and Richard Farkas's impeccable interior layouts and typography? "Thank you" somehow doesn't seem quite enough. I am grateful to my agent, Christopher Schelling, for pairing me with the whole Kentucky team.

Thanks also to those individuals and institutions where I conducted re-

Acknowledgments

search, including the Howard Gotlieb Archival Research Center at Boston University (special thanks to J. C. Johnson); the Margaret Herrick Library of the Academy of Motion Picture Arts and Sciences (special thanks to Stacey Behlmer); the Warner Bros. Collection at the University of Southern California as well as USC's Film and Television Library (special thanks to Ned Comstock); the Billy Rose Theatre Collection at the New York Library for the Performing Arts at Lincoln Center (especially Leslie Ferrari); the Free Library of Philadelphia Theatre Collection (special thanks to Geraldine Duclow); the MacPherson Library, University of Victoria; the Los Angeles Public Library; the Beverly Hills Public Library; the Pasadena Public Library; the Glendale Public Library; the Connecticut State Library; the San Diego Public Library; and the Scottish Regiment, London.

Individuals who provided interviews, information, advice, research leads, photographs, general assistance, friendship, hospitality, and support include Rudy Behlmer, Jay Blotcher, Ronald V. Borst, Ray Bradbury, Kevin Brownlow (for proofreading above and beyond the call of duty), Dr. Sam Carvajal, Keith Clark, Julius Epstein, Susanna Foster, Kevin Gerlock and Sandra Skal-Gerlock, the late Sir John Gielgud, Dr. Julia Gomez, Jack Greene, Aljean Harmetz, Byron Hite, George Hoffman, Clay Hornik, Michael Isador, Scott MacQueen, Bob Madison, the late Roddy McDowall (for photographs as well as an interview), Ronald Neame, Lori Nelson, Terry Nelson, Ted Newsome, Terry Pace, Linda Robinson, Rich Scrivani, the late Vincent Sherman, Joyce Stock and David Cheng, Donna Tattle (major thanks for her patient and generous photographic assistance), Ara Touniyans, the late Richard Valley, Tom Weaver, and JoAnna Wiokowski.

The ebullient original cast recording of *The Drowsy Chaperone* got me through the darkest drudgery of final fact-checking and indexing (Claude Rains himself certainly understood the sustaining and restorative energies of live theatre). Our extended family of feline companions—Whitefoot, Margaret, Louis, and Momcat—offered their constant, calming reassurance, even while draping themselves all over the desk, monitor, and manuscript.

Finally, heartfelt thanks forever to Robert Postawko, whose contributions and support to this and many other projects can never be fully repaid or enumerated.

CLAUDE RAINS

Introduction

RODDY MCDOWALL WAS IN AWE OF Claude Rains. Both were English actors transplanted to Hollywood, but somehow they had never met, socially or professionally. McDowall had started his American career as a juvenile performer for MGM, while Rains worked primarily for Warner Bros., and their paths had simply never crossed. McDowall was one of thousands of British children evacuated to America in 1940 during the Blitz. Rains had already been in the States for more than a decade, but at the height of World War II he had returned to London via military transport to give one of his signature screen roles in Shaw's *Caesar and Cleopatra.* Their lives, careers, and screen personae couldn't have been more different, though they did have a few things in common. One was an elegant former juvenile star; the other, an elegant and mature character actor, one of the most celebrated in the world, who had begun his own career as a juvenile stage manager and performer. One was gay, the other straight—having lived through six marriages by the early 1960s when they finally met.

Offscreen, McDowall had become a noted photographer of Hollywood personalities, and he was especially eager for a portrait sitting with the man who had first electrified the world over thirty years earlier with his appearance (or disappearance) as *The Invisible Man* and who had gone on to act with distinction in a constellation of major films, including *Anthony Adverse, Mr. Smith Goes to Washington, Casablanca, Now, Voyager, Mr. Skeffington, Notorious, Lawrence of Arabia,* and dozens of others.

If it was a classic film, there was a good chance Claude Rains had something to do with it.

"He was perfect," said McDowall. "There's this very small group of actors who seemingly never made a mistake: Walter Huston, Spencer

Tracy, Henry Fonda, and Claude Rains. And if the material was minor they elevated it with incredibly shrewd invention. And if the material was major they just illuminated the author's intent right to the boundaries."

McDowall and Rains met at the home of their mutual friend, actor Richard Haydn. Haydn, an accomplished comedian, kept up a steady stream of amusing patter during the shoot. "It isn't really difficult to photograph anybody on first encounter if you are engaged in conversation," McDowall said. "To photograph Claude was like a dream come true. He was like a little pixie. He was laughing, which seldom happens in photographs. It was one of the great faces ever in the movies. It was also the most volatile face. I mean, the lines were so terrific, just terrific. It was like Mount Rushmore."

About six months after their photo session, McDowall answered his doorbell in New York City. "And there was Claude Rains standing there. I said, come in, sit down, stay. Stay a decade if you want!" McDowall laughed. Rains had the photos McDowall had taken. Could he have some copies made? "I was thrilled. But, I asked, why didn't you just call me up? He said he wanted to ask me this favor in person. It was so sweet. And we sat for a couple of hours and talked. I remember an essence about him. He was then a very sad man. We talked about his wife, who had just died. And I think the photos reveal a lot of his wit and melancholia and also this tremendous fierceness, like a lion, that Rains had. Everything else seemed to float on top of it. It was always capped. But you knew that if you poked him he could wipe you off the face of the earth."

Four decades earlier, Rains had another fervent acolyte in the person of John Gielgud, who was then a gangly, insecure acting student at the Royal Academy of Dramatic Art, where Rains was his "primary and most inspiring" instructor. Both men's careers would gravitate from stage to screen. "Any actor who is very well trained in straight theatre can adapt very quickly to the movies if they have directors who are sympathetic," said Gielgud. "I was very self-conscious in all my early films and very ashamed of them. But as Claude was a very showy actor, it must have been quite difficult for him to temper it down to exactly the right tempo. But he obviously knew exactly how to do it and learned it more and more as he went on. He was a self-made man like Richard Burton and Emlyn Williams who absolutely clawed his way into success by sheer willpower."

Like many people who knew and worked with Rains, Gielgud considered the older man something of an enigma. "I never had a meal with him or went to any house where he lived or met him outside the theatre," he said. But in 1950, when Rains made a triumphant return to Broadway in *Darkness at Noon*, Gielgud caught up with him after a performance. "I came across him all of a sudden one night, and he said he was very pleased to see me, and he said, 'I'm writing my biography. I'm trying to write it and I'm being very hard on myself.' So I think he had a very modest side to him as well as being enormously ambitious."

Nothing of Rains's first attempt at a memoir has survived, except that he intended to call it *Lost and Found*, "the significance being," he said, "that I was lost for many years. I was a wretched little boy, you know, with no education, and for the most part, still am." He took another hopeless stab at a biography with his final wife, an unprofessional writer. But not long before his death, he began collaborating on another biographical project with San Francisco journalist Jonathan Root. Together they produced dozens of hours of audiotaped reminiscences. But Root died suddenly of a heart attack before the project could be realized, and Rains himself died soon after. The untranscribed tapes and fragmentary notes for the book were eventually purchased by the Rains estate.

Root faced many conundrums in dealing with Rains. As Gielgud noted, there was a strange combination of self-effacement and grandiosity about him. Although women threw themselves at him, he was nevertheless self-conscious about his height (five foot six), wore elevator shoes, and developed a way of brushing his hair to add an inch or so to his stature. It's not surprising he played Napoleon four times. Despite his lifelong craving for a stable family life, he was chronically unable to sustain most of his many marriages. He fought off inner demons, which he never acknowledged, with ever-increasing amounts of alcohol, seriously compromising his health. But to the outside world he was the picture of controlled elegance and savoir faire. As J. B. Priestley noted, "I can imagine an American filmgoer, seeing Claude Rains in one of his later Hollywood roles, as an autocrat or smooth villain, feeling certain that here was a man who must have left an aristocratic landed family, somewhere in England, to amuse himself making films." That filmgoer would be startled to learn of Rains's almost Dickensian origins "on the wrong side of the river Thames," his early, debilitating speech impediments, and his brief childhood career as a petty thief. And rather than being amused by his film work, Rains, one of the greatest character actors Hollywood ever produced, could not bear to watch his own screen performances. He had begun making movies out of financial necessity during the Depression, but his real passion was always the stage, and one senses a gnawing inner emptiness after he abandoned the theatre. Until the end of his life, his most vivid memories revolved around the world of live performance, its heady energies, and its bigger-than-life personalities.

In *A Biographical Dictionary of Film* historian and critic David Thomson comments on the many contradictions that fueled Rains's life and career, noting, "It is amazing that this mix of decorum and wildness has not yet inspired a biography."

Finally, it has. Based primarily on his own recorded memories, combined with extensive new research and the recollections of his only child, the extraordinary life story of Claude Rains, in all its decorum and wildness, is presented here for the first time.

There was more to the Invisible Man than ever met the eye.

1

Bloody Idiots Who Couldn't Learn Their Lines

HIS PARENTS COULD NOT AGREE on what to call him. His father, Frederick, wanted a solid English name—William or Harry. And for that matter, what was wrong with Frederick? His mother, Emily, was entranced by the French name Claude, which she had discovered in a romantic novel. It sounded like "cloud," something elevated and dreamy. Something far away from the grim circumstances of their lives in working-class Clapham, south of the Thames. It wasn't that she expected her child to soar above the ordinary. She just wanted him to live. Of the ten children she had delivered in the same brass bed, seven had died at birth or shortly thereafter. In London during the 1890s, children of the poorest classes stood a twenty percent chance of dying before their first birthday. The public water supply was notoriously unsanitary, and infantile diarrhea, measles, and diphtheria were rife.

Claude rhymed with Maude, the name of one of Emily's children who, with her sister Henrietta, had survived. Maude's name, perhaps, was lucky. Emily was completely unaware that the literal meaning of the name Claude was "lame" or "limping." She just liked the sound. And it gave her hope.

They finally reached a compromise. Frederick would call the boy William, while his mother would call him Claude.

In the end, they both called him Willie.

William Claude Rains was born November 10, 1889, the first son of Frederick and Emily Eliza Cox Rains. Frederick Rains was very short, a trait he passed on to his son. He was also arrogant, unreliable, pompous, clever, versatile, vain, and as far as Willie was concerned, sadistically cruel. Frederick Rains had descended from a family of substance in the village of Rainham, in Kent, but had somehow never ascended to respectable employment. He was, in fact, constantly in transition between one temporary occupation and another, propelled by opportunity and necessity. He had been a music hall composer and performer, an organ and piano maker, an insurance agent, and, after studying the subject for a week in the public library, a foreman in a boiler factory. He was discharged from the latter position (as he was from most) for being more knowledgeable than the people who employed him—or so he always maintained. He was also active as a performer in the early British film industry. His *New York Times* obituary in 1945 claimed, quite impossibly, that he had appeared in over eight hundred silent films. It was either a typographical error or grandiosity on an egregious scale.

In any event, the child who would become one of the most revered character actors in the history of motion pictures showed no interest in the burgeoning art form when it was being introduced in London at the turn of the century, quite possibly because of his animosity toward his father and anything he might be involved with. Until Claude Rains actually acted in his first film he claimed, implausibly, that he had never even seen one.

The boy's memories of his father would always be colored by the man's extremes. He could be the expansive host, playing the piano after dinner in a lordly way, with grand flourishes, bellowing songs like one that ended, " . . . and things seem all awry / Some get all and some get naught / Egad, I wonder why." An occasional vaudevillian, Frederick performed his own songs in music halls and, for Christmas pantomimes, cross-dressed as a grand dame, an annual role he played with relish.

Frederick could also be a merciless dispenser of punishment, lashing his son with a leather strap in the garden tool shed while his mother's face floated, like some disembodied mask, in the flat's rear window. More than a half century later, Rains would remember his mother crying, "Oh, Fred, don't hurt him, Fred, please don't hurt him."

But Fred went on hurting him. Rains's earliest memory of corporal punishment was when he was four or five. His mother had presented him with an extravagantly expensive Lord Fauntleroy–style velvet suit, but, in his excitement over the gift and his mother's overflowing delight at the sight of her boy wearing the outfit, he soiled it.

Frederick came home to find the trousers he had paid for drying on the clothesline.

"What's that?" he demanded.

"Willie had an accident," explained his mother.

"Oh, he did, did he?" thundered Frederick, unbuckling his belt.

"I may have been a difficult little boy," Rains would say decades later, perhaps searching for a reason for the harsh treatment. "Those beatings may have been good for me." He was always stoic under his father's thrashings; he never made a sound. He also never trusted his father or bonded with him in any way.

The family moved often, as Frederick's fortunes flowed and ebbed. One of Rains's more pleasant childhood memories was his riding on the tailgate of yet another horse-drawn moving wagon. Wherever the Rains family lived, whether in one of Clapham's neat brick row houses with their window boxes or amid the lesser architecture of nearby Brixton, redeemed by the golden curbside border of laburnum trees, they never sacrificed their emblems of respectability—a scrubbed doorstep, polished brass hardware on the front door, and always a paper fan in the grate when a fire was not burning.

Emily sometimes carried the façade of respectability to the brink of embarrassment. Sunday dinner with a joint of lamb or beef was a ritual as often as it was economically possible, and there were always guests—neighbors or Frederick's occupational associates. After dessert, when Emily had cleared the table, she never failed to inquire, daintily, "Would anybody like a little cheese?" while the family held its collective breath—because there wasn't any cheese, ever. They couldn't afford it. Mrs. Rains never knew whether her guests simply didn't like cheese, or whether they were aware of her little deception, but tactful enough not to call her bluff. In any event, Claude remembered no one ever asking for cheese.

Emily had no use for hollow pride, however, and she did not hesitate to take in boarders when Frederick failed in his latest venture. These nameless lodgers, a stream of faceless strangers in the dining room, brought more shame to the boy than did the lack of money in the family budget.

Claude Rains's first appearance on the stage came in 1898, soon after the outbreak of the Boer War in South Africa and attendant jingoism at home. He and his playmates, all of them age ten or less, were tramping up and down Brixton Road, brandishing wooden swords and wearing helmets fashioned from newspapers. His sister Henrietta trailed behind, decked out in a white cap and Red Cross armband. The clamor attracted the attention of a local minstrel who was then plying his trade on the stage of a nearby music hall, singing patriotic songs. Seeing opportunity, he traversed the neighborhood for parental permission, then shepherded his little troop off to the music hall as a backdrop for his act. Though functioning as little more than a stage prop, Rains never forgot the exquisite thrill of that first applause.

He had absolutely no conception of the legitimate theatre then; his only exposure to live performance had been the music hall. Nobody, however astute, would ever have spotted in this ungainly child the makings of an actor. For one thing, he had considerable difficulty with ordinary vocal expression. He seldom talked at all at home, instead expressing himself with grunts and gestures that only further irritated his father. One particularly idiotic doctor suggested that they simply starve him until he would finally have to ask for food. When he did manage to form words, he sounded like no one else in the family, his words emerging in a whining Cockney dialect that the boy seemed to have plucked from the streets. (His mother had only a slight working-class accent, and his father, given his privileged upbringing, had a more upper-class cast to his voice.) The boy's speech was further marred by r's that sounded like w's; Emily had encouraged a lazy tongue through her reinforcement of her beloved son's baby-talk mannerisms, which she found endearingly "pwetty." His classmates at the Camberwell Green School thought otherwise. One boy in particular began taunting him publicly as "Willie Wains." Rains lay in futile wait for his tormentor for days on end, loudly declaring he would thrash him "as sure as God made little apples." He only succeeded in becoming known for a long time thereafter as "Little Apples."

For all his checkered career, Frederick Rains still enjoyed a certain luster back in Kent, and he turned to his relatives there when his younger daughter, Henrietta, suffered a prolonged illness. The whole family accompanied the little girl to the rural home of Frederick's cousins, a large and agreeable family that lived in a picturesque cottage along a rustic lane and owned a cherry orchard. When the Rainses returned to London that night, Willie was so envious of his sister's escape to a pastoral nirvana that he vowed to somehow free himself from what he saw as his various forms of bondage, the most onerous being his incarceration at the Camberwell Green School.

He achieved his goal the very next morning, by bribing a classmate to report him ill. The bribe consisted of one of his mother's jam tarts, and, for the next month, he exchanged similarly prized portions of his lunch to maintain a life of truancy.

He might eventually have gone back to school had not the proprietor of a W. H. Smith store near the school offered him a job as a news vendor. He accepted, and not long after began to notice a handsome boy about his own age, wearing an Eton suit and a kind of mortarboard cap, walking by the store two mornings a week. Rains, with an instinct for elegance, or simply a hunger for personal advancement, coveted that suit. One morning he stopped the boy and, engaging him in conversation, received a full explanation. The boy was a member of the choir at the fashionable Church of the Immaculate Conception in Mayfair, and the clothes came with the job.

When the boy offered to take Rains along for an audition, he immediately resigned his news vending job, and the two of them walked the four miles across town to choir practice. The church was on Farm Street, just around the corner from Berkeley Square, and it was familiarly referred to as the Farm Street Church. It was the pastorate of the Reverend Father Bernard Vaughan, an eminent Catholic humanitarian and confidante of London's West End theatre demimonde.

Rains was presented to Alfred Bellew, the choirmaster, and was about to demonstrate his vocal prowess—like many people with speech impediments, he had fewer problems singing than talking—when the door opened and Father Vaughan swept in. Like many successful men of limited height, the dynamic little priest carried himself with a majestic air that suggested greater physical stature. He spied Rains nervously preparing himself to sing and he walked over, patting him approvingly on the head.

"Well, young man," he said, "why do you want to be a choir boy?"

Rains, who had seldom been in a church of any kind and had no comprehension of Catholicism, was scarcely able to muster a reply. But he did know that coveting a costume was no way to impress such a formidable authority figure, so he blurted out a subsidiary truth, Cockney accent, misshapen *r*'s, and all:

"Sir, when I sing or recite well at home or in school, I am often given sweets."

Father Vaughan winced at the diction, laughed at the candor, patted the boy once more on the head, and left.

Bellew ran Rains up and down a simple scale or two, found his thin soprano voice up to Farm Street's standards, assigned him a place in the front row, and issued the coveted Etonian suit. Willie learned the hymns and chants by rote and was immensely moved by the solemn pageantry of the mass. The future seemed all spiritual glitter and wonder.

Once home, he confided his success to his mother, who was skeptical. But the suit was real, the church was known to her, and, after she had attended mass once to confirm her son's story, she shared his pride. Of course, he didn't tell her that he was also an outrageous truant. It wasn't long, however, until she found out.

One morning the boy was loitering around his former place of employment, watching bales of hay being unloaded from a wagon, when his father, making his rounds on a bicycle to collect insurance premiums, loomed over one of the bales.

"Why aren't you in school?" he roared.

"Well, sir," mumbled Willie, "I, uh, er, can't get past the hay bales."

"You'll get past!" stormed Frederick, dismounting his bicycle and vaulting the hay bale. Seizing his son by the ear, he tugged him in this fashion most of the way to the school, where he thrust the boy into the classroom like a Roman propelling a Christian to the lions.

"Oh," said the teacher solicitously. "Is Willie better?"

Thus made aware of Willie's truancy, Frederick beat him unmercifully and told all the policemen in the neighborhood of his son's shocking transgression, so that the remainder of the term was a kind of nightmare. No matter which alley or other obscure thoroughfare Willie sought for

10

an unmolested route to school, a bobby was certain to appear, wag his finger, and mournfully declare, "So *you're* the little boy who doesn't go to school."

Rains managed to hold on to his choir position, though not during school hours. One day in August 1900, Bellew, the choirmaster, instructed his charges to bring their lunches to the next practice session. "We're going to the Haymarket," he explained.

To Rains, this implied some kind of day in the country. Ever since that frustrating excursion to Kent and the cherry orchard, he had longed for the green outdoors. But when the great day came, he found himself with his fellow choirboys dancing around a papier-mâché fountain on the stage of the Haymarket Theatre. He was, at least, in rather illustrious company. The play he found himself in was the original production of Paul Kester's *Sweet Nell of Old Drury*, starring Fred Terry, brother of the legendary actress Ellen Terry, and Terry's wife, Julia Neilsen, who played the title role of Nell Gwyn.

For his bewildering efforts on the Haymarket stage, Rains was paid the magnificent sum of ten shillings, a fortune beyond his grasp, but not beyond the need-driven calculations of his parents, whose financial distress was known by this time to Bellew. Frequently called upon to provide children for various theatrical productions, Bellew arranged for Rains to work as an extra in Herbert Beerbohm Tree's production of *Herod*, which occupied the boy for seventy-eight performances at the end of 1900 and the beginning of 1901. Bellew also immediately thought of Willie when he was asked if he knew of a reliable, energetic youngster to work as a call boy at the Duke of York's Theatre. A call boy was responsible for reminding actors of the time remaining before curtain, and for calling places. Few boys had impressed Bellew as much as Rains, whose application toward learning the Catholic liturgy and its music had been exceptional. While Bellew may have had misgivings about suggesting that Willie give up school, he realized that the boy's prospects were likely far brighter in the theatre then as a taunted student adrift in an indifferent educational system.

Accordingly, Bellew approached Rains's parents in the spring of 1902 and proposed that Willie, then twelve years old, carve out a career for himself in the theatre. The proposal came during one of Frederick's downturns in financial fortune, and he and Emily agreed. They wanted their son to be educated, but perhaps he could educate himself. They simply needed the money.

Located in St. Martin's Lane, the Duke of York's Theatre was a handsome, three-tiered playhouse constructed only ten years earlier as the Trafalgar Square Theatre; the name was changed in 1895. The current lessee was the renowned impresario Charles Frohman, who also produced plays on the Continent and in America. The first play to which young Rains provided his services was most likely *The Gay Lord Quex* by Arthur Wing Pinero, followed by a one-night engagement of Henri Meilhac and Ludovic Halevy's *Frou Frou*, which was squeezing out an extra performance following a sold-out run at the Garrick. Among the cast Rains would have encountered was Sarah Bernhardt, whom he had seen the previous year in *Cyrano de Bergerac* at Her Majesty's. He didn't recall who had taken him (it was probably Bellew), but Rains later remembered that the production was performed entirely in French. *Cyrano* had paired France's greatest tragedienne with its greatest comedian, Constant-Benoit Coquelin. "I never understood a word Coquelin said," Rains recalled, "but he made me weep." He remembered almost nothing of Bernhardt's performance except her regal presence as Roxanne, but he never forgot an anecdote related to him at the time, likely apocryphal, that the only English word the great Coquelin knew was "lavatory." Another performance that impressed the boy was that of Sir Henry Irving (recently honored by becoming the first actor to be knighted) in *A Story of Waterloo*. Irving's death scene was so realistic that Willie was momentarily sure he had seen the actor actually die.

The hours of Rains's employment were long, from noon until nearly midnight, and the pay was ten shillings a week. Seven shillings went to help support the family, and three shillings were allotted to the boy for his expenses, which were sixpence a day. The bus fare, aboard a Balls Brothers tram drawn by four horses, was onepence each way. This left him fourpence for supper, and for this amount he could buy tea and bread and butter, plus a haddock or a pair of kippers. It wasn't enough for a growing boy, and, when midnight came, Willie was often so hungry he would spend his bus fare for additional food and walk the four miles home.

By the time Rains was on his third play at the Duke of York's, *For Love of Prim*, by Eden Phillpotts, he had attained professional competence. This, coupled with the knowledge that he was helping support his family, gave him unusual self-esteem for his age. It didn't, however, help with his gnawing nighttime hunger. He would have been cold as well, had not Marie Tempest, a brilliant comedienne of the time, taken pity on his threadbare garments and given him a coat with a velvet collar and cuffs.

His next play was *The Admirable Crichton*, J. M. Barrie's genial poke at Britain's hothouse aristocracy. The star was H. B. Irving, eldest son of Sir Henry Irving. The younger Irving's role involved a number of quick costume changes, requiring his dresser to attend him in the wings rather than in his dressing room. During one performance, Rains passed Irving's cubicle and noticed that the door was ajar. Just beyond the door, a pair of expensive trousers hung on a peg. It was late in the evening, and the boy was hungry. Without even pausing to contemplate his action, he slipped into the room, dipped his hand into Irving's trouser pocket, and extracted a half-crown. It was more than a day's pay. He dined that night on several apples, which he munched happily on the bus, arriving home fairly gorged.

The next night, his foraging in Irving's pocket yielded two shillings and, the following night, a single shilling, which, thanks to the abundance of his earlier thefts, he was able to save. It was still in his pocket the next day when he arrived at the theatre and hung his coat, as usual, in the office of Litchfield Owen, the assistant stage manager.

"Ah there, young Rains," said Owen, in a rare outburst of cordiality. "How are you?" But from this innocent inquiry there followed a line of increasingly pointed questions, the aim of which was soon apparent to Willie.

"I've noticed," said Owen, "that you're looking much better lately. Been eating more, I presume. I remember when you had to spend your bus fare for food and then you walked home. But now you've got money."

Rains could only nod dumbly. "Well," said Owen, "how much money have you got? Let's have a look."

His heart thumping, Rains fumbled in his pockets before displaying in his damp palm the remainder of his sixpence allowance and the stolen shilling. Owen took the shilling and held it up to the boy's face. Rains could see that there was a fresh scratch across the face of the coin.

"I'm sorry we had to do this, but we were suspicious. I know why you did it—because you were hungry." There was a look of compassion on Owen's face, and for an instant Willie hoped forgiveness was in sight. Owen shattered the notion as quickly as it had been born. He beckoned the boy to follow him to the office of Dion Boucicault, the show's producer and one of the West End's more eminent personages. Son of the legendary Irish actor and playwright of the same name, Boucicault was a theatrical force in his own right. As Rains was dragged before him, he could see that the impresario was at his sartorial best, in a black frock coat and striped trousers, his silk hat hanging on a coat tree. He had a formidable countenance that reminded Willie of his father's face, though kinder. After hearing the evidence, Boucicault was soft-voiced but firm.

"Go home," he said sadly, "and tell your mother that you have become a thief."

Willie had never permitted himself tears, even under his father's leather strap, and he did not give in now. He begged for a second chance, but in vain.

"No," said Boucicault. "I don't want to see you any more. If you are not punished now, you will become a criminal."

In later years Rains would be unable to remember exactly how he related the catastrophe to his mother, but the following day she accompanied him back to the theatre to deliver her own entreaties to Owen and Boucicault, practically kneeling in supplication. When it was all over and Boucicault had given his last refusal, he stepped forward.

"Mr. Owen has a little gift for Willie," said Boucicault, and into the boy's hand was placed the scarred fruit of his theft. In addition to the scratch, the coin also bore the freshly etched letters HITBP.

"That means 'Honesty is the best policy,'" explained Owen, as Willie and his sobbing mother were ushered from the room.

The pain of his father's whipping was nothing compared to the shame Rains carried back to school. He dropped out of the Farm Street choir. There was little to relieve the oppressive stigma of his crime, of which his father was only too happy to constantly remind him. He could only wonder how many people, in addition to his parents and his teachers, knew his ugly secret. "I was so ashamed of what I had done, I resolved to die before I would steal again," Rains later recalled. He would keep the marked coin for decades.

Several months after Rains had left the Farm Street choir, Alfred Bellew unexpectedly summoned his former choirboy. Willie appeared at the church, prepared for some further humiliation, but all Bellew said to him was, "Have you learned your lesson?"

Although Rains had fallen from grace at the Duke of York's, he was still remembered as one of the theatre's more industrious call boys, and Bellew was ready to give him a second chance. The same job was open at the venerable His Majesty's Theatre, which was then run by the illustrious Herbert Beerbohm Tree, second only to Henry Irving as England's leading actor-manager.

Thus, Willie was once more liberated from school. For a time he enjoyed the envy of his former playmates and tormentors. As they trudged off to school, he could remain in bed or spend the morning tending to his prolific menagerie of guinea pigs. While the other boys wrestled with curriculum, Willie strode manfully down Brixton Road to the Bon Marché department store, where he caught a horse-drawn tram to the West End. At his destination, of course, his self-importance shrank, and he became what he really was—a boy compelled by circumstances to work.

He was already familiar with Her Majesty's Theatre, having seen Bernhardt and Coquelin in *Cyrano* there. He found the theatre itself glamourless. At first he knew nothing of the actors' reputations or celebrity, having spent almost no time in an audience himself. They were simply strangers he had to work with backstage. They could be majestic, kindly, patronizing, arrogant, demanding, or sometimes drunk. His only comprehension of Tree was that he was a towering man with an equally towering personality. Everybody was afraid of him, always addressing him as "Chief" and referring to him in no less awed terms behind his back.

The son of a London grain merchant and a third-generation Briton of German ancestry, Tree had presided over a dazzling decade at the Haymarket, where he mounted some of the most elaborate (sometimes dismissed as "upholstered") productions of Shakespeare ever produced in England. He was deeply envious of Henry Irving's knighthood (his own would not be bestowed until 1908), and their rivalry was played out in public and in private. Tree's Hamlet was considered inferior to Irving's, but his Falstaff and Malvolio were recognized as triumphs. Irving was lessee of the Lyceum Theatre, where he held court in a private apartment/dining room known as the Beefsteak Club; at Her Majesty's, Tree built a parallel aerie known as The Dome. Rains later recalled a story that exemplified Tree's antipathy for Irving, as well as his wit. On visiting a stable that provided horses for the stage, the Chief was told that one fine specimen had worked once for Irving. "Only once?" Tree inquired. The stableman explained that the animal had experienced a bout of explosive flatulence in the middle of one of Irving's scenes. "Ah," quipped Tree. "He was a critic as well as an actor."

Tree's outstanding commercial success was the 1896 stage adaptation of George du Maurier's best-selling novel *Trilby*, in which he made the role of Svengali, the mesmeric music master, his own. Rains saw *Trilby* nightly from the wings when the Chief regularly revived it, and over a half century later would remember it as Tree's finest role. "I couldn't believe my eyes," he recalled. Du Maurier had personally illustrated his novel in pen and ink, so everyone in London knew exactly what Svengali was supposed to look like. Tree didn't disappoint: he meticulously recreated Svengali's physiognomy with a putty nose and a matted beard, and, as if in homage to the character's graphic roots, drew lines on his face and hands with India ink.

Trilby stunned audiences, and earned enough money for Tree to rebuild and occupy Her Majesty's Theatre, a West End playhouse that had been through multiple incarnations since the eighteenth century. Tree opened his new theatre in 1897, the year of Queen Victoria's diamond jubilee. When Victoria died in 1901 and her eldest son ascended the throne, Tree changed the theatre's name to His Majesty's.

In addition to the customary duties of a call boy at night, Rains also worked as a page boy by day, running errands for the theatre, some on the periphery of Tree's private life. Among his more delicate assignments were delivering messages in one hand to Tree's wife and daughters, and, in the other, gratuities to Tree's mistress in Kensington.

Around the time that Rains became aware of Tree's many indiscretions (he also once encountered the actor in a corridor, casually fondling the bosom of a woman he had just met), the boy himself began to notice the opposite sex. With the help of Willie's steady income, the Rains family moved for a short time north of the Thames to what would be their nicest neighborhood, off Fulham Road on the edge of Chelsea. On his first foray down the block, hoping to impress his contemporaries, Rains spied a fetching, twelve-year-old blonde girl. She was prettily dressed, save for a black armband worn in mourning for a distant kin, and she was surrounded by a handful of Willie's prospective playmates. He eased up to the young lady and, while her more familiar admirers stood back, aghast, demanded a kiss. She was significantly taller than he and glared down at him in contempt. Rejected and humiliated, Rains retreated to the gutter and, in a clumsy attempt to repair his masculine self-image, scooped up a rock and hurled it through a window. A woman named Mrs. Hunt, who lived in the home whose window Rains had broken, immediately summoned his father. Frederick Rains promptly thrashed his son on the front stoop, in full and appreciative view of the blonde girl and her neighborhood retinue. The humiliation was unbearable.

In time, Rains was promoted from call boy to prompter. The promotion was reflected in his paycheck and enabled him, for the first time, to think about more than the basic necessities. It did not, however, give him the opportunity for leisure or fun. His sixty- to seventy-hour workweek at least gave him the grim satisfaction of knowing that he was helping to support his family, an obligation he would carry for much of his life. He also was able to provide his family with some degree of domestic luxury. The first gift Rains remembered buying for his mother was a simple toilet paper holder, reflecting his own resentment over a childhood of paper-littered bathroom floors.

Much of the young man's workday involved his commute. It was a ten-minute walk to the Bon Marché tram stop, and the ride to the West

End was at least an hour—along Kensington Road to Westminster Bridge Road, across the Thames, and up Northumberland Avenue to Trafalgar Square. It was a tedious journey, relieved only by the occasional sight of some illustrious figure from the theatre. Rains by then had developed a keen sense of glamour and personal style, and he understood their central importance in the world of the performing arts. Even at the age of fourteen, he was moved by the splendor of Gladys Cooper, who was at the time the rage of London and the most admired actress of the day, walking smartly along Northumberland Avenue on her way to the theatre, the epitome of worldly chic.

Rains was call boy at His Majesty's Theatre for nearly two years, a period during which he became known throughout the West End for his short stature as well as for his energy, eagerness, efficiency, and intelligence. Perhaps above all, though, he was known for his appalling qualities of speech. Actors winced every time they heard him dropping *h*'s and garbling *r*'s.

About this time, Willie made the acquaintance of Walter Crichton, a dashing gentleman and the son of Mandel Crichton, the Bishop of London. Crichton occupied a vague position in the Tree organization. The term "public relations" had yet to be coined, but it would well describe much of what he did, guiding Tree's public persona through the quicksands of London society and the press. Like many others, Crichton cringed at Rains's wretched diction, but the young man's diminutive stature and air of waiflike vulnerability elicited a protective response, and Rains found himself drawn increasingly into conversation with the older man.

"What do you read, Willie?" Crichton asked him one day.

"I read the plays, the scripts, sir," Rains replied.

"I know, I know. But don't you read for yourself?"

"For myself, sir?" The notion was puzzling.

"Yes. To find out about the world."

Rains had a feeling that his devotion to the illustrated boy's publication *Comic Cuts* was not what Crichton had in mind. But he replied that the comic paper was what he read.

The next day Crichton gave Rains three books, all by Robert Louis

Stevenson: *Travels with a Donkey in the Cevannes; A Child's Garden of Verses;* and *Virginibus Puerisque* ("for girls and boys"), a collection of essays. He also gave the boy a dictionary. Rains read the Stevenson books, more to please Crichton than for any other reason, and when he reported that he had finished the three volumes, he was given more.

By the time Rains went on his first tour with Tree's company, through the British and Irish provinces, he was well on his way through the works of William Makepeace Thackeray. On the train from Belfast to Dublin one day, Rains was alone in his compartment, holding a book in each hand. Tree passed by in the corridor and stopped short.

"What are you doing?"

"I'm reading, Chief."

"Yes, I can see that. Very interesting. Two books at one time."

"I'm reading *The Newcomes*, Chief, but I can't read it without the other."

"Why not?"

"The other book's a dictionary."

Satisfied that Willie was on his way to some sort of literary fluency, Crichton next went to work on his protégé's speech.

"Say 'Mon-day,' not 'Mundy.' Can't you hear it, boy?"

Rains could hear it, all right. But he could not readily mimic the difference. Crichton decided that the young man had merely acquired slovenly habits of speech and taught him how to roll his r's—or, more accurately, compelled him to do so. For weeks the backstage of His Majesty's Theatre echoed with nearly incomprehensible cries of "ever-r-r-r-ybody down for-r-r-r the fir-r-r-r-rst act." Slowly, with these new inflections, Rains's voice began to change for the better. This improvement was either apparent to Tree, or he was informed of it by Crichton. In any case, one day the Chief sent for his prompter.

Rains appeared in Tree's office and stood for several minutes before the great desk, waiting for Tree's attention.

"Ah, yes, young Rains," Tree finally boomed, looking up from some more important task. "Tell me—what are you going to do with your life?"

The question staggered Rains. One worked for a living and supported one's family. Was there anything else?

"What do you mean, Chief?" he mumbled.

"I mean, you can't go on being a prompter."

"I always thought I'd like to be a stage manager," Rains replied. The stage manager made five pounds a week and wore a silk hat.

Tree winced at the idea. "No, tell me what you *want* to be."

"I don't know, Chief," Rains confessed. "I just want to live nice."

"Very interesting. Of course, you could live very nicely if you became a successful actor. Have you ever thought about being an actor?"

"I don't know, Chief," Rains said again, increasingly dumbfounded by the whole conversation. He looked desperately down at his shoe tips, freshly conscious of his lack of height.

"You're small, aren't you? I don't think you could play heroes."

"No, Chief."

"How about *Twelfth Night*. Are you healthy? Can you belch?" He was referring to Sir Toby Belch, one of Shakespeare's best comic characters. "What about Sir Andrew Aguecheek?"

"I think I could, Chief."

"You've seen me play Hamlet. Do you think you could play Hamlet?"

He knew he couldn't, but Tree's tone called for an affirmative answer. "I think I could, Chief."

"Then come to my office at one o'clock tomorrow," said Tree. "Perhaps I can help you."

The next day, Rains appeared at the designated hour and knocked on the door. Tree was in a sporting mood.

"Who is it?"

"It's Rains, sir."

"Who?"

"Rains, sir."

At last admitted, Rains found Tree being costumed for a rehearsal by his dresser, Alfred Trebell, who was trussing him into a corset. With each tug at the lacing around his substantial midriff, Tree let out a groan.

"That's all right, Guv'nor," said Trebell, appraising the displaced girth. "Now it's your chest."

"What do you want, Rains?" said Tree, gasping slightly.

"Chief, you told me to come to your office."

"Why?"

"Well, Chief, we were talking about what I was going to do with my life. You told me to come to your office. You said you wanted to help me."

"I did?" Tree retorted, his voice rising in mock incredulity. "How could I possibly help you?"

"I don't know, Chief. You said I might become an actor."

"Ah, yes, but only if you had books and elocution lessons. But of course you would need the money to pay for them."

Rains hung his head in embarrassed silence as Tree, wearying of the tease, reached under his desk blotter and drew out a check for thirty pounds, which he handed, smiling, to the astonished boy.

The man who was Svengali, who drew the voice of an angel from an ordinary working girl, wanted to do something similar for his young prompter.

The thought of becoming an actor had never entered Rains's mind. He was surrounded by so many giants of the profession that the idea of sharing their occupation seemed unattainable. Yet, by his generous gesture, Tree had indicated to Rains that the stage was not beyond his reach. And Crichton, still pressing him to remedy his diction, must have thought him worth the effort.

Rains bought elocution books and applied himself to the exercises with the same zeal he applied to his job. One exercise required him to press his tongue against the roof of his mouth and blow energetically. Whatever else this accomplished, it must have amused his fellow tram passengers. Singing and reading aloud minimized his stammer.

He began to notice the quality of speech flowing everywhere around him, and began to study the voices that he most admired. There was Basil Gill of the resonant timbre and the rich and splendid enunciation, and Henry Ainley, who some said would have been the greatest of them all had his self-discipline and sobriety been equal to his talent. From the physically unprepossessing Philip Merivale, one of Gladys Cooper's husbands, Rains learned that exemplary posture and a royal bearing could be a perfectly adequate substitute for height and physique. He began to pull back his shoulders and puff out his chest to the point that his back muscles became as weary as those of his tongue, and ultimately as highly developed.

It took eighteen months for Rains to rid himself of his speech impediments. As a reward, he was granted a small part, the role of a page boy named Winkles in a revival of the 1901 play *The Last of the Dandies* by Clyde Fitch, which opened at His Majesty's in the spring of 1904, and ran for a week. The play recounted the notorious exploits of Alfred, Count D'Orsay, the great nineteenth-century fashion plate and libertine. His speech impediments conquered, Rains finally spoke his first lines of dialogue on stage, after setting a footstool for Lady Blessington, Count D'Orsay's mistress: "LADY B: Winkles. You say Miss Power received a letter this afternoon? PAGE: Yes, me lady. LADY B: And it made her cry? PAGE: Yes, me lady. LADY B: And what did you do? PAGE: I cried too, me lady. LADY B: [*Touched*] Why, Winkles? PAGE: 'Cause I love Miss Power, me lady. LADY B: So do I, Winkles." With the role of Winkles, "Willie Wains" was finally consigned to history. The young actor was billed as "Master Claude Rains."

When Tree's assistant stage manager, a Frenchman, returned to Paris, Rains assumed his position. Despite the promotion, prompting remained integral to his duties. In addition to always having a prompter on book, Tree relied on other devices, such as having chorus members memorize his part and stand near him on stage, whispering lines as required. He also utilized chalkboards in the wings, inscribed with dialogue; Rains once incurred Tree's wrath by holding one upside down.

Rains got at least one direct glimpse of Tree's personal life during a lavish 1908 production of *Faust*, an adaptation of the legend by Stephen Phillips, an actor turned playwright whose poetic interpretations of the classics had led many critics to claim him as the salvation of a theatre mired in realism and decadence. Phillips had already given Tree the lyrical productions *Nero* and *Ulysses*, which had earned acclaim. *Faust* was Tree's direct challenge to the legacy of Henry Irving—now two years dead—who had made Mephistopheles a signature role. But Phillips's adaptation was no match for the Lyceum's, and the production had problems from the start.

One day, a technical rehearsal was about to begin and Tree was absent. Rains was dispatched by the stage manager to find him, and he searched from the basement to the Dome, but Tree was nowhere to be found. Rains was passing the royal box on his return to the stage when, from behind the drawn curtains, he heard a woman's giggle. Rains paused, then parted the curtains. There in the dim interior was Tree, mounting a bosomy conquest.

"Excuse me, Chief," said Rains, his cheeks hot with embarrassment.

Tree shot him an outraged look. "Go away, idiot!" he snarled. "You always ruin everything."

Tree was perhaps more amused than annoyed, for discomfiting incidents were something he enjoyed as much as he relished a good joke, which he frequently created if one did not appear. Any actor who played the Artful Dodger to Tree's Fagin in *Oliver Twist* might expect to find a cold kipper in his pocket instead of the stolen bauble specified in the script.

As Tree's assistant stage manager, it was Rains who began to bear the greater brunt of Tree's pranks.

Tree's rehearsals were legendarily chaotic, and onlookers were frequently amazed when the actual performances went smoothly. Tree was often preoccupied with his jokes, and his idea of humor could sometimes turn cruel. He kept J. Fisher White, a noted character actor of the time, sitting around backstage for half a day for the rehearsal of a scene Tree actually had no intention of doing. The incident introduced Rains to what he would later describe as "my first ugly word." White slumped morosely in a chair, fanning himself with a bowler hat, and Rains passed by him several times. White, a man of soft voice and gentle manner, at last brought himself to inquire when he might expect to be called.

"They're not doing that scene today, sir," Rains answered, and was dumbfounded by White's response. The actor emerged from his courtly tranquility like a bull departing an arena chute. He slammed his bowler atop his head, and placed his reddening face up to Rains's. With precise and elegant enunciation, White said, "I hope he dies writhing with cancer in his fucking stomach."

Rains was shocked. It was the only time that White ever revealed a baser side. Years later, it occurred to Rains that White probably had some romantic assignation arranged that day, and that Tree perhaps was aware of it.

Faust put Tree especially on edge. His performance and production would be closely compared to Henry Irving's, and the Phillips script was badly showing its seams in rehearsal. During a scene in which Mephistopheles emerged from Hell, the stage was in darkness except for a flickering red light that flooded upward from behind a small flat painted to resemble jagged rocks that supposedly concealed a terrifying abyss. Tree, more than most actors, was prone to forget his lines; indeed, in every play he did there was at least one scene in which his memory repeatedly went blank. Everyone in the theatre was aware of it, and they grew tense as the problem scene in *Faust* approached: the famous scene on the Brocken, with the stage glowing red and flying witches dangling overhead on wires.

Tree managed the first line or two, then hissed to Rains, who was standing on the left side of the proscenium. "What do I say now?"

As he looked toward his prompter Tree saw a bright white light glaring off the script. "What is that damned light?" he demanded. "It's ruining the scene! Turn it off!"

Rains turned off the light.

"That's better," said Tree. "Now, what do I say?"

"I don't know, Chief."

"What do you mean, you don't know?"

Tree knew full well the reason, but preferred to tease the boy.

"I can't see the book," answered Claude.

"Why not?"

"Because you told me to turn out the light."

"Bloody idiot!" Tree snorted, grinning inwardly.

The rehearsal proceeded, with Rains turning the light on and off. Afterward Tree pulled him aside.

"I've got a marvelous idea," he said. "Why don't you memorize that scene and you can lie on the floor behind the flat and when I need a line, I'll just tap you with my foot and then you give me the line."

Rains hadn't memorized dialogue in four years, but he dutifully took the script home and stayed awake all night learning the scene. The next day, during the final dress rehearsal, he was so tired from lack of sleep that he was almost numb. He crawled behind the flat and lay on his back. The lights dimmed, the red glow appeared, and Mephistopheles loomed above. Tree was well into the scene before he gave Rains a tap in the ribs with his foot. Rains, of course, was half asleep, his mind emptied of the devil's rhetoric. Tree tapped him again, harder. Then another, even more severe tap. *"What do I say?"* the actor hissed. Silence. The taps escalated into outright kicks. Still nothing. The great actor finally lost his patience. "A bloody idiot!" Tree bellowed. "A bloody idiot who can't learn his lines!"

2

Marriages and Mustard Gas

EMILY RAINS WAS NOT A HAPPY WOMAN while her son was growing up, though not because of any failing on his part. On the contrary, he must have been a source of pride for her. After all, in addition to overcoming his speech impediments, his responsibilities at His Majesty's Theatre had expanded impressively, from those of call boy to prompter to assistant stage manager. Rains had become an indispensable part of the production company and toured extensively, giving him considerable exposure to the world outside London. "At various times after I was fourteen years old, I visited and lived in most of the important provincial towns of England and Ireland, and I visited Berlin, Germany in pursuance of my occupation," he later wrote.

But while he was at home he watched his mother's mental state steadily deteriorate. The concept of postpartum depression had not yet been formulated, but there is much in Rains's recollections to suggest the condition. "She'd lost a lot of children," he noted; and her final pregnancy, with Rains's sister Maude Emily, whom the family called Bobby, "had affected a nerve."

"I wouldn't say she was out of her mind, but there's no doubt about it, she needed treatment," he said. He called his father "a damned fool of a husband" who delayed getting his wife medical attention. "I don't know if was on the advice of a doctor or not—I don't know how it was done, and she may have been more seriously ill than I knew. But he took her to a lunatic asylum on Epsom Downs where the famous Derby is run."

Rains recalled his painful memory years later. "And I remember getting on the bicycle, on the weekend—I was working then—and going to see Mother. She had no business being there. She was surrounded by lunatics. She was frantic." For reasons he didn't understand, he was required to sleep with his father during his mother's stay in the asylum. Rains also was forced to become a caretaker for his youngest sister. "I was the only one who could do anything with Bobby," he recalled. Bobby had unrecorded health problems of her own, and didn't survive childhood.

Finally, his mother was released from the asylum. "I remember the joy of her coming back, our joy, my joy, my sister's joy. And then her mind going a bit off again. So this time she thought maybe we'd send her back to Epsom Downs, and she went off and got the Salvation Army to look after her. They did a marvelous job, and she was happy while they were doing it. They had her in some kind of a home, and they cured her all right, took care of her mind."

Not all of Rains's adolescence was preoccupied with family illness and loss. His interest in the opposite sex became serious for the first time at the age of sixteen, when he fell in love with a young walk-on actress at His Majesty's named Elsie Rowbottom. She was only fourteen or fifteen years old and, in Rains's recollection, "an English rose." He saved his money for a long time, then went to the Burlington Arcade in London and bought Elsie a silver bracelet. In a tailor shop on Westminster Bridge Road he spied a suit sure to impress her. He couldn't afford it, but wanted to buy it on time. His father refused to let him, giving him a piece of advice: "If you can't buy outright, don't buy at all."

Rains didn't buy the suit, and he rigorously avoided buying on credit for the rest of his life.

Elsie eventually married Tree's wardrobe master. But the unsuccessful romance made Rains acutely aware that "I wanted a wife and I wanted children."

He may have got one, but not the other, soon after. At the age of sixteen he made the acquaintance of a twenty-year-old seamstress named Rachel Nelson, who lived in the East End but, like Claude, worked in the West End. After a time, Rachel became pregnant, quit her job, and was forced out of her home to give birth. A fictitious paternal name was recorded on the birth certificate. According to surviving members of the Nelson family, a large "severance payment" was made to her, which they have always presumed came directly from Herbert Beerbohm Tree as an accommodation to his indispensable and indefatigable employee.

In 1910, at the age of twenty-one, Rains was assistant stage manager for Tree's acclaimed production of Shakespeare's *Henry VIII*, in which Tree played Cardinal Wolsey. The West End blockbuster ran for nearly a year. *Henry VIII* would mark Rains's last professional association with his mentor.

While the young man's responsibilities had substantially increased, his salary hadn't. He approached the stage manager, who referred him to the business manager, a Mr. Dana.

"What is it you want?" Dana asked.

Rains told him.

"I'll ask the Chief" was the brusque reply.

"When can I know?"

"Soon."

The next day, Dana turned Rains down. "You're getting too big for your britches," Dana said. A raise was a "ridiculous" demand. "Look what we've done for you. You've grown up in this theatre. We've made you an elegant man." Rains said nothing about Rachel, the child, or anything else. He remembered crying at being refused the raise, but he wasted no time approaching other theatres. He was well known and well liked in the business. "They all knew little Rains in the West End," he recalled. Charles La Trobe, stage manager of the Theatre Royale company based at the Haymarket, was sympathetic to his situation and agreed he should be better compensated. The theatre's director, Harley Granville-Barker, had been staging a highly successful production of Maeterlinck's fantasy *The Blue Bird* and was about to tour it to Australia. They needed a stage manager.

Worried about long-range security, Rains at first hesitated. But the next day he returned to the business manager's office at His Majesty's Theatre and submitted his resignation.

"Where are you going?" Dana sneered. "The workhouse?"

On hearing the news, Tree summoned Rains to his office. "What's this I hear about your going away? You can't. It's out of the question." He then called for Dana. What was going on? "Aw, I didn't want to bother you with it, Chief. The boy's getting impossible."

Rains agreed that the situation had indeed become impossible and made his farewell.

Before the Australian tour, his work at the Haymarket included more assistant stage managing, and here he had his first adult stage role, as a beggar named Slag in Lord Dunsany's *The God of the Mountains*.

Rains had also been smitten by a luminously beautiful young actress and singer named Isabel Jeans, who had made her London debut a few years earlier at His Majesty's Theatre in the musical fantasy *Pinkie and the Fairies*. At first he had barely noticed her, but during a Dublin tour, after a period of hard work, he was given a vacation of sorts, on the condition that he also sail to Liverpool to accept shipment of some company scenery. Riding a "jaunting car" (a kind of buggy used in Ireland) on his way out of town, Rains suddenly took notice of one of his traveling companions—Isabel. Later, in the moonlight, on the boat, he was immediately drawn to "this lovely little girl with enormous eyes." The stop in Liverpool led to more conversation, and a courtship soon began. Rains learned that Isabel's life was unhappy and fairly lonely. Her father was a commercial traveler, roaming about London at night selling tea, coffee, and food, with a steady, prime spot at Marble Arch.

Rains quickly decided he wanted to marry Isabel. He would use the Australian tour to finance the nuptials. They gave each other pet names: "Clid" and "Izzy." Rains arranged for Isabel to stay with a family with sons and daughters near her own age. The relationship got off to a bad start when Rains became jealous of one of the family's sons. Although there was no evidence of actual infidelity (just an overly familiar post-card), Isabel had to intercede to prevent Rains from thrashing the other young man with a cane.

For *The Blue Bird*, Rains was sent to Sydney a month ahead to make preliminary arrangements, supervise set construction, and hire child ac-tors and dancers—a dozen of the latter were required for one key scene, to emerge spectacularly from the numerals of a giant clock. Expecting to receive his first paycheck upon arrival, he spent most of his money on some flashy suits, both to celebrate his prestigious new appointment and to impress the Aussies. He had not anticipated that the boat would dock in Melbourne and that he would have to make an overland train connection to Sydney, thus delaying his paycheck by several days. A room had been booked for him, but Rains could afford little more than peaches and water for breakfast, lunch, and dinner. It was a humiliating situation, reminiscent of his starving pickpocket days at Her Majesty's.

This time, though, there would be no thievery. According to Walter Havers, a writer for *The London Magazine* to whom Rains later gave a detailed biographical interview, "False pride and his appalling sensitiveness would not allow him to request an advance of salary, and steadily the craving for more solid food grew upon him. There was only one way to satisfy his hunger, a truly drastic one." He had a ring of no small sentimental value, but he decided to pawn it. He could buy it back after receiving his pay.

"Nervously, he made his way to the nearest pawnshop, " Havers wrote, "only to pass and repass it, unable to pluck up sufficient courage to enter. Timidly he approached the window, and then in desperation, slipping the ring from his finger, turned hastily to enter the shop. Fate, however, was against him, for under the window was an iron grating, and in his excitement the ring dropped from his hands and disappeared into the murky depths beneath." Peaches and water would have to tide him over.

The Blue Bird opened in Sydney, was a hit, and ran for six months. This was followed by a shorter but still successful engagement in Brisbane. Yet in Melbourne the same production was an inexplicable flop. The company decided to replace the offering with a production of Shaw's comedy *You Never Can Tell*, a play perfectly suited to the existing acting company except for one part, which management was loath to cast with an Australian because of the clash of accents.

The business manager pointed at Rains. "You."

"But I'm not an actor."

"You'll play the part."

"But the character's an old man!" Rains protested. Actually, Shaw described the character as between forty and fifty. To Rains, that sounded old.

"Doesn't matter," said the business manager. "Go out and get some striped trousers and a black jacket. Put a lot of white in your hair. You'll play it."

"Oh, what I did to that part!" Rains remembered, laughing. The role was that of Bohun, a surprise mediator in a family dispute who appears in the final act in the most histrionic manner possible—"grotesquely majestic," according to Rains—wearing a hooded cloak, a false nose, and goggles, which he discards in an equally theatrical manner, "rolling up the nose in the domino and throwing the bundle on the table like a champion throwing down his glove." Rains of course could not know that Shaw would eventually become one of his stage specialties. But Shaw's own stage directions described a performance quintessentially Rains-like: "His bearing when he enters is sufficiently imposing and disquieting; but when he speaks, his powerful menacing voice, impressively articulated speech, strong inexorable manner, and a terrifying power of intensely critical listening, raise the impression produced by him to absolute tremendousness."

When Rains returned to England, after an absence of nearly a year, he found himself once again assistant stage manager for yet another *Blue Bird* engagement, this time at the Queen's Theatre. The next few years in Rains's professional life would be marked by a pull between acting and stage managing, with acting eventually taking the lead.

Once back in England, Rains married Isabel, and they settled at Clifford's Inn, London. "In the same year I came to [America], visiting various cities of the East and Middle West for Granville-Barker and the Messrs. Shuberts," Rains wrote. Isabel remained in London.

In 1913, Rains worked as assistant stage manager at the Haymarket for Ibsen's *The Pretenders* and Melchior Lengyel's *Typhoon*; in the latter play he also acted the first of several Asian roles (in which he was presumably cast because of his short stature). Moonlighting from the Haymarket, he was cast in one of his more substantial roles to date, that of Grasset, a Revolution-era French philosopher in Arthur Schnitzler's *The Green Cockatoo* at the Aldwych Theatre. He also stage-managed *Cockatoo*, along with the companion piece, Schnitzler's *Comtesse Mitzi*. Unfortunately, his showy performance in *Cockatoo* was not widely appreciated, since the play closed after only two performances. Much more successful was a guest production by Tree that Rains worked on as assistant stage manager, an adaptation of Bayard Veiller's *Within the Law*, which ran for over four hundred performances. Rains also performed in its one-act curtain-raiser, *A Dear Little Wife*, in a Japanese role.

In 1914, Granville-Barker summoned Rains, eager to have him take his company to America. "You'll act as my representative till I get there. All you have to do is watch the production, make sure that everything is all right on the stage. Clock the audience as it comes in, in order to check the box office, handle finances—ah—make speeches about Mr. Shaw and me before different clubs and organizations—I'd like you to see that the publicity is good, too, and—oh yes, I nearly forgot," he added, "you'll play a small part."

Isabel accompanied her husband on the scouting trip. They returned to England briefly, residing in Hampstead, and recrossed the Atlantic for the 1915 tour, which included *Androcles and the Lion*, *Iphigenia in Taurus*, and *The Trojan Women*. Rains appeared briefly in *Androcles* and as a herdsman in *Iphigenia*. For the latter, the *New York Times* opined that Rains "bounced a good deal" at the Yale Bowl performance; for the subsequent engagement at the new stadium of the College of the City of New York, before some five thousand spectators, the *Times* commented that "Claude Rains seems to have modified somewhat the sheer physical vigor of his performance as the herdsman, but it remains an exceedingly effective contribution to the play, so good, in fact, that many must regret that during the long season at Wallack's, he did all his work behind the scenes."

A Titania was needed for *A Midsummer Night's Dream*, and Granville-Barker sent for Isabel. She adored the tall, thin, brilliant, red-headed producer. "Oh, he's so pink!" Rains remembered her exclaiming.

The previous summer, Archduke Francis Ferdinand of Austria was assassinated by a Serbian student in Sarajevo, precipitating all-out military conflict in Europe. Germany declared war on France and in September set up a nearly impregnable fortress at Vimy Ridge, overlooking the city of Arras.

Rains had received an offer of employment from the American producer Charles Frohman, but declined because of the war. "I was not heroic," he said later. "I just knew I'd be ashamed of myself if I did not go back. I didn't want to be hurt, or hurt anyone else. And a friend over there sent word he could get me a job where I wouldn't have to do either," he recalled, although he ultimately would not be able to avoid the battlefield.

Rains chose to join the London Scottish regiment, in part because of its theatrical uniform and its self-bestowed, bloodthirsty sobriquet "The Ladies from Hell."

"I saw this soldier in his magnificent kilt," Rains recalled. The regiment's kilt was fashioned from the homespun cloth known as Hodden Grey—tartans had been rejected to avoid favoring one clan over another. Besides, as the regiment's first commander, Lord Elcho, observed, "A soldier is a man hunter. As a deer stalker chooses the least visible of colors, so ought a soldier to be clad."

"I wanted to look just like that," Rains said. "It was the actor in me." He often told the story of how he followed the kilted soldier on the street right into an enlistment office.

Rains trained as a marksman and proved a crack shot. He took readily and eagerly to military life; before his deployment to Vimy Ridge in the spring of 1916, he had already attained the rank of lieutenant. Rains was being sent to a place where some 150,000 French soldiers had already lost their lives; he and his fellow British troops faced the same quixotic challenge in attempting to recapture Vimy Ridge. High above the Arras plain—a vast, bleak, vulnerable expanse—the Germans were bunkered behind artillery-proof fortifications and had the clear advantage. Rains's battalion landed at La Havre; it was a hot, terrible march to the Vimy Ridge trenches, almost three days. Once there, he lay for hours by day on coconut matting amidst the mud and desolation of No Man's Land, and sat up late at night with a flashlight, bayonet, and the company of rats. In one raid on German trenches, Rains captured a German sergeant-major, who was furious. On the march back, the German was followed by a British lance corporal, Rains keeping pace alongside. For some reason, as a white flare went up, the prisoner became even more enraged, suddenly seizing Rains by the ear and shaking him. Some bayonet prodding by the lance corporal brought the German back in line.

After Rains's division's colonel was killed, he was replaced by a Scottish army man. Appalled by the appearance of his troops, he began holding parade inspections on trench duckboards and required that his men shave every day.

"My biggest fear was not war per se," Rains recalled, "but that while sitting over the latrine, clinging to the bar, I might be shot and fall in."

The casualties at Vimy Ridge continued to be heavy. One night, while bombs were being thrown in the dark, a lieutenant cried out, "Where's Private Whitehead?" Rains knew where he was, and went to fetch him. He found the young man in a dugout, trembling and hysterical. "Fuck it! Fuck the army! Fuck England! Fuck the King!" he shouted. Rains calmed him down, persuading him to return to the unit and not disgrace himself and the regiment.

Whitehead returned and was almost immediately killed.

In addition to machine guns, the Germans had begun to use aerosol poisons, at first chlorine and phosgene gas, and, beginning in the summer of 1917, the slower-acting, more insidious mustard gas. Rains's battlefield service was abruptly ended by both shrapnel and gas. The last thing he remembered after the shell hit him was the sound of voices saying, "Well, they got Rains." He recalled bleeding profusely. After being hospitalized on the French coast near St. Cecile, he was invalided to Bagthorpe Military Hospital, a converted workhouse in Nottingham. His first visitor, while he was still on a stretcher, was his mother—oddly, in very good spirits. He was almost completely blinded in his right eye, and his vocal chords were paralyzed. The blindness was permanent (and would remain a carefully guarded secret for the rest of his life), but his speech gradually returned. However, he now spoke with a husky new timbre that would forever be his trademark.

In 1917, though, Rains wasn't considering future work in the theatre. After the experience of war, painting one's face for a living seemed a poor excuse for a career. Instead, he seriously contemplated a permanent military commitment. Upon his release from Bagthorpe, he transferred from the London Scottish to a battalion of the Bedfordshire Regiment, which remained in England for the duration of the war. At the time of his discharge, he had achieved the rank of temporary captain.

During the war, Rains's relationship with his wife suffered. Isabel continued acting both during and after the war, appearing in a West End production of *The Man Who Married a Dumb Wife* (1917) and the musicals *Oh! Joy* and *The Kissing Time* (both 1919), making new professional contacts and attracting new admirers. The deterioration of their marriage was made clear one night.

Isabel was playing at His Majesty's in *Chu Chin Chow*, a record-setting box office phenomenon that would only be eclipsed by Agatha Christie's *The Mousetrap* several decades later. One night Rains was entertaining a friend, John Hall, who had been wounded in the field and almost given up for dead. Celebrating his recovery, Rains took Hall to see Beatrice Lillie in the musical *Cheap* at the Adelphi Theatre. They drank heavily between acts, Hall so heavily that he was unable to walk. Rains had planned to dash over to His Majesty's after the show to surprise Isabel, but instead had to take his friend to Victoria Station and put him on a train to Croydon, tipping the conductor and porter to see that Hall got back to his regiment. By then it was midnight and too late to meet Isabel, so Rains decided to go home.

Just as he entered the Underground, a zeppelin raid hit. The tube was plunged into darkness. In the confusion Rains took the wrong train; he had to change at Hammersmith for the next train to Kew Gardens-Richmond. The train was dark. After a while he heard a familiar voice saying "darling" to someone. Then he saw, momentarily silhouetted by a searchlight, Isabel—in the arms of another soldier.

Rains said nothing, but followed the couple when they got off at Kew Gardens. He watched from a distance as they took a long time saying good night. "It was such an indignity," he remembered. He decided to deliberately stride past them on the platform.

"My God, it's Clid!" Isabel exclaimed when she saw him. She broke away from the soldier and ran after her husband down the platform. "What are you going to do?" she asked him when she caught up with him.

"I'm going home."

"Oh, Clid, it's dreadful," she said.

"Yes, it is. I feel dirty. Who is he?"

"He's Gilley. He's the son of the Bishop of Birmingham. He's going to be a barrister."

"How long has this been going on?"

"All the time you were in France. I was terribly lonely."

"Do you want to marry him?"

"Yes."

"How could you? You wrote me all those letters, sent me books, everything I needed or wanted."

"I was lonely."

"You'd better pack up," Rains told his wife. "You sleep upstairs tonight. I'll sleep downstairs. You'll go off tomorrow." Isabel protested that she still loved him. "Don't worry about me," he told her icily. "Worry about yourself."

Isabel would later describe the breakup in rather different terms to her friend John Gielgud, who reported, "I once asked her how she got on with Claude, and I think she said 'He locked me in a cupboard' or something. Anyhow, I think he was a bit brutal with her."

Brutalized or not, three nights later Isabel returned, abject. Rains found her sitting in their living room, surrounded by luggage and boxes, and her canary in a wicker cage. "My heart was beating like hell," he remembered.

"Clid?" she began.

"What are you doing here?"

"I'm unhappy."

"Don't you love Gilley? Aren't you living with him?"

"I'm not happy there with him. Because I know you're so unhappy. Can't you make up your mind to be happy so I can be happy with Gilley?" She was pitiful, clearly wracked with guilt.

Rains and Isabel attempted reconciliation twice, but after she suffered a miscarriage—with Gilley presumably the father of the unborn child—Rains finally divorced her on grounds of adultery in 1918. Rains recalled the divorce as a "dreadful" process. He appeared at the Old Bailey in uniform, and Isabel admitted her infidelity. After the divorce, she married Gilley.

After the war, Rains wrote, "I was demobilized with the rank of [temporary] Captain early in 1919." He completed paperwork for reenlistment with the Eastern Command. "I wanted to live a man's life. I wanted to be a soldier," he said. The move would require him to drop from the rank of captain to lieutenant and take an assignment in Nigeria, but his mind was made up—or so he thought.

All that he still needed was a colonel's signature on his enlistment papers. He was walking down the street with the papers under his arm when he ran into an old theatre acquaintance.

"Why are you in uniform?" Rains's friend asked.

"I'm going to stay in uniform. I'm going into the regular army."

His friend was incredulous. "What for?"

"I'd feel like a sissy if I went back to the theatre."

Rains's friend gave him a sly look. "Come have lunch," he said. He took Rains to the Green Room Club, where Rains had been a member before the war. At the club they encountered directors Stanley Bell and Gilbert Miller, as well as celebrated classical actor Henry Ainley, whom Rains greatly admired.

By the end of the lunch, Rains had accepted a contract as stage manager at St. James's Theatre, where he would also act. His first acting assignment after the war was in Douglas Murray's comedy *Uncle Ned*, starring Ainley, on tour in Sheffield in the spring of 1919, followed by the role of Ivan Petrovitch in *Reparation*, based on Tolstoy's *The Live Corpse*. *Reparation* was staged at St. James's Theatre, and Rains once more found himself acting with Ainley under the direction of Stanley Bell. Rains lived with Ainley and his wife for a time in St. Regent's Park, and the older actor would forever address the younger man not by his given name, but as "Lodger." Rains combined stage-managing with acting in *Julius Caesar* at St. James's in January 1920, first playing the role of Casca and later, on tour, Cassius to Ainley's Marcus Antonius. In April, Rains was loaned out to the Duke of York's Theatre for the lead role in Gogol's comedy *The Government Inspector*.

In addition to his stage work, Henry Ainley had been active in motion pictures since 1914, and it was evidently on his professional coattails that Rains was cast in Ainley's film *Build Thy House*, directed by Fred Goodwins and released by the Ideal Film Company in October 1920. Ainley played a demobilized officer, Arthur Burnaby, who returns to England to take over his deceased father's business interests. Rains played Clarkis, formerly Burnaby's batman, or soldier-servant, now a drunken and jobless casualty of war, who recognizes that this "Burnaby" is an imposter. But instead of developing into a standard crime melodrama, the story takes a sharp turn into a somewhat preachy tract for labor reform. No print of the film, nor any still photographs from the production, are known to have survived. Rains would not appear in another motion picture for thirteen years.

Rains's respect for Ainley was sorely tested during the Wimbledon tryout of Sem Benelli's *The Jest* in the fall of 1920. Benelli set his play in Florence during the fifteenth-century reign of Lorenzo de Medici, but constructed the rip-roaring melodrama in the style of a Jacobean revenge tragedy. Stanley Bell cast Rains in the showy part of Giannetto, a sensitive young painter brutalized by a pair of thuggish brothers, Neri and Gabriello, upon whom he takes a delicious revenge. Ainley played Neri. The roles had been essayed the previous season in New York by John and Lionel Barrymore, and the show was a proven hit. The thirty-year-old Rains was not exactly the ideal choice for the part of a fey youth of seventeen (the role had already been offered to Basil Rathbone and Godfrey Tearle, who were unavailable), but he was a better choice for his part than was Ainley, who had "begun to fill out a bit," recalled Rains, owing largely to an increasing fondness for gin. Though strikingly handsome, the older actor's career had clearly begun to decline, while Rains's was on a rapid ascent. The producers considered ways to adapt the role for Rains. Perhaps instead of being effeminate he could be a hunchback? Because the character already had a servant-dwarf of his own, this idea did not play well. In the end, Rains played the part like a demonic kewpie doll. Rains recalled that his costume and makeup drew the special attention of gay theatre patrons, one of whom was overheard in the lobby: "Did you see Rains? White face, red hair, black tights—and no jockstrap!"

Over four acts, Giannetto sets a series of traps for Neri, who, in his drunken oafishness, steps into each one. The coup de grâce is Neri's fatal stabbing of his own brother, believing him to be Giannetto. Then, in the third act, Giannetto confronts his nemesis, shackled and near-mad in a dark jail cell. "I had the most marvelous speech to bring down the curtain, a speech with a lot of venom in it," Rains recalled. The scene was illuminated by a single lantern, the light of which intensified along with Giannetto's swelling monologue, dramatically illuminating Rains from below. "I was getting good notices," he remembered.

Ainley's performance, however, was called "a little too vigorous, too much of a Viking. He bellowed and shouted and stamped." The actor apparently began taking all the humiliation and abuse heaped upon his character personally and grew jealous of his show-stopping protégé. "Harry was disgruntled about the whole goddamned thing," recalled Rains. It was his own fault, he shouldn't have played the part. He couldn't play Giannetto, he'd grown too big." One night Ainley distracted and upstaged Rains by changing some dialogue in the first act. Then he began to press Rains to eliminate what he called the "ridiculous, comic" device of the lantern in Rains's big scene. As an experienced stage manager, Rains knew it was verboten to change the staging of a production once on tour. Besides, where would light come from in a dark jail cell except from the lantern? Perhaps from pale moonlight through a grate, Ainley suggested. Rains refused.

The next night Ainley took things into his own hands—or feet. He contrived a new entrance that allowed him to stumble over the thing that was giving Rains so much attention. "He kicked out the lamp, smashed it," Rains recalled. Management, alerted in London by phone, finally intervened; the lantern was restored. From then on, said Rains, "it was bloody murder to be in the theatre with him, let alone play a part with him." Yet, he added, "I was sorry for the man. I saw what was happening to him. And I did like him. I tried to help him in so many ways." For instance, Rains would help Ainley into the bathroom when he came home drunk, not an uncommon occurrence. And he managed to convince the older man to bathe instead of just dousing himself with cologne. Ainley's American wife, whom Rains remembered as "a damned good-looking woman," felt the younger actor was a stabilizing influence on her husband.

The London engagement of *The Jest* was ultimately canceled, but in the wake of advance publicity, another management quickly mounted its own production, now called *The Love Thief*, with the waspish character actor Ernest Thesiger as Giannetto. John Gielgud judged that production "a great failure."

Rains never worked with Ainley again. Not long after, Gilbert Miller bought out Ainley's interest in St. James's Theatre.

During this period, Rains's mother had to be committed to a nursing home. "Her mind went," he said. "I don't know how else to describe it. She was lucid just half the time, and needed proper care." Rains and his sister found the home, and Rains paid all the expenses. "She grew to be very happy when her mind was nice and clear, but when it wasn't she was unhappy. She got to know the birds, I remember. She'd talk about them when I went there, point them out, the different birds she'd learned about. She was very loving to me."

One day backstage at St. James's, the phone rang, the caller refusing to identify herself until Rains took the call. It was Isabel. She told Rains she was in some kind of difficulty and convinced him to meet her at a little restaurant on German Street near Piccadilly Circus. There, over dinner, Rains found his former wife "very gay" and well turned out, wearing one of her "wonderful wigs." (Her natural hair, Rains recalled, was very thin.) She didn't even mention the nature of her "trouble" until the check arrived.

"What is it you want, Izzy?" he finally asked.

"I want *you*, Clid."

Her strategy didn't work. Rains had already made the acquaintance of another actress, Marie Hemingway, while touring with *Julius Caesar* and *The Jest*. "She was so beautiful," said Rains, "and because she was so beautiful I thought she must be innocent. I was lonely, we were on tour, the days and the nights after the theatre were empty, and what with one thing after another, I found myself saying, 'Well, I'll marry you if you want me to' or something like that."

Rains admitted that he knew very little about Marie. Nevertheless, he said, "We were married quietly and went down to Cornwall, to her parents' house. Up on the cliffs and the water below. Everything very nice. Had dinner. Went to bed. She excused herself to say good night to mommy and daddy and returned an hour later terribly drunk. Lusty. I wanted nothing to do with her. She said, 'If you won't, I'll throw myself out the window.' I remember her opening the window and standing up on the sill. God, what a first night!"

Things only got worse when they returned to London, to their second-floor flat in Duke Street, St. James. "I finally realized she was an alcoholic. She would hide liquor everywhere, even on top of the old high toilet. Bottles of Three-Star Hennessey." Marie was then playing the lead opposite Sir John Martin Harvey in *The Only Way*. "Somehow she managed to get through rehearsals. Several times she was too drunk to make the theatre and I had to telephone and say she was sick."

Having already had one marriage end disastrously, Rains was not eager for another marital catastrophe. "I tried to make the best of it. I couldn't stand another failure. I hate failure. I tried to live with it."

Rains sought the advice of Marie's family physician, Dr. Lidyard Wilson (who would remain "a marvelous friend" almost to the end of Rains's life). Wilson was blunt. "You've got to get out of this," he said. "I warn you, she will destroy you."

Following the doctor's advice, Rains moved out of the Duke Street flat and into a nearby hotel "where they brought you a brass hip bath and tins of hot and cold water in the morning." He found himself spending much of his time at the Primrose Club in St. James Street, which had made him an honorary member.

But he still stewed over Marie. And he knew she was spending time with another man.

Late one night he got up, got dressed, and resolved to break into the Duke Street flat to confront his treacherous wife and her lover. He even put on tennis shoes for stealth, planning to climb in silently through the bathroom window. But as he passed through the hallway outside the flat, he heard a man's voice inside and lost all composure. "I banged on the door," he said. "Lost my head. I heard the lady phone for the police." He ran across the street and hid in a doorway. He watched the police arrive, go up to the flat, then come back down and leave.

The flat beneath his and Marie's was occupied by Betty Chester, a well-known comedienne. Just as Rains was catching his breath, Betty came down the street. Accompanying her was a friend of his: Noel Coward, then a struggling young playwright, actor, and songwriter who, like Rains, had served in the war. Coward spied Rains in the doorway.

"What's the matter, Claude?" he asked. Rains explained the situation. Betty went inside her building, and Rains and Coward took a walk across St. James's Park. Coward was on his way to his mother's house on the other side of the park, and the late-night stroll allowed for some private conversation.

"I can't bear another failure," Rains told Coward. "I already had one—and now this."

"But everybody knows about her," replied Coward. "She's beautiful and she's very vain, Claude. Do you want to go on with it? You'll only have trouble."

"I can't bear failure," Rains repeated.

By then the two had arrived at the opposite side of the park, by the Queen Victoria monument across from Buckingham Palace. They sat on the coping before the lights and spraying water. "There's only one thing to do," Coward said. "You'll have to go to her and tell her it's *your* fault—that *you're* the difficult one to live with."

Rains pondered this. "But I can't go see her," he said at last.

"Well, then, write her."

It was perfectly logical counsel from one who had such a way with words; but Rains, a nonwriter, wasn't up to the task. His attempts at composing a letter to Marie failed, and he appealed to his friend Coward, who, in the manner of *Cyrano de Bergerac*, dictated a letter for him. "A wonderful thing for him to do," Rains later said.

But high-powered literary ghostwriting got Rains nowhere with Marie. Dr. Wilson told him that Marie was saying "all kinds of things" about him, even accusing her husband of homosexuality, perhaps because of his friendship—which was completely platonic—with Coward. Pushing his idea for a divorce, Wilson presented Rains with a game plan. If Wilson could persuade the volatile Marie to "behave" in court, could Rains contrive some evidence giving *her* grounds for divorce? Rains, recoiling at the idea of parading his wife's alcoholism in public, consented to a ruse. Once again, Noel Coward helped him concoct a scheme.

Rains remembered, "I went to a little hotel in Soho with a very gracious lady who had been a student at the Royal Academy of Dramatic Art, which had been founded by Herbert Beerbohm Tree. 'I'll help you out,' she said. I got a bottle of whiskey and a little bag, and we registered as man and wife. She got into bed. I got into an armchair and got drunk." The next morning, he got up, rang for room service, and hopped into bed with the "gracious lady." When the maid arrived, Rains said, "I want breakfast for Mrs. Rains and myself."

Rains handed over this "evidence" of adultery to Dr. Wilson, who nonetheless was unable to make Marie cooperate. As the divorce proceedings began, the physician rang him up. "What's this about cruelty?" he asked. Rains didn't know what his friend was talking about. Wilson suggested he get a newspaper. When Rains did, he saw the lurid headline: "Cruelty of Actor Husband."

Marie was granted a divorce, but at a considerable cost to Rains's reputation—or at least to his pride. He felt himself to be ostracized, even professionally suspect. "I was a womanizer, a dirty dog, and nobody would have anything to do with me," he remembered. "No decent theatre would hire me." Rains's feelings may have gotten the better of his memory here, however: in fact he had no fewer stage roles in 1921, the year after his marriage and divorce, than he did in 1920.

In January 1921 Rains took the title role in *Daniel*, a work by French playwrights Georges Berr and Louis Verneuil, who was the grandson-in-law of Sarah Bernhardt and who had tailored the play specifically for the aging Bernhardt's physical limitations. At the age of seventy-six, with one of her legs recently amputated, Bernhardt played the title role of a wheelchair-bound morphine addict, covered in stump-concealing rugs, embroiled in a melodramatic love triangle. French audiences suspended multiple layers of disbelief, accepting Bernhardt in the part of a young man nearly fifty years younger than she actually was. When Rains played the role in London, reviewers were less quick to swallow the wheelchair-and-rugs gambit, which contributed nothing to the plot. Nonetheless, Rains himself received plaudits. The *Times* called his performance "a haunting thing," the character of Daniel "an utter wreck, but a picturesque, romantic wreck, a choice curio shattered, the irretrievable ruin of something comely and precious."

Next was the role of "The Stranger" in George Middleton and Guy Bolton's *Polly with a Past* with Noel Coward and Edith Evans, produced, like *Daniel*, at St. James's Theatre. Then came the part of Laurent, the Marquis de Mortain, in *Legion of Honor* at the Aldwych Theatre in August, followed by the Clemence Dane play *Will Shakespeare*, in which Rains played doomed playwright Christopher Marlowe, rendered with a considerable dollop of poetic license by Dane. Shakespeare was played by Philip Merivale, and Ann Hathaway by Moyna Macgill (the future mother of Angela Lansbury); Flora Robson was also in the cast, as Queen Margaret.

The year 1922 provided Rains with only two acting credits: the role of a creepy Japanese butler in Mary Roberts Rinehart and Avery Hopwood's long-running melodrama *The Bat* in January and in the expressionist/experimental play *The Rumour* by C. K. Munro in December. The following year, to supplement his acting income, Rains accepted a teaching position at the Royal Academy of Dramatic Art, which had been founded by his mentor, Herbert Beerbohm Tree, in 1904. When Rains began his association with RADA, it was based in a pair of old houses in London's Gower Street. The school's curriculum was heavily weighted with the disciplines inherited from the era of Tree and Irving—gesture, elocution, fencing, and movement. The more deeply psychological influence of Stanislavski was barely noted by the British theatre establishment. (The Moscow Art Theatre would not appear in London until 1928.) The British theatre had no government subsidies at the time. Because of this, it was a market-driven industry and therefore embraced techniques that were proven commercially. Rains would never have a formal introduction to Stanislavski's "method," though he would later express considerable appreciation for the technique. In fact, he clearly took a similar approach to building his characters, instinctively grounding them in solid psychological motivation.

Cedric Hardwicke, who had been a RADA student a few years before Rains taught there, recalled that "the principal method of tuition was for each class to rehearse some three or four plays, which were eventually produced at the end of the term. It was a good system for the students, and as the girls at the Academy far outnumbered the boys, I gained experience in a wide variety of parts. But it seemed tough luck on the parents and friends whose duty it was to attend the performances!"

Rains was immediately struck, and forever frustrated, by the unevenness of talent, much less professional aspiration, he perceived in many of his female students. "These young students, what were they there for? Fun, having larks, some of them. They put up some kind of good test or they wouldn't have gotten in, but when they were in, it was obvious they weren't filled with the fire or ambition to become real actresses. They'd laugh. I used to get livid."

Like most acting teachers, Rains found that some of his students "were more temperamental than others, some were more adept than others, but nearly all of them had speech difficulties of one kind or another. So at some point during their studies, they could be sure of one particular assignment. It was a tongue-twister, a series of verbal acrobatics from a book of nonsense titles, *Grimm Tales Made Gay.*" He recalled an example, suggested by the legend of Bluebeard:

A maiden from the Bosporus
With eyes as bright as phosphorus
Once wed the wealthy bailiff
Of the Cailiff of Kilatt.
Though diligent and zealous, he
Became a slave to jealousy.
Considering her beauty,
'Twas his duty to do that.

Rains's teaching colleagues included Alice Gachet, who specialized in French drama, and Elsie Chester, a formidable instructor who had lost a leg in a traffic accident and was thereafter reputed to fling her crutch at students who sufficiently displeased her.

Fortunately, Rains had a number of students who didn't displease him at all. One who later expressed special admiration for Rains was John Gielgud. In a 1996 interview, Gielgud recalled, "I'd had one professional job before I met [Rains], in a provincial tour of a West End play with my cousin Phyllis Neilson-Terry, and during that tour an actor in the cast said to me, 'I don't think you're much good, you ought to have another year's training.'" So Gielgud applied to RADA and received a scholarship. "Rains was my principal and most inspiring teacher. He was very attractive, rather stocky, brown hair sort of combed over one eye. Very smart double-breasted dark suits and large knotted ties, and beautiful linen cuffs and so on."

Gielgud thoroughly enjoyed his association with Rains. "He was very agreeable and enthusiastic and not at all bullying. And I became extremely attached to him because he seemed to give me a lot of chances. One of the first things he did with me was a scene from Shakespeare's *Henry IV*. I did it under his direction at a prize-giving session and won the prize."

Rains next gave Gielgud the lead role in a student production of Tolstoy's *The Live Corpse*, the same part Rains himself had played earlier in the West End in the translated version, *Reparation*. "It was a very fine part and I was thrilled to be asked to try it. And we all worked very hard at the rehearsals and borrowed all the props from our homes, and it went very well."

Gielgud avidly followed his teacher's stage work. "I saw him in a number of plays, including *The Doctor's Dilemma* at the Everyman Theatre, in which he was wonderful. I was very envious because in the last act—the fourth act, I think it is—he comes on dying in a wheelchair, and Claude was there in this beautiful dressing gown, with white hands over the edge of the chair, dying, and I thought, this was marvelous."

"I worked as hard as I could and imitated Rains's acting until I became extremely mannered," Gielgud wrote. "I strained every fibre in my efforts to appear violent and emotional and only succeeded in straining my voice and striking strange attitudes with my body." Gielgud, of course, would eventually develop his own inimitable style, but in the interim, Rains "was rather interested in my work and was willing to help me all he could." Gielgud had seen Rains's performance in *Daniel*, and was asked to play the part himself in what he described as a "terrible" 1924 screen adaptation called *Who Is the Man?*

Rains, said Gielgud, "had a twinkling eye and a very good sense of humor. He didn't take himself too seriously, which I think is such a frightfully good thing for an actor. Claude didn't give one the impression of being madly self-centered, even, but he was obviously very hard working and practical, and gathered strength from the people around him." Gielgud thought that Rains "perhaps learned more about his own acting through teaching."

Also among Rains's students was a lumpish young man from Brighton named Charles Laughton. He had come from a family of hoteliers, but had developed a rich imaginative life and a passion for the stage. According to Gielgud, "He had been helping his mother run a small hotel near Scarborough on the east coast and doing amateur theatricals, and [it was] very fortunate for him because nearby lived three people interested in all the arts—the Sitwells, Dame Edith, Osbert, and Sir Gerald. They must have seen his genius."

Laughton's teachers were all struck by the obvious disparity between physique and talent. "When he came to the Academy, he was ten years younger than I and looked ten years older," Rains recalled. Nonetheless Rains, like the Sitwells, recognized talent when he saw it. "There was nothing I could do for him," Rains said. "He was [already] a gifted actor. All I could tell him were the technicalities of the theatre."

"Sir," Laughton once asked Rains, "do you think I could play a romantic part?"

His teacher was direct in his reply: "Well, you could play it, but you wouldn't look like it." Rains felt Laughton was destined for a career in comedy, a mistake in judgment he would later fully acknowledge.

During this time, Rains was living in rooms he rented from a Mrs. Forscutt, who was the mother-in-law of actor O. B. Clarence. She only let rooms to theatre people. Rains recalled, "She did the cooking, and it was a lovely place to live." While under her roof he appeared in *The Love Habit* by Louis Verneuil and Shaw's *The Doctor's Dilemma*.

Next, Rains had the first of two acting engagements with Nigel Playfair, the renowned actor-manager who ran the Lyric Theatre, Hammersmith, and produced throughout the West End. A dozen years earlier, he had assistant stage-managed *The Younger Generation*, starring Playfair, at the Duke of York's Theatre. A few years earlier, Playfair had already translated (with Paul Selver) and produced Karl Čapek's *R.U.R.*, the allegorical fantasy that introduced the word "robot" in its modern sense (in Czech, the word is the rough equivalent of "serf labor"). Čapek and his brother Josef had written another fable, even more politically caustic, which Playfair and Clifford Bax freely adapted from an English translation by Selver. In all the translating and adapting, much of the satirical sting of the original was lost, or deliberately jettisoned, but *The Insect Play* (*And So Ad Infinitum*) was presented at the Regent Theatre for forty-two performances in May and June of 1923. An anonymous London reviewer described the play as "a succession of parables from insect life—in turn of butterflies, beetles, ants, and may-flies, each representing a different phase of human experience."

Rains played three roles. In the first, dealing with the butterflies, he played The Lepidopterist. The London reviewer wrote that the butterflies "are presented as modern frivollers—some in evening dress, some in fancy costume, but all with butterfly wings, squeaky voices, and trembling hands. They have nothing to do but love-making and chase each other in couples flirting and fox-trotting, and spouting little verses round a sort of fairy cocktail bar. Rather a limited view, both of butterflies and humans, and not by any means the best thing in the play."

The Insect Play marked the professional debut of John Gielgud, who played a butterfly named Felix. "I played a small part in the first act," Gielgud recalled in 1996, " and I think I understudied Rains, who played three parts in different parts of the play and was wonderful in all of them. Anyhow, my scenes were rather a failure and I was very much aware that I didn't know how to act at all and he used to give me hints."

The second act dealt with beetles, presented as vulgar, middle-aged Cockneys pushing their giant ball of dung, which they alternately call their "capital" and "little pile." A cricket couple (Mrs. Cricket was played by Angela Baddeley) is stabbed by an ichneumon fly, which feeds their body fluids to its larva (played by Elsa Lanchester as "a huge, sluggish, and also Cockney child"). The larva is devoured in turn by a Parasite, played by Rains. The feasting took place discreetly off stage. Rains returned to reveal the Parasite, hiccupping, "with Elsa inside me," in a rolling, padded get-up he described as resembling the rotund character that advertised Michelin tires. In the third act, Rains played the Chief Engineer, the single-minded supervisor of an assembly line of warrior ants.

During the run of *The Insect Play*, Rains met James Whale, a director, actor, and set designer who had honed his stage skills producing amateur theatricals while interned in a German P.O.W. camp. Whale was enamored—at least platonically—with Doris Zinkeisen, the production's costume designer. Rains considered Zinkeisen "a stunning woman" and remembered her many paintings that adorned the walls of Whale's flat as "trophies of unrequited love." Later, as a Hollywood director, Whale would have a major impact on Rains's career when he cast him in *The Invisible Man*. He would use Zinkeisen as his costume designer for the 1936 film version of *Show Boat*.

Rains played the role of the poet David Peel in John Drinkwater's *Robert E. Lee* (which, despite the title, was not a biographical drama but rather a study of four Virginians during the Civil War). John Gielgud understudied him and played a few performances. Rains's final acting assignment of 1923 was in Seymour Hicks and Ian Hay's *Good Luck* at the Drury Lane.

In 1924 Rains joined the Everyman Theatre in Hampstead for a series of productions that would showcase him in a series of roles, primarily Shavian. The first was Napoleon in *Man of Destiny*, pairing him opposite Jeanne de Casalis in a role suffused with Shaw's trademark battle-of-the-sexes badinage. Next came Shaw's "discussion play" *Getting Married*. A reviewer noted that he was a "first rate" actor of "very considerable possibilities. Unfortunately, the heat-wave caused him to stream with perspiration, although he was supposed to be cool as a cucumber." Rains took a break from Shaw with the role of an Irish dock thief who kills his brother in Ernest George's *Low Tide*, but was soon in Shavian form for *The Devil's Disciple*. "Mr. Claude Rains as Dick Dudgeon adds one more to the very striking series of parts which he has played on this particular stage recently," wrote a reviewer. "Considering how good Mr. Rains used to be (and doubtless still is) at the degenerate type of character, he makes a very satisfactory strong man—and, owing to his quick intelligence, a more than satisfactory Shavian strong man." A stage mishap during the run generated some press attention (if it wasn't generated for just that purpose):

STAGE EXECUTION ALMOST BECAME REAL
WHEN HE LOST HIS BALANCE

While acting as the condemned man in the execution scene in Bernard Shaw's "The Devil's Disciple," at the Everyman Theatre, Mr. Claude Rains had a narrow escape from being hanged.

"The steps leading to the scaffold rest on a little trolley," said Mr. Rains in an interview yesterday, "so that when I am about to die the executioner pushes the trolley and the steps from under me.

"Just as the executioner had placed the rope round my neck I lost my balance. The steps and trolley beneath me began to move, and if the executioner had not noticed it and acted quickly, I am sure my sins would have found me out."

Another paper quipped that "Hanging your leading actor sounds like a drop scene," a groaning pun on the term for painted background scenery hoisted and lowered on ropes.

Rains traded in the noose for an aviator's scarf and goggles for Shaw's *Misalliance*, perhaps a bit too engagingly for the playwright, who sent him a rather cryptic critique by telegram: MY DEAR MR. RAINS. MUST YOU BE SO VERY C-H-A-R-M-I-N-G AS JOEY PERCIVAL? For Everyman's final Shavian outgoing, *The Philanderer*, a comedy about a man dealing with two assertive New Women of the century's turn, a reviewer noted that "it is to Mr. Rains's credit that, while both Miss [Cecily] Byrne and Miss Dorothy Massingham have a material advantage over him in terms of inches, he contrived yesterday to fully hold his own." It was not the first, and hardly the last time the subject of his height would work its way into critical appraisals.

In the midst of Rains's Everyman period, he was approached by his student Charles Laughton. "I was leaving, to get married or something, and Laughton said to me, 'Sir, I'm looking for some rooms. Do you think you could introduce me to Mrs. Forscutt?'" Laughton was wearing a blue suit, shiny with wear, and had little money. However, on Rains's recommendation, Mrs. Forscutt took him in.

Rains was indeed leaving to be married. He had grown used to the attentions of his female students at RADA, but the one especially mad about the boy was Beatrix Thomson, who had been awarded the Academy's silver medal for acting, and with whom Rains had acted, appropriately enough, in *Getting Married*. He described her as an "elfin, charming, tiny thing," and a good actress. She was also rich. Her family lived in a mansion at Effingham, Surrey, the walls hung with Goyas and the work of other masters. Beatrix's father was a close friend of the legendary English art dealer Joseph Duveen and shared his tastes.

Rains was a bit surprised when Beatrix approached him privately one day. "She wanted to take me home for a weekend. She thought I had a glamorous life." They drove down to Effingham one night after a performance to meet her family. "I don't know if they ever really accepted me," Rains said. But he had his own clear opinion about Beatrix's brother Gordon. "Terrible snob, the brother. Never did any work, just went to the Devonshire Club and rowed in the Oxford-Cambridge boat race." His oars and cups were prominently displayed in the house.

The first night of the visit, Rains was still wearing stage makeup, and it rubbed off on his collar. He slept in a guest room, awakening to find the butler standing at the foot of the bed, holding the shirt and "gazing scornfully and with utter distaste" at the unsightly evidence of a life in the theatre.

Despite Rains's apparent discomfort with her family (and theirs with him), in November 1924 Rains and Beatrix Thomson were married. The pair took up residence in a pleasant basement flat with tiled fireplaces in Camden Grove, just beyond Kensington.

Rains's final repertory assignment with the Everyman company was in *Home Affairs*, Norman MacDermott's translation of a Hungarian comedy by Ladislas Fodor, which was produced in January 1925. According to MacDermott,

> The notices were almost the best that any Everyman production
> had; several critics prophesised that it would be transferred

quickly to the West End. Enquiries for transfer started
within days. Three different theatres were on offer. But each
Management wanted to change the player of the leading part
from Claude Rains to some matinee idol. When I refused and
asked for an explanation, they said 75 percent of all audiences
were women; Rains was "too short and stocky" and women
would not see a lover in him! To us, who knew Rains only had
to lift that wicked quizzing eyebrow for every woman present
to give an ecstatic sigh, this was at first a joke; then infuriating
stupidity.

MacDermott finally turned down "two firm offers in which the
change was made a condition," and the play closed.

London audiences next enjoyed Rains in a revival of Richard Brinsley Sheridan's Restoration comedy *The Rivals* at the Lyric Theatre. The
casting proved a bit awkward, in that both his former and current wives
appeared in the production—Isabel Jeans, Marie Hemingway, and Beatrix
Thomson. Whatever discomfort Rains may have experienced did nothing
to deter him from giving a bravura performance as Faulkland, usually considered a thankless part that breaks the comic tone, and one often cut in
performance.

Rains next took the supporting part of a dapper gambler in Godfrey
Tearle's short-lived production of *Salomy Jane*, nominally based on the
Bret Harte story "Salomy Jane's Kiss." But between the play's preliminary
announcements and opening night, Harte's name "was omitted from
the programme—and wisely, for except in superficial things and the California miner in the 'sixties atmosphere, there was little to suggest that
fine writer," wrote one reviewer. "Only one incident did I recognise—the
kissing by a pretty girl of a friendless man about to be hanged." Rains
was spared any critical lynching; one review called his performance "a
brilliant little sketch."

Rains had long been shrewdly adept at garnering the best notices in
inferior plays and productions, but none of his skills could much help
The Man from Hong Kong, a melodramatic potboiler by Mrs. Clifford Mills
that opened at the Queen's Theatre in August 1925. The story concerned

a cocaine smuggler of half-English, half-Chinese heritage named Li-Tong (Rains), who worked out of a "vile little restaurant in Hong Kong" but in England affected the persona of a wealthy Briton living on a houseboat in the Thames. Li-Tong is betrothed to an English maiden, whom he then proceeds to abuse in the best Saturday-matinee tradition. According to one reviewer, "In the third act we witness the Chinese ruffian continuing his evil work upon his fair-haired captive, kissing her, flinging her about, and generally reducing her to the very imbecility of terror."

"Mr. Rains, as the Chinese villain, scowled and deepened his voice and did everything he could think of to suggest the sinister and evil," opined the same reviewer. Another praised him for performing "with much cleverness in the first two acts. In the third the absurdity of the role proved too much for him, and he had to suffer the good-natured mockery which the ending evoked."

Rains wasn't so sure that the derision was good-natured. "The gallery rose with one accord and said 'Boo,'" he confided to a reporter.

Luigi Pirandello's *And That's the Truth (If You Think It Is)* (the title now usually translated as *Right You Are If You Think You Are*), an expressionist parable about illusion and reality, provided a fine acting platform for Rains, Nigel Playfair, and Nancy Price, and garnered better notices at the Lyric Hammersmith than the original Italian production, previously seen in London. Rains played a provincial Italian official whose separate living arrangements with his mother-in-law and wife become the target of gossipy speculation. Pirandello never explains the puzzle, which only adds to the droll philosophical humor. "There is some brilliant acting in this play by Claude Rains, who is probably the most dynamic and eruptive player now before the public," wrote one critic. "I know of no player more charged with electricity. The one danger is that he may sometimes make the sparks fly at the wrong moment. If anybody seems to be bursting to act, that man is Mr. Rains."

In Granville-Barker's talkative drama *The Madras House* at the Ambassadors Theatre in November, Rains shone in the role of an American millionaire named Eustace Perrin State. Rains next appeared, in May 1926, in a new translation of Gogol's *The Government Inspector* at the Gaiety Theatre, reprising the lead role he had played in 1921. The production, directed by Theodore Komisarjevsky, a major talent from Russia, was presented as a fantastic farce rather than as a straight comedy, and was radically stylized. Conventional sets were replaced by a revolving platform with movable windows and doors without walls, and the actors were made up to resemble puppets or toy soldiers. Rains felt he was being slighted by Komisarjevsky in favor of a Russian protégé in the cast, to whom he only spoke in Russian. Rains's costumes during dress rehearsals were uncomfortably ill-fitting, and he wasn't completely sure that it was not by design, just to throw him off.

The actor with whom he shared a dressing room was sympathetic and made a suggestion before the first preview, a matinee. He produced a bottle of scotch. "Why not have a good one?"

Rains was not accustomed to drinking during the day, much less before a performance. But he was sufficiently upset on that particular day to consent to a "good one." As a result, his first, inhibition-relaxed scene, opposite the Russian protégé, was a resounding success. The Russian actor, feeling upstaged, chose to exit the scene with Rains, in essence claiming half the applause. "It was the only thing he could do," said Rains. But his fondness for scotch would increase over the years, with serious consequences.

New in the cast of *The Government Inspector* was Charles Laughton, marking the first time teacher and student acted together professionally. Rains recalled, "I was afraid, when we played together, that he would act me out of the theatre. He was so damned good. He had that extraordinary face you could do so much with." The play had a brief tryout on the London outskirts, to which Rains personally chauffeured his still financially-struggling former pupil, insisting that Laughton bargain hard for a weekly salary of no less than five pounds.

Laughton was still living at Mrs. Forscutt's, but would soon strain his landlady's hospitality to the breaking point. One night Rains dropped by to see her and found that Laughton was no longer living there.

"Where's he gone?" he asked the landlady.

"I'd rather not say" was her cryptic reply. "He was not alone when I brought him tea in the morning. So I thought he'd better go."

Rains assumed that Laughton had been sneaking his well-known, however improbable girlfriend, Elsa Lanchester, into his rooms at night.

But Lanchester, in her autobiography, recalled that Laughton's landlady (whom she misremembered as "Mrs. Foster") was "very attached to her 'lodger'" and that it was impossible for her and Laughton to meet in Laughton's rooms. It was, perhaps, significant that Mrs. Forscutt never told Rains the exact identity of the other party in Laughton's room. Soon after, under another roof, Laughton and Lanchester would be forced into painful private negotiations over acceptable outlets for his closeted homosexuality. In any event, the doting Mrs. Forscutt clearly felt betrayed or jilted—if not in one way, then in some other.

West End propriety was hardly limited to the sexual sphere. Dramaturgical conventions were also stringent, and productions that strayed too far from established notions of the "well-made play" did so at their peril. Just as Stanislavski was resisted, so too were the substantial contributions of German expressionist drama, which had been flourishing in Berlin for more than a decade under the nurturance of producer Max Reinhardt and playwrights like Georg Kaiser, whose *From Morn to Midnight* (written in 1912 and first produced in 1916) finally came to London in 1926 in an English translation by Ashley Dukes.

Expressionist theatre was an aggressive repudiation of realism, and used symbol and stylization to project psychological realities outward. *From Morn to Midnight* is now generally regarded as an expressionist classic, though many of its first audiences outside Germany were more than a bit perplexed by what they beheld. Rains played the Cashier, a character whose impulsive theft of 60,000 marks in the opening scene (a fascinating prefiguration of Alfred Hitchcock's similarly audience-disorienting *Psycho*, especially given that film's expressionist visual energy) detonates a dizzying, day-long exploration of reality and artifice, culminating in the character's public suicide. Despite a significant supporting cast, the play amounted to a one-man performance by Rains, who had to memorize some of the longest sustained speeches in the modern theatrical canon. In the end, he appears in a public hall, stripped of all illusions, scattering the stolen money to a grasping mob.

I've been all day on the road. I confess; I'm a bank cashier. I
embezzled the money that was entrusted me. A good round

sum; sixty thousand marks! I fled with it into your city of asphalt. By this time they're on my track; perhaps they've offered a big reward. I'm not in hiding any more. I confess! You can buy nothing worth having, even with all the money of all the banks in the world. You get less than you pay, every time. The more you spend, the less the goods are worth. The money corrupts them: the money veils the truth. Money's the meanest of the paltry swindles in this world! (*He takes a gun from his pocket.*) Why did I hesitate? Why take the road? Whither am I bound? From first to last you sit there, naked bone. From morn to midnight, I rage in a circle . . . and now your beckoning finger points the way . . . whither? (*He shoots the answer into his breast*)

The Times in particular was not impressed. "We obstinately decline to see more in this play with a vulgar story with a vulgar moral," the anonymous reviewer wrote, rejecting the idea that there was any spiritual dimension in larceny.

In Rains's next play, *Before Men's Eyes* by Ben Fleet and Clifford Pember, he played a drug-addicted surgeon who redeems himself by performing delicate surgery on his wife during a raging thunderstorm. *The Times* described his work in glowing terms: "His touch is light and sure; he has an infectious vitality; he speaks a good phrase always as if it had that moment leapt to his mind." Another reviewer made a blunter assessment: "There must be something radically wrong with the London theatre that it can find no permanent employment for this consummate actor."

Although Rains did not immediately realize it, these were the last notices he would ever receive for his work on the British stage.

3

An Actor Abroad

IN LATE 1926, BEATRIX THOMSON was offered the female lead in the New York production of *The Constant Nymph*, a play based on the best-selling novel by Margaret Kennedy and adapted by Basil Dean. The story of the romantic downfall of a naïve child-woman had been a hit in London, but the original British cast members were unavailable. Beatrix was uncomfortable about traveling alone, and Rains wasn't enthusiastic about cutting his ties with the London stage and with RADA. After an unpleasant confrontation with Beatrix's brother, who insisted that Rains accompany his sister to America for what the family perceived to be a major career opportunity, Rains finally assented.

He wasn't entirely convinced of his wife's stage potential. "She had a false sense of her relationship to the theatre," he would later say. Although Beatrix—or, as he called her, "Trixie"—was undeniably talented, Rains believed her to be too shy and unassertive to succeed in acting. He thought her real calling was in producing and management, and felt that she would probably have been happier running a theatre than performing.

It is unclear whether Beatrix's wealthy family subsidized Rains's accompanying his wife to New York, but it is highly likely. Despite his critical acclaim and the adoration of his students, acting and teaching in London were not providing a steady income. John Gielgud recalled his dilemma. "I said to him, while he was still working in London, why do you want to go to America? He said, 'Well, I can't eat my notices.' He always had wonderful press, but he never became a top star in billing, you know. And I suppose that disillusioned him."

To secure income of his own, Rains accepted the minor role of a butler in *The Constant Nymph*, a demeaning assignment given his substantial London credentials, but he was completely unknown in New York. Besides, this was supposed to be his wife's time in the sun, not his own. Beatrix received respectable reviews, though she was criticized for her diction, and many critics made note of the fact that she was not the first, or even second, choice for the role. Rains himself, however, judged her performance "excellent." In New York, they lived at the New Weston Hotel on Madison Avenue.

But Rains's restlessness for theatrical attention of his own would soon win out. He left *The Constant Nymph* for a short-lived lead comic role as an eccentric musician in Henry Stillman's *Lally* at the Greenwich Village Theatre. The *New York Times* commented on his defection: "His reasons for doing so are probably to be found in the part itself, for it is a florid, showy impersonation, giving any actor abundant opportunity to create a character that at best is none too credible. . . . In fairness to Mr. Rains it should be said that he has probably done as well with the material given him as any male human could do."

Rains and Beatrix returned to London in the summer of 1927 and shortly thereafter gave up their residence at Camden Grove to return to America and go on the road with *The Constant Nymph,* this time with Rains in the male lead. The *Philadelphia Ledger* was impressed by the couple's performance, calling Beatrix "superb" and Rains "equally splendid," but perhaps striking too close to the real-life bone in its observation that "Mr. Rains well presents the picture of the unconventional composer, foolishly caught in a marriage that is imposing rigid, chafing, and inspiration-killing restrictions on his conduct." The income disparities of husband and wife were underscored when, according to one newspaper account, she purchased a parcel of New Jersey real estate as an investment almost on a whim during their Philadelphia engagement.

Their relationship at this point was seriously strained. Rains continued to receive glowing reviews and opportunities, while his wife's theatrical fortunes languished. Despite her excellent British training, *The Constant Nymph* threatened to be an American one-hit wonder for Beatrix.

In the winter of 1927–1928 the couple returned to New York and rented an apartment on East Eighty-Sixth Street. At the time, they were acting in Don Marquis's comedy *Out of the Sea*. In the spring they moved to another apartment, on West Fifty-Seventh Street. Rains recalled, "My wife had been inactive from the early spring up to the time she visited Baltimore to play for a week in Mr. Knopf's repertory about the month of May." Meanwhile, he said, "I had been employed by other managements in New York, namely the Greenwich Village Theatre for a period of two weeks, and by the Messrs. Shuberts for about eight weeks." Then, "with the acquiescence of my wife," Rains signed a three-year contract with the Theatre Guild of New York City, "to commence in the late summer."

The Theatre Guild was the most prestigious producing organization in America, a resident New York ensemble that also toured; it was the first attempt at a truly national theatre company in the United States. The Guild specialized in edgy, serious plays; it was a major force in the career of Eugene O'Neill, as well as being the leading American producer of Shaw. Rains was suggested as the company's replacement for a well-regarded character actor named Edward G. Robinson, who was departing to explore film work in Hollywood.

"Who suggested me?" Rains asked Theresa Helburn, one of the Guild's founders, when she phoned him with the offer.

"Alexander Woollcott," she replied. "He's seen you in England and thinks you should be in the company." Woollcott was the former drama critic of the *New York Times*, now in the same position at the *Sun*. A bigger-than-life character, Woollcott is best remembered today as the inspiration for the acerbic character Sheridan Whiteside in George S. Kaufman and Moss Hart's *The Man Who Came to Dinner*.

"But I don't even know him," Rains replied, flabbergasted.

"Well, he knows you."

That summer, before beginning his work with the Guild, Rains and Beatrix journeyed to Hartford, Connecticut, where they were employed by the Macbane Players, a noted stock company, for a short season, including works by Shaw and Molnar. During their engagement in Massachusetts, Woollcott himself, to Rains's surprise, came backstage to introduce himself. He had a house in the Berkshires and invited Rains for lunch. After the meal, they strolled into the garden, where Woollcott's remarks "became increasingly personal, very sentimental," Rains later recalled, especially on the topic of Ruth Gordon, an actress who was then a member of the Theatre Guild.

"She's the only woman I've ever loved," Woollcott told Rains.

"Why don't you do something about it?" Rains asked.

"You goddamn fool," Woollcott shot back. "Don't you know I've had the mumps?" Side effects of the mumps in adult men can include atrophy of the testicles and impotence. Woollcott had contracted the disease in his early twenties.

"I don't think he ever had a woman in his life," Rains said.

At the end of Rains's summer tour, he returned to New York to take up his work with the Theatre Guild. He began by understudying, and then replacing, Dudley Digges in the title role of Ben Jonson's *Volpone,* as adapted by Stefan Zweig.

Vincent Sherman, another company member and understudy, didn't quite know what to make of Rains at first. "He was very quiet, to himself, reticent. He was very slow, I thought, in picking up what had to be done. And I said, oh, man, this guy will never get it. He would question every line as the stage manager said, now you move over here, now you do this, now you do that, to follow what the principals had done. But I realized, as the days went on and we continued rehearsing, he wanted to know every step of what he was doing and why he was doing it. And then slowly, little by little, I began to see the part begin to take shape. And he brought a kind of wily foxiness to the part of Volpone that even Digges didn't have, and Digges was a very fine English actor. By the time opening night came he was wonderful."

Sherman recalled some of the details that Rains brought to the title role. "If you know the story of *Volpone,* it's an old man who pretends to be dying, so that all the people that want to get a part of his fortune bring him gifts." Rains "put in business that was very funny and got howls of laughter."

On a personal note, Sherman, who was at the time "just a beginner, a youngster at the Guild," recalls that Rains was "very nice to me." Sherman, Rains, and the rising actor Morris Carnovsky all became friendly and often met for coffee or a meal after a performance.

Beatrix, who had returned to New York from her engagement with the Macbane Players a month later than her husband, remained in New York, working in Charles Hopkins's company, while Rains left on tour with the Theatre Guild. The production was *Marco Millions* by Eugene O'Neill, an exotically staged tale of Marco Polo's journey to China. Rains replaced Dudley Digges for the touring version, playing a key advisor to Kubla Khan.

During the runs of *Volpone* and *Marco Millions*, Rains made the acquaintance of an eighteen-year-old bit-part actress named Frances Propper. She was frankly more interested in finding a husband and settling down than in becoming a star. Frances's sister, who had paid for her theatrical training, cautioned her about the instability of the profession. "What's happened to the theatre? Isn't there anyone in it any more who just wants to be an actor?" She knew that several of the Guild actors had aspirations to other careers. There was Johnny Mercer, a struggling young songwriter who was acting in bit parts. There was Vincent Sherman, an aspiring director. And Albert van Dekker, who really wanted to be an artist, but who would eventually drop the "van" from his name and become famous as Hollywood's Dr. Cyclops.

Frances pondered her sister's question about who in the Guild was actually serious about his profession. "Oh, yes . . . there's an attractive older man—I forget his name—something to do with the weather. Oh, yes—Claude Rains."

Her sister laughed. "No actor would have a silly name like that."

It turned out that Rains had noticed Frances Propper and wondered about her name. "And *is* she very proper?" he is said to have asked. Frances later told a journalist, "Maybe it was each of us thinking that the other had such a weird name that brought us together."

Their relationship was not, in fact, at all proper. Rains was still married to Beatrix. But he and Frances began sleeping together shortly after they met. "I was lonely, and she was weary of virginity," Rains said.

In an effort to relieve the tension with Beatrix, he sent her copies of glowing reviews while he was on the road, but to no avail. "In November," Rains later wrote, "when I was playing in Cleveland, Ohio, my wife informed me on the telephone that she no longer loved me, and that she no longer wished to stay in this country. I implored her to remain with me, but she was adamant."

"I remember walking the streets in an overcoat I've still got," said Rains almost forty years later. "God, I was miserable."

By late 1928 he and Beatrix were virtually living apart. Rains later wrote, "Early in December I visited her in New York, and at her request, arranged for her to sail immediately, which she did." Subsequently, according to Rains, Beatrix "wrote to our mutual friend, Mrs. William Adams, of New York City, asking her to inform me how resolute she was never to return to me and confessing her love for another man." In January 1929, Rains signed a three-year lease for a new, Beatrix-free apartment at 159 East Thirty-Third Street, in the Murray Hill district.

In the spring of 1929, Rains appeared with the Guild company in *The Camel Through the Needle's Eye*, a comedy by Frantisek Langer. "Claude Rains makes a capital figure of an irate continental father by the device of playing as if someone had shoved a ramrod down his back," observed the *New York Times*. Rains next had a smaller role in *Karl and Anna*, acting with Otto Kruger and Gale Sondergaard, who would soon be Hollywood bound. Another soon-to-be-Broadway-expatriate, Henry Fonda, played with Rains in *The Game of Love and Death* by Romain Rolland, but Rains won the critical kudos. The director was future Hollywood filmmaker Rouben Mamoulian. "He was wonderful," Rains said. "He knew what to do with me."

In the winter and spring of 1930 Rains played Proteus, the prime minister, in Shaw's *The Apple Cart*, once more earning glowing reviews and a long run. That summer, he later wrote, "I went back to England, where I saw my wife, and with the realization of how hopeless a reunion was, I returned to [New York] on a Visitor's Permit, and continued my bachelor residence." He had decided to make the United States his permanent home. Accordingly, he wrote, "I sailed to England for the purpose of securing a quota number to return to this country as an immigrant."

Rains next played multiple roles in the Guild's production of *Miracle at Verdun* by Hans Chlumberg. The director was Herbert J. Biberman.

"He'd just come back from Russia," said Rains, "and was full of new ideas." These ideas included the acting theories of Stanislavski, innovations in set design, and revolutionary politics. *Miracle* was an ambitious, multimedia event with a cast of seventy, including a sequence in which the dead soldiers of the Great War rise from their graves. Biberman, however, may have been a bit too ambitious for New York audiences—and perhaps for Rains as well. "He combined film and stage techniques, and killed it," Rains said.

In Alfred Savoir's comedy *He*, Rains turned once again to the role of Napoleon—or at least the character of an elevator operator who thinks he is Napoleon. As in many of his assignments, Rains was the one performer who drew critical plaudits. Although he never admitted it, Rains had by this time established an undeniable pattern of regularly accepting poor material—and then, given his trademark intensity of performance, stealing the show. The plays may have been mediocre and had short runs, but Rains almost always attracted the lion's share of critical attention.

The Moon in the Yellow River by Denis Johnston paired him opposite Henry Hull, and was followed by Shaw's *Too True to Be Good*, in which he played the Elder. Meanwhile, the Guild's adaptation of Pearl Buck's Pulitzer Prize–winning novel *The Good Earth*, about a Chinese peasant and his slave-wife, had encountered problems out of town. It appeared that the original leading man "wasn't strong enough" (in Rains's words) to play against the formidable Alla Nazimova as the wife. In fact, Nazimova, a Moscow-trained legend and long a leading presence on the New York stage as well as in silent films, was not so much the problem as a disjointed script by Owen and Donald Davis. Rains nonetheless stepped in.

Before leaving for Pittsburgh to join the company of *The Good Earth*, Rains reconnected briefly with Charles Laughton and Elsa Lanchester. Laughton had earned exceptionally good Broadway notices for his work in productions of *Payment Deferred* and *Alibi*, in which he had been very successful in London, though the plays failed to find audiences in America. After performances, Laughton and Lanchester would come by Rains's apartment. There he would cook them kippers, a dish for which he had a lifelong fondness, in commemoration of their mutual roots. Laughton and Lanchester were considering moving back to London, but Rains wasn't. He had just rented a cottage in Middlebush, New Jersey, and was contemplating putting his savings into a large parcel of New Jersey land. Theatre was always a precarious business, never so much so than in the midst of the Great Depression. If he was ever unable to act, Rains figured, at least he might be able to grow his own food. On the morning of Rains's departure to Pennsylvania (he had to catch a noon train) Laughton phoned.

"Like to see you, sir, before you leave," he said.

The schedule was awkward. Rains was supposed to have brunch at ten o'clock at the home of a doctor who ran a small hospital on Madison Avenue. His wife was the sister of an actress who had played opposite Rains in Shaw's *The Apple Cart*, and he felt an obligation. But as it turned out, Laughton was also taking brunch at the same time, almost next door, so Rains agreed to drop by.

Laughton's brunch companions were Alexander Woollcott, who hosted, Alfred Lunt, Lynne Fontanne, and Elsa. Rains remembered Woollcott in dishabille, wearing a dressing gown, with "books stacked all over the place." After some light conversation, Rains got up and began to leave, only to hear the pattering of feet behind him. He turned. Laughton was standing there, with his hands behind his back.

"Sir, I've never been able, really, to express how I feel what you did for me, and other students, at the Academy. It was wonderful to have had you as a teacher. It's been difficult to know how to do it—how to thank you. I thought of writing a letter, or this, that, and the other, and—well—here, sir!"

Laughton handed him a portfolio, then vanished. The album was filled with etchings of the great French thespian Coquelin—the actor for whom Rains had served as call boy at His Majesty's Theatre years before—in all of his famous roles.

The Good Earth opened in New York on October 17, 1932, to scathing reviews. Perhaps worst of all was the appraisal of Brooks Atkinson, the *New York Times* reviewer, who noted, "Every year our foremost drama organization opens, by special arrangement with God, on a rainy night, and every year it begins with a bad play." The difficulties of adapting Buck's sweeping novel to the stage were compounded at the first performance by

Nazimova's slowing her delivery to a snail's pace, adding almost twenty minutes to the playing time. Whether it was a case of nerves (despite all her success in the theatre, she suffered from chronic stage fright) or a deliberate attempt to milk her stage time is a matter of conjecture. But, in any case, it helped sink the show. "As O-Lan, the slave wife, Nazimova has in the early scenes an interior image of the dumb, clumsy peasant that goes straight to the heart of that magnificent character," Atkinson wrote. "But in the latter half of the play her acting subsides into torture-some grimaces and her speaking becomes a series of primordial sounds." Rains fared little better. "Claude Rains is quite on the surface in his early scenes, and his hind of the fields speaks like a University man. When Wang Lung becomes more like a gentleman in the last part of the play Mr. Rains's style is more suitable." All in all, Atkinson concluded, "In the exact proportion that *The Good Earth* is a full and excellent novel it is an empty and scattered play." It ran for just fifty-six performances.

Emil Ludwig's political satire *Versailles*, retitled *Peace Palace* for its Guild production, was given an out-of-town tryout, with Rains in heavy makeup as Georges Clemenceau, but the show never made it to New York. Rains had renewed his Guild contract until 1933. He requested a raise, which was turned down, and found that few roles were forthcoming. He made a strong impression in a bizarre pacifist melodrama (not produced by the Guild), *The Man Who Reclaimed His Head* by Jean Bart, which opened at the Broadhurst Theatre in September 1932. Rains played Paul Verin, a sickly, disfigured political writer whose idealistic pieces are cynically misused by corrupt war-machine interests, leading eventually to melodramatic revenge (the decapitation telegraphed by the title). The director was Herbert J. Biberman, who had also directed *Miracle at Verdun*; and here, too, he swamped the production with too much stage technology, primarily a carousel-like set, which broke the stiffly written play into ever more mechanical tableaux as it revolved. Rains's performance was likewise over the top, in a manner that was compared to Lon Chaney's Hollywood grotesques. According to Brooks Atkinson, "Claude Rains, who is one of the best actors the Theatre Guild ever had, plays Verin in terms of makeup, deformity, and asthma." The *New York Herald Tribune* called his performance "an abandoned combination of Dracula and Mr.

Hyde." *Catholic World* judged that Rains "accentuated his deformities with a delivery as jerky as his movements. The rest of the cast seems to have caught the habit. They speak their lines as so many automata." Verin's wife was played by Jean Arthur, whom Rains found a "very attractive but very temperamental actress," alternately insecure and abrasive. A silent-era starlet at Paramount, Arthur's career stalled at the dawn of talkies as legions of stage-trained actors (like Rains) began arriving in Hollywood. She reversed the pattern by taking to the stage after her first studio contract was dropped. Although her throaty, often cracking voice would eventually become her screen trademark in screwball comedies, at the time of *The Man Who Reclaimed His Head* the critics were not kind in their appraisal of her vocal skills.

The Man Who Reclaimed His Head closed within a month.

Following a small, thankless part in a single act of the Guild's historical triptych *American Dream* by George O'Neil in February 1933 Rains began to consider other career options. The Guild, for its part, had long been resigned to company members departing for greener pastures, particularly Hollywood.

But Rains would be the first actor to make a move to Hollywood for the specific purpose of *not* being seen.

4

Invisibility and After

DESPITE HIS REPUTATION AS A VERSATILE and often adventurous performer, Claude Rains was oddly indifferent to the medium of motion pictures. He claimed to have seen only a half-dozen films prior to joining the Theatre Guild (and several, perhaps, were less-than-artistic silent vehicles in which his less-than-beloved father Fred appeared). Once in New York, however, he became acutely aware of the precariousness of theatrical life in the Great Depression and watched as Guild alumni steadily headed for Hollywood. Edward G. Robinson, whom he had replaced in the company, had already had a tremendous success in the title role of *Little Caesar*, but other Guild actors weren't so lucky. Peg Entwhistle was a well-regarded performer whose move to California led only to professional disappointment and depression; her most notable achievement in the film colony was her suicidal high-dive from the "Hollywoodland" sign.

Nonetheless, talking pictures were by the early 1930s a firmly established and profitable sector of the American entertainment industry, posing a threat to legitimate theatre as well as vaudeville. For one thing, movies provided a far cheaper form of entertainment. The Guild was under financial strain, had to briefly suspend operations, and had also refused Rains's request for a raise. The nation's dire economic state attracted a number of Guild members to radical politics. Rains remembered being invited by director Herbert J. Biberman to a private reception for a Chinese actress; he escorted Guild founder and company member Helen Westley to the event. When the "actress" was introduced, instead of discussing the theatre, she began to deliver a shrill communist screed. Rains whispered to Westley, "Let's get out of here," and they quietly slipped out.

The limited, irregular income from New York stage work was no match for the potential of motion pictures. Rains engaged Harold Freedman of the Brandt and Brandt Theatrical Department as his agent to explore film work. Freedman was well connected with the studios and represented many New York-based dramatists and performers in the early 1930s, when a great migration from stage to screen (and from east to west) was gaining momentum.

Rains made a screen test for RKO's *A Bill of Divorcement* that was an unqualified disaster. In an attempt to be showy, Rains had chosen a bombastic speech from *The Man Who Reclaimed His Head* that the camera magnified unmercifully—asthma, google-eyes, and all. A second monologue, as Napoleon from Shaw's *The Man of Destiny*, was also unlikely to land him a part in a naturalistic modern drama. Rains himself later described his first performance in front of a camera in twelve years as "the worst screen test in the history of moviemaking." John Barrymore ultimately played the *Divorcement* role opposite Katharine Hepburn. As a kind of consolation prize, Rains took the part on radio in wake of the film's publicity. Meanwhile, legend has it, the awful screen test was circulated in Hollywood as a kind of joke reel.

Freedman, however, believed in Rains's screen potential. He was largely responsible for *Dracula* and *Frankenstein* being purchased and produced by Universal, inaugurating a new era of horror films. Freedman had a well-established relationship with both Carl Laemmle, Sr., and Carl Laemmle, Jr., and had personally shepherded the properties through years of studio indecision and negotiation intrigue, acting as referee between father and son over the potential of weird pictures.

Dracula and *Frankenstein* were hugely successful, arguably saving Universal from insolvency during the worst year of the Great Depression. Junior Laemmle, a proponent of strange stories, embarked on a whole slew of macabre and fantastical photoplays. One of them was *The Invisible Man*, based on the famous novella by H. G. Wells. The director attached to *The Invisible Man* was Rains's old acquaintance from London, James Whale, who had scored a major Hollywood success with *Frankenstein* and was given remarkable freedom in developing his own projects. Many accounts of Rains's being cast in *The Invisible Man* maintain or infer that Whale somehow "discovered" Rains via the RKO screen test ("I don't care who that actor is, but I want that voice!"), but Whale was in fact already fully aware of Rains's talent, reputation, and, most especially, voice.

According to Rains, he was called for a test in New York. He had not even seen a complete script and was unaware of the convoluted journey the screenplay had already taken. *Dracula* and *Frankenstein* had accustomed Universal to play fast and loose in adapting classic thrillers, milking them for name value rather than literary fidelity. Both the Bram Stoker and the Mary Shelley screen adaptations were based on stage plays the novelists would have barely recognized as representations of their work. The original authors were also conveniently dead. H. G. Wells, however, was still very much alive, and he was a major literary figure with a keen interest in the medium of film. Universal acquired the film rights to *The Invisible Man* for $10,000 on September 22, 1931, for a period of ten years (the studio would later purchase the rights in perpetuity). Of this, $6,000 went not to Wells but to the French producer Louis Nalpas, who had originally bought the rights with a silent film in mind but by 1931 was on the verge of retirement.

Paramount had just produced an adaptation of Wells's novel *The Island of Dr. Moreau*, retitled *The Island of Lost Souls* and starring Charles Laughton. Wells was reportedly unhappy with the results. Despite a bravura performance by Laughton in the film, Wells's complicated social/scientific satire had been reduced to the dimensions of a standard horror movie. The British author requested and was granted script approval for *The Invisible Man*.

Wells's novella had all the makings of a terrific film. The narrative was simplicity itself, beginning with the arrival of a bandage-swathed stranger at an English inn in the dead of winter. He is at first taken to be the victim of a terrible, disfiguring accident, but gradually his true condition is revealed. The story plays out as a classic narrative of Faustian hubris. Rather than being rewarded for his amazing scientific discovery, Griffin, the Invisible One, is misunderstood and ostracized, driven to crime, and finally hunted down and killed by a society that cannot accept him.

Universal first intended *The Invisible Man* as a thrills-and-chills vehicle for Boris Karloff. Director Robert Florey and screenwriter Garrett Fort, both of whom had been involved with the script of *Frankenstein*

(Florey had been the directorial choice before Whale), collaborated on a screenplay, which was rejected in the spring of 1932. John L. Balderston (coauthor of the stage versions of *Dracula* and *Frankenstein,* which Universal had purchased) was then tapped for a treatment and three scripts, including an unsuccessful collaboration with director Cyril Gardner. John Huston and script department head Richard Schayer also made contributions, also in vain. Martin Brown contributed an undated treatment, and Laird Doyle, who would later work on many of Rains's Warner Bros. pictures, also turned in a complete screenplay.

Many of the difficulties with story development arose from Universal's having also bought the rights to Philip Wylie's 1931 novel *The Murderer Invisible* and the studio's tortuous attempts to force a hybrid storyline. Wylie's book contained sensational elements undreamed of by Wells—an aquarium battle with an invisible octopus, a nefarious plot to send plague-bearing invisible rats into Manhattan, and so on. Wylie, as it happened, had also worked on the script for *Island of Lost Souls,* and his involvement in the present project, however tangential, could not have endeared him to Wells.

Despite all the rejected scripts, no one was yet speaking up for Wells's work—except perhaps Wells himself.

James Whale, who had been on and off the project, tried his hand at an original treatment. Whale posited that the Invisible Man is motivated to disappear not because of scientific curiosity, but rather out of a desperate attempt to escape the sight of his own terrible facial disfigurement, acquired while selflessly attending the sick. In an agony of religious torment, he makes a Faust-like appeal to God:

> OH THOU WHO ART INVISIBLE
> and to whom nothing is unseen
> who carest for the sick and fatherless,
> who created the earth and all that is upon
> it, to whom there is no mystery in man or
> beast: THOU who gavest and takest away, hear
> the prayer of thy servant, and remove from
> the eyes of mortal man the harmful sight of

this frightful face, that I may be allowed to do
thy will unseen . . .

He discovers the means to invisibility, but at a price. "With all the
arts of Camera and mystery trickery," wrote Whale, "the stupendous
achievement is complete, but our horror grows as we discover that during the transition the mind has completely changed, and now has only a
longing to kill those people he had healed and befriended."

Whale conceived a lurid climax in a church, where the invisible mad-
man stalks down and stabs to death the beautiful girl he once loved, who
is taking novitiate vows. And yet,

> Our meal of horror is not yet complete. The liqueur is still
> to be served. Our eyes must surely pop completely out as we
> watch the knife jerk out of the now unlovely corpse, raise itself
> into mid-air, and plunge itself quivering into the heart of the
> remorseful invisible man. Who, as his life's blood ebbs swiftly
> away, becomes gradually visible, revealing for an instant, a face
> so fantastically horrible that even we who are used to such
> dishes, close our eyes, as the sound of a dull flopping thud
> forces the sickening news through our other senses, that the
> lovers are united at last!

Whale had a flair for Grand Guignol excess, and it's not clear how
much of this treatment he intended seriously. But the concept of invisibility leading to insanity was a deft dramatic stroke and would prove to
have staying power. Whale's proposed story was handed over to accomplished silent film scenarist Gouverneur Morris, who developed it into
yet another full-length script, which, not surprisingly, was met with disap-
proval by Schayer and Laemmle. In addition, Preston Sturges submitted
a Russian-based concept, moving the story to czarist Russia and splitting
the main character in two: a scientist who discovers the invisibility secret (a part intended for Paul Lukas) and a mentally deficient guinea pig
(Boris Karloff).

After all that, it was popular novelist John Weld who discovered that,

despite all the development work to date, Universal didn't even possess
a reference copy of Wells's book. Weld found one at a Hollywood library
and wrote a straightforward adaptation of the novel, which was further
developed by R. C. Sherriff, the celebrated English playwright who had
written the World War I drama *Journey's End* (which had taken Whale as
a director first to New York and then to Hollywood). Sherriff incorporated Whale's insanity conceit, added a romantic subplot (the invisible
man's previously nonexistent fiancée), broadened the humor involving
the innkeepers and villagers, and added a melodramatic revenge twist
involving an automobile crash (Wells's novel was published in 1897, still
solidly an age of horse-drawn conveyances). But the liberties Sherriff took
with Wells's story were dramaturgically sound—at least by Hollywood
standards—and the core of the tale remained intact. Wells is reported to
have bristled initially at Griffin's newfound Hollywood insanity ("Instead
of an Invisible Man, we now have an Invisible Lunatic!"), but the Invisible Man's ascending megalomaniacal tirades enhance the story, offering
the actor playing the part an especially rich opportunity absent in the
Wells original:

> I shall offer my secret to the world, with all its terrible power.
> The nations of the world will bid for it. Thousands! Millions!
> The nation that wins my secret can sweep the world with
> invisible armies . . . Don't you see what it means? Power! Power
> to rule! Power to make the world grovel at my feet!

Casting, too, presented problems. Karloff was involved in a contractual contretemps with the studio, and negotiations on a new agreement
were reaching an impasse. Colin Clive, who had played the monster's
maker in *Frankenstein*, was considered as a possible replacement, but he
was unavailable.

Rains himself initially didn't take the studio's feeler seriously. The
RKO screen test had been humiliating enough. He was finishing his work
in *Peace Palace* in New York and was considering another stage part. As
he recalled, "I dropped in [to Universal's New York office], read the lines
that were given to me, then dashed on to the theatre for my performance.

Imagine my surprise the next day when the Universal man called me on the telephone and told me I was perfectly grand. Would I do the part? Would I arrange to leave for Hollywood as soon as possible? Would I sign the contract?" He remained skeptical until his agent, Harold Freedman, told him the terms of the contract, including the fact that he had negotiated top billing for Rains, plus an onscreen credit above the screen title (though not in advertising) twice the size of H. G. Wells's, and an option on a second picture.

Contract in hand, Rains began packing his trunks, but before leaving the East Coast for Hollywood, he purchased a fifty-eight-acre farm in Lambertville, New Jersey. The Queen Anne–style farmhouse became the repository for all his possessions, including his papers and theatrical memorabilia. If Hollywood failed to provide, Rains figured, he would provide for himself—as a working farmer. His own family's lack of permanent roots had inculcated a deep regard for the value of land ownership and self-sufficiency.

Upon arriving at Universal City, Rains was surprised to be told by James Whale that he would appear throughout the film swathed in bandages, and sometimes only as a disembodied voice. Worse yet, many of the special-effects sequences in which the Invisible Man is partially clothed—some of the film's showiest moments—would be performed by a stuntman, with Rains lip-synchronizing dialogue to a physical performance that was not his own, some of which would be executed after the end of his contract. "I had spent years fighting for my artistic integrity," he later said; and here he wouldn't even have corporeal integrity.

One of the first things Universal required was having Rains's head and shoulders cast in plaster. A mold was needed for two key scenes: first, to provide the understructure for a thin wire cage that perfectly matched Rains's physiognomy, from which bandages could be dramatically removed for two unveiling sequences; and, second, for the hospital death scene where Griffin regains visibility. It was a claustrophobic process, with Rains having to endure breathing tubes inserted in his nostrils, with his head encased in immobilizing plaster, which gave off an uncomfortable degree of heat as it set. He later told his daughter it triggered flashbacks to his war injuries in the trenches and his subsequent hospitalization.

Rains's casting prompted prominent actor Chester Morris to depart the cast. Morris had been slated to play the role of Dr. Arthur Kemp, Griffin's nemesis, but he bridled at taking anything less than top billing. He was replaced by Theatre Guild alumnus William Harrigan, with whom Rains had acted in *The Moon in the Yellow River*. Two other Guild actors, Henry Travers and Dudley Digges (whom Rains had replaced in *Volpone*), also appeared in the film. Ironically, all three supporting actors would be seen on screen far more than Rains, the nominal star.

The Invisible Man provided unique challenges to both performers and technicians. The head of Universal's effects department was John P. Fulton, who, working with the independent Frank Williams Composite Laboratory Company, pushed the "traveling matte" optical printing process to unprecedented levels of ingenuity. In an article for *American Cinematographer* published a year after the film's release, Fulton wrote, "We used a completely black set—walled and floored with black velvet, to be as nearly nonreflective as possible."

> Our actor was garbed from head to foot in black velvet tights, with black gloves, and a black headpiece rather like a driver's helmet. Over this, he wore whatever clothes might be required. This gave us a picture of the unsupported clothes moving around on a dead black field. From this negative, we made a print, and a duplicate negative which we intensified to serve as mattes for printing. Then, with an ordinary printer, we proceeded to make our composite: first we printed from the positive of the background and the normal action, using the intensified, negative matte to mask off the area where our invisible man's clothing was to move.

A second round of optical printing added the moving clothes, and the composite final negative was painstakingly retouched by hand, using opaque dye to eliminate visual imperfections. According to Fulton, "We photographed thousands of feet of film in the many 'takes' of the different scenes, and approximately 4,000 feet of film received individual hand-work treatment in some degree, making approximately 64,000 frames which were individually retouched in this manner!"

A scene in which the Invisible Man stands before a mirror and re-moves his bandages was exceptionally complex, requiring four separate negatives, and was perhaps the most elaborate composite shot ever at-tempted in Hollywood, rivaled only by some sequences in *King Kong*, also released in 1933. "First, there was the shot of the wall and the mirror," wrote Fulton, "with the mirror itself masked out by black velvet; next, a separate shot of the opposite wall of the room, as reflected in the mirror; thirdly, the shot of the invisible man, from the rear, unwrapping his bandages; and lastly, the reflection of him, from the front, doing the same act."

No record exists detailing just how the work was divided by Rains and his double, but the filming was grueling for both. According to Ful-ton, the black-suited scenes were especially difficult. "In some of these scenes, it was possible to leave small eye-holes in the helmet, through which the player could see: but in others—especially the close shots of the unwrapping action—this was impossible, and the player had to act 'blind.' Air had to be supplied through tubes, as in a diving suit—but the tubes were concealed, usually running up a trouser-leg." Midsummer filming, coupled with the intense heat of arc lights, made the work especially un-comfortable. "On at least one occasion," Fulton wrote, "[Rains] fainted in the middle of a scene. Had he not been in splendid physical condition, I doubt if he could have survived the strenuous ordeal of working in such a costume, under such conditions." He continued:

In nearly all of these scenes, though they were made silent, it was difficult—sometimes impossible—to direct the actor, for the helmet muffled the sound from the outside, and the air-tubes made a roaring rumble in his ears, which drowned out any sounds which might filter through the padding. When I used a large megaphone, and shouted at the top of my voice, he could just barely hear a faint murmur! Accordingly, we had to rehearse and rehearse—and then make many "takes"; as a rule, [by] "Take 20" of any such scene, we felt ourselves merely well started toward getting our shot!

77

The optical work proved far more expensive than anyone expected, and it took months following production for Universal and an outside vendor to arbitrate a $2,500 settlement for disputed expenses.

Despite all its technical derring-do, Universal lagged behind other studios in prestige and production values. Gloria Stuart, Rains's leading lady in *The Invisible Man*, recalled in a 1997 interview that Universal was considered a bit "potschke"—a Yiddishism meaning something not serious, or otherwise slapdash. She had earlier been skeptical about accepting a contract for Whale's previous film, *The Old Dark House*. Having worked on stage at the Pasadena Playhouse, Stuart hoped that film work might lead to a career on Broadway. Universal, tucked away in the boondocks of the then-undeveloped San Fernando Valley, with the president's sprawling family billeted in backlot bungalows, was not exactly Stuart's idea of a stepping-stone to prestige. Unlike MGM and Paramount, Universal's bread and butter consisted of popular programmers, with only an occasional "A" picture like *All Quiet on the Western Front* thrown into the mix. Even with its horror-assisted reprieve from bankruptcy, the studio was far from a glamour palace.

Stuart ran into some unanticipated treatment on the set. Rains, his stage ego seriously hampered by a bandaged disguise, responded with some untypically impolite behavior. "He was upstaging me," said Stuart. Rains, she maintained, repeatedly backed her into the camera, rendering *her* invisible—a bizarre situation where neither performer's face could be seen. Apparently, Rains felt that if he couldn't be seen, nobody else should be, either. Whale interceded, according to Stuart. "James said, 'Now, Claude, you are not in the theatre. This is a motion picture set. And we can shoot the scene over and over and over again until Gloria has one half of the shot.'" She recalled that it took three additional takes to finish the scene.

In Stuart's opinion, "Claude Rains was what we would call 'an actor's actor'—and twenty-four hours a day, on a set on a stage, in a bar, going to the loo, baking a cake, he was giving a performance." With Rains, "there was no camaraderie, no feeling or concern about the other actor. He was not one of my favorite people, I'm afraid; he never extended himself in any direction, as far as being gracious or saying 'Hello.'" Since she was taller than Rains, he also had to stand on boxes while she worked in her stocking feet. Still, Stuart acknowledged, "this was Claude's first film, with so much pressure to succeed, and under the kind of technical constraints that would have left a lesser actor flummoxed. He rose to the occasion with that distinctive, expressive voice of his. And it was an honor to have worked with him."

Whale, concerned about Rains's near-total unfamiliarity with film or film acting, had ordered him to start seeing at least three movies a day in the days before he left for California. Rains found a willing movie companion in his Theatre Guild friend Helen Westley. (Westley herself would move to Hollywood and be featured in James Whale's *Showboat* a few years later.)

Vincent Sherman, who had been called to Hollywood to reprise a role he had played on stage in Elmer Rice's *Counselor at Law,* recalled that Rains was staying a posh hotel called the Chateau de L'Elysee on Franklin Avenue during the filming of *The Invisible Man.* Soon after arriving in California, Sherman called Rains to let him know he was in town.

"Well, well, your first trip to California?" Rains asked. "You've never seen the Pacific Ocean?"

"Never."

"Good. Let's have dinner tonight and I'll drive you out."

They dined at Musso and Frank on Hollywood Boulevard, already well established as a leading industry grill and watering hole; after dinner, they drove out to Santa Monica in a snazzy little Ford roadster ("with red wire wheels," Sherman recalled) that Rains had acquired with some of his Universal largesse. Rains and Sherman had a long talk on the beach about their simultaneous good fortune in the film business and what it all might mean, or not mean. Neither had any faith that the role of a character who is never actually seen on screen or that of a communist radical (Sherman's part in *Counselor*) would be tickets to success. Of course, neither could anticipate their later highly successful collaborations as director and actor. The sunset conversation on the beach would be Sherman's last encounter with Rains for seven years.

Rains returned briefly to New Jersey after *The Invisible Man* had wrapped, then traveled back to Los Angeles in September for what he assumed would be the pick-up on his second picture contract option with Universal. Exactly what transpired during this September visit and what film he almost made is not clear, but the option was not exercised. *The Invisible Man* was still in expensive and complicated post-production, and the box office potential of the decidedly quirky picture was not predictable. Rains was still an unproven Hollywood commodity. And James Whale's previous production, *The Old Dark House*, imbued like *The Invisible Man* with the director's eccentric sense of humor, had not done particularly well. In short, Universal could not have predicted that *The Invisible Man*, finally released in November 1933, would become an international sensation and one of its top-grossing films of the year, or that the *New York Times* would name it one of the best ten motion pictures of 1933. Despite this acclaim, *Variety*, the bible of entertainment trade publications, didn't even mention Rains in its otherwise positive review of the film.

Not particularly impressed by his first foray into Hollywood, Rains returned east while *The Invisible Man* was still being edited. He rejoined the Theatre Guild in February 1934 for the role of attorney Nathan G. Rubin in John Wexley's *They Shall Not Die*. The play was based on the recent, explosive Scottsboro trials, in which nine Alabamian black men were sentenced to death on a false accusation of gang rape. Rains's part was based on the real-life defense attorney in the case, Samuel Leibowitz. Cast member Ruth Gordon recalled in her memoirs that Rains was alarmingly "colorless" in rehearsals and "droned" his seven-page, climactic speech. "Everybody worried," she wrote. "He was the pivot of the whole play. Opening night I sat behind the backdrop waiting for the scene to be over. Claude's summation blew the roof off! Even that frosty Guild first-night list had to loosen up and cheer. It's the only time I ever saw an actor wait till opening night to wrap up a show."

Rains's performance drew the attention of Ben Hecht and Charles MacArthur, who were preparing a film based on a story by Hecht that required an actor who could play a flamboyant attorney. Hecht and MacArthur had contracted with Paramount to produce *Crime without Passion* at Astoria Studios in New York. They already had acquired brash, bad-boy reputations on stage and screen; their cynical newspaper comedy *The Front*

Page had already been successfully adapted as a film in 1931. *Crime without Passion* would emerge as an almost perfect example of Hollywood's pre-Code ethos at its most exuberant. The story revolved around a successful but ethically challenged attorney, Lee Gentry, who cold-bloodedly breaks the heart of his Latin dancer girlfriend to make room for a more upscale love interest. A struggle with a gun ensues, and Gentry believes he has accidentally killed his mistress. In reality, the bullet has only grazed her head, but Gentry's desperate attempts to cover his supposed crime lead him to commit a deliberate murder and pay the price for it.

"When the script was finished," Rains recalled, and the character of Lee Gentry was finally settled, "I approached Ben and said: 'Look here! This man's a terrible scallywag. Don't you think he's a little too unsympathetic? Oughtn't I tone the part down a bit?'"

Hecht replied with a couple of choice expletives (he could be "a most forceful conversationalist," Rains said), and then explained his concept of the character. Of course Gentry was a heel, said Hecht. "And that's my idea of a hero! Play him just as he is—and don't take the edge off anything!"

Rains had played many unsympathetic characters, often to great critical acclaim. But he still had lingering doubts about the advisability of lending his face to such a contemptible cad as Lee Gentry. After all, the moviegoing public hadn't really seen his face before. Was this any way to make a first impression?

Rains claimed to have been personally involved in the casting of a Colombian screen novice, Margo, as the dancer Carmen Brown. "Believe it or not," Rains told a reporter, "that girl just walked into the New York office where Ben Hecht and Charlie MacArthur and I were sitting discussing who should play the female lead—and asked for a job. She'd never acted before, either on the stage or the screen; she was a dancer by profession and wanted to try her hand at it." Margo's real name was the unwieldy Maria Marguerita Guadalupe Boldao Castilla y O'Donnell, so her use of a single professional name was perhaps understandable. "Charlie and Ben looked at one another," Rains recalled. "I looked at them both—and at 'Margo'! Then Ben and Charlie looked at me. I nodded." Whether or not the story is completely true or mostly the invention of Paramount's publicity mill, Margo's casting was a major asset in the film. Her melancholy beauty and untutored, almost improvisational acting proved the perfect counterbalance to Rains's studied pyrotechnics and made her character's victimization all the more believable and poignant.

As in *The Invisible Man*, Rains in *Crime without Passion* had to compete on the screen with ambitious special effects. The title sequence almost upstages everything that follows: three modern-day Furies arise from the spattered blood of Manhattan murder victims to wreak their vengeance, swooping through high-rise canyons, shattering glass and wreaking havoc. At one point in the film, Rains had to act opposite himself in a dreamlike interlude that posed considerable technical problems, a "tricky double-exposure sequence in which my logical mental self argues with my illogical emotional self," he told *Film Weekly*. "I played it through once and something went wrong with the lights. I played it through again and something went wrong with the camera. I played it through a third time and something went wrong with the sound. And then I started making mistakes myself. I became mechanical. There was no feeling in my expressions, no meaning in my lines." At that point, he blew up.

"I'm not going on with this!" he shouted. "I'm not a puppet!"

As Rains remembered, "There was an awed silence. Everyone waited respectfully for me to cool down. Then Charlie [MacArthur], quite unperturbed, said quietly, 'O.K., puppet. Let's take a rest.' From then on, he always called me his 'little puppet.' How can you get temperamental with a man like that?"

One day during filming, Rains received a call from his Lambertsville neighbor, Ed Lassels, who, along with a friend, had driven him early that morning to the Trenton train station for his daily commute to Astoria. Lassels and others frequently did favors and ran errands for their actor friend with the rustic house.

"Claude?"

"Yes?"

"It's Ed."

From the odd, hesitant tone of Lassels' voice, Rains immediately suspected something was amiss.

"Yes, Ed?"

"After you left, we went and had a sandwich."

Now he knew that something was wrong. Ed was not in the habit of reporting on his meals.

"Yes, Ed?"

"Well, then we drove out to your place. You know where you leave the pavement?

"Yes, Ed." The property was off the main thoroughfare.

"Well, when we got there—you know the long dirt road?"

"Yes, Ed."

"Well, we couldn't get up."

"Why, Ed?"

"Too many cars coming down. We wondered where they were coming from, Claude."

"Yes, Ed?"

"Well, we were finally able to go up, wondering about the cars."

"Yes, Ed?"

"Well, we finally got to your house."

"Yes?"

"There's no house there."

"What?"

"The house, Claude. It burned down."

"Is Frances all right?" Rains asked. She was, and so were their Irish setter and her ten puppies. The dogs had a little house of their own. But the main house was a total loss; Rains was only able to salvage a pair of andirons and a soot-encrusted rug. The official cause of the blaze was a lightning strike, though Rains never believed it. He immediately suspected arson. He had acquired with the property an "oafish" grounds-keeper, who had lately begun pressuring Rains to let him move into the house full-time. Rains was appalled at the request. "I wouldn't have let him stay in the doghouse," he later said, and he may have been less than diplomatic in his refusal. A few years later he would receive a letter from a former neighbor, belatedly confirming his worst suspicions: "I think you should know who burned down your house." But, in the absence of hard evidence and the absence of the disgruntled, and long-departed, groundskeeper himself, a legal case was never pursued.

Among the many treasures lost was Rains's kilt from his war service. Only its pin survived.

Rains had purchased the property for $2,600, paid $3,500 for improvements, and had approximately $6,000 in personal belongings on the premises at the time of the blaze. His insurance, however, covered only $4,000 of the real estate and approximately $2,000 of personal property. For all practical purposes, he was wiped out.

After the fire, Rains and Frances relocated to Narragansett, Long Island, while he completed *Crime without Passion*. Remarkably, there is no record of Rains's farmhouse disaster having disrupted production in any way. He continued to meet his contractual obligations without any known appeal to his employers.

Crime without Passion received generally excellent reviews (for Rains's performance, at least) and good publicity, most of it centered on the angle of "The Invisible Man Revealed." The *New York Times* lauded Rains's "extraordinarily clear characterization," and the reviewer for *Family Circle* wrote, "I was pretty sure I was going to find Mr. Claude Rains's acting boring, due to his inclination to strut and make fussy gestures. However, as the film progresses, Mr. Rains becomes a more and more interesting character. He's one of those birds who gets under your skin, and it's difficult to explain because he's not an impressive-looking man, nor is his voice particularly easy to take. Maybe it's because he is a good actor." Louella O. Parsons, the powerful Hearst papers columnist, welcomed Rains as a visible screen presence, but dismissed the film as "not a picture for the people. It's a picture for the highbrows and intellectuals who like their entertainment the hard way."

In the wake of *The Invisible Man*'s international success and the positive reception of *Crime without Passion*, Universal approached Rains again, this time with a guaranteed two-picture deal: a screen version of *The Man Who Reclaimed His Head*, in which he would reprise his Broadway role of Paul Verin; and the studio's upcoming adaptation of Charles Dickens's *The Mystery of Edwin Drood*, in which he would play the villainous John Jasper.

Carl Laemmle, Jr., was attracted to *The Man Who Reclaimed His Head* because of its grotesquery, reminiscent of Lon Chaney in his melodra-

Rains's parents: left, Emily Eliza Cox Rains; right, Frederick Rains.

Rains's theatrical mentor Sir Herbert Beerbohm Tree, in and out of his signature stage role, Svengali.

Rains in his Scottish Regiment kilt, circa 1917.

The earliest known
portrait of Rains, as an
army captain, shortly
before he was wounded
at Vimy Ridge.

Actress Isabel Jeans,
Rains's first wife.

Julius Caesar (1920): Rains as Casca (far right), with Clifton Boyne (seated) as Caesar and Henry Ainley as Marcus Antonius.

As Christopher Marlowe in Clemence Dane's *Will Shakespeare* (1921), with Mary Clare.

With Nancy Price in Pirandello's *And That's the Truth (If You Think It Is)* (1925).

Newspaper cartoon of Rains in *The Man from Hong Kong* (1925).

As Faulkland in *The Rivals* (1925).

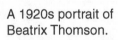

A 1920s portrait of Beatrix Thomson.

Rains around the time of his appointment as acting instructor at the Royal Academy of Dramatic Art.

Rains, with a stoic royal guard, contemplates his inability to "eat his notices" in London.

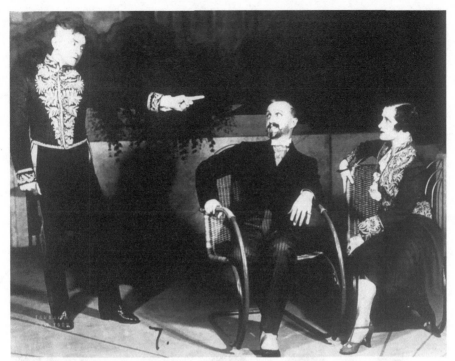

As the Prime Minister in Shaw's *The Apple Cart* (1930), with Tom Powers and Eva Leonard-Boyne.

With Alla Nazimova in the Theatre Guild's New York production of *The Good Earth* (1932).

As a would-be
Napoleon in
Alfred Savoir's
comedy *He*
(1931).

As the asthmatic, deformed Paul
Verin in Jean Bart's *The Man
Who Reclaimed His Head* (1932).

An actor on the move, script in hand, in the early 1930s.

With Gloria Stuart in *The Invisible Man* (1933) (David J. Skal collection).

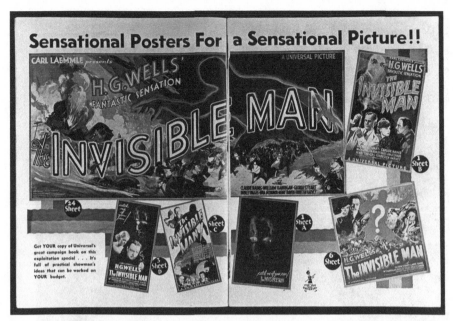

Poster and billboard art for *The Invisible Man* (David J. Skal collection).

Rains's invisibility required a creative approach to publicity photos. With William Harrigan (David J. Skal collection).

With Whitney Bourne in *Crime without Passion* (1934) (courtesy of
Donna Tattle).

Rains takes his revenge on Lionel Atwill in the film version of
The Man Who Reclaimed His Head (1935).

As the drug-addicted murderer John Jasper in *Mystery of Edwin Drood* (1935) (courtesy of Donna Tattle).

With Fay Wray in *The Clairvoyant* (1935) (courtesy of Donna Tattle).

As Napoleon, with Marion Davies in *Hearts Divided* (1936) (courtesy of Donna Tattle).

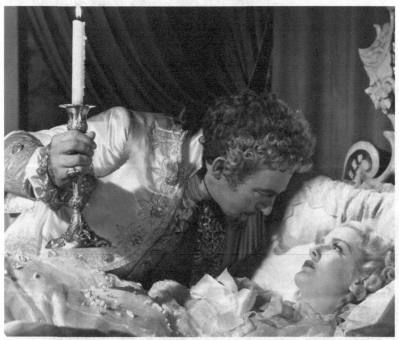

With Anita Louise in *Anthony Adverse* (1936) (David J. Skal collection).

As Sir John in *The Adventures of Robin Hood* (1938), with Melville Cooper (left) and Basil Rathbone (courtesy of Donna Tattle).

With James Stewart in *Mr. Smith Goes to Washington* (1939) (David J. Skal collection).

As theatrical impresario David Belasco in *Lady with Red Hair* (1940) (David J. Skal collection).

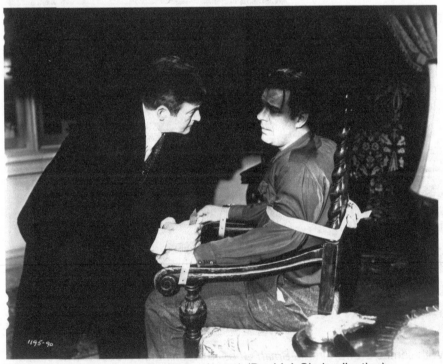

With Lon Chaney in *The Wolf Man* (1941) (David J. Skal collection).

matic revenge films. Oddly, Rains was not the first choice for the film; actor-director Lowell Sherman was mentioned in an early Universal memorandum as likely both directing and performing for a combined fee of $40,000. (In the end, the studio got a bargain: director Edward Ludwig was paid a fee of $3,000, and Rains received $1,750 a week, the total for the two amounting to $10,500.)

At some point it was decided that the film would reinvent Verin as emotionally oversensitive instead of physically malformed. It is likely that Rains himself insisted on the change; he would have wanted to avoid inflating his bombastic screen test into a feature film. Having completed just two talking pictures, he already understood the necessity of under-playing for the screen. As with his stage acting, Rains's screen technique would be self-learned and self-taught, the results in both cases equally effective.

New York Times critic Andre Sennwald opined that the film "has the overwrought and underdone look of a theme which has caused its au-thor's head to whirl with the magnitude of its implications." Sennwald added that, as a "cautious reporter," he was "not prepared to admit that Mr. Rains' portrait of applied hysteria is the brilliant piece of acting that some of his disciples appear to believe. But it is certainly arresting, and is dosed with the kind of virtuoso terrorism that makes it difficult for you to breathe when he is on the screen."

Before returning to California for *Edwin Drood,* Rains filed divorce papers in Trenton, New Jersey, against Beatrix Thomson on the grounds of desertion. It had been four years since their last, unpleasant meeting in London, and nearly six since she had left him. He and Frances planned to marry as soon as his divorce was finalized. Though not yet a citizen, Rains had firmly established American residency; the divorce, therefore, would fall under American jurisdiction.

Around this time Rains apparently either rejected or was rejected for two of the choicest mad scientist roles ever concocted by Hollywood: Dr. Gogol in MGM's expressionist extravaganza *Mad Love,* directed by Karl Freund; and Dr. Pretorious in Universal's *Return of Frankenstein* (eventu-ally retitled *Bride of Frankenstein*), directed by James Whale. Playwright-screenwriter John L. Balderston was attached to both films, and it was likely the efforts of their mutual agent, Harold Freedman, that got Rains's name into trade-paper announcements for the former and onto Universal's preliminary casting lists for the latter.

Rains's communications with Freedman have not survived, but their professional relationship was coming to an end, possibly over the issue of typecasting. His screen roles had so far included one mad scientist, a sociopathic attorney/killer, and a Dickensian opium fiend. No prestige films, roles, or dependable term contracts were anywhere on the horizon. Dripping with all the standard trappings of classic Universal horror (madness, moldering crypts, the San Fernando Valley standing in for the English countryside, a script coauthored by John L. Balderston, with *Dracula*'s David Manners in the title role), *Mystery of Edwin Drood* gave Rains a role that easily could have gone to Boris Karloff. Rains plays John Jasper, an opium-addicted choirmaster who kills his nephew, Edwin Drood, out of an obsession for Drood's fiancée, Rosa, to whom Edwin has been betrothed since childhood. Jasper doesn't know that the couple have a platonic relationship and no real intention of marrying. But the senseless, drug-fueled murder is carried out nonetheless, and Jasper is driven in the end to a spectacular public suicide.

Edwin Drood was based on Charles Dickens's final, unfinished novel (though the solution to the "mystery" was obvious to any but the most obtuse readers). Full of melodramatic blood and thunder, it was Rains's first screen excursion into historical villainy (which he would soon make a great specialty) and fully utilized the actor's knowledge of the barnstorming styles of his Victorian acting mentors. The film was aided by George Robinson's moody, nuanced cinematography and above-average production details. Rains was paid $10,000 for five weeks of work, matching director Stuart Walker's weekly rate.

The reviews were lukewarm; but, as usual, Rains was singled out for praise. *Variety* found the narrative structure weak but noted that "Rains imparts a wealth of weirdness and intensity to the production."

Once more, Universal let Rains's contractual option drop.

Edwin Drood would be a major turning point in Rains's career. Beyond marking his break with the Laemmles, the film foreshadowed the vivid constellation of screen roles that were to come, roles that would frequently draw upon Rains's early professional exposure to some of the most famous English and Continental actors of the late Victorian and early Edwardian age, tempered by a self-taught restraint of technique necessary for the camera.

John Jasper in *Edwin Drood* was also a film role of Rains's that drew the heightened attention of the censors, and it wouldn't be the last. (Singapore, for instance, demanded that the "dope den scenes" be removed from the film, thus rendering Jasper's character incomprehensible.) In later years, Rains would be called upon to use all of his technical skills and personal charm to make palatable other amoral and villainous characters who, had they been undertaken by actors less skilled than he, would likely have attracted the censure of the Production Code Administration.

After *Edwin Drood*, Rains, remaining skeptical about Hollywood and its enticements, was happy to return to the East Coast. Frances and he had their eye on a new farm in New Jersey. (They had netted $1,225.00 on the sale of the burned-out property.) "It's a good thing I didn't move to Beverly Hills like everybody else," he said later, referring to the exodus of New York stage talent to California in the early 1930s. "I would have been lost."

With his work in Hollywood and his home back east, Rains often found himself in transit. After his work on *Edwin Drood* was finished, in Salt Lake City awaiting a connection for a flight home, he was having coffee at the terminal's lunch room when suddenly, he said, "I became aware of this creature striding past." It was Charles Laughton.

"Charles? You remember me? Rains?"

"Yes, yes," Laughton said, dispensing with the formality of a greeting. "I've just had the most extraordinary experience. I've been to the Tabernacle."

Rains then described Laughton's ensuing impromptu performance. "He was doing Brigham Young, up and down the coffee shop."

The two finally boarded the plane, where Laughton proceeded to extol his own Oscar-winning screen performance in Alexander Korda's *The Private Life of Henry VIII* (1933). "He told me how wonderful he was," Rains recalled. The subject eventually turned to Rains's performance in *The Invisible Man*. Laughton became condescending.

"Good God almighty, what did you do that for? A challenge? An extraordinary thing to do. I suppose *you* would accept a challenge like that."

"I got off the plane at Newark and got away from him," Rains said. "It was a long and uncomfortable ride." It would not be the their last uncomfortable encounter.

Rains had not been to England in several years, so he accepted Gainsborough Pictures' offer to play a music hall mind-reader in its film *The Clairvoyant*. Doing so allowed him the chance to visit his family (his mother continued to require nursing home care), renew professional contacts, and, not incidentally, be fitted with some new double-breasted suits from his favorite London tailor.

The Clairvoyant was not a major production by American studio standards, but it was a more than decent British effort for the time. It also provided Rains with a firm employment offer at a time when he had no pending Hollywood work, a rather clever script, and the opportunity to be top-billed over Fay Wray, who had achieved iconic status with *King Kong* two years earlier. But Rains was being asked to undertake still another weirdo part, not as grotesque as a mad scientist, but close to it. Rains played Maximus, a celebrated, but phony, music-hall clairvoyant who, for reasons never explained, suddenly becomes able to actually predict the future, including a catastrophic train wreck in a tunnel for which the skeptical authorities suspect he is responsible.

According to Wray, she had traveled to England to escape her identification with *Kong*. But there was no escape. When interviewed by the BBC soon after her arrival, her first questioner asked her to scream. As for *The Clairvoyant*, she recalled years later, "It had more substance than most of the things I had been doing in Hollywood, so I was very hopeful that it would be a step up in quality." She encountered none of the difficulties with Rains that Gloria Stuart experienced during the filming of *The Invisible Man*. "Claude was a dear, a true gentleman," Wray said, "and very professional. I found him very giving as an actor, and very pleasant. He was also very stimulating to work with. He had those wonderful piercing, burning eyes—I'll never forget them."

Wray elaborated on the unusual power of the Rains gaze. His eyes "seemed to me all the while to reflect the actual thoughts of the character. In other words, he was acting with his eyes." She added, "He has a queer habit, too, of using his eyes without saying a word in real life. If anyone is talking to him and he is tired of the conversation, he will not trouble to interrupt. He will simply look at the person in a way which seems as if he is looking right through him. And the conversationalist will falter, forget what he is talking about, and bring the tedious talk to an end."

Overall, Wray found Rains to be "a rather unexpected mixture of boyishness and seriousness" and "one of the most meticulous actors I have ever known." On several occasions during the making of *The Clairvoyant*, she said, "He would ponder quietly over a scene, then say he felt that the character's reactions would be different from those described in the scenario. And he would always be psychologically correct." She called him "one of the few film stars who could accurately be described as a psychological actor." In Wray's opinion, "Most stage actors, in spite of what they may say for the benefit of publicity writers, really and truly regard the screen as an inferior offshoot of the theatre. But Claude Rains is genuinely enthusiastic about film work. He regards it as an entirely new medium and doesn't try to bring his theatrical mannerisms into his acting. Which helps to explain why he has achieved success in films so quickly."

The Clairvoyant was generally well received, though Rains's notices emphasized his skill at portraying psychological eccentrics. *Film Weekly*'s comments were typical: "Claude Rains dominates every foot of the action with another of his compelling studies of abnormal mentality."

While in London, Rains evidently made contact with Rachel Nelson, likely the mother of his first child, and arranged for several of her family members to work as extras in the train wreck sequence of *The Clairvoyant*. There is no documentation of his meeting with Rachel and her/their son, but present-day members of the Nelson family recall that while Rains was usually referred to euphemistically as some kind of uncle or cousin, he was always regarded warmly and with pride.

Following *The Clairvoyant* Rains experienced one of his longest periods of unemployment. Fortunately, he had Frances, plans for their future, and money in the bank. After nearly six months of professional inactivity, he was considering a contract from Paramount to appear in *The Last Outpost*, a drama of the Great War set in Britain's Middle Eastern and North African fronts.

On March 9, 1935, Rains closed purchase on a forty-acre Pennsylvania farm property called Glen Mills. In the first week of April, the state of New Jersey granted his divorce from Beatrix Thomson, and he and Frances were finally married on April 8. They traveled together to Hollywood in May, looking forward to a long-term relationship with Paramount and the security it would provide for their new life and their new homestead. But even as they headed back to Hollywood, Beatrix Thomson was planning revenge.

5

Mr. Rains Goes to Burbank

RAINS WAS SHOCKED TO LEARN that Beatrix, in Britain, was accusing him of bigamy, challenging the legality of his American divorce and remarriage. In London, on July 16, 1935, she filed a countersuit to his New Jersey divorce action, naming Frances as codefendant. Although Beatrix may have had reason to want to clarify her marital status under British law, a jealous, vindictive streak soon proved to be her true motivation.

Beatrix felt that her ex-husband owed his success to her. Rains, after all, would never have gone to America without her. In her mind, he used her celebrity as a professional stepping-stone, though it was clear to everyone else which of them had the real acting talent. Beatrix's career had never sustained the brief footing she had secured with *The Constant Nymph* in America—and, of course, nobody in England even saw her in the play. She would later appear only sporadically in films.

Through her wealthy family, Beatrix retained expensive legal representation, and soon Rains was embroiled in lengthy and gratuitous cross-Atlantic legal filings, all to prove the obvious: she had deserted him without cause, and he had been steadily and gainfully employed in America under a valid resident permit and was a property owner in the United States, therefore making him subject to American jurisdiction.

Beatrix, however, was not willing to let him off easily. The story had the potential to get her name in the papers, and she saw that it did. And it certainly didn't hurt at all that one of the London plays in which she appeared during the legal proceedings, *Wisdom Teeth*, had a divorce theme. "AM I MARRIED?" ASKS ACTRESS, read a banner headline in the *Daily Sketch*. DIVORCED IN AMERICA BY FILM-STAR HUSBAND BUT STILL "MRS."

"Here is a real-life drama of tangled loves," the article began, "the eternal triangle; a man, newly married in America, a woman at home in England who does not know whether she is still a wife or not: anxiety, unhappiness—and, for her, a waiting that seems like eternity." In a subsequent, boldface paragraph, the actress begged the reader, "Am I a free woman—free to live my own life, and perhaps make a home for myself?" Obviously, Beatrix had answered the question to her own satisfaction when she left Rains for another man in the first place. But readers of the *Daily Sketch* would find no mention of that in the article.

In the midst of this tumultuous year, Harold Freedman secured Rains a role in Paramount's *The Last Outpost* opposite Cary Grant. The result was professional turmoil, made all the more unbearable because the film's production coincided with Rains's epic battle with Beatrix. As the actor later wrote his agent, "The script I was presented with on arriving was a good romantic yarn, which with the proper handling could have been a successful picture of the Bengal Lancer type." He felt that *Outpost* "had a good chance to be exciting and colourful and it had no other pretensions." But he became wary when he met the director, Charles Barton, "a man who had grown up in the studio. And had by slow degrees advanced from office boy to Westerns so you can easily understand his fear of the office and his lack of independence and authority."

Rains was quickly offended when he learned, secondhand, that Barton hadn't been happy with one of his scenes but was too intimidated to ask for a retake. "It was evident immediately that Mr. Barton knew nothing about directing actors, and Cary Grant knew nothing about acting or behaving decently," Rains wrote. Barton was assigned three advisors, including a dialog director from New York, Henry C. Potter, who had never worked in film. But even with the on-set difficulties, "we still thought this glorified Western had a chance." The reports on the daily rushes were positive. "And I came in for my share of the praise. Then we got back to the studio and Miss Gertrude Michael was added to the cast. She and Mr. Grant loathe each other, which didn't help their love scenes, and besides being no actress she insists on being cute."

Rains was promised a viewing of the rough cut. "I waited for three weeks and heard not a word from anybody and needless to say I was beginning to suspect something." When he was finally summoned to the studio, he was told that Barton had been taken off the film, his advisors had been let go, and the film was being half-rewritten, with Louis Gasnier now at the helm and Max Marcin directing dialog for the retakes. The internecine backstabbing escalated. According to Rains, the final indignity came when the producer, E. Lloyd Sheldon, attempted to scapegoat him for ruining the first version of the film. Rains wrote that Sheldon had let it be known that Rains was "too strong" for Barton and that Rains had personally demanded the inexperienced New York dialog director—and, Rains added, Sheldon was relating "many other unpleasant and untrue stories."

Rains insisted on a screening, and upon finally viewing *The Last Outpost*, he wrote, "I was sick. It is very bad and I don't think it has a chance in the world . . . it shows only too clearly I had no direction." Rains was particularly appalled by the insertion of undercranked (that is, silent-era) stock footage "taken years ago and when put in the picture moved to a different tempo and the people scurry around." He met with Paramount production manager Ernst Lubitsch to dispel the finger-pointing and give his side of events. Paramount had an option for a second picture and "unofficially" scheduled him opposite Carole Lombard in the comedy *Hands across the Table*, a role that eventually went to Fred MacMurray.

"Harold," Rains wrote Freedman, "I have a fear that this picture [that is, *The Last Outpost*] will give my film career a bad setback." He asked his agent to convince Paramount to drop their option clause. They did. And Rains dropped Freedman as his film agent.

Despite his apprehensions, Rains's performance received no brickbats, and no less an arbiter than Graham Greene, writing in *The Spectator*, lauded the actor's technical performance, if not the script. "Mr. Rains' low, husky voice, his power in investing even commonplace dialogue with smoldering conviction, is remarkable. He never rants, but one is always aware of what a superb ranter he could be in a part that did not call for modern restraint but only for superb diction."

By the time *The Last Outpost* opened, Rains was in the hands of a new and effective Beverly Hills agent, William Hawks of the Hawks-Volp Corporation, and it was only a matter of a few months before Warner Bros. made an impressive long-term contract offer for his services. An initial, four-picture guarantee would give Rains $4,000 a week for the first two films, with a four-week guarantee with extra pro-rated compensation "for so long as may be necessary." The second two pictures would pay him a flat $4,500 a week with a four-week compensation cap on each film. A one-year extension option provided $5,000 a week, with four pictures guaranteed at four weeks each. A second extension would increase his salary to $6,000 a week on the same four-picture basis. A third would pay him $5,400 weekly, but guarantee a flat five weeks' pay on each project. A fourth extension would restore his base weekly pay to $6,000, a fifth to $6,800, and a sixth to $7,600. He would be perpetually guaranteed "not less than second featured billing, in type at least equal in size to first featured player." Warners would, additionally, pay any British income taxes, and would reserve the right to loan him out to other studios. In short, should all the options be exercised, Warners was willing to pay him approximately $750,000 over seven years.

Rains was understandably suspicious of option clauses, which too often had all the substance of paper props. He was also skeptical about the first assignment the studio was proposing: the role of Napoleon Bonaparte in *Hearts Divided*, a strange semi-musical confection in which Dick Powell would play Napoleon's singing younger brother, sent to America incognito to negotiate the Louisiana Purchase and falling in love along the way with a character played by Marion Davies, the real-life mistress of newspaper mogul William Randolph Hearst, who was bankrolling the production. Rains had played Napoleon three times on stage: in Shaw's *Man of Destiny*, in a one-act comedy called *Napoleon's Barber*, and as the delusional alter ego of an elevator operator in the Theatre Guild production of *He*. Reviewers of these performances invariably made comments about his height, or the lack of it, and Rains was well aware of the limitations his stature imposed on his career.

The contract also included a potentially troubling morals clause, in light of his still-unresolved legal issues with Beatrix Thomson and her public accusation of bigamy: "The Artist agrees to conduct himself with due regard to public convention, and agrees that he will not do or commit any act or thing that will tend to degrade him in society or bring him into public hatred, contempt, scorn or ridicule, or that will tend to shock, insult or offend the community or ridicule public morals or decency or prejudice the producer or the motion picture industry in general."

Moreover, once Rains signed the contract, he, like other studio contract players, would have no control over casting. Was *Hearts Divided,* and whatever fevered studio concoctions that might follow, really the best career move for him?

His agent was not alone in being aghast that Rains had any hesitation about appearing in a Hearst picture.

Why, Rains asked, is everyone so surprised by his reluctance?

"Louella Parsons—you need her" was the reply.

"And why is that?" he asked. Rains never read his own reviews, much less the writing of Hollywood columnists, and he was genuinely unaware of Parsons's powerful position as the lead entertainment journalist in the Hearst newspaper empire. He had very few contacts in the film colony outside of his immediate studio coworkers and often joked about his hermitlike existence with interviewers.

Rains signed the Warner Bros. contract on November 27, 1935, and commenced work on *Hearts Divided* in Burbank on December 2. In spite of generally mixed reviews, Rains garnered such critical kudos for his Napoleon that the studio intimated in press squibs that it was planning a full-scale biographical film with Rains in the role. (This proved illusory.) Louella Parsons praised both his performance and the film: "In addition to being a tender romance, *Hearts Divided* takes on the dignity of an important historical production with Claude Rains probably the best Napoleon who has ever been seen on the screen or stage. One of the most delightful scenes in which he figures is the bathroom episode, where he issues commands in the midst of his ablutions." (For true Rains fans, this would, sadly, remain one of the only bathtub or seminude appearances in the actor's film career.) Rains's role was well written, with one especially wry theatrical aside. One of the characters asks if Napoleon's success in convincing the Marion Davies character to give up Dick Powell for the greater glory of France was a matter of strategy. No, he replies, it was simply a matter of dramaturgy: "An amazingly good actor met an amazingly receptive audience."

Rains made an even showier costume-picture splash as the lascivious

Don Luis in *Anthony Adverse* (1936), based on Hervey Allen's best-selling novel. Early in the movie, Don Luis discovers that his wife has been having an affair while he has been receiving treatment for gout. The treatment successful, Don Luis kills the lover and firmly reasserts his conjugal rights. The scene in which he makes his intentions clear raised obvious censorship flags, and director Mervyn LeRoy was willing to cut it. But Rains provided a reading of the scene perfectly tailored to both industry propriety and spectator prurience. As British writer W. H. Mooring noted in *Film Weekly*, "In the hands of an actor who was anything less than a genius, the whole scene might have been transformed into a most disgusting spectacle of senile passion gone riot. . . . Rains carried the scene right to the very edge of that narrow border which divides good drama from bad taste . . . not one actor in a thousand could have suggested it without a suggestiveness which would have turned our stomachs."

Rains's next film, *Stolen Holiday* (1937), saw Rains once again playing a mustached scoundrel, this time Stefan Orloff, an unscrupulous Russian financier in the world of Parisian high fashion, loosely based on the career of Serge Alexander Stavisky (a role later essayed by Jean Paul Belmondo in Alain Resnais's *Stavisky*). *Stolen Holiday* did not make many waves, although it marked Rains's first collaboration with director Michael Curtiz, with whom he was destined to do much more celebrated work. Although leading lady Kay Francis and Rains made an attractive screen couple, he found her to be a "hoity-toity" actress and, at one point, oblivious to his professional needs. During the shooting of cutaways (inserted, individual close-ups that aid the editing of a previous take involving more than one person), it is considered good form for the off-screen performer to feed lines to the on-camera actor in order to maintain continuity. When Francis repeatedly failed to make eye contact, Rains finally asked, "Miss Francis, could you please look at me?" She did, but only after making her umbrage and annoyance perfectly clear. It was the kind of petty disregard that rankled Rains professionally, and always would. About *Stolen Holiday*, the *New York Times* said only, "If the picture is at all distinguished, it is because Claude Rains does a superb job with the character."

Beatrix Thomson's divorce complaint was still unresolved at the time

Stolen Holiday was released in early 1937, and Rains had been advised by his attorney that she would likely sue for legal costs and damages. "She didn't need the money," Rains recalled. "She was rich as Croesus. It was all spite." He began work on Warners' *The Prince and the Pauper* not knowing how much of a pauper he was likely to be by the time the film wrapped.

Based on Mark Twain's perennially popular novel, *The Prince and the Pauper* had been twice produced for the silent screen. In this classic tale of dual identity, Prince Edward, son of Henry VIII, has a (completely unexplained) identical twin named Tom Canty, born to London beggars. The boys meet by accident and agree to exchange identities. Rains played the Earl of Hertford, who discovers the boys' scheme and exploits it for his own political advantage, forcing the false prince to be his pawn: "You don't want that pretty head of yours chopped off, do you? Nor to have your mother see the crows tearing tufts from a skull on London Bridge and know that it's her son's hair in which they will nest? Then never forget that you are Edward the Sixth of England and that to ever again become Tom Canty is to die!" The film was a star vehicle for Errol Flynn, who overshadowed everyone involved as Miles Hendon, a soldier of fortune and protector of Prince Edward. In an unusual twist, the film cast real-life identical twins Bobby and Billy Mauch in the title roles, giving their scenes together a naturalism not attainable with the standard split-screen camera tricks of the time.

Rains's next assignment, in *They Won't Forget* (1937), was a virtual reversal of his stage role in *They Shall Not Die*. Based on a true case of racial injustice and lynching in the deep South by way of a novel by Ward Greene, *They Won't Forget* featured Rains as a politically ambitious prosecutor instead of a heroic defense attorney. Despite his vocal gifts, Rains never managed to master a credible Southern accent and played the part with his usual mid-Atlantic locutions. *They Won't Forget* was Rains's second outing with Mervyn LeRoy as director and was a bigger critical and box office success than *Anthony Adverse*. It was named one of the year's top ten films by the *New York Times* and the National Board of Review. The *Times*'s Frank Nugent wrote of the film: "For its perfection, chief credit must go to Mr. LeRoy for his remarkably skillful direction—there are a few touches as fine as anything the screen has done . . . and to all the cast, but notably to Mr. Rains, for his savage characterization."

Beatrix Thomson was finally granted a divorce by the British courts on July 26, 1937. Rains reluctantly made a settlement of $25,000—virtually all of his cash assets. No copy of the specific settlement terms has survived, but the divorce was treated quietly by the press (fortunately for Rains, the word "bigamist" never appeared in print). After the divorce, Beatrix never made a public statement of any kind about Rains again. She died in 1986, after a long, if not especially distinguished, stage career and after making a handful of forgettable motion pictures in the 1930s and 1940s.

Despite Rains's steady employment at Warner Bros., the divorce settlement put a severe strain on his finances. His nonstop work in Hollywood required that he obtain a California residence in addition to his Pennsylvania farm, so he mortgaged a modest, country-style home on Evanston Street in the fashionable Brentwood district of West Los Angeles. He and Frances were anxious to start a family, but they were having difficulty conceiving. Rains, approaching fifty, underwent fertility tests, which revealed no abnormalities. Ever since his adolescence, Rains had been eager to have children, and now, on the verge of finally having the resources to comfortably support a family, the fertility problem was especially frustrating.

Rains's next picture, *Gold Is Where You Find It*, was his first in Technicolor, and it provided him with a sympathetic part after his having portrayed several villains. Rains plays a California farmer battling industrial miners who are destroying agricultural land through their hydraulic blasting for gold. The *New York Times* found an uncomfortable disconnect between the story and its glitzy production values. Reviewer Frank Nugent called it "a story of ugliness—of greed and mud, exploitation and destruction . . . Technicolor's roseate approach is as indecorous as a Maypole dance at a funeral."

His next film was one far more appropriate to Technicolor. With a hefty budget ($2 million), *The Adventures of Robin Hood* starred Errol Flynn, Olivia de Havilland, Basil Rathbone, and Rains as the scheming Prince John. At first, Rains didn't know how to approach the part; it seemed from the script to be just another standard costume villain without much depth. He told the press that he had a major epiphany when he learned the part would include an eye-catching red wig and beard. But he later told his daughter privately that all the henna, ermine, and brocade gave him a cue to play the prince as tacitly homosexual. Roddy McDowall was always convinced that Rains based his performance on the stylized voice and mannerisms of another Warners contract performer, Bette Davis. McDowall, in fact, asked Rains years later if this was the case, but Rains's only answer was an enigmatic smile.

Rains's next two pictures did little to further his career, though they were lucrative. In *White Banners* he took a back seat to Fay Bainter, who received a best supporting actress Academy Award nomination for the film (one of two that year for Bainter; she won for *Jezebel*). Rains played the befuddled head of a midwestern family, a science teacher–inventor whose disorganized home is benevolently colonized by a housekeeper (Bainter), who manages the household mess and dispenses inspirational advice and assistance to everyone in sight, despite her own clouded past. In *Four Daughters*—another collaboration with director Michael Curtiz, based on a story by Fannie Hurst—Rains played a music professor overseeing the emotional entanglements of his single-parent female quartet. The film earned an Academy Award nomination for best picture, as did John Garfield for best supporting actor, and *Four Daughters* made the *New York Times* ten-best list.

By the second half of 1938, Rains and his agent were growing increasingly concerned about Warners' living up to its contractual obligations. Rains was maintaining residences on two coasts. He had committed a sizable amount of his annual studio income to Beatrix Thomson in their divorce settlement. His wife, Frances, had just given birth to the baby they had longed for, a daughter they named Jennifer. But the studio was not giving Rains the four yearly assignments stipulated in his contract. Nor was Warners lending him out to other studios, despite its financial incentive to do so. (Studios frequently negotiated higher fees for loan-outs than they were contractually obligated to pay their contract players.)

Moreover, Rains's latest assignment, the role of a hardboiled New

York detective in *They Made Me a Criminal,* was particularly not to the actor's liking. Rains sent a telegram to Jack Warner on August 31, 1938:

> Dear Jack. Having thoroughly enjoyed my association with the studio and toed the line to cooperate to the best of my ability, I feel you should know of my inability to understand being cast for the part of Phelan in "They Made Me a Criminal." Frankly, I feel I am so poorly cast that it would be harmful to your picture. You have done such a good job in building me up that it seems a pity to tear that down with such a part as this, and I am confident that your good judgment will recognize this. Dogs delight to bark and bite and I think I have been a good dog for three years, so perhaps you will give me five minutes to talk it over.

In the end, Rains was forced to be a good dog once more, and *They Made Me a Criminal* indeed proved to be one of his least successful parts.

In an interoffice communication on November 7, 1938, Warners general counsel Roy Orbinger noted, "Under our contract with Claude Rains we were to have produced four pictures during the year ending Dec. 1, 1938. To date, we have only produced two." In order not to breach the contract with Rains, Orbinger stated that he got the studio "out of this embarrassing situation" by agreeing to advance the full $48,000 for Rains's next two pictures by the end of December 1938. Surviving correspondence suggests that this offer was later significantly modified: a $24,000 advance would be paid to Rains on January 6, 1939, for services for 1939, plus a special fee of $7,500 for one week's work on the film *Juarez,* the movie being considered an "outside" production. On December 9, Orbinger wrote, "We have received considerable concessions from Claude Rains, inasmuch as he really had us over a barrel for 2 unproduced pictures. . . . The billing clause of Rains was quite an issue, and Rains only made the above concessions with the understanding that he would get the billing which I outlined to you . . . it would be useless to try to ask Rains for any further concessions, as I know that he would definitely not grant them."

In what seems to be another concession by the studio, Rains received star billing in the Technicolor short *Sons of Liberty*, playing Haym Salomon, the Jewish patriot of revolutionary America. Another "outside" project, directed by Michael Curtiz, *Sons of Liberty* won an Academy Award for Best Short Subject.

For *Juarez*, despite his relatively small screen time, Rains received second featured billing, below headliners Bette Davis and Paul Muni, and following Brian Aherne. Rains played Napoleon III, who schemed to retain France's grasp on Mexico. Muni and Davis played Benito Juarez, the elected Mexican president, and his wife, Carlotta, who urges him to declare himself king of Mexico rather than abdicate to the French.

Although Rains could have tossed off the role like the side project it was, he did his usual careful preparation and was fully in character for his first scene with Davis, his character's detested nemesis. The ferocious stare he conjured so unsettled Davis that she stopped the scene. "His performance was so real I thought he found me an inferior actress. He scared me to death," Davis recalled. "That was our initial contact, and that I got through it at all was a miracle. When Claude played a character, he was the consummate actor. It was always monumental theatre with him."

As filming progressed, however, Davis found looking at Rains easier and easier. "Thank God you're married," she told him, only half jokingly. He responded by bringing his baby daughter to the set the next day as a protective prop. When his daughter was older, Rains told her that Davis alarmed him "because she devoured men the way she devoured cigarettes." "Every now and then, I would kid Claude," Davis recalled. "I would say to him, you marry all these women, why do you *never* marry me? He would just smile, and that was that. I think he was basically enormously sexy. It reeked! He had that in any role he played."

The Warners front office did not, evidently, find Rains sexy; at least, they certainly did not see him as a leading man. In addition to an ongoing dearth of films (including a planned loan-out to Goldwyn for a Gary Cooper film in 1938, which failed to materialize), Rains and his agent continued to squabble with the studio over billing. "It has come to my attention that you have expressed dissatisfaction with respect to the billing which has been accorded you in connection with some of your recent pictures," Jack Warner wrote to Rains on February 24, 1939. "While I am satisfied that there has been no intentional disregard by any of our departments as to our contractual obligations with respect to billing, it is possible that some inadvertencies may have been committed. Therefore, I am again impressing upon the minds of all of the officials of this studio who play any part in setting up the billings in our various pictures to adhere strictly to the obligations established in our contracts, and have every confidence that if there has been any cause for complaint in the past, such conditions will be corrected and not occur hereafter."

Warner Bros. continued to cast around half-heartedly for loan-out contracts, and made a press announcement that Rains might portray Edgar Allan Poe in a biographical feature that—again—never materialized. William Dieterle, who had directed *Juarez*, wanted Rains to play the role of the villainous Archdeacon Frollo in RKO's lavish production of *The Hunchback of Notre Dame*, starring Charles Laughton as Quasimodo. But before the deal was completed, Rains recalled later, "I met [Laughton] by accident on the Universal lot. I recalled the old relationship fondly at the sight of him."

Rains walked up to him to say hello, but the much taller Laughton just looked down and said with a sneer, "Hello, you little shit."

For Rains, it was too much. "He was condescending to me," he later said—an understatement if there ever was. Rains refused the part in *Hunchback*; Cedric Hardwicke ultimately played it. Rains and Laughton never spoke again. "I didn't want to have any trouble with him," Rains said. "It was the end of our relationship."

Rains also passed on the title role in Universal's *Son of Frankenstein* opposite Boris Karloff. Peter Lorre had also refused it, and the part was finally taken by Basil Rathbone. Rains's decision probably had less to do with his reluctance to appear in a monster movie than the virtually unfilmable mishmash of a script Universal was offering. (Rathbone, despite a bravura performance, didn't even mention the film in his memoirs.)

In 1938, the nightmare of Beatrix Thomson behind him, Rains became a naturalized American citizen, and he traded his small Pennsylvania farm for a much larger property in nearby Chester County called Stock Grange. It was the working farm he had always dreamed of—a bucolic place that would ultimately comprise 600 acres, with an eighteenth-century stone farmhouse that he and Frances filled with antiques. "Stock Grange was one of the greatest prides of my father's life," Rains's daughter remembered. "He just couldn't wait to get back to it after he had competed a film. It was beautiful Pennsylvania land and resembled the English countryside."

After *Juarez*, Warners cast Rains in *Daughters Courageous*, a Michael Curtiz film cast in the mold of *Four Daughters*. Rains, who was given second billing after John Garfield, played Jim Masters, a smooth-talking father attempting to ingratiate himself to the family he abandoned twenty years earlier. It was a plum of a role, excellently written by Julius and Philip Epstein, but, despite Jack Warner's earlier assurances, there were more problems with Rains's billing: large billboards displayed Rains's name at only 20 percent the size of John Garfield's and buried it at the bottom of the poster.

Hawks, Rains's agent, fired off an angry message to the studio on August 2, 1939: "I do not believe that Mr. Enfield or the New York office mean any of the promises that have heretofore been made to me or Claude, and in this particular instance, they have deliberately broken the contract. This is a very serious breach of contract, coupled with the previous breaches, and very frankly Warner is in a serious position." He continued, "I believe that not only is there apology due me for this deliberate slap in the face, but unless there is satisfactory change, I am really going to enjoy a good fight. Please remember that Claude has been paid for his next picture in advance."

The money covered a loan-out to Columbia for Frank Capra's *Mr. Smith Goes to Washington*. Rains was to play Senator Joseph Paine, a silver-haired, silver-tongued, and ultimately corrupt politician who ensnares a political naïf, Jefferson Smith (James Stewart), in a high-level land fraud scheme. The part was not specifically tailored for Rains. As Capra recalled,

> We leafed and leafed through the Players Directory, pored over names in the lists of clients agents sent us. None raised blood pressure until one of my henchmen casually remarked,

"I just thought of an actor that'd *look* like a senator—Claude Rains." Boing! Not only could that distinguished British actor add grace and luster to any nation's Upper House; he had the artistry, power and depth to play the soul-tortured idealist whose feet had turned to clay.

Warners' Steve Trilling memoed Hal Wallis on March 23, 1939: "Bill Hawks 'phoned they had been over to see Frank Capra, and the part in 'MR. SMITH GOES TO WASHINGTON' was the best thing that CLAUDE RAINS has ever been offered since he has been in pictures—equally as important as James Stewart's and Jean Arthur's roles and they were therefore loath to pass it up." Hawks's and Rains's attitude was actually more that Warners would prefer Rains doing the movie to add to his prestige and name value for the studio's own future benefit.

Capra's screenwriter, Sidney Buchman, created a showpiece role for Rains, even though the part was not specifically conceived for him. Rains's role, the corrupt Senator Paine, was an ambiguous character—once idealistic, now cynical, ever scheming, yet supremely guilt-ridden—and Rains gave it his all. After working in motion pictures for just a little over five years, he had mastered a subtler technique, acting with his eyes and reining in the declamatory stage techniques on which he had been raised. Never again would he feel the need to back an actress into the camera. Unlike the many mediocre scripts he had elevated with his presence, in *Mr. Smith Goes to Washington* his talents were placed in the service of a genuinely fine piece of screenwriting.

Perhaps Rains's most impressive speech in the film is the one he delivers to James Stewart as the young senator, Jefferson Smith, who has begun to ask inconvenient questions about the propriety and legality of the federal appropriation of land in his home state. Rains summons Stewart for a meeting and proceeds to deliver one of the longest monologues in the film:

Listen, Jeff—you—you don't understand these things—you mustn't condemn me for my part in this—for my part in this without—you have no experience—you see things as black and white—and a man as angel or devil. That's the young idealist in you. And that isn't how the world runs, Jeff—certainly not Government and politics. It's a question of give and take—you have to play by the rules—compromise—you have to leave your ideals outside the door, with your rubbers. I feel I'm the right man for the Senate. And there are certain powers—influence. To stay there, I must respect them. And now and—for the sake of that power—a dam has to be built—and one must shut his eyes. It's—it's a small compromise. The *best* men have had to make them. Do you understand?

Jeff is silent, and the senator continues, in desperation:

I know how you feel, Jeff. Thirty years ago—I had those ideals, too. I was *you*. I had to make the decision you were asked to make today. And I compromised, yes! So that all these years I could stay in that Senate—and serve the people in a thousand different ways!

Rains rivets the viewer by beginning his speech in a quiet, avuncular manner, then building slowly into a full-scale Faustian confession. The senator is trying to convince himself of his personal virtue as he attempts to persuade the young idealist to sell his soul for political expedience. Mr. Smith refuses to go along, and Senator Paine denounces him on the floor of the Senate as corrupt and unworthy of his office. Jeff responds with a marathon filibuster—perhaps the most memorable scene in James Stewart's career, and one of the most memorable in Rains's—which leads to Paine's attempted suicide in the Senate cloakroom. There follows an extraordinary, if not quite believable, scene in which Paine recants his trumped-up accusations against Jefferson Smith. "Expel *me!* Not him! *Me!*" the senator cries. "Every word that boy said is the truth! I'm not fit for office! I'm not fit for any place of honor or trust in this land! Expel me—!"

Screenwriter Buchman hated the suicide attempt and the confession, which Capra insisted upon. Although the sequence stretches credulity, it does serve to bring the audience back to the more reassuring territory the director had staked out in *Mr. Deeds Goes to Town* and so many other films. In real life, the senator would never have confessed, but Capra knew his audience and sent them out of the theatre smiling.

Mr. Smith proved both prestigious and controversial, actually drawing fire from the Senate floor. Both Capra and Columbia's publicity department were no doubt delighted when the film was denounced by Republican senator Alben B. Barkley of Kentucky, who spewed his venom for the *Christian Science Monitor*. The film, he said, was a "grotesque distortion" of the congressional process. "It was so grotesque it was funny. It showed the Senate made up of crooks, led by crooks, listening to a crook. . . . It was so vicious an idea it was a source of disgust and hilarity to every member of congress who saw it." Barkley's comments set in motion even more vociferous criticism. Democratic senator James F. Byrnes of South Carolina stated that *Mr. Smith* promulgated an outrageous image of legislative corruption that was exactly what "dictators of totalitarian governments would like to have their subjects believe exists in a democracy." According to Capra, even the American ambassador to London, Joseph P. Kennedy, wired Columbia's head honcho Harry Cohn in protest.

At the time of the film's release, newspapers all around the country editorialized at length about the film, mostly positively. The media attention did nothing but drive more audiences into theatres. In addition to the film's technical merits, superior script, and direction, Claude Rains's understated performance hit a home run. (One can only imagine how a lesser actor, playing the part like a standard Hollywood bad guy, would have damaged the film's impact.)

Jean Arthur played the secretary, one of those hardboiled-with-a-heart-of-gold roles that she performed to perfection, at least as far as audiences were concerned. But on the set she was almost pathologically insecure, literally cowering in her dressing room between takes. As Frank Capra observed, "Those weren't butterflies in her stomach. They were wasps." Capra recalled that she often vomited before or after shooting a scene. Fortunately for Rains, "We only had one or two scenes together." He never understood "this pain that was gnawing at her inside." Once, during a publicity photo session, he was shocked when Arthur, annoyed with a minor delay in the lighting set-up, abruptly announced, "I don't see why I have to be here," and walked out. Rains maintained his professional distance throughout the production: "I never called her 'Jean,'" he recalled.

Mr. Smith garnered Academy Award nominations for best picture, as well as for James Stewart (best actor) and Rains (best supporting actor). None won, but Warners was effectively on notice that other studios were ready to make better use of Claude Rains than the one to whom he was under contract.

Four Wives, at Warners, was Rains's final assignment for 1939. This film, a sequel to *Four Daughters*, with Rains once more in the father role, gave Rains an amiable enough part, but it was certainly no *Mr. Smith Goes to Washington*.

Rains began renegotiating his Warner Bros. contract in early 1940. This time, he agreed to two films a year, at $6,000 a week for the first two years, $6,800 for the third year, and $7,600 a week for a fourth year. All films would have five-week guarantees. But unlike his earlier contract, the new one would give him the right to do two freelance pictures per year. And, unlike a headline star like Bette Davis (who was in no sense a "good dog" and battled endlessly and obsessively with studio brass over her assignments, culminating in a disastrously unsuccessful lawsuit filed in England to break her American contract), Rains, according to his daughter, was given limited right of script refusal—he could pass on two films, but was expected to take the third, if offered. (It is remarkable that this clause doesn't actually appear in the contract; according to Rains's daughter, the actor used his personal charm and consummate professional reliability to obtain extra-contractual concessions to his advantage.) Warners recognized Rains as a valuable and nontemperamental studio asset.

After signing the new agreement, Rains dropped Bill Hawks as his representative and hired Hollywood agent M. C. "Mike" Levee as his business manager. No record exists of Rains's specific dissatisfaction with Hawks, who continued to collect his commission for Warners projects. Levee concentrated on outside assignments until the Hawks contract finally lapsed in 1945.

Warners kept its original bargain with Rains for the balance of 1940, casting him in *Saturday's Children, The Sea Hawk, Lady with Red Hair,* and *Four Mothers* (completed in 1940, released in 1941). *Saturday's Children* marked his professional reunion with Theatre Guild alumnus Vincent Sherman, who had recently broken into directing with Warners' *The Return of Doctor X* (1938), Humphrey Bogart's single foray into the horror genre. *Saturday's Children* was based on a Pulitzer Prize–winning play by Maxwell Anderson that had already been twice adapted for the screen; Rains gave an unusually downbeat performance in yet another father role. "Do you know when I stopped living?" Rains, the beleaguered bookkeeper, asks his daughter. "When I was forty-three. I realized then what the end of my life would be—exactly what it had been up to then: repetitious, dull, and completely worthless to anyone." The line was ironic, since Rains had made his memorable screen debut when he was forty-three.

In *Lady with Red Hair* Rains had a plum role that drew upon his personal experience with turn-of-the-century theatrical impresarios. As producer David Belasco, he played opposite Miriam Hopkins, who starred as Chicago socialite Caroline Carter, a real-life character who bulldozed her way into the New York theatre world despite her lack of formal training. The film has a decidedly *Pygmalion*-like flavor and remains one of the most delicious backstage comedy-dramas Hollywood has ever produced.

Warners next cast him in the title role of *Here Comes Mr. Jordan,* as a heavenly administrator who oversees the reincarnation of Robert Montgomery. Rains is wry, impish, and ironic in this original screen version of the play by Harry Segall, *Heaven Can Wait.*

Rains's new agent, Mike Levee, arranged for his client to receive top billing in Universal's *The Wolf Man,* in the supporting, but pivotal, role of Sir John Talbot, a Welsh aristocrat-astronomer. Talbot, improbably, has an American-raised telescope technician son twice his size named Larry (played by Lon Chaney, Jr., with no trace whatsoever of English breeding), who is bitten by a cursed gypsy (Bela Lugosi) and subsequently turns into a rampaging werewolf.

The screenwriter, Curt Siodmak, acceded to the familial conceit despite the absurdity of the studio's request. He had originally written Chaney's part as a visiting American. Siodmak was a gifted but practical scenarist who knew how to choose his fights. "I targeted the screenplay to be delivered as late as possible," he wrote. "That gave the front office no time to engage another writer, who could mess up my screenplay. Universal was stingy and didn't like to spend money for rewrites. That was the secret of getting a 'classic.'"

Siodmak's script was significantly retooled in other ways as well to accommodate Rains's star billing. In Siodmak's first draft, the Wolf Man is killed by the dashing, up-and-coming contract player Patric Knowles; but the shooting script gave the honors to the top-billed Rains, who bashes in the lycanthrope's brain with a silver wolf's-head cane in a ferocious struggle.

Rains returned to Warner Bros. for a difficult part in *Kings Row*, based on the best-selling novel by Henry Bellamann. Set in turn-of-the-century America, the book was the *Peyton Place* of its time, with a strong dose of *Winesburg, Ohio* thrown over the flames—a lurid melodrama of small-town secrets that immediately raised the ire of both the press and the film censors. *Los Angeles Daily News* columnist Ted Le Berthon wondered "how anybody could possibly clean up 'Kings Row,' and why anyone outside of a booby hatch could have regarded it as screen material." He continued:

> In this book, spiced with harlots, idiots, nymphomaniacs, and homosexuals, there are three fathers who become sexually enamored of their daughters, one hangman who derives erotic pleasure from hanging people by the neck until they are dead, a sadistic doctor who performs unnecessary operations for the gloating pleasure of seeing his patients suffer to the human breaking point, and a whole horde of half-witted creatures preoccupied with sex. And the scene of all this is a Missouri town of some 5,000 population which seems to take on some of the dark mood of a state mental asylum . . .

Rains played Dr. Alexander Tower, portrayed in the original book as a reclusive physician who no longer has patients, having retired to a gloomy house with a mad wife and a beautiful daughter, Cassie, with whom he is incestuously involved and whom he kills before committing suicide. Joseph Breen informed Jack Warner in April 1941 that the script—which had already removed the incest (instead making Cassie a nymphomaniac), as well as harlots, idiots, the hangman, and any suggestion of homosexuality—was still "definitely unacceptable under the provisions of the Production Code and cannot be approved." The production of *Kings Row*, said Breen, "may well be a definite *disservice* to the motion picture industry for, no matter how well the screenplay is done, the fact that it stems from so thoroughly questionable a novel is likely to bring down upon the industry, as a whole, the condemnation of decent people everywhere." Nonetheless, the very next day, a meeting between Breen, executive producer Hal Wallis, screenwriter Casey Robinson, and associate producer David Lewis resulted in a compromise: all suggestions of incest and nymphomania would be replaced with the theme of hereditary schizophrenia.

Rains was not the original actor chosen for the role of Dr. Tower. When British actor James Stephenson, who was scheduled to play the part, suffered a heart attack, Hal Wallis called Rains—who, Wallis said, "declined instantly. But we tried again, rushed him the book, and he finally agreed to break off his much-needed vacation and make the long train journey west." According to Wallis, Rains's "refusal to fly meant a considerable delay in our schedule."

Casting Dr. Tower's doomed daughter presented difficulties. Hal Wallis wanted Ida Lupino, but the actress proved difficult, objecting to the relative smallness of the role. Bette Davis wanted the part and briefly was a shaky front runner, but was eventually passed over. Olivia de Havilland was also approached, and at one point the script was even sent to Ginger Rogers. Betty Field, a contract player from Paramount, was finally cast.

Most of Rains's scenes were opposite Robert Cummings as Parris Mitchell, an aspiring psychiatrist whom Dr. Tower takes under his tutelage and who falls in love with Cassie. (An interwoven story line had Ronald Reagan in an even worse fix with another disturbed doctor-father—a surgeon who unnecessarily amputates Reagan's legs after an accident, just to settle a score involving the doctor's daughter, played by

Ann Sheridan.) Rains's scenes all have a melancholy intensity, accentuated by James Wong Howe's moody cinematography. Dr. Tower often
seems to be engulfed by the shadows of his house as the nightmare of his
wife and daughter's mental instability closes in. He foreshadows his own
demise with fatalistic observations shared with the idealistic young doctor-
to-be, almost as if warning him of the tragic limitations of the healing arts.
"In this modern, complicated world," the turn-of-the-century doctor says,
"man breaks down under the strain, the bewilderment, the disappointment, disillusionment; gets lost, goes crazy, commits suicide." And, as if
anticipating the tragic arc of the twentieth century, "Mankind's building
up the biggest psychic bellyache in history."

Indeed: Pearl Harbor had already been bombed.

6

Now, Contract Player

A PRIOR ENGAGEMENT WITH BETTE DAVIS prevented Claude Rains from attending his own mother's funeral.

Eliza Cox Rains died on May 13, 1942, during the production of *Now, Voyager*, Warners' latest Bette Davis vehicle. Based on a best-selling novel by Olive Higgins Prouty, *Voyager* had begun production on April 7, with retakes continuing through June. There is no record of Rains having made any request for bereavement leave or, for that matter, his discussing his mother's death with anyone. Aside from his contractual commitments, the logistics of making an emergency transatlantic crossing during wartime would have been formidable. Years later he would sadly recall, "She shouldn't have died, I'm sure." He put most of the blame on his father. "I don't know what he'd done with her, or about the doctor or anything. But I know that he didn't know how to look after her. He didn't realize the importance of it all." Rains's sister reported that Frederick Rains had said of his famous son, "He's a great success. He's earning money. He can look after me." Rains suspected that some of the money he had been sending for his mother's care may well have been diverted. "I'd pay the nursing home and send the checks to him. If he did any work, I didn't know about it. Tiny parts in pictures. People knew him. I remember his going to Paris, or France, anyway, and coming back with beautiful clothes. I'm quite sure, from what I heard about him and his general behavior, he was killing himself," Rains said, alluding to his father's alcoholism.

Now, Voyager was a welcome assignment. Rains had just returned to Burbank after a loan-out to Twentieth Century-Fox for *Moontide* in a largely superfluous role supporting French heartthrob Jean Gabin in his American film debut. The assignment at Fox did, however, give Rains the chance to begin an enduring friendship with the film's screenwriter, novelist John O'Hara—despite O'Hara's having written Rains an enigmatic, walk-through part the actor could do little with. In contrast, *Now, Voyager* would be specifically developed and expanded to showcase his talents.

Warners wanted Rains to play Dr. Jaquith, an eminent psychiatrist. Jaquith effects a swanlike transformation of a mother-ridden ugly duckling named Charlotte Vale (Davis), who ends up romantically exchanging cigarettes with her star-crossed lover, played by Paul Henreid. But the studio once more attempted to cajole contractual concessions from Rains and his agent, on the basis that the role, though pivotal, was relatively small and the shooting schedule would exceed Rains's five-week guarantee. In his autobiography, Hal Wallis wrote that Rains "turned down the part, insisting it was too sketchy. [Screenwriter] Casey Robinson built up the role and Rains agreed to do it for the then enormous salary of $5,000 a week. I offered him $25,000 for six weeks but his agent Mike Levee was adamant and we went ahead with the required arrangement."

It was hardly a victory for the actor and his agent, since *Now, Voyager*'s production fell in the third year of Rains's contract, which stipulated that in that year his salary would be $6,800 per week. Warners obviously intended to continue, outrageously, to renegotiate terms picture by picture. But for the moment, Rains knew he had a terrific part. He left it to Mike Levee eventually to settle the financial score.

Unlike Rains, whose role was specially tailored for him, Bette Davis was cast only after Irene Dunne, Norma Shearer, and Ginger Rogers had fallen by the wayside. Davis would earn an Academy Award nomination for her role in this film. *Now, Voyager* was seen as groundbreaking on the topic of psychiatry, especially in its implications for women. The subject matter was provocative for its time, although it still indulged in some Freudian clichés about domineering mothers, as reflected in this scene between Rains and Davis's mother, played by the indomitable Gladys Cooper:

JAQUITH: She is most seriously ill.
MRS. VALE: Charlotte is—?

JAQUITH: Thanks to you.

MRS. VALE: Did you say—?

JAQUITH: My dear Mrs. Vale, if you had deliberately and maliciously planned to destroy your daughter's life, you couldn't have done it more completely.

MRS. VALE: How? By having exercised a mother's rights?

JAQUITH: A mother's rights—twaddle! A child has rights. A person has rights—to discover her own mistakes, to make her own way, to grow and blossom in her own particular soil.

MRS. VALE: Are we getting into botany, Doctor? Are we flowers?

Unlike later screen psychiatrists, whose own demons often manage to rise uncomfortably close to the surface, Rains plays Dr. Jaquith as solid, professional, and compassionate. The New York Times praised Rains's "polished and even-tempered performance." Davis herself was so taken with the character of the psychiatrist that in later years she opined that Charlotte Vale and Dr. Jaquith should have married and run his sanitarium together.

By the time he worked on Now, Voyager, Rains had some demons of his own and could perhaps have benefited from the professional services of a Dr. Jaquith. He was developing a serious alcohol problem, beginning to drink at noon and alternating scotch with Guinness stout. Still, not a single professional colleague ever recalled an occasion in which he seemed to be impaired, on the set or off, which only made the problem more insidious. Rains was a master actor who could convincingly play being sober. But the long-range effects would be devastating.

Casablanca, Rains's next film, could easily have been a mess of a movie. Based on an unproduced stage play, Everybody Comes to Rick's, Warners' original announcements named Ronald Reagan and Ann Sheridan to play star-crossed lovers in a wartime melodrama set in French Morocco. The central character is Rick Blaine, a world-weary ex-lawyer from the states, who now runs the Café Americain in Casablanca. Ilsa Lund, Blaine's former heartthrob in Paris, shows up with a new love interest, a Czech resistance fighter named Victor Lazlo, whom she has married. Both are seeking elusive exit visas to escape Nazi-occupied territory.

The play outlines the bones of the story as we now know it; a major difference is that the Bergman character was originally an American named Lois Meredith. The studio wisely replaced the originally announced cast with Humphrey Bogart (after considering George Raft, who lobbied for the part) and Ingrid Bergman (Louis B. Mayer refused to loan out the services of Hedy Lamarr). Bogart and Bergman were both leery of committing their services to an unfinished script and wanted to escape the assignment as late as a week before principal photography began. Bergman was then under contract to David O. Selznick and complained to him vociferously about the loan-out: "You cannot sell me for something when you don't even know the story!" Indeed, there was no finished story or script; Warners had assigned the screenplay to Julius and Philip G. Epstein, who produced several treatments before going on to greener pastures. The completion of the script was the responsibility of a junior screenwriter, Howard Koch. Koch recalled sweating bullets at the prospect of turning forty preliminary pages into a finished screenplay within a matter of weeks.

Production on *Casablanca*, as the project was now called, commenced with half a script, and no one—producer, director, writer, and least of all the actors—had any idea where the story was heading. "I didn't know from one day to the other what we were going to do," Bergman recalled.

> I had a problem as there were two men, played by Paul Henreid and Humphrey Bogart, who were both in love with me, so I said to the writers, "Now which of these two men do I end up with?" And they said, "We haven't decided yet and are going to shoot it two ways." "But this is impossible," I said. "You must tell me because, after all, there is a little bit of difference in acting toward a man you love and another man for whom you just may feel pity or affection." "Well, they said, don't make it too much of anything. Play it in between, you know, so we can decide in the end."

Rains avoided the fray, to the point of brown-bagging his lunches and avoiding the studio commissary and its personalities and politics. He had been cast as the impish and charmingly corrupt prefect of police, Louis Renault (Rinaldo in the play). Industry censors had difficulty with implications in the original script that Renault was trading exit visas for sexual favors, and certain adjustments were made. For instance, in the shooting script, a desperate, beautiful woman without money begs Rick, "It used to be a villa at Cannes, or the very least, a string of pearls—now all I ask is an exit visa." Rick rebuffs her, and Renault comments cynically, "How extravagant you are—throwing away women like that. Someday they may be rationed." The Breen office insisted that "rationed" be changed to "scarce." Another Rains line that the censor objected to (this one delivered to the Nazi major played by Conrad Veidt): "You enjoy war. I enjoy women. We are both very good at our jobs." Breen asked that "enjoy" be changed to "like." And so on.

Although a supporting role, the Renault character is pivotal to the plot. The audience knows he is compromised and therefore doesn't know whether to trust him until the very end of the film, when he betrays the Nazis and permits Ilsa and her husband to escape. Rains toys with the characters (and the audience) throughout the picture, maintaining suspense.

Rains greatly admired Bogart, who, like Rains, had done serious stage work in New York. After hours, Rains and Bogart occasionally drank together. Bogart drank by himself during working hours, at first discreetly and later indiscreetly. But during *Casablanca*, Bogart showed no obvious effects of alcohol, unlike his then-wife Mayo Methot, whom Rains (and everyone else in the studio) immediately recognized as a sloppy and aggressive drunk. Bogart's drinking had more subtle effects, such as an obsessively dictatorial manner, which expressed itself one day when Rains received a memo from Jack Warner, reprimanding him over some trivial matter. Rains was willing to laugh it off, but Bogart, suddenly menacingly serious, insisted that the actor immediately confront Warner, that he march directly to the front office and take the studio head to task for the "son of a bitch" he was. "You have to do it now!" Bogart ordered him, again and again, his voice rising. Rains found himself very nearly following the crazy instructions. "He was very persuasive."

Quite unlike his friendly rapport with Bogart, Rains had taken an immediate dislike to second male lead Paul Henreid, whom he privately called "Paul Hemorrhoid." The precise reason for their mutual animosity is unclear, but both men seem to have felt that the other was a pampered, demanding performer. Their next, and last, pairing, in *Deception* (1946) with Bette Davis, would give both actors the chance to play out their real-life conflict in a melodramatic context.

Actor Leonid Kinskey, who played the bartender at Rick's, remembered that Rains "always kept to himself and rarely participated in those little superficial conversations that take place between 'takes,'" although he recalled "a warm, genuine smile" that emerged whenever Rains talked about his farm. "Looking back," wrote Kinskey in 1972, "I have the impression that he loved uniforms and costumes. On our picture he glanced at himself in any mirror that his eye caught, constantly adjusting the military cap and tunic of his impeccable French uniform."

Peter Lorre, who played the visa trafficker Ugarte in the film, recalled Rains's perfectionism and his "constantly studying" the script. At one point Lorre saw the chance for a prank that might break what the cast regarded as Rains's overly serious demeanor. A scene having nothing whatsoever to do with *Casablanca* was concocted and memorized by Lorre and others. "When he came in the next day and saw us rehearsing the scene," recalled Lorre, "he was frantic. He called me aside and said, 'Peter, something terrible has happened to me. I can't remember a single line.' We all broke up and he wasn't even mad—just relieved that his memory wasn't failing."

Rains enjoyed working again with Michael Curtiz (his most frequent director), though he didn't always agree with him about the interpretation of certain scenes. Once, to cut the tension after Curtiz asked him repeatedly to make an entrance with "more energy," he responded by energetically bursting through the door on a bicycle.

"Mr. Rains is properly slippery and crafty as a minion of Vichy perfidy," opined the *New York Times* in its original review of *Casablanca*. Louis Renault became a signature role for Rains, and his famous lines "Round up the usual suspects" and "I'm shocked, *shocked*" (to discover gambling at Rick's while simultaneously pocketing his own winnings) have deeply embedded themselves into the American vernacular.

Oddly enough, Rains's preference for Pennsylvania farm living may have secured the film's indelible final scene, in which Bogart looks forward to "the start of a beautiful friendship" with Rains as they walk away from the camera into a foggy airfield on the Burbank backlot. Because *Casablanca* was completely shot in Burbank, a foggy airstrip needed to be improvised on a soundstage. "They wanted a tremendous long view of the airport," Bergman remembered. "so they had midgets in the background so that the people would look very small."

According to Aljean Harmetz, the definitive *Casablanca* historian, "Claude Rains inadvertently saved the ending of the film. When the picture was finished and just about ready to be released, the Allies invaded North Africa. And that gave Warners the idea that they should change the ending of the movie. And they wrote a new scene, and in it Bogart and Claude Rains and a host of extras were on the deck of a freighter about to disembark on North African soil." In a memo dated November 11, 1942, Hal Wallis wrote, "Rains is in Pennsylvania, and I'm asking Levee to get him out here as quickly as possible as I want to make these scenes this week if possible." Given the wartime shortage of commercial air flights, getting Rains back that quickly proved impossible. And on November 12, David O. Selznick, who had seen the final cut, wired Wallis, praising *Casablanca* to the rafters and urging him not to touch the film, which had generated ecstatic audience responses at preview screenings. Wallis relented, and one of the most memorable final scenes in motion picture history was saved. Another late decision made the moment: "We needed a good punch line for the ending at the airport," recalled Wallis, and Bogart recorded two alternates for his fade-out with Rains. The first—"Louis, I might have known you'd mix your patriotism with a little larceny"—was jettisoned in favor of the line that would become world-famous: "Louis, I think this is the beginning of a beautiful friendship."

In the end, Bogart and Bergman carried the show, but Rains supplied his usual ample support. It is rare indeed when such an assemblage of such perfectly cast, top-drawer talent (including Veidt, Sydney Greenstreet, and Lorre) has been brought together for a single film. And rarely has any motion picture become quite so iconic, still drawing intense fascination and analysis more than sixty years after its release. The film won the Academy Award for best picture of 1943. Screenwriters Julius Epstein, Philip Epstein, and Howard Koch received an Oscar for the screenplay. Bogart and Rains were nominated for best actor and best supporting actor (Rains's second nomination), but neither won. The film was also nominated for best film editing (Owen Marks) and best music (Max Steiner).

Rains's next film, RKO's *Forever and a Day* (1943) was a well-meaning but rather muddled Hollywood tribute to the indomitable spirit of the British during the Blitz, and Rains was one of dozens of English actors in Hollywood who donated their services to the film, the proceeds of which were earmarked for the British War Effort and American polio research (President Roosevelt's charity of choice). Seventy-eight actors, twenty-one writers, and seven directors were involved in the epic, which took nearly two years to complete. Charles Laughton had a role, though no scenes with Rains. *Forever and a Day* used an air raid on Britain as a framework for a flashback-structured film recounting the history and inhabitants of an English manor house threatened by German bombs. Rains played a nineteenth-century villain with limited screen time. *Variety* gave him a rare pan: "Claude Rains . . . does not impress as the menace."

While negotiating his client's latest Warners contract option, Mike Levee persuaded Rains to accept the title role in Universal's lavish Technicolor remake of *Phantom of the Opera*. Rains had reservations. He would be third-billed under Nelson Eddy and the eighteen-year-old soprano starlet Susanna Foster. The original 1925 film, starring Lon Chaney, was notable for its having one of the most grotesque makeup designs in Hollywood history, a living death's-head painfully constructed out of putty, wires, and Chaney's masochism.

Rains eventually accepted the role, with the proviso that the makeup would not be extreme. He was seriously concerned that a too-strong identification with the horror genre would impede his future chances of being cast in leading roles. A long series of negotiations with director Arthur Lubin and Universal's makeup head Jack Pierce ensued. Lubin was frustrated, knowing that the public wanted any remake of *The Phantom* to include a horrific visage. The unmasking scene and the chandelier crash were essential set pieces audiences would expect and demand. A studio that would eliminate either would do so at its box office peril.

Rains might have been more comfortable with Universal's earlier treatments of the remake. As early as 1936, the studio envisioned Boris Karloff in the role and considered making the Phantom's disfigurement psychological instead of physical—the traumatic result of World War I shell shock. Then, Universal's pairing of Deanna Durbin and Charles Laughton (then the newest "new Lon Chaney" in RKO's *Hunchback of Notre Dame*) in *It Started with Eve* led the studio to believe that Laughton's flair for grotesquerie and Durban's musicality might be a winning combination for a new *Phantom*.

No photographs of Jack Pierce's initial makeup tests on Rains exist, but Arthur Lubin remembered that the plans were repeatedly modified to accommodate Rains's comfort zone. Rains never commented on the makeup except to tell one reporter that it amounted to no more than a scar on his cheek. Unlike the original story, the Phantom's ugliness in the shooting script was not congenital but the result of an acid-burn disfigurement. As Erique Claudin, veteran first violinist of the Paris Opera, Rains is dismissed because of an arthritic left hand. He falls back on composing in order to support the singing career of his long-lost daughter, Christine, who has never known him. But when he mistakenly believes the score of his masterwork concerto has been stolen, he strangles a music publisher, whose assistant-mistress promptly throws a pan of engraving acid in his face. Hideously burned, he takes refuge in the catacombs of the Opera, where he descends into murderous dementia.

Lubin told film historian Scott MacQueen that Rains was so concerned about his burn makeup and its potential effect on his career that the director was forced to employ a hidden camera to capture needed footage during the unmasking scene. The initial shot, in which Susanna Foster rips off the mask, was compromised by a slightly out-of-focus zoom-in. Two perfectly focused head shots of Rains were subsequently inserted; these, apparently, are the surreptitious footage Lubin described. Rains never talked about his collaboration with Pierce, who was notoriously testy and autocratic. As it turned out, the final makeup was uncannily similar to the typical effects of the World War I gas that had blinded Rains in one eye, which doubtless added to his discomfort. Since he insisted on being masked until the very end of the film, Rains created a dilemma for himself somewhat parallel to being similarly unseen in *The Invisible Man*, and he held out for the most flattering mask possible. Lubin remembered "a great deal of argument" about the "testing of the damn mask." But the result was brilliant—a pale blue, almost feline stylization of Rains's own face, allowing the actor to be perfectly recognizable even while disguised. The mask is believed to have been executed by Pierce's assistant (and later his successor at Universal), Bud Westmore.

In addition to Rains's anxiety over the makeup for his character, Lubin also recalled that Rains wanted to be certain that the scenes in which he played the violin and piano be completely convincing, and the actor practiced fingering techniques for weeks in advance of shooting. It was yet another example of the meticulous preparation so many of Rains's coworkers would comment upon throughout his career.

Reminiscent of the censor's concerns about *Kings Row*, Rains's *Phantom of the Opera* also pushed some incest buttons. In a scene deleted from the finished film, Nelson Eddy discovers the secret of Christine's paternity, but the audience has been led to believe that Claudin is romantically fixated on the young woman. The deletion only confused matters, though more than one newspaper reviewer intuited that Claudin was Christine's protective father, not her unrequited lover.

Rains's real-life daughter recalls a memorable Halloween following the release of the movie. Her father borrowed his costume from the Universal wardrobe department. Unable to find the original, custom mask, he substituted a Zorro-style one. He then proceed to take his daughter and two of her playmates on the rounds of neighbors' houses. The girls hid under his cape as he rang each doorbell. When the householder opened the door, there was the Phantom of the Opera in person, intoning an old poem about All Hallow's Eve. The recitation complete, the Phantom threw open his cloak and the children, dressed as gremlins, jumped out, squealing "Trick or treat!" The gremlins were then invited inside for food, and the Phantom for drink, a ritual enacted a good number of times throughout the evening. Frances was the designated driver.

Back at Warners, Rains was cast in *Passage to Marseilles*, an ill-advised attempt to recapture some of *Casablanca*'s box office magic by reassembling several of the previous film's key performers—Bogart, Rains, Greenstreet, and Lorre, as well as director Curtiz—for a preachy wartime tale of French-Fascist conflict, with an escape from Devil's Island thrown in. Confusingly structured by screenwriters Casey Robinson and Jack Moffitt with flashbacks inside of flashbacks, *Passage* gave Rains (second-billed) more screen time than Bogart, who played a doomed airman in the Free French Air Squadron. Rains played a dapper, eye-patch–sporting French captain who narrates the Bogart story line.

After Paul Henreid turned down the title role in Vincent Sherman's *Mr. Skeffington* opposite Bette Davis, Rains stepped into the part. The film was embattled from the start. During pre-production, Davis's second husband, Arthur Farnsworth, died under circumstances that have never been completely explained. Farnsworth collapsed on a Hollywood sidewalk and was dead two days later. A postmortem examination showed that the cause of death was a skull fracture suffered at least two weeks earlier. One theory, advanced by Davis biographer Charles Higham, posited that her husband had been attacked in retaliation for an extramarital affair and never reported the injury that ultimately killed him.

The tragedy only fed Davis's famously histrionic tendencies. She returned to work only a week after Farnsworth's death, and shortly thereafter began an affair with director Sherman, possibly as a power ploy. She did everything she could to seize control of the production. Jack Warner asked the Epstein brothers, who had written the screenplay, why the production was behind schedule. Their sardonic reply: "Because Bette Davis is a slow director." As Rains later remembered Davis's general demeanor on the set of *Mr. Skeffington* and the other films in which they worked together, "She wants to photograph the thing, she wants to direct it, she wants to light it, and all that. But when it comes to her fellow players, she's wonderful." Of Bette herself, he said, "I'm very fond of her and I'm

*

123

very sorry for her. She doesn't know how to live with a man. She needs one badly. She makes mistakes all the time, puts men up on pedestals, but once they're up there—bam! None of them could take it."

According to Rains, Mr. *Skeffington* was shot over a period of twenty weeks, a schedule he found excessive. Although he ultimately only worked his contracted weeks, the protracted production effectively prevented his being cast in other projects for the duration. Rains played Job Skeffington, a Manhattan stockbroker who falls under the charms of Fanny Trellis, a beautiful but monstrously self-centered socialite whose ne'er-do-well brother has stolen money from Skeffington. To protect her sibling, she seduces and marries the powerful, but nebbishy, financial magnate. Her humiliated brother exiles himself to the front lines of World War I and is promptly killed. Fanny blames Skeffington and proceeds to treat him like dirt until the next world war, during which he enlists and becomes missing in action. Fanny contracts diphtheria, which ravages her once-legendary beauty and repels her entourage of sycophantic, would-be suitors. At the end of the war, Skeffington returns, a shell of his former self, broken and blinded in a German camp. Fanny welcomes him back, as he—a blind man—is the only person who can appreciate her for something other than her lost physical charms.

Mr. *Skeffington* was one of only a handful of World War II Hollywood films to address anti-Semitism, however gingerly. Rains had strong personal feelings on the topic; his wife was Jewish, and he believed there might be Jewish blood far back in his own lineage. He had difficulty playing a scene with Davis, in which the custody of their daughter is at issue. On the verge of being deployed to wartime Europe, Skeffington resists taking his half-Jewish daughter with him (for obvious reasons, which he sensitively explains to the child in what is arguably the film's only emotionally realistic scene). Rains, whose own daughter was half-Jewish by way of her mother, bridled at performing the scene as written, which startled Davis. "He forgot his character and I sat there in absolute shock. My great friend, whom I would have done anything on God's earth for in a scene, turned on me personally. I shook all over. I was so frightened of him in that scene, it was unbelievable."

Still, director Vincent Sherman had nothing but accolades for Rains.

"Rains had great concentration, knew his attitude in each scene, played with his partner, and created an inner life for his character. He was a professional in the best sense of the word. While he came on the set prepared, he always left room for the director to create with him."

Critics were appalled by the glamorization of such a thoroughly unsympathetic creature as Fanny Skeffington. In his review of Mr. Skeffington, James Agee opined that the character (and, by extension, Davis herself) "demonstrates the horrors of egocentricity on a marathonic scale." Despite the film's deficiencies, Rains was nominated a third time for an Academy Award for best supporting actor; once again, he lost.

With Rains employed steadily during this time, the family found themselves spending an increasing amount of time at their home in Brentwood. As his daughter recalled, "Jimmy Stewart lived across the street. The only interaction we had with him was to say hello when he came shuffling down the driveway in his bathrobe and slippers to pick up the newspaper. Lee Strasberg lived across the street, about three doors down. His daughter Susan and I were very good friends. A great teacher, but a very odd man. He never sat down during dinner; he'd just stand there at the table, reading to himself." The Henry Fonda family also lived nearby, and Jennifer was friendly with young Jane.

Rains detested Hollywood pretension. He enrolled his daughter in the Brentwood Town and Country School, which had a reputation for not treating movie stars' children like movie stars' children. One neighborhood parent, James Mason, was rumored to have bought the school simply in order to fire sycophantic teachers.

If the Rainses' neighborhood had a social queen bee, it was Joan Crawford, also a Warner Bros. star, with whom Rains had oddly never been paired by the studio, although he would be briefly considered for the role Sydney Greenstreet played opposite her in 1947's Flamingo Road. Around the time she won the Oscar for Mildred Pierce, Crawford called Frances, inviting Jennifer to attend a birthday party for her adopted daughter Christina. Frances said her daughter would be happy to attend. How should she dress? Dungarees would be fine, Crawford said.

When Jennifer arrived at the party—an elaborate backyard affair, complete with a pony—she was humiliated to find that she was the only girl wearing jeans. The other Hollywood mothers had dressed their daughters competitively in elegant pinafores. Jennifer looked like the farm girl she actually was. Christina dutifully took her to meet her mother, who was reclining on a chaise in a white robe and turban, attended by both a manicurist and a pedicurist. Both girls curtsied. Crawford looked Jennifer up and down. "It was very nice to meet you," she said, one eyebrow slightly raised. "And now, you may leave."

Christina took Jennifer to see her doll collection, which was housed in a cabana-style structure adjacent to the swimming pool. Jennifer loved dolls and looked forward to playing with Christina's collection, the largest, most exquisite one she had ever seen.

"Oh, no," said Christina, sadly. "We can't ever touch them. We can only look." Then she closed the door on the strange mausoleum of the dolls, and the girls returned to the party. Jennifer never visited again.

Her father's next freelance assignment was in an ill-timed ideological film, *Strange Holiday* (1945), an impassioned screed by Arch Oboler, a radio drama maven perhaps best known for his legendary series *Lights Out.* Oboler's script railed at American complacency about the Nazi threat, but the film was released after the war had actually ended and did poor business. The project had started as a short subject and was unwisely expanded to feature length, with Rains called upon to provide ineffective padding in a tale of a fantastic, fascistic takeover of America. In its way, *Strange Holiday* was not unlike the cold war propaganda films of the 1950s. Despite the film's shortcomings, Rains greatly admired Oboler, and it would not be the last time they worked together.

In *This Love of Ours,* produced by Universal in 1945, Rains was second-billed under Merle Oberon, playing a sardonic café caricaturist. The script was based on a play by Luigi Pirandello and directed by William Dieterle, who had earlier wanted Rains for *The Hunchback of Notre Dame* at RKO. The *New York Times* opined that Rains "is altogether delightful and contributes some mildly amusing moments in an otherwise doggedly tragic drama."

By 1945, Rains was not happy with his languishing situation at Warner Bros. and the lackluster outside work he was forced to take. Therefore, when Mike Levee asked him if he would consider the male lead in the British film version of Shaw's *Caesar and Cleopatra*, to be shot in wartime England with Vivien Leigh as his costar, he wasted no time in accepting. He didn't know at the time that the assignment would have unforeseen intrigues and convolutions leading to his becoming the most highly compensated performer in film history.

The heavily armed, four-engine Avro Lancaster bomber set down at Prestwick, Scotland, shortly before noon on an overcast day in May 1944. It had been decided that military air transport across the Atlantic was the only safe option for Rains's travel. Within an hour the actor was aboard a commercial aircraft bound for London, where a limousine and an elegant emissary of the J. Arthur Rank Organization was waiting for him. This splendid figure, with striped trousers, frock coat, bowler, furled umbrella, and lemon kid gloves, seemed oblivious to the grim grey mantle of war and the noisy death that was raining down. The Battle of Britain had long since been decided, but the V-1 and V-2 rocket bombs continued, hurtling earthward, erratic and unannounced.

The Rank envoy's only reference to the war during the long drive into London was his apology for not being able to find quarters in the country, "where it is safe." Instead, Rains would be housed temporarily in a suite at the Savoy. Rains's only concern at the moment was to find a police station near the Savoy and register, as the law required, as an alien.

"A police station? Good lord, Mr. Rains, what have you done?"

"I haven't done anything, except become an American citizen. I am required to register."

For all his decorum, the Rank man could not disguise his disgust. "Bloody nonsense," he said with a snort. "Once an Englishman, always an Englishman." The subject was not discussed further.

By the time the limousine had reached the Strand and was in sight of the Savoy, a covey of rockets was evidently looming overhead, for antiaircraft batteries suddenly began to thunder. Rains noticed a perceptible increase in the walking speed of pedestrians; some were scurrying toward shelters. As the car pulled up to the hotel entrance, fragments of the bursting flak shells were falling in the streets, a kind of metallic hail.

"Good evening, Mr. Rains," said the doorman, seemingly unperturbed. "I trust you've had a comfortable journey." His voice was steady, if pitched a trifle above the din. He made no reference to the buzz bombs or falling shrapnel.

Rains asked if there was a bomb shelter. There was, but the doorman didn't think he'd be comfortable there. "It's crowded, and there's not much air. Why don't you do what I do?"

"What do you do?"

"Well, sir, I go to bed, put a pillow over my face and a pillow over my vitals. And pray."

There would be frequent food shortages during his stay, but one of the hotel waiters was an admirer and personally brought the actor special meals from his partially bombed-out home. Rains was struck by the man's unruffled stoicism and asked him how he personally dealt with the relentless bombardment and omnipresent possiblity of death.

"To be honest about it, sir," the waiter replied, "sometimes I just shit my pants."

Rains had been in London nearly two weeks, conferring occasionally with Gabriel Pascal, the producer and director of *Caesar and Cleopatra*, and visiting the studio at suburban Denham, before he was finally summoned by George Bernard Shaw for a meeting at his venerated estate at Ayot St Lawrence in Buckinghamshire, an hour's drive from London. Shaw's wife had died, and the old playwright was living with only his housekeeper. Pascal met Rains at the door as the limousine arrived and escorted him to the study, where they waited in relative silence for several minutes. Shaw, wearing a tweed jacket and knickers, finally entered, shook Rains's hand with reasonable enthusiasm, and then retreated to a small wooden armchair facing the fireplace. Pascal moved quickly to an adjoining chair, leaving Rains in the center of the room, staring awkwardly at their backs. Rains felt a mounting mixture of humiliation and anger. Perhaps he can't stand the sight of me, he thought. After all, Shaw had written the play for Johnston Forbes-Robertson, a handsome, manly giant, and now he is confronted with the prospect of a relative dwarf in the role. Rains was wondering whether he should leave the room when Shaw, without moving or even turning his head, spoke.

"I understand you're now a *movie* actor," spitting out the key word with sufficient force to convey his frequently stated contempt for Hollywood.

"Yes, Mr. Shaw," Rains replied softly.

"I also understand you have a farm, and that you're happy. You also have a child. You always wanted a child. You were unhappy in this country."

"Yes, Mr. Shaw."

Rains assumed that Shaw was maliciously toying with him, but refrained, with some difficulty, from saying so. He only glared at the pair of bunched backs before him. "Tell me about yourself," said Shaw. "How many of my plays have you done?"

Haltingly, Rains recited a list of eight or nine.

"Do you remember the first time we met?"

"Yes, Mr. Shaw. I was a tutor at the Royal Academy, and we were doing one of your plays. I asked you to come and lecture the class, and you did."

"Oh, no," replied the great man. "We met long before that. At His Majesty's Theatre. You were a boy of sixteen. Frederick Whalen was doing one of my plays at his afternoon theatre. I went to the rehearsals and sat in a box to the right of the proscenium. Don't you remember? I became ill one day with a kidney stone. You went for the doctor. Do you remember the doctor's name?"

Rains paused uncomfortably as he tried to ferret the doctor's name from the ashes of memory, marveling that Shaw, nearing ninety, could recall such ancient trivia.

"Yes," Rains said, awed at his own sudden recollection. "It was Dr. Matthews. In Suffolk Street. I ran all the way."

Another long silence followed. Pascal squirmed in his chair.

"You were at His Majesty's all those years," resumed Shaw. "You must have met a lot of interesting people. Does any one of them stand out in your memory?"

"Yes, Mr. Shaw. I remember Basil Gill and his rich, rolling voice. It was the first voice that impressed me."

Shaw waved his hand irritably.

"Never mind the men. Tell me about the women."

"Well, of course, there was Ellen Terry . . ." Rains smiled inwardly, for he knew Shaw had carried on an ardent correspondence with the actress, who had been Henry Irving's most celebrated leading lady. Rains himself always thought that Terry was overrated as a performer, but he kept that bit of information to himself.

At the mention of Terry's name, Shaw leapt to his feet in a surprising display of agility for a nonagenarian. He pulled his chair away from the fire and gave it to Rains.

"Let's talk about her," said Shaw, seemingly rejuvenated and grinning mischievously.

After they had exhausted the subject of Terry, Shaw turned the discussion to Mrs. Patrick Campbell, the actress who had created the role of Eliza Doolittle for Shaw's original production of *Pygmalion* in 1914. Shaw had also had a passionate correspondence with Campbell, one that amounted to an unrequited love affair. Shaw, a strict vegetarian, recalled a comment Campbell had made about his larger appetites. "She once said to me," whispered Shaw, "'The day you eat a steak, G.B.S., God help the women and children.'"

Shaw cackled delightedly over the anecdote, then turned to Pascal, whose presence at the meeting had been manifested by no more than an occasional fidget. "It is time," Shaw told him, "to send for the tea and crumpets." Pascal rose and headed for the door.

When Rains left Ayot St Lawrence, Pascal told him that he and Vivien Leigh were scheduled to meet the press the following morning in the lobby of the Savoy.

"I can't make a speech," Rains protested.

"You don't have to. Just be chatty. The press thinks very highly of you, you know—coming over here from safe California in the middle of the air raids just to make a film."

Indeed, Rains was so disarmed by the reporters' deference that he impulsively told them, in some detail, of his encounter the day before with Shaw.

"I don't think he really wanted me," Rains said. "I think he was asking me all those questions and deliberately embarrassing me just to find out what kind of man I am."

His remarks, of course, appeared in print, and Shaw promptly issued a denial. Rains received a postcard. "Dear Mr. Rains," wrote Shaw. "You are quite mistaken. I made up my mind about you in the first split second."

Rains, however, was unconvinced. While Shaw might deny that he was testing the actor, what other explanation could there be for his odd behavior? Pascal reassured him. "Actually, he made up his mind long before you ever got here."

This was true only to a point. Pascal didn't tell Rains that the role had first been offered to John Gielgud, who turned it down because of his personal dislike of Pascal. When Rains's casting became common knowledge in theatrical London, Pascal related, a coalition of actors he refused to identify approached Shaw to lodge a protest. Rains was no longer a British actor, they told him, merely an expatriate Hollywood curiosity. They even sought to cast doubt on his professional competence and attempted to demolish Rains's stature in Shaw's mind. They reminded him that the actor's personal life was anything but blemish-free. He had left England only to cause a highly publicized marital scandal; he had been married two other times; and, frankly, he was known to be a bit of a rogue with the ladies. Shaw and the reputation of his film would suffer by association with Rains. Why not Laurence Olivier? Why not Paul Scofield? Why not *anybody* else?

Shaw pondered the impassioned accusations for several minutes while the committee of actors glared unhappily. Then Shaw leaned forward in his chair and cleared his throat.

"What you're saying," he said, "is that Rains has balls. Well, Caesar has balls, and Rains shall play him."

Rains granted interviews with the press as the Rank Organization requested, but after the *London Star* quoted Rains as saying jovially that he and Shaw had talked for hours on everything but the subject of *Caesar and Cleopatra*, Shaw interceded testily. On April 27, 1944, he wrote Pascal. "This press foolishness must stop immediately. You and I, Rank and Rains, have a first-class publicity which cannot be improved on; but it can be spoilt and made offensive by such silly rubbish as appears in the papers today, the work evidently of the press agent whom you so wickedly planted on me on Tuesday." Henceforth, "unless our proceedings are treated as sacredly private I will take no part in them. A report of what passes at rehearsal or production is worse than the betrayal of a confession. The Americans do not know this; they have no sense of privacy; but you must not Americanize the British studios. Get rid of all your press people: they damage you every time, and offend everyone else."

Caesar and Cleopatra was originally performed on the London stage in 1907. On one level an arch historical comedy, the play is also a gentle sociosexual satire. Unlike Shakespeare's telling of the tale in *Anthony and Cleopatra*, in Shaw's play Caesar is not infatuated with the Egyptian queen. Rather, he is amused by her kittenish demeanor and enjoys her eventual coming of age, acting as her avuncular mentor.

Caesar's avid supervision of Cleopatra's transformation prefigures Henry Higgins's more vigorous efforts to make a lady out of Eliza Doolittle in *Pygmalion*. It was *Pygmalion* that first brought Shaw and Pascal together. The director had been a devotee from an early age, when he first read Shaw's plays in translation in his native Hungary. He began his film career in Germany in 1922 and produced his first English-language feature in 1936. He dogged Shaw relentlessly, hoping for a chance to film his plays. Pascal was the only producer who made it clear he had no intention of compromising Shaw's texts. As Shaw recalled,

> Until he descended on me out of the clouds, I could find nobody who wanted to do anything with my films but mutilate them, murder them, give their cadavers to the nearest scrivener, without a notion of how to tell the simplest story in dramatic action, and instructed that there must be a new picture every ten seconds, and that the duration of the whole feature must be forty-five minutes at the extreme outside. The result was to be presented to the public with my name attached, and an

assurance that nobody need fear that it had any Shavian quality whatever, and was real genuine Hollywood.

Shaw turned down Samuel Goldwyn, who had made an offer for the screen rights to his plays, in favor of the virtually unknown Pascal, who in 1938 produced a remarkably faithful screen adaptation of *Pygmalion* for the Rank Organization starring Wendy Hiller and Leslie Howard. Since Shaw did the screenplay himself, the textual fidelity is hardly surprising. *Pygmalion* proved wildly popular and lucrative for its backers. *Major Barbara* followed in 1941, also starring Wendy Hiller. Like *Caesar and Cleopatra*, it was shot in Denham against a real-life background of German air raids, which repeatedly interrupted production.

In his writings, Shaw often waxed enthusiastic about the possibilities of film as a new dramatic medium, but his own adapted screenplays amounted to workmanlike, slightly elaborated transcripts of his stage work with no real cinematic innovation, and he demanded approval of almost every aspect of production, no matter how small. Changes that cost very little in a stage production take on a completely different dimension on a major motion picture set, with hundreds of people on the payroll. Fussing with the makeup or hair color or costume of a supporting player after photography has begun can create major problems, both in budget and continuity. Shaw never acknowledged his own responsibility in the soon-to-be-legendary cost overruns on *Caesar*, but his participation certainly contributed to the problem. Although Shaw described Pascal as "one of those extraordinary men who turn up occasionally, say once in a century, and may be called godsends in the arts to which they are devoted," the playwright attempted to deflect blame away from himself. "He shocks me by his utter indifference to the cost," he said of Pascal; "but the result justifies him. The man is a genius."

Still, wrote Shaw, "I pity poor Rank," adding, "The film will cost a million. On Thursday there were hundreds of men in the studio; and only twelve at most had anything to do but take snapshots and pick up scraps of my conversation for sale to the papers. Most of them did not even do that much. Were they all on the payroll?" Shaw also objected to the number of retakes that were required, some the result of Vivien

CLAUDE RAINS

Leigh's supposedly sloppy enunciation. Leigh, who had expected to begin work on the film a few years earlier, seemed to have lost much of her passion for the part. She quibbled with Shaw over a line involving Rains. In Shaw's play, Cleopatra calls Caesar "old and stringy," which Rains obviously wasn't. Shaw, who retained iron control over his dialogue, told Leigh to instead say, "You are hundreds of years old, but have a nice voice." But in the finished film, she says, "You are old and rather wrinkly." Exactly how this compromise was reached is not documented.

Meanwhile, Pascal's competence to manage the huge production as well as direct it came under increasing fire, not only from the cast and crew but from the press as well. Flora Robson, who played Cleopatra's nurse, Ftatateeta, complained directly to Shaw, bluntly telling him that he "should not have a director of an English film who does not understand English. He makes actors overact to explain the meaning to *him*." Although Pascal was proficient in English, it was not his first language, and he spoke with a strong Hungarian accent. Robson recalled that Both Rains and Leigh complained directly to the Rank Organization about the ponderous pace of shooting and equally ponderous direction, which, they felt, completely undermined Shaw's comedy. Rank officials disagreed, and Rains eventually gave up protesting. "What else can we do?" he asked Robson.

Rains bickered with Pascal and Shaw over his on-screen headwear; the actor wanted more screen time with his helmet or laurel crown, which was denied. The reason for Rains's concern is obvious: the close-cropped Caesar haircut made impossible the trick he had developed of combing his hair back and up to add an inch or so to his height. The helmet and laurel leaves created an illusion of additional stature. Pascal was doing little, if anything, with the camera to mitigate the obvious disparity between Rains's height and that of the rest of the cast. Rains offered a different explanation for his concern about the headgear. "The first authority I looked up was Plutarch," Rains told an interviewer. "He said Caesar was a very good dresser, very fussy about his hair. He combed it a lot because he was going bald."

In the actor's opinion, Pascal "drowned" Shaw's story in spectacle. He was especially critical of the director's treatment of Caesar's farewell to Cleopatra, which he felt should have been handled intimately: "Pascal

134

staged it grandly on a staircase and killed the poignancy of the scene."
Rains never commented on his working relationship with Vivien Leigh,
whose temperament could be the equal of Bette Davis's. But he could
not have been unaware of her miscarriage (her second), which halted
production for nearly six weeks—she had slipped on a marble floor while
flogging a slave in a scene involving Rains—or of her tormented marriage
to Laurence Olivier, or of the gnawing manic depression that would be-
devil her until her death. One of her first manic episodes occurred on
the set of *Caesar and Cleopatra*; she subsequently apologized to the entire
company in writing for disrupting the production.

The weather also made for problems, necessitating additional weeks
of delays when the sun refused to shine and making it impossible to
match outdoor scenes with previously shot footage. Pascal made the radical decision to move the production, in the middle of the shoot, to Egypt.
Among other things, this necessitated transporting a miniature sphinx,
which figured prominently in several completed scenes and, as Pascal's
widow, Valerie, noted, "had no counterpart in Egypt." The fact that so
much valuable cargo space was allocated to transporting movie props
during the war incensed both the press and members of Parliament, who
were already outraged at the film's runaway budget during a time of ra-
tioning and privation for most of the British population.

Valerie Pascal recalled that a rumor was begun in the press that Pascal was importing sand to the Egyptian desert as well as props. But reality
was even stranger, she wrote. "The sun was shining in Egypt, all right,
but the natives somehow got access to the props, found the glue of the
papier-mâché shields nourishing, and ate them up." The starving, poorly
paid Egyptian extras did indeed find the paste, a simple mixture of flour
and water, to be edible. More than three hundred new shields had to be
fabricated in England and shipped, causing more delays.

All the principals grew restless. Marjorie Deans, the official chronicler of the film, took a catty swipe at Rains in her book *Meeting at the
Sphinx*, perhaps reflecting the contretemps with the press and Shaw's dis-
pleasure. "Professionally he is not an easy man to deal with," she wrote.
"One has the impression, indeed, that he has never found himself easy to
deal with! He has none of Vivien Leigh's facility and grace."

Pascal, who had been a favorite of Shaw ever since his film of *Pygmalion*, let the production grow out of control in a way that would only be eclipsed by Fox's bloated production of *Cleopatra* two decades later. *Caesar and Cleopatra* was plagued by expensive delays and technical problems from beginning to end. The expense, however, benefited Shaw, Pascal, and Rank, each in his own perverse way. Shaw, whose antipathy to Hollywood was legendary, finally had the power to call the shots. Pascal was able to feed his inflated sense of self in his deluded belief that he was an equal collaborator with Shaw. Rank, who was already planning his own defection to Hollywood, believed that *Caesar and Cleopatra* would be his calling card—proof that British films and filmmakers could compete in terms of budget and extravagance with anything the American industry had to offer.

The filming schedule overran Rains's British work permit, necessitating huge wartime taxes that drove Rains's official compensation to over a million dollars, though his own net receipts were on par with his usual Hollywood contracts ($100,000 for nine months' work). Nonetheless, Claude Rains, a mere Hollywood contract player, suddenly found his earnings surpassing those of the biggest stars in the industry—at least on paper. The Rank Organization never made public its final accounting on *Caesar and Cleopatra*, but a reasonable estimate of costs, based on trade magazine speculation, was about £1,500,000, with the wartime exchange rate being approximately £4 to each dollar. Red ink at the time of the first American release was believed to be in the vicinity of $3 million.

One day during shooting in Denham, Rains passed by a pool of extras. To the astonishment of the actor who "couldn't eat his notices" in London, he saw that he was now supported by almost half the talent of the darkened West End. One of the day players was an old acquaintance. It was Henry Ainley, who hadn't made a film in eight years and was in the last year of an alcohol-ravaged life. Ainley's jealousy was just as acute as it had been when he had tried to sabotage Rains's performance in *The Jest* almost a quarter century earlier. Encountering the younger actor, Ainley glowered.

"That part should have been mine," he asserted.

"There was really nothing I could say," Rains remembered; so he simply walked away.

The profligate cost overruns, poor box office, and mixed critical reception of *Caesar and Cleopatra* effectively ended Gabriel Pascal's career; today, many standard motion picture biographical references don't even mention his name. Shaw reportedly disliked Leigh's performance and wished he hadn't cast her in the first place. But the film garnered Rains enormous publicity (most of it exaggerating his salary) and set the stage for one of his best roles in Hollywood, in the hands of another famously controlling director.

7

MacGuffins, Deceptions, Domestic Recriminations

MIKE LEVEE, RAINS'S AGENT, called his client one day. Alfred Hitchcock had expressed interest in Rains's services. Could he have a meeting?

Hitchcock was casting a film called *Notorious,* a tale of postwar intrigue and espionage revolving around an expatriate Nazi cell in Rio de Janeiro, starring Ingrid Bergman and Cary Grant. Bergman would play Alicia Huberman, a woman with a checkered background who is conscripted by American intelligence to seduce and marry a mother-dominated Nazi, Alexander Sebastian, who is suspected of trafficking in uranium. A performer of special elegance and cosmopolitan charm was required. Rains was intrigued.

"Tell me," said Hitchcock. "How will you play this fellow? With a German accent?"

"Oh, no. You've got real Germans. This man has been to Heidelberg, the Sorbonne, and I was thinking about Oxford."

"And Brixton?" Hitchcock asked bluntly.

Rains was slightly startled. "How did you know?"

"I found out everything about you. I *wanted* to know."

Hitchcock's first choice for the role had been Clifton Webb, whose arch screen persona would likely have underscored the subtextual implications of homosexuality in the mother-dominated character. But the story called for Sebastian to be genuinely, achingly in love with the Bergman character, and Webb would arguably have been not quite believable in the part. Rains would play it with great subtlety and convincing pathos.

Hitchcock then changed the subject. "What about this business of being a midget?"

"What do you mean, a midget?" There were no midgets mentioned in the script.

"Your wife, Miss Bergman, is very tall. There are occasions when we can build a ramp, but have you ever worn elevated shoes?"

Rains, recounting the story years later, said that at this, "My pride took a bit of a setback. I protested, but he insisted in a gentle way and I bought them." He added, "I finally got used to them, and I've used them many times since."

Most accounts of the making of *Notorious* mention Rains's use of lifts in his shoes and ramps to bring him up to Bergman's stature (Humphrey Bogart famously wore platform footwear for several scenes opposite the actress in *Casablanca*). On the first day of shooting, Rains was talking to Bergman. Hitchcock crept up and jerked up the cuff of Rains's trousers, displaying the shoes. "The shame of Rains," he intoned.

A close viewing of the film reveals very little obvious chicanery with Rains's height. Hitchcock in fact uses the disparity in height to visually underscore the shifting power dynamics between characters. There are several long shots of Rains and Bergman walking together at what appears to be their natural height (Rains was about 5'6" and Bergman about 5'9"); these are scenes in which Bergman's character seems to be gaining confidence and control. But in other key scenes, such as Sebastian and Alicia's first meeting in a restaurant, as well as the bedroom scene in which Sebastian almost discovers his wife's crucial theft of a key, Hitchcock brings his performers to a level plane. At one scene in a restaurant, Rains seems to be sitting on the equivalent of a telephone book, the better to look Bergman directly in the eye.

Notorious is a sterling example of Hitchcock's use of the "MacGuffin," his pet word for an inanimate object or other arbitrary device that drives the story. In this case, it was a bottle in Sebastian's wine cellar filled with granulated uranium. This was not a particularly good way to transport a radioactive substance, but it was an excellent way to stage a suspenseful sequence in which Rains painfully realizes he has been set up by Bergman and American intelligence.

Rains made no recorded comment about working again with Cary Grant, who had made such a poor impression on him during the filming of *The Last Outpost*; for *Notorious*, Rains was content simply to walk away with the show. As one Canadian reviewer noted, "It is difficult not to find Rains' baggy-eyed, shrewd-face villainy more interesting, and therefore more sympathetic, than the virtue of Cary Grant."

Notorious earned Rains his fourth, and last, Academy Award nomination. He lost again, but never made a comment to anyone about his obvious disappointment. Meanwhile, he and Hitchcock developed a social relationship. "At dinners at his house," Rains remembered, "he'd fill himself with beef and wine and we'd all go into the living room, indulging in a little light conversation. Suddenly you'd look at Hitch and he'd be sound asleep. But such a joy. A warm, understanding man. His wife and daughter would be there, carrying the conversation. A dear man." One evening, with the director snoring and the conversation growing thin, Rains quietly suggested to Frances that it might be time to leave. Hitchcock woke instantly. "What?" he asked. "Am I *boring* you?" Rains recalled "unusual things, charming things" that Hitchcock would do, including "putting a box of my favorite cigars in the car seat so I would find it when I drove home. Or bottles of wine."

If Rains's next assignment, as Nick in *Angel on My Shoulder* for United Artists, came across as the flip side of the heavenly emissary he played in *Here Comes Mr. Jordan*, it should have come as no surprise. Both films were based on original stories by the same writer, Harry Segall, who wrote the screenplay for *Angel* in collaboration with Roland Kibbee. In *Angel*, Rains played the devil, with fellow Theatre Guild alumnus Paul Muni as a murdered gangster condemned to hell. Rains offers Muni a deal: he will let him return to earth in the form of a prominent, do-gooding judge for whom the gangster happens to be a perfect double. The gangster thus has the opportunity to carry out revenge on his killer, and the devil has the chance to use the possessed judge to spread earthly corruption and evil and thereby increase the population of the nether world.

Rains plays the demon with sardonic relish, thanks to an exceptionally witty screenplay, his black-clad presence heightened by the moody shadows and angled lighting of cinematographer James Van Trees. Seldom has the glow of hellfire been used to such atmospheric effect. But the overall fun of the finished picture was marred by what seemed to be a jinx. Both Muni and lead actress Anne Baxter were waylaid by illness; an assistant director died; and, to top it all off, the body of a studio technician, who had apparently fallen drunkenly from a catwalk, was discovered behind the papier-mâché inferno set during the film's wrap party, generating lurid headlines.

Immediately following *Angel on My Shoulder* Rains was assigned one of his best Hollywood roles, one that deserved to earn him another Oscar nomination (but that inexplicably failed to do so). In Warners' *Deception* he was cast opposite Bette Davis in a screenplay based on the drama *Jealousy* by Louis Verneuil, son-in-law of Sarah Bernhardt, in several of whose plays Rains had acted in his London days. The original play involved a married female artist who was compromised, both sexually and artistically, by a relationship with her mentor. It had previously been produced as a silent (and now lost) film with Fredric March and Jeanne Eagels in 1929. The play's audacious conceit was to never depict the mentor, just the conflict between husband and wife. Hollywood, however, had different ideas. In *Deception*, the mentor is fleshed out as a monstrous, but genius, composer, Alexander Hollenius, who contrives to destroy the musical career of his protégée-lover's former romantic interest, who was believed to have been lost in the war but miraculously turns up alive at the start of the film. Rains was given dominance in scene after scene, with some of the most deliciously wicked dialogue ever written for him. Davis's character seems pallid in comparison. Rains was also given the chance to torment his professional nemesis, Paul Henreid, especially in a scene (reportedly done in one take by Rains, to the applause of the crew) in which Hollenius plays cat and mouse with the Davis and Henreid characters in a restaurant, where he orders course after course, discussing gastronomy instead of the master concerto he has composed and Henreid is desperate to play.

After the first read-through, Davis said drily, "That's quite a part you've got there, Claudie."

The film was not a critical success, and Davis took most of the brickbats. "The censors ruined it," she would later complain. And, indeed, the industry moral guardians caviled endlessly about the essentially amoral triangle at the center of the story and demanded change after change. Finally, to square things up, Davis murders Rains and gets her criminal comeuppance. Director Irving Rapper objected to the ending, but maintained that it was Davis who demanded the blood and thunder. Rapper felt the film "should have been concluded as a comedy, and the writer, John Collier, intended it that way. It was to have a gay, light, natural 'So what?' ending. The three people walk off as friends. But Bette wanted a dramatic conclusion; she insisted on it, and I didn't care very much either way, so I gave in."

The critics found the story ludicrous, but no one found fault with Rains's performance. As *Newsweek* observed, "It is the character of Hollenius, epicure, egomaniac, and sadist, that lifts the film from its soap opera situation. For [John] Collier and his collaborator [Joseph Than] have improved on the French playwright by turning this vague, offstage figure into a sinister and highly articulate menace. And in playing the role Rains has one of the best roles of his career."

The part was so vividly portrayed that many viewers assumed it had been based on a real music celebrity. As Rains recalled, "A friend of [Leopold] Stokowski came on the set one day and said, 'I know who that is, that's Stokowski.' And then another day someone who knew [Arturo] Toscanini said, 'I know who that is, that's Toscanini.' I was told that the man resembled [Jean] Sibelius a little. But I know little about Sibelius, and Hollenius certainly was not based on him. John Collier, as good a writer as there is, did a wonderful character on paper. If the character is based on anyone, it's based on John Collier's."

Not long after *Deception*'s release, Davis paid a visit to Stock Grange. Her first words, delivered with great good humor: "You son of a bitch, you stole the picture." Years later, she would elaborate: "Claude Rains rightfully stole the picture. It was up to him to work against the dialogue and to make the audience understand, through his jealousy, that they had been having a hot affair, and that he was not just her piano teacher. He worked like ten men on that movie."

Despite Rains's Herculean efforts in *Deception*, Warners chose not to renew his long-term contract. The final straw came before the film's release, when Mike Levee wrestled once more with Jack Warner about Rains's billing and salary. Levee wrote Warner:

> In view of the fact that Mr. Rains has been co-starred with Vivien Leigh in a five million dollar picture, "CAESAR & CLEOPATRA" and is being co-starred with Paul Muni in "ANGEL ON MY SHOULDER" in the same size type as Paul Muni, and because it is my intention that I will not, in the future, commit him to any other outside picture without receiving co-star billing, I wonder if I cannot prevail upon you to grant him the assurance that when "DECEPTION" is released that he will be co-starred with Bette Davis and Paul Henreid.

Rains received same-line, same-size billing for *Deception*, but Warner balked at Levee's insistence on a $75,000 guarantee per picture, and the studio declined to renew its option on Rains's services. The following year, the actor returned briefly to the studio for his first and only top-billed assignment for Warners, teaming with Michael Curtiz for their last picture together. *The Unsuspected* was an unabashed piece of hokum in which Rains plays a popular radio personality, Victor Grandison, whose weekly mystery program milks a real murder, about which Grandison has far too much personal knowledge. Stylishly shot in brooding noir style, the film was a financial, if not a critical, success. For Rains, though, *The Unsuspected* was only the palest shadow of his best work at Warner Bros. The studio had been making less and less use of his talents, to the actor's frustration. (Bette Davis was struggling with the same issue and would be released from her contract not long after Rains's departure.) For the time being, at least, Rains was happy to be a free agent, and more than happy to give up his residence in Los Angeles and base himself, Frances, and Jennifer permanently in Pennsylvania. Thereafter, when asked by her schoolmates what her father did for a living, Jennifer would reply, "He's a farmer."

Jennifer loved full-time life on the farm. In addition to helping with planting and harvesting, she learned from her father how to shoot a rifle and, like Rains in his Scottish Regiment days, became a crack shot, expert in picking tin cans off a fence. "Growing up as the only child of an actor noted for his beautiful speech was a burden—oddly enough not for me, but for my father," she remembered. "He was determined that I would not have the Pennsylvania accent, that I would pronounce my words 'succinctly,' and in that he was successful." For a short time when she was about seven she began stammering, just as her father had as a boy. "The cure for stuttering was to sing everything. I remember us sitting around the dining room table. The cook would enter the room with a silver dish holding the vegetables. 'Here are the peas, Mr. Rains,' she would sing in her gospel-singer's voice. Enjoying this therapy immensely, my father would belt out, 'Pass them to Jennifer first, she must eat the peas before she eats the lamb chops.' Fa Fa, as I called him then, thought this was all absolutely hilarious. My mother, a little tone deaf, as I recall, also joined in. His other aim was to develop a daughter with a ballet-straight back. Before dinner I had to stand with my spine touching the wall. Then I had to pronounce in a well-articulated voice, 'How now, brown cow? G-r-r-azing in the g-r-r-een, g-r-r-een g-r-r-ass." Eventually she lost her stammer.

In early 1948, not long after arriving in England to film *The Passionate Friends* for producer David Lean, Rains was surprised to receive an unsolicited script in the mail. The sender was Beatrix Thomson, with whom he had had no contact, direct or indirect, since their nightmarish divorce saga. She was producing the play, she wrote, and was appealing awkwardly to some imagined sense of British duty in an attempt to lure Rains back to the London stage. But he, happy to be an American, was unimpressed by his ex-wife's attempt to exploit his name in what he saw as a bid to recapture her lost status in the theatre. In an impersonal reply, Rains expressed his lack of interest and returned the script. He never heard from Beatrix again.

Based on the novel of the same title by H. G. Wells, *The Passionate Friends* would be released in America under the title *One Woman's Story*. (As Rains would later quip, Americans apparently didn't understand passion.) The plot revolved around an adulterous triangle between an international banker (Rains), his wife (Ann Todd), and her former and current flame (Trevor Howard).

The original director, Ronald Neame, clashed with Todd, a glacial blonde in the Hitchcock mold (she had, in fact, appeared in Hitchcock's *The Paradine Case*) who was involved in her own adulterous affair with Lean. Lean agreed to switch assignments with Neame and direct the film himself.

"David Lean liked Claude very much," Neame recalled in 1999, "and not only liked him very much but thought he was a consummate actor. David was a wonderful director with actors who were secure. He made them better and better and better. Quite aside from his talent, Claude was very disciplined. He always knew his lines. He was always on time. He took direction beautifully. And he was a reliable, solid rock of Gibraltar in anybody's film."

Rains also greatly admired Lean. "I can't say enough about the man as a director," he said. "He's magnificent." But the actor was concerned about his director's personal life, which seemed to be interfering with his work on the film. Lean, he also knew, was seeing a psychoanalyst.

"David," Rains asked him at one point, "what's going on? What are you up to?"

"Claude, I'm going to get into awful trouble," Lean said. He then told Rains about his ongoing affair with Ann Todd and the mess he had made of his marriage to actress Kay Walsh. Rains disliked Todd, who he felt had wasted everyone's time through her prima donna behavior with Neame over the script and Neame's direction. As Lean later told his biographer, Kevin Brownlow, "I said I was going to stop the picture. We couldn't go on spending money at that rate. We had commitments to Claude Rains, and we had permission to pay him in dollars. You don't realise how difficult that was. That had to be a top-level decision. He'd already been sitting there doing nothing for most of the time he'd been in the country."

Rains had already admonished Todd privately about the need to show up on the set every morning, whether she was immediately needed or not. But as he observed the dynamics of her relation with Lean, his dislike of Todd only increased. Todd was a man-eating "machine," in Rains's opinion. "By God, she took every cent from him. I don't think anyone could live happily with that woman. She took every damn thing away from him. He ended up with nothing except an old car. He was broke by the time he did *The Bridge on the River Kwai*."

It is testimony to Rains's professionalism that his personal feelings about Todd didn't influence his performance with her. It was Lean, in fact, who convinced him to reconsider his interpretation of the pivotal scene in which his character discovers his wife's infidelity (she neglects to hide a pair of unused theatre tickets, giving away the fact that she has, of course, been somewhere other than the theatre.) Rains had prepared to play the scene as a wounded spouse, but Lean wanted to infuse the scene with a minor bit of deviltry, Rains's character subtly taking the upper hand in a game of cat and mouse. Rains, embarrassed at having misread the scene ("I'm a fool," he told Lean), immediately returned to his hotel to prepare a new interpretation. The sequence was smoothly reshot the next day, and Lean considered it Rains's best scene in the film.

Lean recalled that "Claude always amused me because he carried timing to an almost absurd degree. You can almost put a Claude Rains scene to numbers: 'Yes,' pause of one, two, three, 'I'm not so sure.' Cross legs, two, three. 'What do you think?' And so on." But Lean regarded timing as an essential technique of acting. "You ain't got timing, you ain't got anything."

In Hollywood, Rains never used alcohol on the set, but the British film industry had different standards. "I knew he was a heavy drinker," said Neame. "But I was, too. We might have been valiantly drunk, but nobody ever knew we were. I think there are people who can hold [their] drink a lot. And the British are pretty good at that, by the way. You Americans are hopeless. You don't have a bar in any of your film studios because you'd all get drunk after a couple of drinks. Whereas we'll go into the bar at lunchtime and drink three gin and tonics and discuss the scene that we were doing in the afternoon."

At the beginning of filming, before Frances and Jennifer joined him for an extended stay at London's Connaught Hotel, Rains was housed temporarily at Great Fosters, a Tudor-era estate that at the time provided accommodations to an exclusive clientele. Late one night, he heard a loud commotion outside his room. Peering through his cracked door, he saw a ghostly figure in a nightshirt and nightcap, leaping and pirouetting up and down the hallway. When he made inquiries of the staff the next day, he learned that the nocturnal performance had been given by none other than legendary dancer Vaslav Nijinsky. Long disabled by schizophrenia, traveling with his wife and a male nurse, he was "dancing for the ghosts," according to a hotel employee. Two years later, Nijinsky would join the ghosts permanently.

With *The Passionate Friends* completed, Rains and his family returned to the States, where he worked on two films in 1949, both for Paramount: *Rope of Sand* and *Song of Surrender*. A story of intrigue in the South African diamond trade, *Rope of Sand* also featured Burt Lancaster, Paul Henreid, and Peter Lorre. Rains plays a scoundrel and makes the most of a wealth of close-ups. *Song of Surrender*, by contrast, was a semi-musical directed by Mitchell Leisen. In this film, Rains played a New England museum curator whose much younger wife is being seduced by a New York lawyer. As he had done so reliably in the past, Rains did his best with problematic material.

In 1950, the Universal horror and fantasy classics of the 1930s and '40s were theatrically redistributed by RealArt Pictures, and ultimately reached rural Pennsylvania. Rains's daughter, who was then around twelve, recalled a memorable night at the movies. One night, "My father said to me, 'Get dressed, I'm taking you out.' And I said, 'Where are we going?' He said, 'Just get dressed and get into the car.' We drove for eight miles to a little movie theater. It was winter, and he had a coat and his homburg hat and a scarf, which he wrapped around his face because it was cold. Actually, he looked a lot like the Invisible Man in the opening scene of the film. So we went up to the theater and he said to the cashier, 'I'll have two tickets.' And the man who was selling the tickets, who was also the owner of the theater, who was also the man who tore the tickets, who was also the man who showed you to your seats, immediately recognized the voice and said, 'Oh no, Mr. Rains, I certainly couldn't let you pay.' And my father said, 'Absolutely not. I must pay for myself and my daughter.' I don't remember who won this argument, but we did go in to see *The*

Psychiatrist Rains shares a luncheon of Freudian frankfurters with Bette Davis in *Now, Voyager* (1942) (courtesy of Donna Tattle).

Rains's performance as the long-suffering title character in *Mr. Skeffington* (1944), another tour de force with Bette Davis, earned the actor his third Academy Award nomination (courtesy of Donna Tattle).

As Captain Louis Renault, with Conrad Veidt, in *Casablanca* (1943) (David J. Skal collection).

Poster art for *Phantom of the Opera* (1943) (David J. Skal collection).

Rains as Erique Claudin, a.k.a. the Phantom (courtesy of Donna Tattle).

Rains's burn makeup, created by Jack Pierce (courtesy of Ronald V. Borst/Hollywood Movie Posters).

Rains's fourth marriage,
to Frances Propper,
proved his most
enduring union.

Sharing a script with his
only child, Jessica, later
an actress in her own
right.

With Vivien Leigh in *Caesar and Cleopatra* (1946) (David J. Skal collection).

George Bernard Shaw, Rains, and director Gabriel Pascal.

With Paul Muni in *Angel on My Shoulder* (1946) (courtesy of Donna Tattle).

Murdered by Bette Davis in *Deception* (1946) (David J. Skal collection).

As a Nazi mama's boy: Rains with Leopoldine Konstantin in Alfred Hitchcock's *Notorious* (1946) (courtesy of Donna Tattle).

Rains with David Lean and Ann Todd on the set of *The Passionate Friends* (1949) (courtesy of Donna Tattle).

In *Song of Surrender* (1949) (courtesy of Donna Tattle).

The main house at Stock Grange, Rains's Pennsylvania homestead.

Rains with one of his favorite steers.

Rains's triumphant
return to Broadway
in *Darkness at Noon*
(1951).

Broadway, 1954: T. S.
Eliot's *The Confidential
Clerk.* Left to right: Richard
Newton, Joan Greenwood,
Ina Claire, Rains.

With Clint
Eastwood in
Rawhide episode
"Incident of
Judgment Day"
(1962).

With Keir Dullea and Richard Conte in "The Outpost" for *DuPont Show of the Week* (1962) (courtesy of Donna Tattle).

Arch Oboler's *Night of the Auk* (1956).

With space helmet sans faceplate in *Battle of the Worlds*
(1960) (David J. Skal collection).

With fifth wife, Agi Jambor.

With sixth and final wife,
Rosemary McGroarty,
and her son, Schuyler
(courtesy of Donna Tattle).

With Peter O'Toole in David Lean's *Lawrence of Arabia* (1962).

With David Lean on the set of *The Greatest Story Ever Told* (1965), with inscription to Rains from Lean.

Rains's final publicity portrait, by Roddy McDowall (courtesy of Roddy McDowall).

Claude Rains's headstone at Red Hill Cemetery, near Sandwich, New Hampshire.

Invisible Man, which was the first film that I had ever seen him in, even though you don't see him until the end."

They sat in the back, and Rains proceeded to explain the technical details of the film to his daughter in a very audible—and recognizable—voice. "This is the part where they put straws in my nose, so that they could make a cast . . ." She went on: "He was explaining the film to me for the whole hour and eleven minutes. There were maybe thirty people in the theater, and they weren't watching the movie at all. They were all turned our way, watching my father talk about how they made this film."

The school Jennifer attended was about ten miles from Stock Grange, and her father usually drove her, mornings and afternoons. En route, she would run lines with him from whatever script he was currently studying. Increasingly, they were television scripts. Many Hollywood actors boycotted the small screen in the early 1950s, sensing an industry threat, but Rains's close proximity to New York City, where most live television drama was then being produced, provided a natural connection. Jennifer disliked the debilitating car sickness she experienced while reading scripts along bumpy Pennsylvania back roads, but didn't complain. She was surprised to learn that her father didn't merely memorize his own lines. He memorized entire scripts. As a young boy, it had been his habit, as a prompter for Beerbohm Tree's company, to commit to memory everybody's dialog, and it was a technique he employed for the rest of his life.

Rains also continued to work in films, and in 1950 he did two for RKO, *The White Tower* and *Where Danger Lives*. The former, shot in Technicolor, was a mountain-climbing drama set in the Swiss alps; Rains played a heavy-drinking French stereotype, adrift in a cast of other international stereotypes, including a Brit (played by Cedric Hardwicke), a German (Lloyd Bridges), an American (Glenn Ford), and a Swiss local (Oscar Homolka). The film has the rare distinction of being one of the few that resulted in a bad notice for Rains. Bosley Crowther of the *New York Times* stated flatly, "Claude Rains, as a garrulous weakling, is something of a bore, and Sir Cedric Hardwicke, as another, is pathetic." Rains's primary memory of the uncomfortable location shoot was enduring near-frostbite and receiving full-body brandy rubdowns from a nurse.

Where Danger Lives was a preposterous melodrama concocted to show-case RKO owner Howard Hughes's obsession with raven-haired actress Faith Domergue, then being groomed by the studio as "the new Jane Russell." Rains took on the thankless role of Domergue's supposed father (actually her husband), who is suffocated by his psychopathic daughter/wife in the opening sequence, but not before warning her suitor (Robert Mitchum) against marrying her. "You want her?" says Rains. "You can have her, only first I think you should know what you're getting." What amounted to a cameo for Rains was puffed up in the advertising for the film, using Rains's name in an attempt to guarantee box office for a film that was thoroughly unworthy of his talents. Hughes and his staff wanted to secure a long-term commitment from Rains. But the actor instinctively knew that Hughes was only interested in him as a trophy acquisition, and he declined the offer.

Rains had long been considering a return to the theatre, but he was understandably apprehensive. In 1950, seventeen years had passed since he last acted in a play. After nearly two decades of "murmuring my way through the movies," as he put it, Rains's technique had changed radically. Could he succeed in live performance?

When playwright-director Sidney Kingsley, who was preparing a stage adaptation of novelist Arthur Koestler's powerful indictment of totalitarianism, *Darkness at Noon*, approached Rains, the actor was surprised. Would he consider playing Rubashov, the idealistic Russian revolutionary turned upon and crushed by the communist party? The part would be prestigious, but exceedingly demanding, with Rains onstage for almost the entire play. The script was only partially finished, and the actor would be consulted for input as the adaptation progressed. Rains decided it was an extraordinary opportunity, offering him material far superior to his recent films. And although he would frequently tell interviewers he was "crazy" about film acting, his heart was dedicated to the immediacy and electricity of the stage.

What Rains didn't know (and would never know) is that he may have been Kingsley's second choice for the part. Edward G. Robinson, who had recently come under fire by the House Un-American Activities Committee and seemed like a natural for the role, was Kingsley's first choice. Robinson wasn't sure about whether to accept the offer. "I searched my soul," he later wrote. "Could I do it? Or would it be too obvious for me to appear now in an anti-Communist play; would it be a kind of inverse confession, even though, God knows, I had nothing to confess?" Robinson agonized over the decision, but in the end, "I sent my regrets. Claude Rains, that beautiful actor, played it instead, and it was a hit."

More than twenty years after Robinson's memoirs were published, Kingsley would bluntly call the actor's account "lies." Kingsley also claimed that California communists "worked on Claude Rains, trying to frighten him, and telling him if he appeared in it it would ruin his career." In any event, Rains had no idea of what a problematic personality he was bargaining with when he agreed to appear in *Darkness at Noon*.

Rains immersed himself in the project, and "practically memorized" Koestler's novel, consulting with Kingsley from Stock Grange by telephone and letter. They became "warm friends," according to Kingsley. Difficulties arose, however, when rehearsals began. Rains realized that Kingsley's adaptation and direction were skewing the story toward red-scare theatrics at the expense of the book's ideological complexity. The novel is a scathing indictment of Stalinism, but it doesn't exactly repudiate the communist dream. Rains understood a subtle paradox when he saw one, but Kingsley maintained that "Claude had a double problem of hating direction and being fearful of coming back to the stage, needing direction every moment."

The cast brought together old-school and new-school acting talent, Rains of course in the former category, with Kim Hunter (who had just appeared as Stella in the film version of *A Streetcar Named Desire*) and Walter J. (later Jack) Palance representing the Actors Studio and its "Method." Palance proved especially difficult in rehearsals, both for Kingsley and for Rains. In one confrontational scene that wasn't going very well, Rains finally told Palance, who played Rubashov's nemesis, Gletkin, "Just grab me by the collar and pull!" Palance complied vigorously, but when he tore some buttons off Rains's costume, he immediately burst into tears. Some of the new school–old school conflicts proved as dramatic as anything in the play. As actor Richard Seff, who played Prisoner 302, remembered, one day, when Kingsley asked Jack to turn left and face Claude, Jack replied that there was no "Jack" or "Claude" on stage, only their characters.

> Sidney blinked, but he accepted it. "All right, Gletkin. Turn left on that line and face Rubashov."
> "Why?" "Gletkin" asked.
> "Because it looks good," Sidney sent back.
> "I can't turn left because it looks good," Jack said quietly. When Jack was quiet, he was at his most frightening.
> "It's menacing. I want you to face him when you say that line. It has no threat in it with your back to him."
> "Bullshit," Jack said, and left the stage. Everyone winced. This was 1950. Claude was stunned. Stunned, and insulted.

Rains thought Palance was "mad," and demanded that he be replaced by the understudy, Brian Keith (then Robert Keith, Jr.). But Kingsley insisted that Palance's barely contained volatility, like a "coiled cobra," was exactly what the part required. Palance apologized, took direction as given, and went on to win the New York Drama Critics Circle Award for his performance.

Rains became increasingly irritated with Kingsley's attempts to micromanage and flatten his performance, but did his best to insulate the rest of the cast from his disputes with the director. According to Hunter, "He'd always put Sidney off, insisting that they discuss the point, or points, *after* rehearsal." She didn't know the half of it. Frances Rains told her daughter that her husband ultimately refused to talk to Kingsley at all, and she personally had to act as a go-between for the director's increasingly obsessive communications, which Rains ignored. Hunter recalled that Kingsley relentlessly gave the whole cast (including Palance and Alexander Scourby) excruciatingly detailed notes after every performance, despite the play's triumphant opening and stunning reviews. Following a matinee performance a few weeks into the run, Kingsley went to

Rains's dressing room. "What happened, Claude?" he asked. "You were quite good this afternoon." As Hunter remembered Rains's response: "Well, I just went onstage and said to myself, 'Fuck Sidney Kingsley.'" The director got the message; he never went backstage again during the show's run.

Darkness at Noon was played on an innovative, multilevel set designed by Frederick Fox, utilizing scrims that could represent the concrete walls of a prison when lit from the front and that dissolved into nothingness when lit from behind. The staging allowed for seamless transitions between the grim Moscow trials of 1937 and flashbacks to Rubashov's heady, forward-looking days as a revolutionary. The intense shifts in time and mood were taxing to Rains, who claimed to have given up drinking for the duration of the run to maintain his stamina. Given his long-term alcohol dependence, this assertion isn't quite believable, but the role was certainly a physical and emotional challenge. Rains's daughter recalled that he sequestered himself in his dressing room for hours before each performance.

"I find it quite a job," he told *The New Yorker*. "The other Russians I've represented were complicated but they weren't in a class with this one. Today I'd probably regard the mad poet in Tolstoy's 'The Living Corpse' or Chlestakov in 'The Inspector General' as a fairly light assignment, although when I played them they seemed formidable. As a matter of fact I'm not too nervous about the prospect of playing a modern Christ, which Darryl Zanuck proposes to have me do this summer." (The "Christ" role was to have been Klaatu, the alien emissary who rises from death to save the world in Robert Wise's *The Day the Earth Stood Still*. Rains's Broadway commitment made it impossible for him to accept the part, which went instead to Michael Rennie.)

Although Rains didn't socialize with the company outside the theatre, Richard Seff recalled him as being warm, generous, and surprisingly candid about his life and career. "Claude used to gather us around him before the play each night and regale us with tales of *Caesar and Cleopatra*, Vivien Leigh, Bette Davis, and his early days in England." Rains took a particular shine to Seff and invited him for a weekend at Stock Grange. Showing him around the property, he confessed to the younger man, "Unfortunately, Dickie"—"He always called me that," Seff recalled—"I have no talent other than acting. I can't write, direct, I certainly can't produce. I thought I could farm a little, but it turns out being a gentleman farmer isn't very fulfilling, so others do the farming and I just watch." Seff registered his surprise. "I'm not complaining," Rains replied, "just ruminating. When you reach a point in your career where you can afford to turn down things that don't interest you, and you reach a certain age, well—you don't work all that much. And frankly, I get bored. I'd love to have had a second, parallel career, something meaningful to do between pictures. I enjoy the stage, but it's tough."

The five-month New York run of *Darkness at Noon* was indeed taxing on the actor, and, as Seff remembered, "it sort of dribbled to an end."

This was an era when a hit musical might run a year at most, a hit play a season. But Claude's contract provided an out on July 1—he simply couldn't play this arduous role in the summer's heat. He'd spent the winter complaining about the weight of his sweater, yet the costume required it, for we were all in dank, freezing, damp Lubyanka Prison. Poor man ended each show wringing wet. His big concern was always his voice—one of his great assets, but after years in film, not as strong as it had once been. We were announced to close on June 23rd, but when the Drama Critics Prize and the Tonys came through, business leaped again and we were extended to June 30th. But on June 20th, a Wednesday, after two performances, Claude's voice simply disappeared.

Rains's understudy, character actor Will Kuluva, took over; but as Seff noted, *Darkness at Noon* "was created for a star, and audiences demanded one. Business collapsed, and we played the final four performances to half houses."

Rains had riveted audiences, and his performance generated reverent admiration in the theatrical community. No less a star than Mary Martin, then playing nearby in *South Pacific,* was frequently seen, still in costume, backstage at the Alvin to watch bits of the show whenever she could steal time away from her musical. *Darkness at Noon* earned Rains all of the major New York theatre awards, including the Tony for best actor in a drama, the New York Drama Critics' Annual Best Actor Poll, the Comedie Matinee Club's Bronze Medal, the Donaldson Award, and a Good Speech Medallion from the American Academy of Arts and Letters.

One night near the end of the run, Rains noticed Edward G. Robinson sitting in the front row. Robinson had been chosen to play Rubashov on the road after Rains, exhausted by the production, had turned down the tour. He had never met Robinson during their Theatre Guild years—Rains was Robinson's company replacement—but he had seen the actor in the Guild's production of Franz Werfel's *Juarez and Maximilian* (the basis of Rains's film *Juarez*) and had admired Robinson's performance. They later met socially in Hollywood.

After the performance, Robinson came backstage. "I don't know what to say to you," he said, taking a seat on a dressing room trunk. "I've never seen anything like it in the theatre."

On New Year's Eve in 1951, Rains was at the farm when he got a call from Robinson in Chicago, where the play had opened the previous night. Robinson asked Rains for some technical advice on transitions and bridges, and then said, "The critics have made some ugly comparisons, and I say this in all sincerity." Rains, a bit taken aback, called it "a humble confession."

According to Robinson, Kingsley had turned against him after the first read-through. "It seemed to me he wanted me to give a carbon copy of the Claude Rains performance. I saw Rubashov differently than Rains; maybe I was bringing something of myself into it. Claude had not been born in Romania; Claude was not a Jew; Claude could not possibly understand the agony of a world turned against him—and that was an experience I was still going through." Robinson played the part for a year on the road. Despite the plaudits both actors received, neither was invited to reprise their work when the play was produced for television. Instead, Kingsley chose Lee J. Cobb.

Rains would return to Broadway twice in the 1950s, first in a production of T. S. Eliot's *The Confidential Clerk* in 1954, a dry, blank-verse comedy of manners involving mistaken paternity and maternity. The play received a lukewarm reception, although Rains loved to recount an exchange he had with a scene-stealing Ina Claire. "Why don't you just stand on your head?" he asked her once. "If I could, Mr. Rains," she replied, "I would."

In September 1954, after *The Confidential Clerk* closed and while Rains was contemplating another stage outing, New York producer Robert Whitehead invited him to the opening night performance of Shaw's *Saint Joan* in Wilmington, Delaware, at the beginning of a thirty-week, pre-Broadway tour. The star was Jean Arthur. Whitehead knew that Rains was an expert Shavian, and he also knew that Rains had also worked with Arthur. "I want you to tell me what you see," he said to Rains. Wary of Arthur's volatility, Rains smelled trouble. His suspicions were confirmed during the performance he attended. "I didn't say much," he remembered, but "it just wasn't Joan of Arc." He declined Whitehead's invitation to visit backstage ("I didn't know how I'd be received"). Rains was appalled, but not surprised, when Arthur, claiming illness, walked out on the production several weeks later, without saying a word to the nearly two dozen cast and crew members she was throwing out of work. Throughout his career, Rains was infuriated by unprofessional conduct. He never crossed paths with Jean Arthur again.

Rains's next Broadway outing came two years later with another blank-verse play, *The Night of the Auk*, a futuristic drama set on the first spaceship to the moon and its problematic return to an earth ravaged by nuclear war. The playwright was Arch Oboler, best known for his radio suspense series *Lights Out*. He had also directed Rains years earlier in the film *Strange Holiday*, and Rains had performed in two of his radio plays. He liked Oboler and thought *Auk* "a damned good play," but the critics were savage and the production closed in short order. According to *TIME* magazine, the cast, which, in addition to Rains, included Christopher Plummer, Wendell Corey, and Dick York, was "unhappily squandered on a pudding of a script—part scientific jargon, part Mermaid Tavern verse, part Madison Avenue prose—that sounded like cosmic advertising copy."

One summer night in 1955, when Jennifer was seventeen, she awoke to the sounds of a terrifying argument between her parents. She had never heard them fight before. Words like "fuck" and "shit"—which they had never before uttered in her presence—now flew everywhere and seemed to stick in the walls. Her mother came to her room and told her she was leaving for good. Did Jennifer want to come with her?

Jennifer said no. She had too many friends nearby, and she loved Stock Grange. She was also about to go to college.

Neither of her parents revealed to her the specific reasons for their divorce, although Frances intimated to film historian Aljean Harmetz that the split was fueled in part by the twenty-year difference in their ages. She was more candid with her daughter. Frances had begun a relationship, at first platonic, with the owner of an upscale women's dress shop in a nearby town. The two would later marry.

Ronald Neame remembered being stunned on hearing of the split. "Whenever I came to New York, the first telephone call I made was always to Claude and to Frances. And it was always Frances that answered. And invariably if he was acting in the theatre, which a lot of the time he was, we would go and see the show. And then one day I telephoned and a housekeeper answered." Frances called him back a few hours later. "And she said, 'Well, Ronnie, I have something to tell you that you may not like very much, but Claude and I have parted.'"

Frances asked for Neame's reassurance that they could still remain friends. "I said, 'Good gracious, Frances, I love Claude and I love you. And it's not going to change anything.' But I was very surprised indeed. However, I think that Claude was probably a very difficult man to live with because he did have to be the center of attention all the time. He was very demanding of the people that were around him. And I think you would have to describe him as chauvinistic, perhaps in a quiet way. And I think Frances probably had quite a few moments in that marriage when she had to cover up. As perhaps we all do, of course."

"This wasn't a family that talked about feelings much," Jennifer remembered. "I don't know how many did at the time. My mother told me later that she had been unhappy with the marriage for at least five years, but didn't want to divorce before I was ready to go to college. I must have been an idiot not to suspect something. I was at a boarding school only fifteen miles away, but they would always alternate Sunday visits, never coming together."

The ensuing summer was "nasty," Jennifer recalled. On the day the divorce was final, her father, having been drinking, ran his treasured Bentley into a ditch, wrecking it. It was a miracle he lived. According to his neighbor Harrison Wetherill, "They found him near the car, too drunk to move. The car was on its top and on fire." On his tax return for the year, he claimed the loss of a "1953 Bentley Convertible Coupe, purchased in 1953 [for $10,800]. Destroyed by fire in a country road accident—no other person or car involved—in August." Insurance paid him $8,500 and, given the expenses of the divorce, he replaced the trophy vehicle with a much less expensive Chevrolet convertible.

But the drinking didn't stop. Rains began (or continued) a strange, sad affair with another alcoholic, the wife of a local farm owner, who personally dropped off his spouse at Stock Grange for alfresco assignations at the farm's private pond (the woman was supposedly there to go swimming). On one particularly unpleasant occasion, Rains asked his daughter to help his lover/drinking partner to be sick in the bathroom, an experience that thoroughly disgusted her. That fall, Jennifer enrolled at Bennington College. Two years later, the daughter of her father's mistress also enrolled—an awkward situation, given that Jennifer found it difficult to avoid her on a campus of just four hundred students.

Rains continued doing television. Given the circumstances of his life at the time, it is a bit surprising that he accepted a role of an alcoholic, unemployed actor for an *Alfred Hitchcock Presents* episode called "The Cream of the Jest." In it, the Rains character desperately pleads with a former producer for a second chance. Although not literally autobiographical, his lines underscore the basic insecurity experienced by many professional actors:

> I'll take anything, even walk-ons. I've got to get back on the
> stage, don't you understand that? You know, sometimes when I
> sit in my room I go to the mirror and try to see who *me* is. And
> all the characters I've ever played pass in front of me. And I'm

every one of them. But there's no real me, only the characters.
. . . Then I go back and I sit, and I wait, I wait for somebody
to call me back to life again. Somebody like you. I'm only real
when I'm acting. The rest of the time I'm nothing. That's why
I drink.

The Hitchcock episode also provided a rare filmed record of Rains
delivering Shakespearean verse: the "Tomorrow and tomorrow" soliloquy
from *Macbeth*. (In 1952 he had appeared in, and audio recorded several
selections from, the American Shakespeare Festival's gala *An Evening with
Will Shakespeare*, with Eva Le Gallienne, Nina Foch, and others.)

Aside from his droll signature introductions, Hitchcock was not directly involved in the television series, except for a few episodes he directed (two with Rains), but he did supervise the series. One day, following Hitchcock's surgery for an umbilical hernia and other abdominal
problems in the late 1950s, Rains recalled, he found himself on the same
set with the director. "He had just had the operation. He was sitting there
in that puffed, pouting pose. 'Claude,' he said, 'they've taken my navel
away.' And he hiked up his shirt to show it."

One of Rains's best appearances on the Hitchcock series—he appeared in a total of five episodes—was in the role of a murderous ventrilo-
quist in an adaptation of Ray Bradbury's short story "And So Died Riabouchinska." Bradbury himself was in awe of the performance, so much
that he was at a loss for words when he met Rains on the set, completely
forgetting to ask the actor his long-burning questions about *The Invisible
Man* and other favorite films.

On January 10, 1957, Rains sold Stock Grange to Harrison Wetherill
for $130,657. The divorce settlement allowed Frances to purchase and
renovate a historic carriage house on picturesque Panama Street in
Center City, Philadelphia (where she and her ex-husband would have a
somewhat awkward reunion on the occasion of their daughter's marriage
to Edward Brash). Rains reluctantly moved to a smaller West Chester
property called Hawthorne House at 400 South Church Street. He had

loved Stock Grange, he told the *New York World Telegram and Sun* in 1962. "When the play closed, or the movie was finished, I went right back to that farm," he said. "Knowing it was there sustained me. But my doctor convinced me about five years ago that I didn't need all the burden of that land."

8

New Stages and
Final Curtains

RAINS'S RELATIVE ISOLATION IN PENNSYLVANIA did nothing to lessen the ceaseless stream of fan mail, from which the actor could have easily inferred that the years had enlarged rather than diminished his professional stature and that women of all ages still thrilled to his polished, rich, and sensual voice and to the memory of all those screen portrayals of urbane wickedness and gallantry.

There seemed no reason that he should have been especially attracted to a pale pink envelope that appeared in the profusion of his mail one morning. But something attracted him to it, and he opened this envelope first. The writer identified herself as a West Chester housewife named Rosemary McGroarty, and she inquired, with great deference, if Rains would be willing to address a local theatrical group called The Footlighters.

Although Rains received many such requests (and frequently granted them), he telephoned Mrs. McGroarty immediately, intending to tell her he was leaving the following day for some engagement. Her voice, he recalled, was both melodious and vivacious, and he suddenly found himself inviting her to visit. It was an invitation he regretted the moment he gave it, for he realized he had merely succumbed to the pleasure of her voice. "Now, why did I do that?" he muttered to himself.

His housekeeper would not arrive until nearly noon, so he put the coffee on the stove himself and waited irritably for his visitor. It was eleven o'clock before the doorbell rang. Rains braced himself, in the manner of a star confronting a stage door congestion of fans, and resolved to say that, as much as he would like to accommodate The Footlighters, it was not possible.

He was stunned as he pulled open the door, for instead of the frumpy village matron he had expected, there stood a willowy blonde woman in a bright yellow coat and an immense paisley-banded picture hat—"this glorious creature," he later recalled. A decorous hour ensued, wherein Mrs. McGroarty sat demurely at the old pine table by the kitchen fireplace, discussing aspects of the theatre and Rains's career. She was familiar enough with his work to accurately quote one of his more memorable lines from *Deception*.

Rains was both flattered and impressed, and he resolved to himself to telephone her as soon as he returned from Hollywood and the filming of *This Earth Is Mine,* a bucolic melodrama set in California's wine country, in which he played a bearded, irascible patriarch to Jean Simmons, Dorothy McGuire, and Rock Hudson.

Rains's daughter and her friends at Bennington were especially curious about the male lead in *This Earth Is Mine*. Several of them crowded into a phone booth when she called her father long distance. "Is it true that Rock Hudson is homosexual?" they wanted to know.

"Of course not," said Rains, deadpan. "He's perfectly charming. He always says 'Good morning, Claudie,' and gives me a friendly pat on the behind."

This Earth Is Mine was Rains's first film for Universal since *Phantom of the Opera,* and "the first one that has a pleasant title. I was starting to believe they would only engage me for horror pictures," he told studio publicist Bob Rains, whom industry people often assumed was some relation to Claude, perhaps his son. Rock Hudson had introduced the non-namesakes to each other. Bob asked Claude if he knew anything about London's Rains University, which had been obliterated in the Blitz. Bob's great-grandfather had taught journalism there. Claude wasn't familiar with the school, but he took a liking to Bob and, on two subsequent trips to London, sent the publicist gag photos, the first with an attached note: "I still can't locate the Rains University. I trust this will suffice until I do." The photo showed Rains standing in front of the Tower of London holding a hand-lettered sign reading RAINS UNIVERSITY. A few years later came a follow-up: "They say if you don't succeed, try, try again. And I have tried and tried and tried. I really think I am getting too old to look for the Rains University. But I guess that fathers should never stop trying to help their sons." The photo this time showed Rains outside Buckingham Palace, with a new sign: SORRY, THIS ISN'T IT!

After Rains returned to Pennsylvania from Hollywood, he never managed to telephone Mrs. McGroarty, possibly because soon after his return, through what he only described as "some West Chester social accident," he made the acquaintance of Agi Jambor, a distinguished pianist-composer who taught music at Bryn Mawr College. Jambor was fifty-one, a Hungarian Jew who had fled the Holocaust (one of her best-known compositions was the piano solo "Sonata for the Victims of Auschwitz"); her specialty was Bach. Rains and Jambor shared several dinners with friends and also shared their memories of the war. According to Rains, Jambor was soon begging him to marry her. Impulsively, he agreed, and they wed on November 4, 1959, six days short of his seventieth birthday.

His friends were puzzled by the match. Rains told them, "She's a wonderful artist. I can listen to the music." Agi said that her husband had a good musical ear; he often offered her suggestions, which were always correct. He was delighted by her accent, which reminded him of the Gabor sisters. But an undercurrent of depression also seems to have fueled the decision to marry. Both were lonely—Agi had lost her first husband ten years before—and Rains was melancholy. "It's getting on towards the end," he said. "I'm through." He felt a final marriage to an artist might "be calm and peaceful."

It wasn't. Problems started on their wedding day. On their way to the ceremony, Agi insisted on delaying the nuptials and returning home because she had forgotten to wear the underwear in which she had previously been married, and which had sentimental value. "She was imperious with me," Rains said. "Her habits were not nice. I'll put it that way. They were dreadful." Having a pianist in the house, for instance, was hardly the soothing experience he expected. "She drove me crazy," he said, as she practiced on a silent keyboard; he couldn't stand watching her hands flying around with no music to appreciate. But Rains's own habits weren't nice, either. He had an explosive temper and was given to throwing things. Also, according to Agi, he was "an incredibly heavy drinker." "My heart would bleed for him," she said, "because he was so insecure. He never enjoyed his success."

Rains was stingy with money, even to the point of claiming he was broke (which was hardly the case, although most of his assets were tied up in investments and annuities). When Agi would ask for more grocery money (she claimed, improbably, that he gave her a grand total of $9.40 for food shopping during their entire marriage), he told her she should earn additional money of her own. This was sheer spite: Agi already had a modest income from lecturing at Bryn Mawr and making occasional concert appearances; she soon understood that Rains would never really tolerate a wife with a career of her own. Paradoxically, though, he never discouraged her from working, on the basis that "One does not waste a talent."

Rains soon grew to dislike his wife's spicy Hungarian cooking as much as she balked at his predilection for bland English cuisine (which may explain the constant arguments about groceries). Rains also claimed that she brought pornographic books into their bedroom in an attempt to excite her seventy-year-old husband, who was past his sexual prime. This only repulsed him. "She was sexually starved," he said. According to his daughter, "He was extremely moralistic, and pornography appalled him. Once, when I was visiting in New Hampshire, I was reading the [at that time, expurgated] diaries of Anaïs Nin, at his recommendation. He was reading ahead of me and became so scandalized that he confiscated the book and told me I was never to finish it." One of the few posthumous compliments Agi would pay him was to call him "a very moral man."

Eventually, while Rains was in California on a television assignment, he impulsively called his handyman and told him to change the locks on all the doors while Agi was out shopping. "I was sewing costumes for an off-Broadway show," recalled his daughter, "and suddenly got a call from Agi, saying that she came back from the market, couldn't get into the house, and didn't know what was happening. But I immediately knew what was happening and told her to call my father's lawyer."

Rains also called his lawyer from Hollywood with a frantic plea to "Get me out of this." He was determined. "I don't care what it costs," he said, "and I don't care what she says about me." The latter was not precisely true. He had been married so many times that the notoriety of another divorce would distress him greatly. Yet he bore it all with outward equanimity, even in the relative privacy of the company of his friends. Jambor, locked out of the house and forced to relocate, filed for divorce in May 1960. Her petition charged that, in "violation of his marriage vows and of the laws of this Commonwealth, the defendant has over a period of time commencing on or about November 5, 1959 offered such indignities to the person of the plaintiff as to render her condition intolerable and life burdensome." In his response, Rains denied the charges and demanded proof. Evidently, sufficient proof was provided; Jambor was granted her divorce on July 28, 1960. The terms of the financial settlement were never made public. Rains only said, "I let her make her charges and paid her off."

Rains had been shuttling back and forth between Pennsylvania and California several times in the six months between his meeting Rosemary McGroarty and marrying and divorcing Agi Jambor. He had nearly forgotten about Rosemary when he happened to see her one day in the spring of 1960. He was in his driveway, discussing the problems of his Mercedes 300 SL with a West Chester mechanic who had come to take it away, when he noticed a movement of feminine raiment. He turned in time to see Rosemary walking briskly by the house. He did not recognize her immediately, and by the time it dawned on him who it was, she was already gone.

He dismissed the mechanic and went into the house, wondering what he had done with her initial letter, fretfully trying to remember her name. He was rummaging through the drawers and slots of his Chippendale desk, marveling at his sudden longing to see the lady again, when the telephone rang. It was she. The sound of her voice made him feel like a timorous teenaged swain.

"I hope I'm not disturbing you," she began, with appealing diffidence. "I wasn't aware that you spend much time here. But I did see you earlier today, and as long as you are here now I would like to talk to you again about The Footlighters." There was more, but the conversation never progressed beyond this impersonal level. Rains invited her to breakfast the very next day, somewhat alarmed at his eagerness to see her.

He awoke at dawn as usual and fidgeted impatiently for the three hours before her arrival, assembling a menu of bacon, scrambled eggs, and grilled tomatoes, setting the old pine table with antique sterling and blue willow ware, and finally building a fire in the kitchen fireplace.

When Rosemary arrived, she was even more lovely than Rains had remembered, and the breakfast that followed was a tense, mutually self-conscious, exploratory conversation during which, he noted, her hand trembled whenever she raised her coffee cup.

It was only after she had gone that he could consider with any detachment the emotional tempest her presence had occasioned. She was a divorcée in her early forties—nearly thirty years his junior—and she had three children: a daughter who was a freshman at Bryn Mawr; one son, nearly grown; and another barely ten. She had only recently moved to West Chester from Wilkes Barre, where she had spent most of her life, apart from an extensive art education at Moore's Academy, the Pennsylvania Academy of Fine Arts, and the Barnes Foundation, all in Philadelphia. During a subsequent series of tête-à-têtes in the Rains kitchen that spring, Rosemary indicated that she might like to be his biographer, even though she was not a professional writer and had no significant contacts in the publishing world. Nonetheless, he relished the attention.

They only met in private. Divorce litigation with Agi was still pending, and Rains dared not be seen with another woman in public. He tried to explain this to Rosie one morning, but it came out like this: "I wish I would have known you six months ago. I did a very foolish thing which I might not have done. I married a lady I shouldn't have married."

This implied proposal of marriage elicited some candor from Rosemary as well. She admitted that she had written him only because she wanted to meet him. Her association with the amateur theatrical group was tenuous at best. It had, in fact, all been a ruse. She later disclosed to Rains that her sole reason for moving to West Chester was just to be near him. She had already told friends in Wilkes Barre that her goal was to marry him. Rosemary was not the first, and would certainly not be the last, obsessive fan to romantically stalk a Hollywood star in his declining years.

Rains by this time was old, alone, and drinking more heavily than ever. He never questioned Rosie's intentions. He was starved for company and companionship. Around this time he returned to Hollywood to play Professor Challenger in Irwin Allen's remake of *The Lost World* for Twentieth Century-Fox, based on the novel by Arthur Conan Doyle. (The film, originally touted as a state-of-the-art spectacular with stop-motion special effects that would put the original, silent *Lost World* to shame, in the end was just a tacky spectacle with optically inflated lizards running rampant on miniature sets.) The cast included Jill St. John, Michael Rennie, David Hedison, and Richard Haydn, who later became a close friend. Rains spent several evenings at Haydn's pleasant home in Santa Monica Canyon, where he talked incessantly about Rosemary.

Shortly after Rains arrived in Hollywood, the Screen Actors Guild called a strike, which halted production of *The Lost World*, so the actor returned to West Chester. Marriage was now a tacit understanding between Rains and Rosemary, although he still had doubts that he could make a success of it. Was he wildly romanticizing and idealizing her, as he had done with his five other wives? The couple began taking weekend trips to Bucks County and beyond, booking double accommodations to avoid scrutiny. Once, at the Swiftwater Inn in the Poconos, they were treated with such lavish hospitality that they decided to be married there when the Jambor divorce was final.

Rains soon went west again to finish *The Lost World*. Rosemary wrote him letters of stirring encouragement and astonishing ardor. Each night, when he returned from the studio to his suite at the Beverly Hills Hotel, he would telephone her to exchange love talk and the trivia of the day.

One night when he returned to the hotel after work, he found outside his door a single, fresh lily. Inside the door was a handsome, dark-haired, middle-aged woman he had previously seen staring at him in the hotel dining room. He left the suite door open and silently gestured for her to leave. Resolute hostility, he had learned, was the best way to repel amorous fans.

"I only want to talk to you," she pleaded.

"Please get out," Rains replied stiffly.

Then the telephone rang. It was Rosemary. Rains put his hand over the receiver and glared at the woman, who had now moved brazenly to the center of the room, staring back at him.

"I'll scream," the woman threatened.

"I don't care what you do," Rains answered. "Just get out. If you don't leave immediately, I shall call the manager."

"You're very rude," the woman said haughtily. She left without screaming, but slammed the door behind her.

"What was that?" Rosemary asked.

Rains told her, dismissing the incident as a common hazard for celebrities. But Rosemary smelled sexual competition, and her voice rose several decibels. "When it comes to you," she said, "I can be savage."

After the phone call, the spurned intruder returned, with ferocity of her own, and began banging on Rains's door, furiously demanding an audience. Rains called hotel security and had the screaming woman removed.

He returned to Pennsylvania. *The Lost World* had hardly been worth his effort and time, and it did nothing for his professional reputation. The film generated sarcastic and dismissive reviews, as per *Time*'s critique: "'The Lost World' exhibits Claude Rains in a red fright wig, and Jill St. John in—just barely—a pair of pink slacks. These wonders notwithstanding, the most intriguing performers, as is only proper in a Good-Lord-Professor-Can-It-Be? film, are several dinosaurs." The *New York Times*, which almost always championed his work, called his performance "a caricature."

Claude Rains married Rosemary McGroarty in August 1960. His daughter said later, "He told me that there were some problems in the marriage." According to her, Rosemary "had expected to be the wife of a movie star, and of course he wasn't living that kind of life." Rains was busy with television in Hollywood, and Rosemary accompanied him to Los Angeles while he worked on episodes of *Naked City, Rawhide,* and a Hallmark Hall of Fame adaptation of *Lost Horizon* called *Shangri-La.* She disliked southern California as much as he did, complaining especially about the stale-tasting water. The television assignments, perfunctorily produced, were nothing like the prestige productions he had done under the now-defunct studio system.

Rosemary pressured Rains to accept what turned out to be a terrible assignment in an Italian science fiction movie, *Battle of the Worlds*. The movie would be remembered largely for the camp spectacle of Rains wearing a helmet without a faceplate, despite being in deep space. But at least it would include a semi-glamorous vacation. Jennifer and her husband, Eddie, were traveling in Europe that summer and met Rains and Rosemary in Rome. The studio sent a limousine for the four of them. Rains sat in front with the driver, and Jennifer, Eddie, and Rosemary were seated in the back. As they passed the Appian Way, Rosemary could not contain herself. "Do you *know* who this is?" she asked the driver excitedly, pointing at Rains. "Julius Cesare! Julius Cesare!" The driver, who barely spoke English, had no idea what she was saying, even with her attempt at an Italian accent. "We were all mortified," recalled Jennifer. Rains's daughter had remained on friendly terms with Agi Jambor and was not at all impressed with her father's sixth wife.

Ariane Ulmer, the daughter of film director Edgar G. Ulmer, was working at a post-production facility in Rome at the same time Rains was doing voice synchronization for *Battle of the Worlds*. She was then engaged to an Italian whose family strongly disapproved of their son's choice. When Ulmer entertained Rains and his wife at her Rome apartment, she found Rosemary to be "extremely cool," but Rains, ever the romantic, encouraged her to proceed with the marriage despite the family friction. Ulmer was touched by his concern and advice, which she followed. "It was like having Mr. Skeffington suddenly walk into my life," she recalled. "He was a total sweetheart, the romantic of all romantics."

After returning to the States, Rains appeared onstage with the Philadelphia Orchestra, reading Tennyson's narrative poem *Enoch Arden* to Richard Strauss's score. The concert was well received, and Schuyler Chapin, head of RCA Records, invited Rains to record his performance in collaboration with famed Canadian pianist Glenn Gould. Rains was flattered. He greatly admired Gould's work, but the recording session proved an ordeal. Gould was an idiosyncratic talent who had withdrawn from the concert stage to the protection of the recording studio, where he could exert complete technical control over his performances.

Rosemary attended the recording session in New York, and a collision of one obsessive personality against another was inevitable. "Mrs. Rains was quick to imagine slights to her husband," Chapin wrote in his memoir *Musical Chairs*. Soon the performers were working separately in the same studio, concealed from each other behind screens. According to Chapin,

> They set to work with mutual suspicion. Gould would romp through florid piano parts while Rains rolled out the language with suppressed chokes and sobs that were so much a part of nineteenth-century declamation. Mrs. Rains was constantly furious and the conversations between the artists were peppered with her comments. . . . But they did finish it and at the end stiffly acknowledged that they had both done some service to Tennyson and Strauss.

Rains's only comment on the episode was that Gould was "the most temperamental performer I have ever known."

In 1961, Rains and Rosemary traveled to Spain for his small but nonetheless memorable role of a British diplomat in David Lean's film *Lawrence of Arabia*, which was released the following year. Stanley Kauffmann, reviewing the film for *The New Republic*, observed, "Playing a diplomat, Claude Rains, always a fine and now vintage actor, is simply not on the screen long enough to suit us." However minimal his participation, Rains, for the last time, enhanced the prestige of a film that would go on to receive great acclaim, winning seven Academy Awards, including Best Picture.

Following his work on *Lawrence of Arabia*, Rains had dinner with his daughter's Brentwood playmate Susan Strasberg, who was then an actress and avatar of her father's method. Jennifer had also studied with Susan's father Lee Strasberg, and was convinced that her own father was essentially a method actor himself, whether he acknowledged it or not.

Susan Strasberg, who barely remembered Rains as a neighbor in the Brentwood days, said of his screen work, "Oh, Mr. Rains, I've been at your feet for years."

"I've been at yours recently," he replied. "I'm very much like you. I think a lot about what I'm doing. People might say I'm a method actor. If I don't have a reason for doing or saying something, I don't do or say it. I think a lot about what I'm doing. I like to think I've marched with the times."

"Many actors were left behind when acting changed," Rains said later. "I recognized the change about the time I did Clemence Dane's *Will Shakespeare* in 1921. Many actors speak off the cuff. They're not concerned too much about the thoughts of the characters. They're concerned about getting the line over. I work hard and I get the man into my guts."

Despite his compliment to Susan Strasberg and his obvious, if self-taught, affinities with Stanislavski, Rains could be critical of so-called method actors: "These method bastards *think*, but it's become so mannered it's no longer what they intended it to be."

In 1963, shortly after receiving his Academy Award for *Lawrence of Arabia*, David Lean called Rains in West Chester and asked for a personal favor. Before returning to England, the director was ghost-directing a prologue to George Stevens's biblical epic *The Greatest Story Ever Told* and needed a seasoned character actor for a few days' work.

"I want you to play that old bastard who killed all those kikes," Lean said.

"Do you mean—Herod?" Rains ventured.

"Yes, that's his name," Lean replied. Rains knew that Lean was not anti-Semitic but could be profoundly tone-deaf on social, cultural, and historical issues. According to his biographer Kevin Brownlow, Lean "was on another planet politically. He barely noticed World War II." Given this, it is not surprising that Lean never comprehended the postwar controversy that arose over Alec Guinness's hook-nosed Fagin in Lean's adaptation of Dickens's *Oliver Twist*; the uproar led to the film's being banned in Israel, with calls raised for its suppression in America and elsewhere.

Rains accepted the assignment and immediately flew to Los Angeles. Lean's prologue to *Greatest Story* is now generally regarded as the artistic highlight in a generally overblown film. The historical record of the old king Herod contains no mention of the slaughter of Jewish children, but Rains effectively played his part of the biblical account in a semi-improvised sequence. Lean felt that some kind of unscripted flourish to Herod's death scene was needed and suggested that Rains throw forward Herod's staff at the moment of his demise. Rains didn't understand the motivation, but trusted Lean's direction and complied, to good effect.

Rains's final film role (though not the last to be released—*Greatest Story* would have many post-production delays) was in *Twilight of Honor* for MGM. Rains played Richard Chamberlain's crusty legal mentor, an alcoholic who perversely indulges his addiction by getting other people drunk, after which, he says, "I stagger up to bed and sleep it off."

Rains and Rosemary left Pennsylvania in the summer of 1963 for a new home in Sandwich, New Hampshire. According to his daughter, "He bought something that needed to be restored or fixed up. That's what he loved to do."

Around this time Jennifer embarked on an acting career in New York, only to learn that a "Jennifer Rains" was already registered with Actors' Equity. She chose a new name: Jessica.

Rains's next acting assignment reunited him with his costar in *Twilight of Honor*, Richard Chamberlain. In January 1964 Rains was again back in Hollywood, shooting an episode of *Dr. Kildare*. He and Rosemary usually wrote each other several times a week when he traveled, but during his last week at the Beverly Hills Hotel, he didn't receive any letters. When Rains returned home he found his wife uncharacteristically withdrawn. A few days later she discovered a lump in her chest. Tests conducted in New Hampshire were negative, but the lump was real. They consulted a doctor in New York, who performed exploratory surgery at Roosevelt Hospital. "The news isn't good, Claude," the doctor told him. The cancer had metastasized to a point where the doctor couldn't determine where it had begun. Eventually Rosemary was diagnosed with advanced pancreatic cancer.

Neither Rains nor her doctor told Rosemary that she had cancer. She took an apartment on East Ninth Street in order to begin a series of injection treatments with her New York physician, but she soon found she was unable to climb the building's stairs. Rains arranged for her to stay at the Algonquin Hotel in a suite with twin beds. "I didn't think there was going to be any more loving," he said. In March, Rosemary returned to New Hampshire, but she continued to lose strength. At one point, when Rains used a euphemism in discussing her illness, Rosemary told him, "Please don't do that to me any longer. I know what I've got."

In August Rains bought a lake cottage a few miles from the house so that Rosemary could see and be near water. But the weather proved inclement, and in September they returned to the main house. Over the next several months Rosemary's condition steadily declined. She could only navigate stairs by crawling on all fours. Her daughter was a steady presence, giving her mother Demerol injections for the pain. Through it all, Rosemary remained stoic, even humorous. Once, when Father Paris, Rosemary's priest, visited, he commented on her intravenous feeding tube. "You're eating very slowly," he said. "Luck of the Irish," she replied.

Rosemary died on the morning of New Year's Eve, 1964. Rains designed her headstone himself, a traditional upright marker in black granite. For her epitaph, he combined the opening lines of Christina Georgina Rossetti's poem "Song" with a slightly altered refrain from the funeral hymn "Now the Laborer's Task Is O'er" (1871) by John Lodge Ellerton:

ROSEMARY McGROARTY RAINS
1917–1964
The Beloved Wife of
Claude Rains
"When I am dead my dearest
Sing no sad songs for me.
Rather, in thy gracious keeping
Leave me now
Thy servant sleeping."

At the funeral at nearby Red Hill Cemetery, the officiating priest said, "As a result of her divorce and remarriage, Rosemary was not a Catholic in good standing. But when she discovered she had cancer, she made her peace with her God and with her Church, and was thus enabled to enjoy once again the consolations of her faith during the last months of her life." During his wife's illness, Rains had considered converting to Catholicism, but ultimately was not up to the task. As he said later, "Before marriage, we had no religious discussion. I told her I was not a religious person." He was, however, instrumental in having the church reinstate her. After her death, he sent the local Catholic church a check for an unknown amount.

After Rosemary's death, Rains recalled, "I thought I couldn't sleep in the old gothic bed, but I said to myself, you damn fool, you have to." The housekeeper insisted on making up the bed with four pillows as before. Rains pinned a copy of the last letter Rosemary ever sent him to her pillow. It had been written in October 1964 and concluded with a quotation from Shakespeare's *Richard II*: "But heaven hath hand in these events, God, to whose high will be bound our calm content."

Rains was not inclined to save fan mail, but he did preserve one letter from a woman in Revere, Massachusetts, because of its mention of Rosemary:

Dear Mr. Rains,

Last August, when we were on vacation in Saunders Bay, N.H., we were shopping in Laconia. As we were riding, I yelled out to my family in the car, "There's Claude Rains coming out of the hotel dining room!" Well, they thought I was crazy but we turned around and attempted to follow you, which wasn't very nice, but as we are terrific fans of yours, maybe we will be excused. . . . You had parked at a market and we asked the lady who was with you as you passed our car if it was Claude Rains, and she said yes, and it was also her husband. What a wonderful gracious person she was and we were all so sorry to hear that she had died. I will always remember that day. [She] told us how sick she had been from her operation, and she said, I'm not pregnant, pointing to her stomach. . . . We got out our pens and paper and as you came out of the market, your lovely wife said, honey, these people are waiting to see you and talk to you. She was so very down to earth because she could have well given us the brush off. You were such a perfect gentleman. You talked to us and signed our papers, and you will remember chiding my daughter because all she had was an envelope stamped and you didn't want to use that but she said she didn't care and you wrote on it, "waste not, want not." Then you told us of your coming television play and I guess we were about the happiest family in the city that day. We all agreed you were just like on the screen, so natural and so mannerly. Your wife had gone on to the car after saying goodbye to us and my daughter was interested in your car and she went to look at it and again your wife took the time and trouble to tell her all about it, which was so interesting. We were brought up in the old fashioned way of manners, kindness and consideration and to meet show people who returned the same was such a thrill for us. . . . Our sympathy to you in the loss of that lovely gracious lady who took the time to be nice to a very appreciative family. We have long been fans of yours and will continue to be.

Not long after Rosemary's death, Jessica's marriage to Edward Brash failed. Although she and her father were never comfortable talking about emotional issues, she thought he might be able to provide some insight or support, given his own five divorces. Rains was ill and in bed when she told him the news. He sat bolt upright, and boomed in his world-famous voice: *"Tell me—was it sex?"*

During Rosemary's illness, in the summer of 1964, Jonathan Root, a well-regarded reporter for the *San Francisco Chronicle*, happened to be in the projection room of a Hollywood film laboratory with his friend Dick Berg, producer of *Bob Hope Presents the Chrysler Theater* for NBC. The two men were waiting to see the finished print of "Something About Lee Wiley," a dramatization of the mid-career blindness of the Jazz Age singing sensation. The principal roles were performed by Claude Rains, Piper Laurie (as Wiley), and Steven Hill. As they got ready to watch the start of the drama, Berg nudged his friend.

"Now," he whispered excitedly, "watch a real pro."

As Root recalled, "The screen brightened and Rains appeared abruptly in its luminescent center, in an instantly rich and virile portrayal of a self-made midwestern millionaire, seething with the omnipotence of raw wealth. The performance so impressed me that I reflected on it and came to conclude that Claude Rains was as much a cinematic institution as the medium itself"—not to mention an excellent subject for an authorized biography. Root had already published a well-received chronicle of explorer-author Richard Halliburton and was looking for a new project.

Dick Berg had been instrumental in convincing Rains to do television at a time when many Hollywood stars were shunning the medium. He broke Rains's resistance by driving to his farm with a script for him to read, then refusing to leave until he read it. When Berg learned of Rosemary's death, he immediately called Rains and asked if he could come to LA at once to do another *Bob Hope Chrysler Theater*. He knew that for Rains, work was the only antidote to the grief he was suffering. The script was a farcical comedy called "Cops and Robbers." Rains would costar with Bert Lahr and Eduardo Cianelli, affect a broad Italian accent, and generally have a good time.

"I asked Father Paris and he said, go," Rains remembered. As usual, he showed up at NBC punctually and was thoroughly prepared, his lines memorized. But Hollywood no longer held any charm for Rains, if it ever did. "I was never happy in Hollywood," he said. "The way people lived. I didn't like the country. Bare and cold to look at." On his last night in Los Angeles, he had dinner with Berg. Rains recalled, "I got drunk and he drove me to the airport. I restrained myself, didn't let him know what was going on inside me. I don't even remember getting on the plane."

Concerned about Rains, Berg encouraged Root to pursue a biography with the actor. Soon after, while in New York on other business, Root telephoned Rains in New Hampshire. As Root later wrote, "He was flying down to New York the next day, he told me in that haunting voice, for a press conference with the Theatre Guild about a play in which he would be starring in the fall of 1965, and he would be pleased to meet me at the Savoy-Plaza Hotel, where he was staying." The next day, Root recalled, "He met me at the door to his suite with urbane graciousness, arched an eyebrow eloquently and beckoned me inside." A waiter was already serving chicken sandwiches and coffee at a small table. "It's nearly tea time," Rains said, "and I thought you might be hungry."

Root immediately noticed the way Rains's regal bearing suggested a much taller man. He remembered him wearing "an impeccably tailored light grey suit, a white shirt with a soft collar, and a somewhat large and colorful tie."

"They're tearing down this old hotel," Rains said. "Going to put up an office building or something. I expect this is the last time I'll stay here."

Rains walked to the window and stared silently for a moment, surveying the rooftops and squinting at the grey hulk of the Queensborough Bridge in the distance.

"Yes, the last time," he said, turning away. "And that makes me sad."

Then he smiled abruptly, rubbed his hands together, and gestured for Root to sit at the table. "The time passed with irritating haste," Root wrote, but he was at least able to outline his ideas for a biographical project, to which Rains seemed receptive. But finally he looked at his watch and announced, apologetically, that he must leave or be late for his appointment at the Theatre Guild. "Do you know Joel Schenker?" Rains asked.

"No," Root replied.

"He's producing this play for the Guild. It's by the Italian, Ugo Betti, adapted by Henry Denker. It's a marvelous play. It has some wonderful things to say about our times. About all times, for that matter. Joel waited a year for me, until I was available. Isn't that remarkable?"

Probably more sensible than remarkable, Root replied.

"Oh, no," Rains protested. "There are many actors who could have done it beautifully."

Root remembered Rains pulling a double-breasted black chesterfield coat from the closet. The garment dated from his early years in London. "He slipped into it not unlike a monarch donning his robes, plucked a black Homburg from the closet shelf and ushered me out the door." As they stepped into the elevator, the operator, "a pleasant, slender, fortyish woman," broke into a rapturous smile. "Oh, Mr. Rains," she said. "How very nice to see you again."

Rains responded with a beatific grin. "Thank you, my dear," he said.

"But I'm very sad because you're tearing down my hotel." At that point, recalled Root, "Any further discussion of the hotel's demolition was halted by a stop midway in the descent," when "half a dozen men wearing convention badges oozed into the car, and began to stare at Rains in unison."

At the curb of Fifty-Eighth Street, a beaming doorman flagged a cab and swept open its door with a flourish. A bitter winter wind grabbing at his homburg, Rains shook Root's hand and agreed to continue their conversations about the biography. They corresponded over the next six months and agreed to proceed with a formal book proposal. In July 1965, Root returned to New York and boarded a nine-passenger Statewide Airways plane for New Hampshire.

"We landed at dusk and Rains was standing at the edge of the tarmac," Root wrote. "There's Claude Rains," announced the pilot. "He's quite a guy. Flies with us all the time."

Rains, now seventy-four, insisted on carrying half of Root's luggage to his Jeep station wagon and drove him thirty miles to Sandwich. "We drank some Scotch, ate some cold chicken, and talked for a long time," Root reported. "We talked for several weeks at intervals during the following year," he wrote, "much of the conversation in the book-lined study overlooking his rose garden, or in the huge, maple-paneled kitchen, under the omnipresent solicitude of Lillian White, his non-taciturn Yankee housekeeper." Among the treasures he shared with Root were a pair of theatrical scrapbooks maintained by a devoted English fan who gave them to Rains during World War II for protection from possible destruction during the Blitz. Over the next year, Root audiotaped most of his and Rains's discussions, finally clocking more than two dozen hours. The tapes were augmented by extensive written notes, taken in person as well as by telephone and correspondence.

Rains and Root decided that their book, provisionally titled *The Love Habit* after the romantic comedy by Louis Verneuil in which Rains had performed in the 1920s, would be anchored around an idyllic account of Rains's marriage to Rosemary. "I've loved many women, but only one loved me back," Rains said, in a line that could have been concocted by a dust-jacket copywriter. Root was historically scrupulous in most of his interviews and research, as was Rains in his career recollections, but Rains had a blind spot when it came to Rosemary, and Root's notes contain a certain number of quotations unsupported by audiotape that, frankly, seem trumped up for book proposal purposes. "You're a very attractive woman," Rains supposedly tells Rosemary, who has just confessed to relentlessly stalking him. Nonetheless, "Suddenly, I found myself in her arms . . ."

Rains's highly anticipated return to the stage received much publicity and prompted Bette Davis to send him a handwritten note:

> Claude dear,
> You can't know how greatly I admire you—your performance—your courage—and just *you!* I wish you so much success with the play—watching you give a performance is always a privilege to me—I am so lucky I have worked with you so many times. It made me homesick for those days.
> Always my love—and I look forward to New Hampshire one day.
> Bette

But Rains's health was failing, and the run of Ugo Betti's *So Much of Earth, So Much of Heaven* at the Westport Country Playhouse was short-lived. Rains played a dictator in self-exile called upon to lead his people again during the threat of a world holocaust. He acted from a wheelchair (as per the script), and actress Joanna Miles, playing his nurse, was on-stage with him at all times. It soon became clear he was forgetting his lines. The company revered Rains, and watching a great actor falter was "terrifying," she recalled. During rehearsals, he had been in good spirits, even accompanying the cast to a local club, where he seemed to enjoy the performance of an unusually artistic drag performer. It would be the last bit of theatre Claude Rains ever witnessed.

The reviews of the play were not good. *Variety* opined that "it is torpid theatre, and impresses neither in content nor form. . . . As a vehicle for Claude Rains, absent from the Broadway scene for almost ten years, the offering also misses." After the fourth performance, Rains was re-placed by an understudy, and the Theatre Guild dropped its plans for a New York transfer. On September 10, 1965, Rains's attorney, Nochem S. Winnet, wrote to Root: "I regret to tell you that the play Claude Rains was in was too much for him. I saw him Monday night at the opening and it was no surprise to me to get a message from him today that he is in the Coatsville Hospital at Coatsville, Pennsylvania. It looks as though he will be there for about ten days and then he plans to go back to New Hampshire. Claude wanted me to get the message to you."

"People sent flowers from all over the world," Miles remembered, so much so that they lined the corridor and spilled into other patients' rooms. Rains minimized his condition to the medical staff and visitors, explaining, for instance, that his vomiting "blood" was simply the result of eating too many beets.

The press was told that Rains was withdrawing due to a bleeding peptic ulcer. In reality, advanced cirrhosis was creating a backup of blood in his liver, resulting in internal hemorrhaging. Surgeons created a por-tacaval shunt, diverting blood flow from his diseased liver to other blood vessels. Jessica was told that the operation might be able to prolong her father's life, but whenever the bypass failed, he would die.

There is no record that Rains discussed his medical condition with Root, who continued to interview him regularly until at least October 1966. The actor claimed to have finally gotten over the grief of Rose-mary's death, retaining only the warm memories. But a certain darkness was descending. "I can't stand the winter nights here alone," he told Root, and said he was considering yet another relocation. "You know how alive water is? I think of something near water. Lillian will come to me a certain distance. I think also about Rye and Portsmouth—they smack of captains and ships. Water is terribly alive. This place is dead. It's all dead."

These were the last words Claude Rains ever gave to an interviewer for publication.

The biographical project stalled because of Rains's failing health, and Root never finished his book proposal. He groused to himself on some of the tapes in which he dictated research transcriptions, complaining of the project's lack of funding. In March 1967, while vacationing in Capri, he suffered a massive heart attack and was airlifted to a hospital in Naples, where a second heart attack proved fatal. He was forty-three years old. Rains covered his own distress at the loss of a cherished confidante and his biographical project by flippantly telling his daughter that Root, who was homosexual, had probably been pushed into a Italian canal by some jealous lover. A veteran, Root was given a stateside military funeral.

Two months later, Rains collapsed in his garden and was taken to Lakes Region Hospital in Laconia. Jessica was contacted and rushed to New Hampshire. "I was told he was bleeding," she said. "I went up and stayed in a little hotel just down the street from the hospital. He was very brittle, very little. The very last thing he said to me was to go home and that he was going home, too. 'Get me my hat and get me my shoes, I'm getting out of here.' And two days later the doctor called me in New York and said, 'Your father is in a coma and won't live.' It was impossible to travel overnight because of limited transportation to Laconia, and I asked him if it would make any difference if I came up in the daytime. He said my father wouldn't recognize me in any case. He called back at 5:30 in the morning to tell me my father had passed away."

Claude Rains died on May 30, 1967, of an intestinal hemorrhage subsequent to liver failure. Jessica requested a cremation, but no facilities were available in the small New Hampshire town. She discovered that her father had designed his own tombstone. It would match Rosemary's and carry an inscription from a poem by Richard Monckton Milnes:

> All things once
> Are things forever,
> Soul, once living,
> Lives forever.

Rains had abandoned an attempt to convert to Catholicism, Rosemary's faith, but her priest nonetheless officiated at his funeral. Jessica, who had no black wardrobe to speak of, wore white instead. "It was surreal," she said. "A very lonely spot with a few close friends attending. I think there were eleven people at the tiny funeral in the little chapel."

Rains left an estate of approximately $400,000, including a trust fund for his daughter and a $25,000 bequest to the Actors Fund of America.

Following the burial, Jessica returned to the house, where she met a woman who had not attended the service. She introduced herself as a "friend." Jessica vaguely remembered her father mentioning this woman, who was a schoolteacher. After offering her condolences, the woman asked a favor, which Jessica granted. Would it be possible for her to have one of Claude's nightshirts as a keepsake? It would remind her of their happy times together.

Like many, Claude Rains died leaving behind loose ends and unrealized dreams. Among his papers was the final shooting script of My Fair Lady. Watching Stanley Holloway charmingly strut and sing his way through "With a Little Bit O' Luck" and "Get Me to the Church on Time," one finds it easy to imagine Rains even more charmingly essaying the role of Eliza Doolittle's father, a role he coveted. The producers, he said, wondered if he could "handle" a Cockney accent. "But I am a Cockney!" he protested. He had cultivated such an elegant voice, it's not surprising if he wasn't quite believed. One also can't help wondering what Rains would have done, earlier on, with another Shavian role, that of Henry Higgins in Pygmalion.

John Gielgud admired Rains's achievements in Hollywood, but felt the stage suffered a great loss when Rains abandoned the theatre for the screen before having claimed some of the great classical roles as his own. And indeed one can only imagine Rains's interpretations of Iago, Macbeth, Richard II (one of his favorites), Richard III—or even Lear, had he the stamina in his later years. ("You have to be superhuman," Rains once said of Lear. "All that madness!") Not long before his death, Rains told Jonathan Root that he had always yearned to play in The Merchant of Venice on Broadway and believed his daughter Jessica was talented enough to play Shylock's rebellious daughter (also named Jessica) opposite him. But he never told this to his daughter, despite her own aspirations in theatre and film. He knew the often heartbreaking vicissitudes of the acting life and was fiercely protective of his only child.

Unlike many once distinguished, but now forgotten, character actors, Claude Rains's reputation has only deepened. It is almost inconceivable that some of his best work—in *Casablanca*, for instance—received only perfunctory notice by the reviewers of the time, while today every nuance of that performance is indelibly etched into the minds of cinephiles everywhere. That he never won an Academy Award remains a crime, but the respect for his professionalism and craftsmanship continues unabated. Vincent Sherman once observed, "He was an immaculate actor, clean, precise, and exact in everything he did. There was no floundering about until he got the feel of a role, but a studied analysis with a design in the background that built bit by bit until the total architecture became visible."

That consummate architect of acting lingers still, from the ubiquity of Louis Renault's supremely cynical "I'm shocked, *shocked . . .*" (certainly one of the most quoted lines in movie history) to an invisible character on the television series *Heroes* who calls himself "Claude Rains," to obsessively surreal homages in films like Alejandro Jodorowsky's *Santa Sangre* and novels like Rick De Marinis's *A Lovely Monster: The Adventures of Claude Rains and Dr. Tellenbeck*, in which a mistreated Frankenstein-like creature names himself after Rains and escapes by disguising himself in bandages from head to foot ("I feel like Claude, moving through the countryside, beyond the rage and fear of the villagers. Beyond their tricks and bad dreams. And almost home").

Four years after Rains's death, Bette Davis briefly hesitated when asked by Dick Cavett if Claude Rains had been a happy person. "As happy as . . ." she began; then, obviously moved by the question, rephrased her response. "As a group, I don't think actors are what I'd call happy people. I think we're very moody people. I think we have great ups and great downs. . . . If something turns out badly you're depressed for days. I think we're terribly peculiar that way, and rather lonely people, actually. So Claude I could not say was a happy person. He was witty, amusing, and beautiful, really beautiful. And thoroughly enchanting to be with. And brilliant."

A few years later, after having introduced a potential Rains biographer to Bette Davis, Jessica received a summons from the diva herself.

Davis was working in television in Culver City, in her decline, and long
removed from her Warner Bros. heyday. Still, she could not forget Claude
Rains.

"Close the door before we talk about Claude," she said, in her famous, clipped cadences as Jessica entered her dressing room. Davis then
proceeded to talk for two hours about people and studio intrigues of
which Jessica had almost no comprehension. But Davis's unrequited passion for Jessica's father remained clear. Dr. Jaquith in *Now Voyager*, for
instance—surely he and Charlotte Vale, Davis's character, eventually married, said Davis—as if the film characters were real people. She poured out
anecdotes, jabbing the air with her trademark cigarette. Her memories
of Rains bringing Jessica and her mother to the set of *Now, Voyager* to
deflect her lust. Her personal crisis during the production of *Mr. Skeffington*, alleviated by Rains's support and professionalism. Her initial terror
of his intensity on the set of *Juarez*. *Deception* ruined by the censors, and
Rains's upstaging her in that film. Jessica, as a child, sworn to secrecy
about the identity of her family's famous houseguest at Stock Grange.
Rains's intelligence as an actor. His lack of temperament. His refusal to
play the Hollywood game ("He never went to a goddamn premiere in his
life!"). His elegance. His sex appeal—especially his sex appeal. The way he
would automatically remove his horn-rimmed glasses the moment any
pretty young thing set foot on the set. His subsequent, seemingly courtly,
flirtations. Her own jealous certainty that Rains's dressing room, so far
from the Pennsylvania farm in those Warners days, must have been "as
busy as Gimbels at Christmas." As for his drinking: "If only he would
have let *me* get him drunk."

When Davis's two-hour monologue about Claude Rains was finished, she turned to Jessica, batted her legendary eyes, and closed their
meeting just as her screen rival Joan Crawford once did, so many years
before.

"And now," said Davis, with a final, thoroughly theatrical flourish,
"you may go."

Appendix

The Work of Claude Rains

Theatre Work

Opening and closing dates have been included whenever verifiable; otherwise, only opening nights are indicated. In early to mid-twentieth-century British theatre, the term "producer" was generally synonymous with "director"; credits here are given as they appeared in original programs and clippings.

1900

SWEET NELL OF OLD DRURY
A comedy in four acts by Paul Kester, adapted by J. Hartley Manners. HAYMARKET THEATRE, London, August 8–October 13 (51 performances).

CAST: *Nell Gwyn* Julia Neilsen; *Lord Jeffreys* Louis Calvert; *Charles II* Fred Terry; *Percival* Lionel Brough; *Lacy* Malcolm Cherry; *Captain Graham Clavering* Fred Volpe; *Lady Olivia Vernon* Lilian Braithwaite; *Sir Roger Fairfax* C. M. Hallard; *Lady Castelmaine* Constance Collier.

NOTE: Claude Rains made his first stage appearance as an unbilled child extra "running around a fountain."

1900–1901

HEROD
A historical play in three acts by Stephen Phillips. HER MAJESTY'S THEATRE, London; October 31, 1900–January 22, 1901 (78 performances). PROPRIETOR AND MANAGER: Herbert Beerbohm Tree. PRODUCER: Herbert Beerbohm Tree. SCENERY: Hawes Craven. COSTUME DESIGN: Percy Anderson. MUSIC DIRECTOR: Andrew Levey.

CAST: *Herod, King of the Jews* Herbert Beerbohm Tree; *Gadias, Chief Councillor* C. W. Somerset; *Pheroras* F. Percival Stevens; *Aristobulus* Alfred Mansfield/Norman Tharp; *Marianne, Queen and Wife to Herod* Maud Jeffries; *Salome, Sister of Herod*

Eleanor Calhoun; *Bathsheba* Rosalie Jacobi/Nannie Bennett; *Cypros, Mother of Herod* Kate Bateman; *Judith, a Lady of the Court* Frances Dillon; *Sylleas, a Blind Man* J. Fisher White; *Hagar* Lillian Moubrey; *Envoy from Rome* C. F. Collings; *A Physician* Charles Fulton; *A Priest* S. A. Cookson; *A Captain* Edward Fielding; *Cupbearer* Julian L'Estrange; *Servant* Cavendish Morton; *Dancer* Ellen Goss; *Extras* Francis Chamier, Godwin Hunt, Cecil King, Henry Lesmere, Alfred E. Calver, Eric Leslie, Frank Gurney, Ernest Leigh, Claude Rains (unbilled child extra).

1904

LAST OF THE DANDIES
A play in four acts by Clyde Fitch. HIS MAJESTY'S THEATRE, London, April 30–May 6 (8 performances). PROPRIETOR AND MANAGER: Herbert Beerbohm Tree. MUSIC: Andrew Levey; STAGE MANAGER: Cecil King; ASSISTANT STAGE MANAGER: Louis Mercanton; MUSIC DIRECTOR: Adolf Schmid; GENERAL MANAGER: Henry Dana; ASSISTANT MANAGER: Angus MacLeod.

CAST: *Count D'Orsay* Herbert Beerbohm Tree; *Lord Ascot* Eugene Mayeur; *Lord Westerbury* Dawson Milward; *Sir Edward Bulwer-Lytton* S. A. Cookson; *Tom Raikes* Cecil Rose; *Mr. Marlby* L. Ericson; *Mons Piquot* Harvey Long; *Ferdinand* Compton Coutts; *Winkles* Master Claude Rains; *Lord Raoul Ardale* Basil Gill; *Lord Harbury* Francis Chamier; *Mr. Disraeli* Eric Leslie; *Mr. Weatherby* F. Wood; *Hon. Richard Bailey* A. C. Grain; *Peters* J. Fisher White; *Mr. Snipps* Frank Stanmore; *Octavio* William H. Day; *John B. Nicholls; *Lady Summershire* Mrs. Sam Sothern; *Lady Carrollby* Lena Brasch; *Deaf Old Lady* Mrs. Stanislaus Calhaem; *Henrietta Power* Isabel Collier; *Hon. Mrs. Weatherble* Elaine Inescourt; *Countess Guiccioli* Dorothy Thomas; *Jane* Hilda Gray; *Lady Blessington* Marion Terry.

NOTE: "Winkles" was Rains's debut speaking role in the theatre.

1910–1911

HENRY VIII
A play by William Shakespeare. HIS MAJESTY'S THEATRE, London, September 1–April 9 (279 performances). PROPRIETOR AND MANAGER: Sir Herbert Beerbohm Tree. SCENERY: Joseph Harker. DESIGN: Percy MacQuoid. MUSIC: Edward German. MUSICAL DIRECTOR: Adolf Schmid. PAGENTRY: Louis N. Parker. STAGE MANAGER: Cecil King. ASSOCIATE STAGE MANAGER: Stanley Bell.

NOTE: Although Claude Rains has been credited elsewhere as assistant stage manager for this production of *Henry VIII*, his name is not included in the original program.

1911

THE GODS OF THE MOUNTAIN
A play in one act by Lord Dunsany. HAYMARKET THEATRE, London, June 1–July 14 (37 performances). LICENSEE AND MANAGER: Frederick Harrison. PRODUCER: Norman Page. DIRECTOR: Herbert Trench. SCENERY: William Clarkson, L.&.H. Nathan, Miss Pitcher. LIGHTING: J. Digby. MUSIC: Norman O'Neill. STAGE MANAGER: Charles La Trobe.

CAST: *Oogno* E. A. Warburton; *Thahn* Reginald Owen/Claude Rains; *Ulf* H. R. Hignett; *Agmar* Charles V. France; *Thief* Lawrence Hanray; *Mlan* R. P. Lamb; *Oorander* G. Dickson-Kenwin; *Akmos* Ernest Graham; *Slag* Charles Maude; *Illanaun* Grendon Bentley; *Báshara* F. G. Clinton; *Thulek* G. Carr; *Thoharmas* Kenneth Dennys; *Haz* B. Hatton Sinclair; *Theedes* A. Jones; *Ackarnees* Norman Page; *Dromedary Man* W. Black; *Lirra* Muriel Lake/Anne Carew; *Eselunza* E. Risdon; *Thonion Alára* V. Whitaker; *Ylax* M. Ronsard; *Nennek of the Meadows* Enid Rose; *Others* E. Lyall Swete, A. Webster, K. Black, H. Cooper, E. Leverett, G. Wilkinson, J. O'Brien.

THE BLUE BIRD
A fantasy in six acts by Maurice Maeterlinck. Australian tour, Melbourne and Sydney. PRODUCER: Harley Granville-Barker. STAGE MANAGER: Claude Rains.

followed by:
YOU NEVER CAN TELL
A play in four acts by George Bernard Shaw. Australian tour, Sydney. PRODUCER: Harley Granville-Barker. STAGE MANAGER: Claude Rains (who also acted the role of Bohun).

NOTE: *You Never Can Tell* was substituted for Maeterlinck when *The Blue Bird* failed to repeat its Melbourne success with Sydney audiences.

1911–1912

THE BLUE BIRD
A fantasy in six acts by Maurice Maeterlinck and Norman O'Neill (music), translated by Alexander Teixeira de Mattos. QUEEN'S THEATRE, London, December 26–February 3 (70 performances). PRODUCER: E. Lyle Swete. SCENIC DESIGN: F. Cayley Robinson, S. H. Sime, Joseph Harker. COSTUME DE-

SIGN: F. Cayley Robinson. MUSICAL DIRECTOR: Norman O'Neill. STAGE MANAGER: Charles La Trobe. ASSISTANT STAGE MANAGER: Claude Rains.

NOTE: The connection, if any, between this production and Granville-Barker's Australian tour version is unclear, except for Rains's involvement in them both. The settings are identical to the production staged at the Haymarket Theatre in 1909 and 1910.

1912

THE GOLDEN DOOM
A play in one act by Lord Dunsany. HAYMARKET THEATRE, London, November 19–December 12 (28 performances). PRODUCER: E. Lyle Swete. DESIGN: S. H. Sime. SCENERY: Joseph Harker. COSTUMES: L. & H. Nathan. STAGE MANAGER: Charles La Trobe. ASSISTANT STAGE MANAGER: Claude Rains.

CAST: *First Sentry* Allan Jeayes; *Stranger* Leonard E. Notcutt; *Chamberlain* E. Lyall Swete; *First Prophet* Ralph Hutton; *Chief Prophet* Ewan Brook; *Second Sentry* G. Dickson-Kenwin; *Boy* Master Eric Rae; *King* Henry Hargreaves; *Second Prophet* Frank Ridley; *Spies* Claude Rains (also assistant stage manager), Gerald Jerome, Cyril Hardingham; *Attendants* M. Brier, R. Lewis, C. Miles, G. Playford; *Girl* Eileen Esler/Dorothy Manville.

THE WALDIES
A play in four acts by G. J. Hamien. HAYMARKET THEATRE, London, December 8–9 (2 performances). PRODUCER/DIRECTOR: Norman Page, for the Incorporated Stage Society. STAGE MANAGER: Claude Rains.

1912–1913

THE YOUNGER GENERATION
A comedy in three acts by Stanley Houghton. HAYMARKET THEATRE, London, November 19–February 8; DUKE OF YORK'S THEATRE, London, February 10–March 3 (131 performances). LICENSEE AND MANAGER: Frederick Harrison. STAGE MANAGER: Charles La Trobe. ASSISTANT STAGE MANAGER: Claude Rains. MUSICAL DIRECTOR: Norman O'Neill.

1913

THE PRETENDERS
An historical drama in five acts by Henrik Ibsen (original title: *Kongsemnerne*), translated by William Archer. HAYMARKET THEATRE, London, February

13–March 15 (35 performances). LICENSEE AND MANAGER: Frederick Harrison. PRODUCER: E. Lyall Swete. SCENIC DESIGN: S. H. Sime and Joseph Harker; COSTUMES: S. H. Sime. STAGE MANAGER: Charles La Trobe. ASSISTANT STAGE MANAGER: Claude Rains.

COMTESSE MITZI
A comedy in one act by H. A. Hertz (translation of Arthur Schnitzler's *Komtesse Mitzi*). ALDWYCH THEATRE, London, March 9–10 (2 performances). PRODUCER: Clifford Brooks, for the Incorporated Stage Society. STAGE MANAGER: Claude Rains.

Performed on a double bill with:
THE GREEN COCKATOO
A "grotesque" in one act by Penelope Wheeler (translation of Arthur Schnitzler's *Der grüne kakadu*). ALDWYCH THEATRE, London, March 9–10 (2 performances). PRODUCER: Norman Page, for the Incorporated Stage Society. STAGE MANAGER: Claude Rains.

CAST: *Grasset* Claude Rains; *Prosper* Luke Forster; *Grain* Norman Page; *Jules* Herbert Alexander; *François, Vicomte de Nogeant* Ralph W. Hutton; *Albin, Chevalier de la Trémouille* P. Perceval Clark; *Emile, Duc de Cadignan* H. B. Waring; *Marquis de Lansac* G. Dickson-Kenwin; *Stephen* Eric Lugg; *Lebrêt* Leonard E. Notcutt; *Inspector of Police* Allan Jeayes; *Scaevola* Benedict Butler; *Henri* Leon Quartermaine; *Guillaume* Ewan Brooke; *Rollin* Terence O'Brien; *Bathazar* Bernard Crosby; *Maurice* Charles A. Straite; *Léocadie* Caroline Bayley; *Michette* Norah Beresford; *Flipotte* Hilda Davies; *Séverine* Violet Farebrother; *Georgette* Joan Bennett.

TYPHOON
A play in four acts by Laurence Irving, from Melchior Lengyel's *Taifun*. HAYMARKET THEATRE, London, April 2–May 23; QUEEN'S THEATRE, London, April 26–July 12; GLOBE THEATRE, London, July 14–Sept 6; NEW THEATRE, London, September 8–27 (202 performances). LICENSEE AND MANAGER: Frederick Harrison. PRODUCERS: Laurence Irving, A. S. Tsubouchi, Yoshio Markino. SCENERY: Joseph Harker. COSTUMES: Doeuillet Ltd., Debenham and Freebody, L. & H. Nathan. STAGE MANAGER: Charles La Trobe. ASSISTANT STAGE MANAGER: Claude Rains. MUSICAL DIRECTOR: Norman O'Neill.

CAST: *Baron Yoshikawa* Robin Shiells; *Takeramo* Laurence Irving; *Kobayashi* Henry Crocker; *Omayi* Claude Rains/Basil Sydney; *Kitamaru* Azooma Sheko; *Ya-*

moshi Charles Terric; *Hironari* Leon M. Lion/Wilfred Fletcher; *Amamari* Arthur Stanley/Wenlock Brown; *Miyake* S. Isogai /R. Matsuyama; *Tanaka* A. Tsuchiya; *Yoshino* K. Sumoge; *Yotomo* George Carr; *Georges* H. O. Nicholson/Frank Collins; *Reinard-Beinsky* Leon Quartermaine/Bertram Forsyth; *Professor Dupont* E. Lyle Swete/Herbert Heweson/H. Appleby; *Benoit* Arthur Whitby/Murray Carson; *Marchland* Allan Jeayes/Alfred Sangster; *Simon* Herbert Heweson/H. Appleby; *Usher* Stuart Musgrove; *Therese* Marjorie Waterlow/Ruth Bower/Winifred Turner; *Hélène* Mabel Hackney.

1913–1914

WITHIN THE LAW
A play in four acts by Frederick Fenn and Arthur Wimperis, adapted from Bayard Veiller. HAYMARKET THEATRE, London, May 24–May 8 (426 performances). LICENSEE AND MANAGER: Frederick Harrison. PRODUCER: Herbert Tree. SCENERY: R. C. McCleery, Joseph Harker. COSTUMES: Madame Raymond; STAGE MANAGER: Charles La Trobe. ASSISTANT STAGE MANAGER: Claude Rains. MUSICAL DIRECTOR: Norman O'Neill.

with:
A DEAR LITTLE WIFE
A comedy in one act by Gerald Dunn. HAYMARKET THEATRE, London, June 6–May 8 (412 performances). STAGE MANAGER: Charles La Trobe. ASSISTANT STAGE MANAGER: Claude Rains. LICENSEE AND MANAGER: Frederick Harrison. SCENERY: Joseph Harker. COSTUMES: L. & H. Nathan; MUSICAL DIRECTOR: Norman O'Neill.

CAST: *Hagiyama* Leon M. Lion; *Takejiro* Douglas Gordon/Claude Rains/George Owen; *Sugihara* Muriel Pope/Nellie Dale/Nellie Briercliffe.

NOTE: *A Dear Little Wife* joined *Within the Law* as a curtain-raiser on June 6.

1915

ANDROCLES AND THE LION
A comedy by George Bernard Shaw. WALLACK'S THEATRE, New York, January 27. PRODUCER: Harley Granville-Barker. SCENIC DESIGN: Albert Rothenstein. TOUR MANAGER: Claude Rains.

CAST: *Editor* Eric Blind; *Lentulus* Horace Braham; *Ferrovious* Lionel Braham; *Call-Boy* Cecil Cameron; *Megaera* Kate Carolyn; *Centurion* Ernest Cossart; *Lion* Phil Dwyer; *Secutor* J. H. Green; *Retiarius* Gerald Hamer; *Androcles* O. P. Heggie; *Menagerie Keeper* Edgar Kent; *Spintho* Arnold Lucy (understudy/replacement:

Claude Rains); *Captain* Ian McLaren; *Ox-Driver* Hugh MacRae; *Lavinia* Lillah McCarthy; *Ensemble* Walter Creighton and Wright Kramer.

NOTE: Granville-Barker's repertory season at Wallack's also included *The Man Who Married a Dumb Wife* by Anatole France and Shakespeare's *A Midsummer Night's Dream*, both prominently featuring Rains's wife, Isabel Jeans.

IPHIGENIA IN TAURUS
By Euripedes, translated by Gilbert Murray. YALE BOWL, New Haven, Connecticut, May 15; HARVARD STADIUM, Cambridge, Massachusetts, May 18; PIPING ROCK COUNTRY CLUB, Long Island, circa May 25; CITY UNIVERSITY OF NEW YORK, May 31 and June 5; UNIVERSITY OF PENNSYLVANIA, Philadelphia, June 8; PRINCETON UNIVERSITY, Princeton, New Jersey, June 11. PRODUCERS/DIRECTORS: Lillah McCarthy, Harley Granville-Barker. MUSIC: David Stanley Smith. TOUR MANAGER: Claude Rains.

CAST: *Iphigenia* Lillah McCarthy; *Orestes* Ian Maclaren; *Pylades* Leonard Willey; *Thoas* Lionel Braham; *Herdsman* Claude Rains; *Messenger* Philip Merivale; *Pallas Athene* Mary Forbes; *Leader of the chorus* Alma Kruger.

REVIEW: "Of the two messenger speeches, Mr. Rains did rather better with his than Mr. Merivale. Mr. Rains bounced a good deal, but the fire was there. Mr. Merivale was apparently unstrung by the effect of his costume on the audience." (*New York Times*, May 16, 1915)

Performed in repertory with:
THE TROJAN WOMEN
By Euripedes, translated by Gilbert Murray. HARVARD STADIUM, Cambridge, Massachusetts, May 19; CITY UNIVERSITY OF NEW YORK, New York, 29 May and June 2, UNIVERSITY OF PENNSYLVANIA, Philadelphia, June 9; PRINCETON UNIVERSITY, Princeton, New Jersey, June 12. PRODUCERS/DIRECTORS: Lillah McCarthy, Harley Granville-Barker. MUSIC: David Stanley Smith. TOUR MANAGER: Claude Rains.

NOTE: Rains's wife, Isabel Jeans, was a chorus member in both productions.

1919–1920

REPARATION
A drama in three acts by Leo Tolstoy (translation of *The Live Corpse* by Mr. and Mrs. Aylmer Maude). ST. JAMES'S THEATRE, London, September 26–January 1 (114 performances). MANAGERS: Gilbert Miller and Henry Ainley. PRO-

191

DUCER: Stanley Bell. SCENERY: J. A. Fraser (from the Moscow Art Theatre's original settings). COSTUMES: Henriette, B. J. Simmons & Co. MUSIC: Norman O'Neill. STAGE MANAGER: Claude Rains. ASSISTANT STAGE MANAGER: George Ayre.

CAST: *Anna Pavlovna* Agnes Thomas; *Alexandra* Meggie Albanesi; *Victor Karenin* E. Ion Swinley; *Lisa Protasov* Athene Seyler; *Ivan Petrovitch* Claude Rains; *Feyda* Henry Ainley; *Masha* Alice Moffat; *Gipsy Leader* Anna Filipova; *Ivan Makarovich* Henry Morrell; *Natasia Ivanovna* Dora Gregory; *Prince Sergius Abreskov* Otho Stuart; *Anna Karenin* Marion Terry; *Voznesensky* Julian Courtville; *Petushkov* Sydney Bland; *Artemeyev* Ernest Milton; *Magistrate* Howard Rose; *Policeman* Leonard Sickert; *Officer* Richard Greenville; *Nurse* Anna Russell; *Maid* Dulcie Benson.

UNCLE NED
A comedy in four acts by Douglas Murray. LYCEUM THEATRE, Sheffield, March 24; ST. JAMES'S THEATRE, London, March 27–April 8 (49 performances). MANAGERS: Gilbert Miller, Henry Ainley. LICENSEE: Gilbert Miller. COSTUMES: Henriette, Hanan-Gingell Shoe Co. FURNITURE: M. Harris & Sons. MUSICAL DIRECTOR: J. H. Squire. STAGE MANAGER: Claude Rains.

CAST: *Edward Graham* Henry Ainley; *Henderson Burke* G. Lawford Davidson; *Dawkins* G. W. Anson; *Sir Robert Graham* Randle Ayrton; *Mears* Claude Rains/ Ernest Digges; *Gibson* Ernest Digges/Robert Russell; *Maid* Phyllis McTavish; *Miss Manning* Irene Rooke; *Gypsy Graham* Edna Best/Phyllis McTavish.

NOTE: A supporting role in *Uncle Ned* on tour in Sheffield in the spring of 1919 marked Rains's return to the stage after being wounded in action during World War I. *Uncle Ned* was revived by the same company and cast in March 1920.

1920

JULIUS CAESAR
A play in three acts by William Shakespeare. ST. JAMES'S THEATRE, London, January 9–March 20 (83 performances). PRODUCER: Stanley Bell. STAGE MANAGER: Claude Rains.

CAST: *Julius Caesar* Clifton Boyne; *Marcus Antonius* Henry Ainley; *Popilius Lena, Varro* Sydney Bland; *Cassius* Milton Rosmer; *Trebonius* Howard Rose; *Decius Brutus* Ernest Milton; *Cinna, Claudius* Julian Courtville; *Lucius* George Hamilton/ Norman Walter; *Servant to Caesar* Stanley Vine; *Citizen, Ligarius, Pindarus* Henry Morrell; *Octavius Caesar* Henry C. Hewitt; *Publius* Leonard Sickert; *Marcus Bru-*

Appendix

tus Basil Gill; *Casca* Claude Rains; *Metellus Cimber* Henry Oscar; *Artemidorus* Ernest Digges; *Servant to Octavius Caesar* Arthur Keane; *Calpurnia* Esmé Beringer; *Portia* Lilian Brathwaite.

THE GOVERNMENT INSPECTOR
A comedy by Nikolai Gogol, translated by T. H. Hall. DUKE OF YORK'S THEATRE, London, April 13–May 8 (30 performances). PRODUCER: Theodore Komisarjevsky.

CAST: *Anton Anton'itch (the Governor)* Maurice Moscovitch; *Anna Andreyevna (his Wife)* Mary Grey; *Marya Antonovna (his Daughter)* Jane Amstel; *Lyapkin-Tyapkin* Edwin Greenwood; *Spyokin* Reginald Bach; *Bobtchinski (Landed Proprietor)* George Desmond; *Dobtchinski (Landed Proprietor)* Alec Thompson; *Ossip* Naylor Grimson; *Korobkin, Waiter at the Hotel* Alfred Wilde; *Police Inspector* William Home; *Second Policeman, Abdoolin (a Merchant)* Lionel Fridjohn; *First Policeman, Gendarme, Second Merchant* Matthew Forsyth; *Third Merchant* W. Herbert; *Klopoff* Leyton Cancellor; *Klopoff's Wife* Mignon O'Doherty; *Zemlyanika (Charity Commissioner)* Roy Byford; *Klestakoff* Claude Rains; *Hueber (District Doctor), Rastakoffski* E. W. Wilson; *Third Policeman* R. Forsyth; *Sergeant's Wife* Chris Castor; *Fitter's Wife* Florence Buckton; *Mishka (Governor's manservant)* Reginald Denham; *Avdotya (Governor's maidservant)* Gwen Evans.

THE JEST
A melodrama in four acts by C. B. Fernald, adapted from *La cena delle buffe* by Sem Benelli. WIMBLEDON THEATRE, London; opened August 9. PRODUCER: Stanley Bell. DIRECTOR: Henry Ainley.

CAST: *Neri* Henry Ainley; *Giannetto* Claude Rains; *Fazio* Murray Kinnell; *Gabriello* Stanley Vine; *Calandra* H. C. Hewitt; *Trinca* Alexander Sarner; *Tornaquinci* Howard Rose; *Cintia* Florence Buckton; *Fiamatta* Henrietta Goodwin; *Laldomine* Lydia Andre; *Lisabetta* Mrs. Ainley; *Ginerva* Marie Hemingway.

REVIEWS: "The performance of Mr. Claude Rains as the Poet was exceptionally good. There was a grave danger of making the character such an utter coward that the audience would lose all interest in his troubles, but Mr. Rains avoided this very effectively. He had some difficult scenes to play, notably that in which he is telling the mistress the deception he has practiced on her. He did it with such skill that fully justified those who believed that Mr. Rains's performance as Casca [in *Julius Caesar*] was but the beginning of much good work. Miss Marie Hemingway looked positively charming as the lady who was loved by all the protagonists in turn, though she has had much more sympathetic parts to play."(*The*

Times, August 10, 1920) Another reviewer noted: "Histrionically, this farrago of fury will be memorable for the sinister figure drawn by Mr. Claude Rains as Giannetto. Mr. Rains gives a powerful portrayal of the vengeful poet. The character has qualities of introspection to which the character gives admirable expression. Mr. Rains will probably go far in his profession." Another praised Rains's "fascinating performance . . . winning his ends by devilish subtlety, as if all the doubtful morals and amazing diplomacy of Machiavelli were embodied again. Mr. Rains, in fact, was the most Italian of the cast—his personal appearance helped him." (Rains scrapbook)

1921

DANIEL

A drama by Louis Verneuil and Georges Berr; English adpatation by Sybil Harris. ST. JAMES'S THEATRE, London, January 15–February 26 (45 performances). PRODUCER: Stanley Bell.

CAST: *Albert Arnault* Lyn Harding; *Doctor* C. Aubrey Smith; *Jerome* George Elton; *Etienne Bourdin* Henry Oscar; *Daniel Arnault* Claude Rains; *Maurice Granger* Leslie Faber/Walter Pearce; *Francois* Garrett Hollick; *Marguerite Arnault* Alexandra Carlisle; *Mme. Girard* Edith Evans; *Suzanne Girard* Alice Moffat; *Red-Headed Girl* Gladys Gray.

REVIEW: "[Rains] is seated, immovable, his legs enveloped by a rug, amid weird Oriental ornaments and idols. Indeed, in his black kimono, he looks rather like an Oriental idol himself, his face a dead white, his eyes black-rimmed, a *macabre* figure—what the vulgar call a living corpse. He has a sick smile, his utterance is tremulous, his movements are a mere languid shivering. Evidently he has not long to live, and our curiosity is excited as to what he is going to do before the end comes. As we shall see, he goes a good deal." (*The Times*, January 17, 1921)

POLLY WITH A PAST

A comedy by George Middleton and Guy Bolton. ST. JAMES'S THEATRE, London, March 2–June 4 (110 performances). PRODUCER: Stanley Bell.

CAST: *Clay Collum* Noel Coward; *Harry Richardson* Henry Kendall; *Polly Shannon* Edna Best; *Rex Van Zile* Donald Calthrop; *Mrs. Davis* Helen Haye; *Myrtle Davis* Alice Moffat/Nancye Kenyon; *Stiles* Arthur Hatherton; *Mrs. Van Zile* Edith Evans; *Commodore "Bob" Barker* Paul Arthur; *Prentice Van Zile* C. Aubrey Smith/Robert Horton; *Parker* Nancye Kenyon; *Stranger* Claude Rains.

LEGION OF HONOUR
Historical drama by the Baroness Orczy, based on her novel *A Sheaf of Bluebells*. ALDWYCH THEATRE, London, August 24–September 10 (21 performances). PRODUCER: Edward Lytton Productions Ltd.

CAST: *Ronnay de Maurel* Basil Gill; *Comte de Puisaye* St. John Hamund; *Comte de Courson* William Lugg; *Laurent, Marquis de Mortain* Claude Rains; *Baron de Ritter* Ivan Berlyn; *Mattieu* G. Laverack Brown; *Mathurin* Fred Russell; *Paul Leroux* John F. Traynor; *Pierre Desprez* Charles F. Lloyd; *Gervais* Gerald Blake; *Marcel* Horn Conyers; *Jacques* Herbert Barrs; *Mme. La Marquise de Mortain* Mary Rorke; *Annette* Agnes Imlay; *Fernande de Courson* Gwendoline Hay.

1921–1922

WILL SHAKESPEARE
Historical drama/invention in four acts by Clemence Dane. SHAFTESBURY THEATRE, London, November 17–January 7 (62 performances). PRODUCER: Basil Dean.

CAST: *Will Shakespeare* Philip Merivale; *Henslowe* Arthur Whitby; *Kit Marlowe* Claude Rains; *Child Actor, Boy Master* Eric Spear; *Stage Hand, Shylock* Gilbert Ritchie; *Landlord, Clown* Ivor Barnard; *Secretary, Antony* Arthur Bawtree; *Othello* Herbert Young; *Prince Arthur* Master Eric Crosbie; *Hamlet* Neil Curtis; *King Lear* Fred Morgan; *Anne* Moyna Macgill; *Mrs. Hathaway* Mary Rorke; *Queen Elizabeth* Haidee Wright; *Mary Fitton* Mary Clare; *Lady-in Waiting* Joan Maclean/Nora Robinson; *Ophelia* Lennie Pride; *Desdemona* Gladys Jessel; *Queen Margaret* Flora Robson; *Rosalind* Phyllis Fabian; *Cleopatra* Mai Ashley; *Three Fates* Norah Robinson, Gladys Gray, Beatrice Smith; *Extras* Colin Ashdown, Mai Ashley, Ivor Barnard, Arthur Bawtree, James Bond, A. Coombs, Gladys Gray, C. Jackson, Gladys Jessel, Fred Morgan, E. Negus, Lennie Pride, Gilbert Ritchie, Flora Robson, Herbert Young, Masters Eric Spear, Eric Crosbie.

REVIEW: "[There is] one intensely dramatic moment, when, while Marlowe lies dead on the tavern bed, tipplers dance round his corpse thinking him asleep, and lift his body to make him share in their revels; but for all that it is merely a show exploiting great names and lending those names to a collection of puppets. The puppets, however, are equipped with sufficiently fine rhetoric and placed in sufficiently telling situations to afford scope for good acting. It is not Mr. Claude Rains's fault that not much is made out of Marlowe . . ." (*The Illustrated London News*, November 26, 1921)

1922

THE BAT

A mystery by Mary Roberts Rinehart and Avery Hopwood. ST. JAMES'S THE-ATRE, London, January 23–October 4 (327 performances). PRODUCER: Collin Kemper.

CAST: *Billy* Claude Rains/George Carr; *Anderson* Arthur Wontner/Allan Jeayes; *Richard Fleming* C. Stafford Dickens/William Kershaw; *Brooks* George Relph; *Dr. Wells* A. Scott-Gatty; *Reginald Beresford* Herbert Bolingbroke; *Unknown Man* Allan Jeayes/Howard Sturge; *Cornelia Van Gorder* Eva Moore; *Miss Dale Ogden* Nora Swinburne; *Lizzie* Drusilla Wills.

REVIEW: "A queer-looking, queer-speaking fellow . . . Mr. Claude Rains [makes] a most uncanny Japanese. . . . the audience last night were agreeably excited . . ." (*The Times*, January 25, 1922)

THE RUMOUR (A STUDY IN ORGANIZATION)

A play by C. K. Munro. GLOBE THEATRE, London, December 3–4 (2 performances). PRODUCER: Alan Wade and the Incorporated Stage Society.

CAST: *Ned* Gilbert Ritchie; *Hon. Algernon Moodie* Edmond Brion; *Mr. Lennard* A. S. Homewood; *Jones* Reginald Dance; *Smith* Alfred A. Harris; *Sir Arthur Cheston, Jackson* A. Caton Woodville; *Torino* Edmund Willard; *Deane* Harcourt Williams; *Prime Minister* Frederic Sargent; *La Rubia* Claude Rains; *Mons Raffanel* Milton Rosmer; *Sir George Darnell* Douglas Jeffries; *Sir Robert Mortimer* Fred Lewis; *Clergyman, Banker* Howard Rose; *Mr. Grange* Alfred Clark; *Luke* Henry Ford; *Konchak, General Moberly* A. Corney Grain; *Saintsbury, Burasto* Charles Hordern; *Walter* Charles Staite; *Jimmy* Arthur Harding; *Pooshpin, Old Sorestil, Expert Adviser* J. Leslie Frith; *Another Prizimian* Ronald Sinclair; *Laminok, Priest, Prime Minister's Secretary* John H. Moore; *Paro* J. Drew-Carran; *Kaprikan, Millard* Cyril Fairlie; *Checkram* Matthew Forsyth; *Chancellor of the Exchequer* P. Percival Clark; *Ruby* Edith Evans; *Aramya* Marget Yarde; *Lena Jackson* Elizabeth Arkell.

REVIEW: "It is a clever piece of satire swamped by political oratory . . . It was efficiently acted by a large cast, among whom Mr. Claude Rains, Mr. Milton Rosmer, Mr. Edmund Breon, Mr. Harcourt Williams, and Mr. Frederic Sanger were conspicuous." (*The Times*, December 6, 1922)

Appendix

1923

THE LOVE HABIT (A PIECE OF IMPERTINENCE)

Romantic comedy by Louis Verneuil, adapted from the French by Seymour Hicks. ROYALTY THEATRE, London, February 7–March 24 (53 performances). PRODUCER: Seymour Hicks.

CAST: *The Upsetter* Seymour Hicks; *Alphonse Du Bois* Dennis Eadie; *Max Quantro* Claude Rains; *Mathilde* Elizabeth Watson; *Julie* Frances Carson; *Rozanne Pom Pom* Alix Dorane.

REVIEW: "Neither Miss Alix Dorane as the light o' love, nor Mr. Claude Rains as her dancing partner, gets much opportunity of distinction. Indeed, the sole opportunity of the play is Mr. [Seymour] Hicks's. But that will entirely content the many admirers of this brilliant comedian." (*The Times*, April 3, 1923)

THE DOCTOR'S DILEMMA

A play by George Bernard Shaw. EVERYMAN THEATRE, London, April 2–April 28 (28 performances). PRODUCER: Norman Macdermott.

CAST: *Redpenny* Michael Sherbrooke; *Emmy* Esmé Hubbard; *Schutgmacher* Michael Sherbrooke; *Sir Patrick Cullen* Ivor Barnard; *Cutler Walpole* Reginald Dance; *Sir R. B. Bonnington* Brember Wills/Edward Rigby; *Blenkinson/Newspaper Man* Harold Scott; *Mrs. Dubidat* Cathleen Nesbitt; *Louis Dubidat* Claude Rains; *Minnie Tinwell* Madge Compton; *Mr. Danby* Thurlow Finn.

REVIEW: "Mr. Claude Rains makes Dubidat more robust a man than our own imagining of him, but his curious mingling of ingenuousness and guile, of satirical humour and childlike protest, gives light to the third act." (*The Times*, April 3, 1923)

THE INSECT PLAY (AND SO AD INFINITUM)

A play by Karel and Josef C. Capek in three acts and an epilogue, translated from the Czech by Paul Selver and freely adapted by Nigel Playfair and Clifford Bax. REGENT THEATRE, London, May 5–June 9 (42 performances). PRODUCER: Nigel Playfair.

CAST: *The Tramp* Edmund Willard; *Lepidoterist, Parasite, Chief Engineer* Claude Rains; *Otto* F. Kinsley Peile; *Felix* John Gielgud; *Victor, Robber Beetle* Algernon West; *Mr. Beetle, Woodcutter* A. Bromley-Davenport; *Ichneumon Fly, Inventor* Ivan Berlyn; *Mr. Cricket, Second Snail* Andred Leigh; *Blind Timekeeper, First Snail*

Geoffrey Wilkinson; *Second Engineer* Harvey Adams; *First Messenger* W. M. Norgate; *Second Messenger* Brandon Philp; *Signal Officer* R. Atholl Douglas; *Yellow Commander* Harvey Adams; *Boy* George Aylward; *Butterflies* Maurice Braddell, Brandon Philp, W. M. Norgate, Geoffrey Wincott,; *Clyytie, Country Woman* Ann Hyton; *Iris* Noelle Sonning; *Chrysalis* Joan Maude; *Mrs. Beetle, Flag Seller* Maire O'Neill; *Larva* Elsa Lanchester; *Mrs. Cricket* Angela Baddeley; *Girl* Alice Mason; *Butterflies* Elsa Lanchester, Margot Sieveking, Muriel Winstead *Mayflies* Margot Sieveking, Muriel Winstead, Noelle Sonning, Elsa Lanchester, Gwen Elphin, Angela Baddeley, Margot St. Leger.

REVIEW: "'Are we alive after all this satire?' cried Ben Johnson on a notable occasion, but at the Regent a more natural cry would be 'Are we awake?'" (*The Times*, May 7, 1923)

ROBERT E. LEE
Historical drama by John Drinkwater. REGENT THEATRE, London, June 20–September 22 (109 performances). PRODUCER: Nigel Playfair.

CAST: *Major Perrin* Harvey Adams/Atholl Douglas/Eric Lugg; *Orderly, Jefferson Davis' Secretary* Geoffrey Wilkinson; *General Scott* F. Kinsley Peile/Leo G. Carroll; *Robert E. Lee* Felix Aylmer; *Tom Buchanan* Tristan Rawson; *Ray Warrenton* Harold Anstruther; *David Peel* Claude Rains; *Duff Penner* Henry Caine; *John Stean* Atholl Douglas/Frank Martin; *Captain Mason* Atholl Douglas/Gerald Jerome; *General J. E. B. Stuart* Leo G. Carroll; *His Aide* Geoffrey Wincott; *Aide to General Lee* John Gielgud; *Sentry* Frank Martin; *Captain Udall* Maurice Braddell/Basil Cunard; *General "Stonewall" Jackson* Edmund Willard/Stephen T. Ewart; *Colonel Hewitt* Harvey Adams/Atholl Douglas/J. Adrian Byrne; *Jefferson Davis* Gordon Harker; *Girl* Alice Mason/Gwen Elphin; *Elizabeth* Anne Hyton; *Mrs. Stean* Margot Sieveking/Molly Fairfax; *Mrs. Meadows* Natalie Lynn; *Ladies* Molly Fairfax, Gwen Elphin, Muriel Swinstead, Oriel Ross.

REVIEW: "Mr. Claude Rains is good as the philosopher . . ." (*The Times*, June 21, 1923)

1923–1924

GOOD LUCK
A sporting drama by Seymour Hicks and Ian Hay. DRURY LANE THEATRE, London, September 27–May 10 (260 performances). PRODUCER: Arthur Collins.

CAST: *Captain Travers* Jevan Brandon-Thomas/Randolph McLeod/Henry Thompson; *Honorable Hughie Weldon* Alan Lister/E. Watts Phillips; *Strusson* Sydney Benson;

Appendix

Grieg Augustus Bowerman; *D'Arcy Bristowe* Julian Royce; *Derek Vale, Earl of Trenton* Claude Rains; *Reverend Godfrey Blount* Henry Hallatt/Leonard Ashdowne; *Mr. Maloney* Arthur Mack; *Sir Anthony Wayne* Langhorne Burton; *Leo Swinburne* Edmund Gwenn; *Lewis Harris* C. W. Somerset; *John Collett* Gordon Harker; *Sir Percy Ford* Arthur Treacher; *Belsey* Rothbury Evans; *First Warder* Leslie Nelson Clare; *Second Warder* Stanley Pearce; *Third Warder* G. Aubyn Bourne; *Governor of Prison* John Keating; *Old Convict* Evan Berry; *First Fisherman* Charles Cecil/Fred May; *Second Fisherman* Norman Ash/Harry Paxton; *Armstrong* Bob Cornell; *Tom Treece* Henry Bonner; *Lord Anglin* William Forrest/Leonard Ashdowne/Walter Durden; *Convict 39* Leonard Ashdowne; *Holden* Wilson Gunning; *Convict 56* George Butler; *Bates* Jack Stephens; *Silas Eldred* Claude Allister; *Quartermaster* George Aubyn; *Dick Frampton* George Wilson; *Sir James Gregory* Andrew Calvert/James Rothbury; *Honorable Jane Ambledon* Kathlyn Clifford; *Vivi Carmichael* Edna Bellonini; *Honorable Mary Carstairs* Joan Maude/Phyllis Bellonini; *Honorable Anne Belben* Carlito Ackroyd/Nora Edwards; *Lady Larkhall* Vivienne Whitaker; *Lady Patricia Wolseley* Ellis Jeffreys; *Rose Collett* Dorothy Overend; *Lady Angela Vale* Joyce Carey/Violet Graham/Olwen Roose; *Wife of Convict 39* Gladys Erskine; *Mrs. Eldred* Dora Slade.

REVIEW: "Mr. Rains contrives to extract a good deal of pathos from a thankless part." (*The Times*, September 28, 1923)

1924

THE MAN OF DESTINY
A play in one act by George Bernard Shaw. EVERYMAN THEATRE, London, June 11–June 23 and August 27–September 10 (28 performances). PRODUCER/DIRECTOR: Norman MacDermott.

CAST: *Napoleon* Claude Rains; *Giuseppe* Aubrey Mather; *Lieutenant* Wilfrid Seagram; *Strange Lady* Jeanne de Casalis.

REVIEW: "Mr. Claude Rains's Napoleon is a man to laugh at but not a fool to despise." (*The Times*, June 12, 1924)

GETTING MARRIED
A play by George Bernard Shaw. EVERYMAN THEATRE, London, July 9–August 9 (33 performances). PRODUCER/DIRECTOR: Norman MacDermott.

CAST: *General Bridgenorth* Frederick Moyes; *Reginald Bridgenorth* Claude Allister; *Bishop of Chelsea* Campbell Gullan; *St. John Hotchkiss* Claude Rains; *Cecil Sykes* Harold Scott; *Soames (Father Anthony)* W. Earle Grey; *The Beadle* Thurlow Finn;

Mrs. Bridgenorth Irene Rooke; *Lesbia Grantham* Auriol Lee/Nell Carter; *Leo* Beatrix Thomson; *Edith Bridgenorth* Margot Sieveking/Grizelda Hervey; *Mrs. George Collins* Edith Evans.

REVIEW: "So very little was done for the actors by the author that a tremendous strain was put on them, if they were to fill out their parts, and this they were not always able to do. When Mr. Hotchkiss (Mr. Claude Rains) and Mrs. George Collins (Miss [Edith] Evans) were acting, the scene became much more lively and the stage properly occupied. At other times, we merely seemed to be assisting at a rather tedious tea-party." (*The Nation & Atheneum*, July 19, 1924)

LOW TIDE
A play by Ernest George. EVERYMAN THEATRE, London, August 12, 1924. PRODUCER: Norman MacDermott.

CAST: *Pat Donovan* Claude Rains; *Nora Bailey* Ethel Coleridge; *Mary Donovan* Olive Sloane; *Dan Donovan* Ivor Barnard; *Joe Briggs* Gordon Harker; *A Policeman* Aubrey Mather; *Father Doyle* Granville Darling; *Detective* Thurlow Finn.

REVIEW: "Mr. Claude Rains mixes suavity and suspicion with excellent judgement." (*The Times*, August 13, 1924)

THE DEVIL'S DISCIPLE
A melodrama in three acts by George Bernard Shaw. EVERYMAN THEATRE, London, September 24–October 18 (26 performances). PRODUCER/DIRECTOR: Norman MacDermott.

CAST: *Mrs. Dudgeon* Cicely Oates; *Essie* Elizabeth Arkell; *Christopher Dudgeon* Harold Scott; *The Reverend Anthony Anderson* Campbell Gullan/Michael Hogan; *Judith Anderson* Hazel Jones; *Lawyer Hawkins* Ivor Barnard; *Uncle William, A Sergeant* Aubrey Mather; *Uncle Titus* C. J. Barber; *Richard Dudgeon* Claude Rains; *Major Swindon* Frederick Moyes; *General Burgoyne* W. Earle Grey; *Chaplain Brudenell* Michael Hogan/Russell Sedgwick; *Extras* E. Doddington, E. Dowson, L. Harding, A. McCulloch, Jabez Messenger, W. McOwan, S. M. Dauncey, B. Cochran-Carr, D. B. Baxter, R. Fair, E. Rose, R. Sedgwick, A. H. Doddington, J. E. Doddington, Ursula Spicer.

REVIEW: "Mr. Claude Rains rightly made no attempt to suggest any reason for Dick's sacrificing of himself than that Dick had an overwhelming sense of the theatre—which is in fact a human as well as a theatrical reason." (*The Times*, September 25, 1924)

MISALLIANCE

A "debate in one sitting" by George Bernard Shaw. EVERYMAN THEATRE, London, October 27–November 8 (14 performances). PRODUCER/DIRECTOR: Norman MacDermott.

CAST: *Johnny Tarleton* Frank Vosper; *Bentley Summerhays* Ivor Bernard; *Hypatia Tarleton* Leah Bateman; *Mrs. Tarleton* Margaret Yarde; *Lord Summerhays* Felix Aylmer; *Mr. Tarleton* Alfred Clark; *Joey Percival* Claude Rains; *Lina Szczepanowska* Dorothy Green; *The Man* Harold Scott.

1924–1925

THE PHILANDERER

A comedy in four acts by George Bernard Shaw. EVERYMAN THEATRE, London, December 26–January 10 (18 performances). PRODUCERS: Norman MacDermott and Milton Rosmer. DIRECTOR: Norman MacDermott.

CAST: *Leonard Charteris* Claude Rains; *Joseph Cuthbertson* Fred O'Donovan; *Colonel Daniel Craven* Stanley Drewitt; *Dr. Paramore* Felix Aylmer; *Page* George Walker; *Sylvia Craven* Nadine March; *Julia Craven* Dorothy Massingham; *Grace Tanfield* Cecily Byrne.

1925

GUILTY SOULS

A four-act drama by Robert Nichols. RADA THEATRE, London, dates undetermined. PRODUCER: The Three Hundred Club.

CAST: *Oswald Bentley* Claude Rains; other players included Ivor Barnard, Ernest Milton, Muriel Pratt, Stanley Lathbury, and Dorothy Holmes-Gore.

HOME AFFAIRS

A comedy in four acts by Ladislas Fodor; English version by Norman MacDermott. EVERYMAN THEATRE, London, January 20–February 7 (20 performances). PRODUCER: Norman MacDermott.

CAST: *Justin* Frederick Moyes; *Adolphe, Baron Martin* Harold B. Meade; *Brigitte* Claire Keep; *Lionel d'Avencourt* Claude Rains; *Susanne* Hilda Bayler *Jacques Morrell* Felix Aylmer; *Duvert* Mervyn Johns; *Poulin* Andrew Wight; *Margot Latreux* Nadine March; *Lucien Tirlemont* Lauderdale Maitland; *Dechamps* George Merritt; *Robert* Charles Thomas; *Adrienne* Elizabeth Arkell/Chris Castor; *Vaubert* William Bradford.

REVIEWS: "Mr. Claude Rains acted the husband with great buoyancy and a fine light-hearted sense of humor that fitted the part," wrote one critic. "Hilda Bayley looked so delicious as the wife that I envied Claud[e] Rains the frequent and passionate kisses he bestowed on her," wrote another reviewer. "It is not, however, jealousy which makes me say Rains was not altogether suited for the part. However, a fine actor is always worth watching, and Rains in undoubtedly a brilliant actor." (Unsourced clippings, Rains scrapbook)

THE RIVALS
A comedy in three acts by Richard Brinsley Sheridan. LYRIC, HAMMERSMITH THEATRE, London, March 5–May 23 (93 performances). PRODUCER: Nigel Playfair.

CAST: *Sir Anthony Absolute* Norman V. Norman; *Captain Absolute* Douglas Burbidge; *Faulkland* Claude Rains; *Acres* Nigel Playfair/Miles Malleson; *Sir Lucius O'Trigger* Guy Lefeuvre; *Fag* Geoffrey Wincott; *David* Miles Malleson/Alfred Harris; *Thomas* Scott Russell; *Mrs. Malaprop* Dorothy Green; *Julia* Isabel Jeans/Griselda Hervey; *Lydia Languish* Beatrix Thomson.

NOTE: According to John Gielgud, Rains's second wife, Marie Hemingway, joined the cast for at least part of the run, farcically bringing Rains's first three wives together in a single dressing room.

REVIEWS: J. B. Priestley would later recall Rains's interpretation of Faulkland in his memoir, *Particular Pleasures* (1975): "As a rule this neurotically jealous character is played as if he were rather a bore, clearly part of a sub-plot, but in this particular production, with Rains playing him, he dominated the piece" (p. 137). As one 1925 critic observed, "The most that any actor has aspired to in this part has been a decent failure; Mr. Rains has made it a blazing success." Another reviewer noted that Rains "almost burlesques the part; but he does it with such sincerity and depth of feeling as almost to turn the comedy to tragedy. Here is a man who is at once ridiculous and suffering agonies. You laugh immoderately, and end by laughing on the wrong side of the mouth. After all, you say to yourself, there are moments on the stage when acting is revealed as an Art really Fine. This is one of them." (Unsigned, unsourced reviews, Rains scrapbook)

SALOMY JANE
A play by Paul Armstrong, after a story by Bret Harte. QUEEN'S THEATRE, London, June 24–July 4 (11 performances). PRODUCER: Godfrey Tearle.

CAST: *Colonel Starbottle* Allan Jeayes; *Low* Eugene Leahy; *Yuba Bill* Tom Reynolds; *Willie Smith* Lewis Shaw; *Mary Ann Heath* Peggy Livesey; *Anna May Heath* Becky Woolf; *Salomy Jane Clay* Dorothy Seacombe; *Rufe Waters* Franklyn Bellamy; *Jack Marbury* Claude Rains; *Larrabee* Gordon Harker; *Madison Clay* H. St. Barbe West; *A Man* Godfrey Tearle; *Lize Heath* Miriam Lewes *Red Pete Heath* Edward O'Neill.

REVIEW: "A romantic play, as you see, with a company of English actors, all taking shots, with varying success, at the full and fruity American accent of 1860, and yep-yepping with, for all we know, authentic Californian gusto. . . . Miss Miriam Lewes, an accomplished actress too rarely seen of late on the London stage, made the best of a small part. So did Mr. Claude Rains." (*The Times*, June 25, 1925)

THE MAN FROM HONG KONG
A play in three acts by Mrs. Clifford Mills. QUEEN'S THEATRE, London, August 3–August 22 (24 performances). PRODUCER: Franklin Dyall.

CAST: *Li-Tong* Claude Rains; *Lo-San* Kenneth Kent; *Yen-Sen* H. R. Hignett; *The Man Behind the Screen* Arthur Goullet; *Chang Fu* J. J. Bartlett; *Lieutenant Anthony Travers, R.N.* Percy Hutchison; *Lieutenant Blake, R.N.* Patric Curwen; *Max* Eric Lugg; *Jocelyn Carsdale* Lawrence Ireland; *Owen Morrison* Ronald Sinclair; *Police Officer* Gerald Saffery; *Storker* Tom Redmond; *Bartly* Eleanor Street; *Mrs. Carsdale* Margaret Scudamore; *Vivien Carsdale* Mary Merrall; *Pearl Morrison* Madeline Seymour.

REVIEWS: "Mr. Claude Rains is a gifted actor, but Li-Tong is too much for him. He is neither satisfactorily English nor convincingly Chinese." (*Westminster Gazette*, undated clipping, Rains scrapbook) "It ought to be thrillingly romantic. In fact, it is at times an embarrassing joke." (*The Times*, August 4, 1925)

AND THAT'S THE TRUTH (IF YOU THINK IT IS)
A play by Luigi Pirandello, translated by Arthur Livingston. LYRIC, HAMMERSMITH THEATRE, London, September 17–October 10 (28 performances). PRODUCER: Nigel Playfair.

CAST: *Lamberto Laudisi* Nigel Playfair/Frederick Lloyd; *Signora Frola:* Nancy Price; *Signor Ponza* Claude Rains; *Signora Ponza* Dorothy Green; *Commendatore Agazzi* Guy Lefeuvre; *Amalia* Margaret Scudamore; *Dina* Paula Cinquevalli *Signor Sirelli* J. Leslie Frith; *Signora Sirelli* Dorothy Cheston *The Prefect* Frank Allanby; *An Inspector* Scott Russell; *Signora Cini* Minnie Blagden; *Signora Nenni* Mary Fenner; *A Manservant* Alfred Harris; *First Gentleman* Arnold Pilbeam; *Second Gentleman* Julian Browne.

REVIEWS: "The acting of this play is good all round, and in the chief two parts something more than good. It has gained from the fact that Pirandello's own company recently performed the play here in the original tongue, but neither Miss Nancy Price as Signora Frola nor Mr. Claude Rains as Ponza has been content merely to imitate an Italian prototype. Each has borrowed an outline, and filled in that outline in a manner entirely personal and original. Each scores a well-deserved and very great success." (*London Telegraph*, undated review, Rains scrapbook) "The acting as a whole struck me as better than Pirandello's own company gave of this play. Claude Rains as Signor Ponza, who pretends to be mad because his mother-in-law imagines he is, played with any amount of fire and energy." (Unsourced, undated review, Rains scrapbook) "Miss Nancy Price's Signora is tenderly pathetic and suggests the mental infirmity of the poor harassed woman much more successfully than her Italian predecessor's. Mr. Claude Rains, too, made a striking thing out of the lady's fellow martyr, Ponza." (*The Times*, September 26, 1925) Another reviewer wondered "Whether in the two leading roles Mr. Claude Rains' intensity is not a little too intense. And Miss Nancy Price's pathos a little too affecting for the balance of the play, Pirandellists must be left to decide." (*Illustrated London News*, September 26, 1925)

1925–1926

THE MADRAS HOUSE
A comedy in four acts by Harley Granville-Barker. AMBASSADORS THEATRE, London, November 30–February 27 (97 performances). PRODUCER: Harley Granville-Barker.

CAST: *Henry Huxtable* Aubrey Mather; *Katherine Huxtable* Frances Ivor; *Laura Huxtable* Christine Jensen; *Minnie Huxtable* Winifred Oughton; *Clara Huxtable* Susan Claughton/Valerie Wyngate; *Julia Huxtable* Ann Codrington; *Emma Huxtable* Marie Ney; *Jane Huxtable* Lois Heatherly; *Major Hippisly Thomas* David Hawthorne; *Philip Madras* Nicholas Hannen; *Jessica Madras* Cathleen Nesbitt; *Constantine Madras* Allan Jeayes; *Amelia Madras* Irene Rooke; *Eustace Perrin State* Claude Rains; *Marion Yates* Doris Lytton; *Mr. Brigstock* Stafford Hilliard; *Mrs. Brigstock* Mary Barton; *Miss Chancellor* Agnes Thomas; *Mr. Windlesham* Ernest Milton; *Mr. Belhaven* Robert Burnard; *Three Mannequins* Winifred Ashford, Helene Barr, Elyse King; *Maid at Denmark-Hill* Ruth Povah; *Maid at Dorset Square* Gladys Gaynor.

REVIEWS: "Mr. Claude Rains and Mr. Ernest Milton were other notables in the cast, though it seemed to me that the two last, as the American millionaire and as Mr. Windlesham, largely overdid it." (Unsourced, undated clipping, Rains scrapbook) "Mr. Claude Rains, made up rather like Augustine Birrell, was a little hampered by the American accent he had to affect." (Unsourced, undated clipping, Rains scrapbook) "Had it not been my particular fortune to have met a 'boss' American business man in the flesh, I should probably have accused Claude Rains of exaggeration. As it is, I can only affirm that in the limning of this type of individual no exaggeration is possible." (Reginald Hargreaves, undated clipping, Rains scrapbook)

1926

FROM MORN TO MIDNIGHT
A play in seven scenes by Georg Kaiser, translated from the German by Ashley Dukes. REGENT THEATRE, London, March 9–March 20 (15 performances). PRODUCER: Peter Godfrey.

CAST: *Bank Cashier* Claude Rains; *Clerk* A. C. Bute; *Boy* Stanley Greville; *Stout Gentleman, Third Jewish Gentleman* Nat Lewis; *Lady* Colette O'Niel; *Bank Manager* Arthur Layland; *Porter* C. E. Hart; *Son, Fourth Jewish Gentleman, First Salvation Army Soldier* Norman Shelley; *First Jewish Gentleman, Third Penitent* John Melville; *Second Jewish Gentleman, First Penitent* Neil Curtis; *Waiter, Third Salvation Army Officer* Henry Ford; *Policeman* H. E. Hutteroth; *Serving Maid, Wife, Second Penitent* Caroline Keith; *First Daughter, First Mask* Irene Barnett; *Second Daughter, Fourth Mask* Gillian Lind; *Salvation Lass* Ellen Pollock; *Second Mask, Second Salvation Army Soldier* Nancy Pawley; *Third Mask* Mildred Howard; *Mother, Salvation Army Officer* Betty Potter.

REVIEW: "The plain truth is, we found the play noisy, garish, and tiresome. Mr. Claude Rains shouted himself hoarse (and thereby gained the applause of the usual crowd which mistakes 'slogging' for cricket) with a zeal worthy of a better cause. He is a true artist, as playgoers well know, and it was disconcerting to find him on this occasion at a disadvantage compared to the unnamed actor who performed on the megaphone." (*The Times*, March 10, 1926)

THE GOVERNMENT INSPECTOR
A comedy in five acts by Nikolai Gogol, translated by Arthur A. Sykes. GAIETY THEATRE, London, May 22–June 19 (33 performances). PRODUCER: Theodore Komisarjevsky; PRODUCTION SUPERVISOR: Philip Ridgeway.

CAST: *Swistunov* Elliot Seabrooke; *Luka Lukich* Dan F. Roe; *Herr Hubner, Abdullin* Sidney Benson; *Bobchinski* Frederick Lord; *Ivan Kusmich* Neil Curtis; *Osip* Charles Laughton; *Waiter, Second Merchant* John C. Laurence; *Derzhimorda* James Lomas; *Ammos Fyodorovich* Stanley Drewitt; *Artemi Philipovich* Kimber Phillips; *Anton Antonovich* Alfred Clark; *Dobchinski* Jack Knight; *Ivan Alexandrovich Khlestakov* Claude Rains; *Third Merchant, Gendarme* Brian Watson; *Anna Andreyevna* Hilda Sims; *Avdotya* Jane Ellis; *Sergeant's Wife* Patricia O'Carroll; *Marya Antonovna* Stella Freeman; *Locksmith's Wife* May Agate.

BEFORE MEN'S EYES
A play by Ben Fleet and Clifford Pember. "Q" THEATRE, London, August.

CAST: *Hester Maynard* Irene Rooke; *Worcester* Herbert Leonard; *Monica Maynard* Gwen Ffrangcon-Davies; *Sir Henry Allison* Felix Aylmer; *Dr. Maynard* Claude Rains; *Maid* Molly Tyson.

REVIEWS: "Mr. Rains gives a very polished performance, and in spite of great temptation was just sufficiently restrained to make his part real." (Unsourced clipping, Rains scrapbook)

MADE IN HEAVEN
A play in three acts by Phyllis Morris. EVERYMAN THEATRE, London, October 5–16 (13 performances). PRODUCER: Raymond Massey.

CAST: *Martin Walmer* Claude Rains; *Olga Lessiter* Gwen Ffrangcon-Davies; *Jane Chute* Marda Vanne; *Martha Helmsgrove* Adrianne Allen; *Lawrence Saunders* Miles Mander; *Daniel Rourke* H. O. Nicholson.

NOTE: *Made in Heaven* marked Rains's last appearance on the London stage.

1926–1927

THE CONSTANT NYMPH
A play in three acts by Margaret Kennedy and Basil Dean, adapted from Kennedy's novel. SELWYN THEATRE, New York, December 9 (148 performances). PRODUCERS: George C. Tyler and Basil Dean. DIRECTOR: Basil Dean. SCENIC DESIGN: George W. Harris. INCIDENTAL MUSIC: Eugene Goosens.

CAST: *Lewis Dodd* Glenn Anders; *Linda Cowlard* Marion Warring-Manley; *Kate Sanger* Olive Reeves-Smith; *Katerina* Loretta Higgins; *Karl Trigoran* Paul Ker; *Paulina Sanger* Helen Chandler; *Teresa Sanger* Beatrix Thomson; *Jacob Birnbaum* Louis Sorin; *Antonia Sanger* Clara Sheffield; *Roberto* Claude Rains; *Susan* Gloria Kelly; *Florence Churchill* Lotus Robb; *Charles Churchill* Edward Emery; *Millicent Gregory* Jane Saville; *Sir Bartlemy Pugh* Sidney Paxton; *Peveril Leyburn* Leo Carrol; *Erda Leyburn* Olive Reeves-Smith; *Dr. Dawson* J. H. Brewer; *Lydia Mainwaring* Loretta Higgins; *Robert Mainwaring* Barry Jones; *An Usher* William Evans; *A Clerk* Harry Sothern; *A Fireman* Thomas Coffin Cooke; *Madame Maes* Katherine Stewart.

Appendix

NOTE: Following his appearances in *Lally* and *Out of the Sea* (see below), Rains assumed the lead role of Lewis Dodd opposite his wife for an east coast and midwestern tour.

1927

LALLY

A comedy in three acts by Henry Stillman. GREENWICH VILLAGE THEATRE, New York, February 8 (63 performances). PRODUCERS: Carl Reed, in association with Norman C. Stoneham. DIRECTOR: John D. Williams.

CAST: *Lally* Claude Rains; *Judith* Anne Morrison; *Isolde* Patricia Barclay; *Archibald Higgins* Gerald Hamer; *Izzyitch* Benedict McQuarrie; *Malvinski* Joseph Granby; *Felicia* Zolya Taima; *Cranston Thompson* Wallace Erskine; *Ronald Byrde* Reginald Malcolm; *Elsa* Eve Casanova; *Matilda* Kate McComb; *Aunt Elizabeth* Augusta Durgeon; *Giovanni* Owen Meech; *Angelique* Genevieve Dolaro; *Brunhilde* Helen Kingstead; *Stravinski* Robert Collier.

REVIEW: "The title role is portrayed by Claude Rains, a well-known British actor and the husband of Beatrice [sic] Thomson, the Tessa of 'The Constant Nymph.' As a matter of fact, he quit acting Roberto in that play for the present part. His reasons for doing so are probably to be found in the part itself, for it is a florid, showy impersonation, giving any actor abundant opportunity to create a character that at best is none too credible. . . . It is pretty difficult to indicate genius by flying into temperamental rages, by continually ordering other people to get out of the room, by registering perpetual abstraction, by playing plaintive tunes on a mechanical piano and by making frequent references to Debussy, Stravinsky, Strauss and the whole catalog of modern composers." (J. Brooks Atkinson, *New York Times*, February 9, 1927)

OUT OF THE SEA

A play in four acts by Don Marquis. ELTINGE FORTY-SECOND STREET THEATRE, New York, December 5 (16 performances). PRODUCER: George C. Tyler. DIRECTOR: Walter Hampden.

CAST: *Mark Tregesal* Lyn Harding; *John Marstin* Rollo Peters; *Isobel Tregesal* Beatrix Thomson; *Timbury* O. P. Heggie; *Arthur Logris* Claude Rains; *Hockin* Reginald Barlow; *Mrs. Hockin* Octavia Kenmore; *Coastguard Dunstan* Thomas Coffin Cooke; *Physician* Guy Cunningham; *First Fisherman* Richard Simson; *Second Fisherman* William Burnett.

REVIEW: "In addition to Mr. Harding and Mr. Peters, the rest of the cast in-

cluded Beatrix Thompson [*sic*] as Isobel, O. P. Heggie as an old salt, Claude
Rains as a Cornish gentleman, and the necessary footmen and servants. They all
smooth the plush-velvet of the drama as lovingly as they can." (J. Brooks Atkinson, *New York Times*, December 6, 1927)

1927–1928

AND SO TO BED
A play in three acts by James Bernard Fagan. SHUBERT THEATRE, New York,
November 9 (189 performances). PRODUCERS: James B. Fagan and Lee Shubert. DIRECTOR: James B. Fagan.

CAST: *Sue* Moon Carroll; *Boy to Pepys* Emlyn Williams; *Samuel Pepys* Wallace
Eddinger (replaced by Claude Rains); *Doll* Roberta Brown.

1928

NAPOLEON'S BARBER
A comedy in one act by Arthur Caesar. GREENWICH VILLAGE THEATRE,
New York; opened February 26. DIRECTOR: Douglas Wood.

CAST: *Napoleon's Barber* Douglas Wood; *Napoleon* Claude Rains; *The Barber's
Wife* Rolinda Bainbridge; *The Barber's Son* George Offerman, Jr.

NOTE: *Napoleon's Barber* shared a bill with an overture by the Greenwich Village
Orchestra, dramatic dances by "The Misses Marmein," and opera singer Myra
Sokolskaya, the live program being a curtain raiser for the feature film *Variety*
starring Emil Jannings.

MACBANE PLAYERS
PARSON'S THEATRE, Hartford, Connecticut, June–July. Claude Rains and
Beatrix Thomson (along with Leo G. Carroll) were featured in a four-play season
including *The Swan* by Ferenc Molnar, *Children of the Moon* by Martin Flavin,
Grumpy by Horace Hodges and T. Wigney Percyval, and the first American production of *The Government Inspector* by Nikolai Gogol.

NOTE: Rains returned to Hartford the following summer and presented an
informal evening of Shakespearean readings for Macbane company members
and invited guests.

VOLPONE
A comedy in three acts by Ben Johnson; adapted by Stefan Zweig, translated
by Ruth Langner. GUILD THEATRE, New York, April 9 (160 performances).

Appendix

PRODUCER: The Theatre Guild. DIRECTOR: Phillip Moeller. SETTINGS AND COSTUMES: Lee Simonson.

CAST: *Maid to Colomba* Mary Bell; *Judge* Morris Carnovsky; *Corvino* Ernest Cossart; *Corbaccio's Servant, Court Attendant* John C. Davis; *Volpone* Dudley Digges (understudied and replaced by Claude Rains); *Colomba* Margalo Gilmore; *Slave to Volpone* John Henry; *Voltore* Philip Leigh; *Mosca* Alfred Lunt; *Clerk of the Court* Sanford Meisner; *Leone* McKay Morris; *Second Groom* Mark Schweid; *Court Attendant* Vincent Sherman; *Corbaccio* Henry Travers; *Captain of the Sbirri* Albert van Dekker; *First Groom* Louis Veda; *Canina* Helen Westley.

NOTE: The Theatre Guild revived *Volpone* in 1930, with Sydney Greenstreet (later Rains's co-player in *Casablanca*) in the title role.

MARCO MILLIONS
A play in a prologue, three acts and two scenes by Eugene O'Neill. GUILD THEATRE, various locations. PRODUCER: The Theatre Guild. DIRECTOR: Rouben Mamoulian. SETTINGS: Lee Simonson. MUSICAL SUPERVISOR: Emerson Whithorne.

CAST: *Marco Polo* Alfred Lunt; *Kukachin* Margalo Gillmore; *Kublai, the Great Kaan* Baliol Holloway; *Chu-Yin* Dudley Digges (tour replacement: Claude Rains); *Maffeo* Ernest Cossart; *Nicolo* Henry Travers; *Teldado/Ghazan, Kaan of Persia* Morris Carnovsky; *Christian Traveler/Buddhist Priest/Paulo Loredano/Tartar Chronicler* Philip Leigh; *Magian Traveler/One Ali Brother/Confucian Priest* Mark Schweid; *Buddhist Traveler/Messenger from Persia/Buddhist Priest* Charles Romano; *Mahometan/General Bavan* Robert Barrat; *Corporal/Domincan Monk/Emmisary from Kublai* Albert Van Dekker; *Donata* Natalie Browning; *Knight Crusader* George Cotton; *A Papal Courier* Sanford Meisner; *Older Ali Brother/Boatswain/Moslem Priest* H. H. McCollum; *The Prostitute* Mary Blair; *A Dervish/An Indian Snake Charmer* John Henry; *Tartar Minstrel* William Edmonson.

NOTE: The Guild toured its 1928–1929 season to Baltimore, Boston, Cleveland, Pittsburgh, and Chicago. On tour with *Marco Millions*, Rains met his fourth wife, Frances Propper, who played a small role in the production.

1929

THE CAMEL THROUGH THE NEEDLE'S EYE
A play in three acts by Frantisek Langer; book adapted by Philip Moeller. MARTIN BECK THEATRE, New York, April 15 (196 performances). PRODUCER: The Theatre Guild. DIRECTOR: Philip Moeller.

CAST: *Mrs. Pesta* Helen Westley; *Pesta* Henry Travers; *Street Urchin* Norman Williams; *Susi* Miriam Hopkins; *Counselor Andrejs* Joseph Kilgour; *Director Bezchyba* Morris Carnovsky; *Marta Bojok* Catherine Calhoun-Doucet; *Alik Villim* Elliot Cabot; *Servant* Percy Warham; *Lilli Bojok* Mary Kennedy; *Joseph Villim* Claude Rains; *A Medical Student* Walter Scott; *Servant Girl* Rose Burdick.

REVIEW: "Claude Rains makes a capital figure of an irate continental father by the device of playing as if some one had shoved a ramrod down his back." (*New York Times*, April 16, 1929)

KARL AND ANNA

A play in four acts by Leonhard Frank; translated by Ruth Langner. GUILD THEATRE, New York, October 7 (49 performances). PRODUCER: The Theatre Guild. DIRECTOR: Philip Moeller. SETTINGS: Jo Mielziner.

CAST: *Guard* Charles C. Leatherbee; *Karl* Otto Kruger; *Richard* Frank Conroy; *First Prisoner* Claude Rains; *Second Prisoner* Philip Leigh; *Sister's Husband* Herbert J. Biberman; *Another Guard* Robert Norton; *Marie* Ruth Hammond; *Anne* Alice Brady; *Marie's Sister* Gale Sondergaard; *Sister's Husband* Larry Fletcher; *People in the surrounding action* Lionel Stander, Helen Gunther, Laura Straub.

1929–1930

THE GAME OF LOVE AND DEATH

A play in three acts by Romain Rolland, translated by Eleanor Stimson Brooks. GUILD THEATRE, New York, November 25, 1929 (48 performances). PRODUCER: The Theatre Guild. DIRECTOR: Rouben Mamoulian. SETTINGS AND COSTUMES: Aline Bernstein.

CAST: *Sophie de Courvoisier* Alice Brady; *Claude Vallée* Otto Kruger; *Jérôme de Courvoisier* Frank Conroy; *Lazare Carnot* Claude Rains; *Denis Bayot* Edward Rigley; *Lodoiska Carizier* Laura Straub; *Chloris Soucy* Anita Fugazy; *Crapart* Charles Henderson; *Horace Bouchet* Allan Willey; *Soldiers and Citizens* Robert Norton, William Earle, Lizbeth Kennedy, Katherine Randolph, Kitty Wilson, Clinton Corwin, Frank DeSilva, Paul Farber, Henry Fonda, Leopold Gutierrez, Daniel Joseph, Charles C. Leatherbee, P. Lapouchin, Hughie Mack, Lionel Stander, Mike Wagman, J. E. Whiffen.

REVIEW: "The play is almost saved by a single performance—the precise dominating acting of Claude Rains, who, as Carnot, contributes magnificently to one scene." (J. Brooks Atkinson, *New York Times*, November 26, 1929)

1930

THE APPLE CART

"A Political Extravaganza in Two Acts and an Interlude" by George Bernard Shaw. FORD'S THEATRE, Baltimore, February 17; MARTIN BECK THEATRE, New York, February 24 (88 performances). PRODUCER: The Theatre Guild. DIRECTOR: Philip Moeller. SETTINGS: Lee Simonson.

CAST: *Pamphilius and Sempronius, Private Secretaries to King* Thomas A. Braidon, Rex O'Malley; *Boanerges, President of Board of Trade* Ernest Cossart; *Magnus, the King* Tom Powers; *Alice, the Princess Royal* Audrey Ridgewell; *Proteus, Prime Minister* Claude Rains; *Nicobar, Foreign Secretary* Morris Carnovsky/Edgar Kent; *Crassus, Colonial Secretary* George Graham; *Pliney, Chancellor of the Exchequer* John Dunn; *Balbus, Home Secretary* William H. Sams; *Lysistrata, Postmistress-General* Helen Westley; *Amanda, Postmistress-General* Eva Leonard-Boyne; *Orinthia* Violet Kemble-Cooper; *The Queen* Marjorie Marquis; *Mr. Vanhattan, the American Ambassador* Frederick Truesdell.

REVIEW: "Claude Rains finds just the right mixture of master and charlatan as the prime minister." (J. Brooks Atkinson, *New York Times*, February 5, 1930)

1931

MIRACLE AT VERDUN

A play in seven scenes by Hans Chlumberg, translated from the German by Julian Leigh. MARTIN BECK THEATRE, New York, March 16 (49 performances). PRODUCER: The Theatre Guild. DIRECTOR: Herbert J. Biberman.

CAST: Scene One (Petit Cimetière at Verdun): *Smith* Caryl Gillin; *Jackson* Robert Middlemass; *Sharpe* J. W. Austin; *Marshall* Thomas A. Braidon; *Miss Greeley* Shirley Gale; *Dorothy* Valerie Cossart; *Violet* Hilda Chase; *Verron* Owen Meech; *Mme. Verron* Marion Stephenson; *Remusat* Jules Epailly; *Lerat* Carlos Zizold; *Mme. Lerat* Miriam Elias; *Mme. Duvernois* Germaine Giroux; *Dr. Pates* Edward Arnold; *Frau Paetz* Helene Salinger; *Von Henkel* Con Macsunday; *Frau Von Henkel* Joan Grahn; *Fritzchen* David Gorcey; *Brohl* Max Willenz; *Spaerlich* Sydney Stavro; *Heydner* Claude Rains. Scene One, Part Two (A Company of the Resurrected): *Wittekind* Hans Hansen; *Hessel* Alexander Ivo; *Weber* Jacob Bleifer; *Sonneborn* Walter Dressel; *Schroeder* George Brant; *Lehmann* Michael Rosenberg; *Schmidt* Anthony Baker; *Vaudemont, the Captain* John Gerard; *Andre Verron* Peter Wayne; *Morel* Clement Wilenchick; *Dubois* Ali Youssoff; *Roubeau* Akim Tamiroff; *Baillard* Percy Woodley; *General Lamarque, French War Minister* Carlos Zizold; *General Von Gadenau, German War Minister* Max Willenz; *French Officers* Alexander Danarov, John

Hoysradt; *German Officers* Joseph Lazarovici, Francis Schaeger; *Vernier, cemetery attendant* Edouard La Roche; *Messenger* Claude Rains. Scene Two (Celebrations in Paris and Berlin—1934): *Premier Delcampe* Jules Epailly; *Interrupter* Georges Magis; *Radio Announcer* John Hoysradt; *Reich Chancellor Overtuesch* Edward Arnold; *Interrupter* Jacob Bleifer. Scene Three (Bedrooms in Paris—Berlin—London): *Premier Delcampe* Jules Epailly; *Odette Lefevre* Germaine Giroux; *Reich Chancellor Overtuesch* Edward Arnold; *Frau Overtuesch* Helene Salinger; *Lord Grathford, English Prime Minister* J. W. Austin; *Leeds, his valet* Thomas A. Braidon. Scene Four (A Field in the Suippe; screen only). Scene Five (Shop of the Cobbler, Paul Vadinet—A Village on the Marne): *Paul Vadinet* Carlos Zizold; *Mme. Vadinet* Miriam Elias; *Jacques, an apprentice* John Hoysradt; *Jeannette* Germaine Giroux; *Policeman* Georges Magis; *Pastor* Juan de la Cruz; *First Villager* Edouard La Roche; *Second Villager* Hilda Chase; *Third Villager* Martin Cravath; *Morel* Clement Wilenchick. Scene Six (Quai d'Orsay): *Lord Grathford, Prime Minister of England* J.W. Austin; *Michel Delcampe, Premier of France* Jules Epailly; *Dr. Overtuesch, Chancellor of the German Reich* Edward Arnold; *Lamparenne, Prime Minister of Belgium* Claude Rains; *General Lamarque, French War Minister* Carlos Zizold; *General Von Gadenau, German War Minister* Max Willenz; *Clarkson, American Ambassador* Robert Middlemass; *Bertolotti, Italian Ambassador* Salvatore Zito; *Yoshitomo, Japanese Ambassador* Kuni Hara; *Cardinal Dupin, Archbishop of Paris* Juan de la Cruz; *Superintendent General Palm* Douglas Garden; *Chief Rabbi Dr. Sorgenreich* Sydney Stavro; *Professor Dr. Steppach, scientific authority* Con Macsunday; *Secretary* Thomas A. Braidon; *Young Prelate* Ari Kutai; *Tsatanaku, Japanese Premier* Hanaki Yoshiwara; *Yoshitomo* J. C. Kunihara; *Representative of Roumania* Robert Deviera; *Representative of Yugo-Slavia* Joseph Green; *Representative of Poland* Lucien Giardin; *Representative of Czecho-Slovakia* Mario Lajeroni; *Trolliet* Edward de la Roche; *Charrier* Georges Magis. Scene Seven (Petit Cimetière at Verdun, ten minutes after Scene One; screen only.)

REVIEW: "Neither the play nor the production requires much from individual actors, although Claude Rains, as the Prime Minister of Belgium, makes himself heard above the general din and gives a splendid, potent performance." (J. Brooks Atkinson, *New York Times*, March 15, 1931)

HE
A comedy in three acts by Alfred Savoir, adapted by Chester Erskin. GUILD THEATRE, New York, September 24 (40 performances). PRODUCER: The Theatre Guild. DIRECTOR: Chester Erskin. SETTING: Aline Bernstein.

CAST: *Bartender* Leslie Hunt; *Elevator Man* Claude Rains; *Monsieur Matard, Hotel Proprietor* Cecil Yapp; *Professor Coq* Eugene Powers; *The Invalid, His Daughter*

Viola Frayne; *Miss Scoville* Edith Meiser; *Commander Trafalgar* Edward Rigby; *He* Tom Powers; *Princess* Violet Kemble Cooper; *Bell Boy* Lester Salkow; *Monsieur Ping* William Gargan; *Hotel Doctor* Le Roy Brown; *First Porter* Lawrence Hurdle, Jr.; *Second Porter* Charles W. Adams.

REVIEWS: "Claude Rains is vastly enjoyable as the servant who fancies himself Napoleon." (J. Brooks Atkinson, *New York Times*, September 22, 1931) "Among the actors nobody except Claude Rains seemed aware of the philosophical hits of the speeches. Mr. Rains as the Napoleonic egoist knew what he meant. The rest of the company played away blindly with their several methods." (Stark Young, *The New Republic*, October 7, 1931)

1932

THE MOON IN THE YELLOW RIVER
A play in three acts by Denis Johnston. GUILD THEATRE, New York, February 29 (40 performances). PRODUCER: The Theatre Guild (Production Committee: Helen Westley and Lawrence Langner). DIRECTOR: Philip Moeller. SETTINGS: Cleon Throckmorton.

CAST: *Agnes* Josephine Williams; *Blanaid* Gertrude Flynn; *Tausch* Egon Brecher; *Aunt Columba* Alma Kruger; *George* Edward Nannary; *Captain Potts* John Daly Murphy; *Dobelle* Claude Rains; *Willie* Barry Macollum; *Darrell Blake* Henry Hull; *Larry, one of Blake's men* Wylie Adams; *Another of Blake's men* John O'Connor; *Commandant* William Harrigan; *A Soldier* Paul Stephenson; *Another Soldier* Desmond O'Donnovan.

REVIEW: "The acting and direction do what they can for a work that purposefully eludes clarification. Claude Rains and Henry Hull, although inclined to overelaborate a bit, give excellent performances as the railway engineer and the leader of the revolutionists." (J. Brooks Atkinson, *New York Times*, March 1, 1932)

TOO TRUE TO BE GOOD
A play in three acts by George Bernard Shaw. GUILD THEATRE, New York, April 4 (57 performances). PRODUCER: The Theatre Guild (Production Committee: Theresa Helburn and Philip Moeller). DIRECTOR: Leslie Banks. SETTINGS AND COSTUMES: Jonel Jorgulesco.

CAST: *The Monster* Julius Evans; *The Elderly Lady* Minna Phillips; *The Doctor* Alex Clark, Jr. *The Patient* Hope Williams; *The Nurse* Beatrice Lillie; *The Burglar* Hugh Sinclair; *Colonel Tallboys, V.C., D.S.O.* Ernest Cossart; *Private Meek* Leo G. Carroll; *Sergeant Fielding* Frank Shannon; *The Elder* Claude Rains.

REVIEW: "Claude Rains, who has recently taken the unactable part of the lugubrious atheist, roars his lines with a cutting crispness." (J. Brooks Atkinson, *New York Times*, April 5, 1932)

THE MAN WHO RECLAIMED HIS HEAD
A melodrama in three acts and sixteen scenes by Jean Bart. BROADHURST THEATRE, New York, September 8 (28 performances). DIRECTOR: Herbert J. Biberman.

CAST: *Jean Richard Barrows; Fernand Demoncey* Romaine Callender; *Paul Verin* Claude Rains; *Linette Verin* Evelyn Eaton; *Curly* Carleton Young; *Mimi* Janet Rathbun; *Margot* Emily Lowry; *Pierre* Paul Wilson; *Jack* Allen Nourse; *Adele Verin* Jean Arthur; *Henri Berthaud* Stuart Casey; *Gendarme* C. Elsworth Smith; *Waiter* Allen Nourse; *Antoine* Paul Wilson; *Baron de Montford* Lionel Braham.

REVIEW: "Mr. Rains, by exceptional performances of comparatively unimportant parts with the Theatre Guild, has won a deserved reputation as one of America's ablest actors. His appearance in a significant role that would give his talents full play has been eagerly awaited. But the effort to provide him with an inspired vehicle was forced. Apparently producer and playwright believed that through him those rare old days when 'acting was acting' could be revived. For, from the moment that the misshapen figure and hideous face of the little French political genius are revealed by the dim light of the doctor's apartment at midnight, the feeling created is that of a *tour de force*, an attempt to proclaim such a virtuosity as Irving must have displayed in enacting Poe's *The Tell-Tale Heart.* Mr. Rains, in so extravagant a makeup as irresistibly to recall some of the cinema impersonations of Lon Chaney, plays so skillfully, with so cunning a use of understatement, that he almost brings his character to life." (Carl Carmer, *Theatre Arts*, November 1932)

THE GOOD EARTH
A play in three acts and ten scenes, by Owen and Donald Davis, based on the novel by Pearl S. Buck. THE GUILD THEATRE, New York, October 17 (56 performances) PRODUCER: The Theatre Guild. DIRECTOR: Philip Moeller, under the supervision of Lawrence Langner and Lee Simonson. SCENIC DESIGN: Lee Simonson.

CAST: *Wang Lung* Claude Rains; *Wang Lung's Father* Henry Travers; *The Gatekeeper* Homer Barton; *A Peach Vendor* Conrad Cantzen; *A Beggar* William Franklin; *The Old Lord* Harold Thomas; *His Son* A. Francis Karll; *The Fifth Lady* Marel Foster; *A Slave* Joan Hathaway; *Cuckoo* Marjorie Wood; *The Ancient Mistress* Kate Morgan; *O-Lan* Alla Nazimova; *Wang Lung's Uncle* Sydney Greenstreet;

Wang Lung's Aunt Jessie Ralph; *Ching* Clyde Franklin; *Wang Lung's Son* Freddy Goodrow; *Two Strangers* Jack Daniels, Vincent Sherman; *A Tall Beggar* Harry M. Cooke; *A Poor Man* Albert Hayes; *Another Poor Man* Conrad Cantzen; *A Young Speaker* Vincent Sherman; *The Rich Man* Homer Barton; *The Fool Child* Helen Hoy; *Lotus* Gertrude Flynn; *A Slave* Nola Napoli; *A Doctor* Mark Schweld; *Yi Ling* Donald MacMillan; *Wang Lung's Eldest Son* Harry Wood; *The Bride* Geraldine Kay; *A Taoist Priest* Philip Wood; *Priests* Harry Barfoot, M. W. Raie.

REVIEWS: "Those who have been wondering how 'The Good Earth' could be translated into a play have their answer now at the Guild . . . [it] is a complete failure on the stage." (Brooks Atkinson, *New York Times*, October 18, 1932) "The acting displayed some of the inconsistencies so often obvious when Western players hide in the guise of almond-eyed and pigtailed Orientals. . . . Between the low, studied gutturals of Madame Nazimova as O-Lan, the slave wife, and the clipped syllables of Claude Rains as Wang Lung, there must be a more happy medium." (Herschel Williams, *Theatre Arts*, January 1933)

1933

AMERICAN DREAM
A trilogy of one act plays by George O'Neil, set in the years 1650, 1849, and 1933. GUILD THEATRE, New York, February 21 (39 performances). PRODUCER: The Theatre Guild. DIRECTOR: Philip Moeller, under the supervision of Lee Simonson and Helen Westley.

CAST: The First Play (1650): *Roger Pingree* Lee Baker; *Martha* Josephine Hull; *Daniel Pingree* Douglass Montgomery; *Luke Pingree* Wilton Graff; *An Indian* Frank Verigun; *Lydia Kimball* Gale Sondergaard; *Celia* Gertrude Flynn. The Second Play (1849): *Daniel Pingree* Stanley Ridges; *Susannah* Leona Hogarth; *Abbie Pingree* Helen Westley; *Ezekial Bell* Claude Rains. The Third Play (1933): *Daniel Pingree* Douglass Montgomery; *Gail Pingree* Gale Sondergaard; *Henri* Sanford Meisner; *Vladimir* Manart Kippen; *Beth Harkness* Edith Van Cleve; *Richard Biddle* Philip Barber; *Eddie Thayer* Stanley Ridges; *Sarah Culver* Helen Westley; *Mrs. Schuyler Hamilton* Josephine Hull; *Lindley P. Carver* Spencer Barnes; *Julius Stern* Lester Alden; *Murdock* Erskine Sanford; *Amarylis* Gertrude Flynn; *Tessa Steele* Mary Blair; *Lincoln Park* Wilton Graff; *Mrs. Harry Tsezhin* Mary Jeffery; *Harry* Frank Verigun; *Jake Schwarz* Samuel Goldenberg.

PEACE PALACE
A play in eight scenes by Emil Ludwig (original title: *Versailles*), adapted by John W. Gasssner. WESTCHESTER COUNTY CENTER, White Plains, New York, June 5. DIRECTOR: Herbert J. Biberman.

CAST: *Georges Clemenceau* Claude Rains; *Mandel* Otis Sheridan; *David Lloyd George* A.P. Kaye; *Marshall Ferdinand Foch* Juan de la Cruz; *Woodrow Wilson* Richard Hale; *Vittorio Orlando* Frank Tweddell; *Makino* H.L. Donau; *General Jan Smuts* Edward Fielding; *W. F. Massey* Charles E. Douglas; *William Morris Hughes* Victor Beecroft; *Ignace Jan Paderewski* Henry Warwick; *Arthur Balfour* J. W. Austin; *Colonel Edward M. House* William H. Lynn; *General Tasker Bliss* Eskine Sanford; *Fridtjof Nanzen* Montagu Love; *Sir Basil Zacharoff* St. Clair Bayfield; *Secretary to Wilson* Ralph Beech; *Mrs. Wilson* Mary Morris.

REVIEW: "Claude Rains of the Theatre Guild has the part of Clemenceau, and if the reactions of the county's citizens are any pointer, he turned into 'Peace Palace' a codicil that was excellent. The part is a difficult one." (L.N., *New York Times*, June 6, 1933)

1934

THEY SHALL NOT DIE
A play in three acts by John Wexley. ROYALE THEATRE, New York, February 21–April (62 performances). PRODUCER: The Theatre Guild. DIRECTOR: Philip Moeller. SCENIC DESIGN: Lee Simonson.

CAST: *Cooley* William Lynn; *Henderson* John L. Kearney; *Red* Tom Ewell; *St. Louis Kid* Fred Herrick; *Blackie* Frank Woodruff; *Deputy Sheriff Trent* Ralph Theadore; *Jeff Vivian* Ralph Sanford; *Lewis Collins* Bob Ross; *Walter Colton* William Norton; *Virginia Ross* Linda Watkins; *Lucy Wells* Ruth Gordon; *Luther Mason* Hale Norcross; *Benson Allen* L. M. Hurdle; *Roberts* George R. Hayes; *Purcell* Alfred Brown; *Walters* Bryant Hall; *Warner* Grafton Trew; *Heywood Parsons* Al Stokes; *Roy Wood* Allan Vaughan; *Andy Wood* Joseph Scott; *Morris* Joseph Smalls; *Moore* Frank Wilson; *Killian* Eddie Hodge; *Oliver Tulley* Robert Thomsen; *Dr. Thomas* George Christie; *Captain Kennedy* Frederick Persson; *Sergeant Ogden* Ross Forrester; *Mrs. Wells* Helen Westley; *Russell Evans* Dean Jagger; *Principal Keeper* Charles Henderson; *Lowery* Carroll Ashburn; *William Treadwell* Brandon Peters; *Reverend Wendell Jackson* Fred Miller; *Warden Jeffries* Leo Curley; *Rokoff* Louis John Latzer; *Cheney* St. Clair Bayfield; *Nathan G. Rubin* Claude Rains; *Johnny* Hugh Rennie; *Mr. Harrison* Frank Wilson; *Frank Travers* Douglas Gregory; *Judge* Thurston Hall; *Dr. Watson* Robert J. Lawrence; *Attorney General Dade* Ben Smith; *Seth Robbins* Harry Hermsen; *Circuit Solicitor Slade* Carl Eckstrom.

REVIEW: "Claude Rains does jeopardize his opening scene with histrionic flamboyance. But in the courtroom scene, which is the crucial one, the part catches up with him and he plays magnificently." (Bosley Crowther, *New York Times*, February 22, 1934)

Appendix

1948-1949

A LINCOLN PORTRAIT

A symphonic work with narration by Aaron Copland. ACADEMY OF MUSIC, Philadelphia, October 15-16, 1948 (2 performances); CARNEGIE HALL, New York, April 19, 1949 (1 performance). Rains was the narrator; the Philadelphia Orchestra was conducted by Eugene Ormandy.

1951

DARKNESS AT NOON

A play in three acts by Sidney Kingsley, based on the novel by Arthur Koestler. AL-VIN THEATRE, New York, February 13-March 24; ROYALE THEATRE, New York, March 26-June 23 (168 performances). PRODUCER: The Playwrights' Company. ASSOCIATE PRODUCER: May Kirshner. DIRECTOR: Sidney Kingsley. SCENIC DESIGN AND LIGHTING: Frederick Fox. ASSISTANT TO MR. FOX: Margery Quitzau. COSTUMES: Kenn Barr. PRODUCTION STAGE MANAGER: David Gray, Jr. STAGE MANAGER: William McFadden. ASSISTANT STAGE MANAGER: Norman Roland. MUSIC: "Moscow" composed by Dan and Dm. Potras, used with the special permission of Edward B. Marks Music Corporation.

CAST: *Rubashov* Claude Rains; *Guard* Robert Keith, Jr.; *402* Philip Coolidge; *302* Richard Seff; *202* Allan Rich; *Luba* Kim Hunter; *Gletkin* Walter J. Palance; *First Storm Trooper* Adams MacDonald; *Richard* Herbert Ratner; *Young Girl:* Virginia Howard; *Second Storm Trooper* Johnson Hayes; *Ivanoff* Alexander Scourby; *Bogrov* Norman Roland; *Hrutsch* Robert Crozier; *Albert* Daniel Polis; *Luigi* Will Kuluva; *Pablo* Henry Beckman; *André* Geoffrey Barr; *Barkeeper* Tony Ancona; *Secretary* Lois Nettleton; *President* Maurice Gosfeld.

REVIEWS: "Mr. Kingsley has chosen his cast judiciously and is fortunate in Mr. Rains' acting. When he last performed in New York, Mr. Rains was not an actor of much eminence. He was a showy actor, to be frank about it. But his study of the destruction of Rubashov from courage and honor to obsequiousness and futility is a sensitive, intelligent, skillful and absorbing piece of work." (Brooks Atkinson, *New York Times*, January 15, 1951) "Rains plays a trying role with a sure and quiet power that dominates the stage at all times . . . Unfortunately, for both Rains and the play, it is difficult to work up anything more than an academic sympathy for a man so justifiably hoist on a petard of his own fashioning; given unqualified pity, Rains' characterization of the involuntary penitent might have been a truly shattering experience." (*Newsweek*, January 22, 1951) "Claude Rains appears to understand his role and the book better than Mr. Kingsley. His performance as Rubashov is marked by a steadily rising tension; at the end he even looks as if he had been through an actual, not a simulated ordeal." (Margaret Marshall, *The Nation*, January 27, 1951) "In the extremely large role of Rubashov, Claude Rains gives a brilliant performance, nicely counterpointed by Walter J. Palance's chilling Gletkin." (*Time*, January 22, 1951) "Being a man of the thirties, Kingsley has a penchant for liberal social preachment. He has, however, no psychological insight, no poetic elegance, no capacity to convey the quality of any inner state. . . . Claude Rains as Rubashov is always sincere, dignified and intelligent. If he strikes one as an impassioned and idealistic English college professor rather than a steel-willed Russian political figure, the fault is not his." (Harold Clurman, *The Nation*, February 5, 1951)

1952

MERELY PLAYERS
A theatrical benefit gala for THE MERELY PLAYERS SOCIETY, London, March 30. In an eclectic evening of scenes, skits and songs, Rains appeared in Act I, Scene II of *Julius Caesar*.

CAST: *Cassius* John Gielgud; *Brutus* Geoffrey Teale; *Casca* Claude Rains.

JEZEBEL'S HUSBAND
A biblical comedy in two acts by Robert Nathan (world premiere). POCONO PLAYHOUSE, Mountainhome, Pennsylvania, followed by THEATRE BY THE SEA, Matunuck, Rhode Island; opened August 4. DIRECTOR: Sherman Marks.

CAST: *Jonah* Claude Rains; *Jezebel* Carmen Mathews; *Judith* Claudia Morgan; *Micah* Ben Gazzara; *Prince Azariah* Robert Emhart. With Ruth McDevitt, Judith Parrish, Ossie Davis, Vinie Burrows, Tony Dowling, and Harry Worth.

REVIEWS: "Rains, who has been an actor since childhood, used every trick of the stage to attain a polished interpretation. His every action, his gestures, dramatic pauses and beautifully clear, clean-cut diction, together with his impressive facial expressions, must have indeed made the director, Sherman Marks, as proud of the star of his show as was the audience." (*Scranton Tribune*, August 5, 1952) "Claude Rains' performance is electrifying and enchanting. It is one of his most satisfying characterizations." (*The Daily Record* [Morris County, New Jersey]; undated clipping)

AN EVENING WITH WILL SHAKESPEARE
A benefit evening for the American Shakespeare Festival and Academy. PARSON'S THEATRE, Hartford, Connecticut, December 5. DIRECTOR: Margaret Webster.

CAST: Claude Rains, Leueen MacGrath, Arnold Moss, Wesley Addy, Eva Le Galliene, Faye Emerson, Nina Foch, Staats Cotsworth, Richard Dyer-Benoit.

REVIEW: "In evening clothes against a simple backdrop they read, recited, and enacted excerpts from nearly a dozen of the Bard's most celebrated and familiar works. They received an enormous hand from a packed house even though 'the flood was playing a revival outside in the night.'" (*New York Times*, December 7, 1952)

1954

THE CONFIDENTIAL CLERK
A comedy by T. S. Eliot. MOROSCO THEATRE, New York, February 11–May 22 (117 performances). DIRECTOR: E. Martin Browne. SETTINGS, COSTUMES, AND LIGHTING: Paul Morrison. PRODUCER: Henry Sherek and the Producer's Theatre.

CAST: *Sir Claude Mulhammer* Claude Rains; *Eggerson* Newton Black; *Colby Simpkins* Douglas Watson B. *Kaghan* Richard Newton; *Lucasta Angel* Joan Greenwood; *Lady Elizabeth Mulhammer* Ina Claire; *Mrs Guzzard* Aline McMahon.

NOTE: Rains's first wife, Isabel Jeans, played the role of Lady Elizabeth Mulhammer in *The Confidential Clerk*'s 1953 Edinburgh premiere.

1956

THE NIGHT OF THE AUK
A play by Arch Oboler. PLAYHOUSE THEATRE, New York, December 1–8 (8 performances). PRODUCER: Kermit Bloomgarden.

CAST: *Colonel Tom Russell* Wendell Corey; *Lieutenant Mac Martman* Dick York; *Lewis Rohmen* Christopher Plummer; *Doctor Bruner* Claude Rains; *Lieutenant Jan Kephart* Martin Brooks.

REVIEW: "[Oboler] is a rhetorical writer. Stirring up scientific jargon with portentous ideas, he writes dialogue that is streaked with purple passages and sounds a good deal like gibberish. . . . As the most experienced actor in the lot, Claude Rains plays the scientist with becoming thought and sobriety, speaking the dialogue as though in a moment everything might come clear." (Brooks Atkinson, *New York Times*, December 4, 1956)

1959

FOR THE TIME BEING
A Christmas oratorio by Martin David Levy with text by W. H. Auden. CAR-

NEGIE HALL, New York, December 7. NARRATOR: Claude Rains. With the Collegiate Chorale Symphony of the Air, conducted by Margaret Hillis, with guest vocalists from the Metropolitan Opera.

1961

ENOCH ARDEN

A piece for narrator and orchestra by Alfred Lord Tennyson and Richard Straus. ACADEMY OF MUSIC, Philadelphia, March 20. NARRATOR: Claude Rains. With the Philadelphia Orchestra, conducted by Eugene Ormandy.

1965

SO MUCH OF EARTH, SO MUCH OF HEAVEN

A play in three acts by Henry Denker, adapted from *The Burnt Flower Bed* by Ugo Betti, based on the original translation by Peter Wexler. JOHN DREW THEATRE, East Hampton, New York; WESTPORT COUNTRY PLAYHOUSE, New Hope, Pennsylvania. August–September. PRODUCERS: Theatre Guild Productions, Inc., and Gerard Oestreicher, presented (at Westport, August 30–September 4) by James B. McKenzie, Spofford J. Beadle and Ralph Roseman. DIRECTOR: Edward Parone. SETTING AND LIGHTING: Paul Bertelsen. COSTUME SUPERVISOR: Patton Campbell; costumes executed by Costume Associates.

CAST: *Giovanni* Claude Rains; *Luisa* Leueen MacGrath; *Tomaso* Larry Gates, *Nicola* Lester Rawlins; *Rosa* Joanna Miles; *Emilio* Howard Honig; *Raniero* Harris Yulin.

Film Work

1920

BUILD THY HOUSE

STUDIO: Ideal Film Co. RELEASE DATE: October 1920. LENGTH: Five reels. DIRECTOR: Fred Goodwins. SCREENPLAY: Eliot Stannard, from a story by S. Trevor Jones.

CAST: *Arthur Burnaby* Henry Ainley; *Helen Dawson* Ann Trevor; *Jim Medaway* Reginald Bach; *Burnaby* Warwick Ward; *John Dawson* Jerrold Robertshaw; *Mrs. Medaway* Adelaide Grace; *Marshall* Howard Cochran; *Clarkis* Claude Rains; *Mr. Cramer* R. Van Courtlandt; *Miss Brown* Mrs Ainley; *Florence Burnaby* V. Vivian-Vivian.

Appendix

1933

THE INVISIBLE MAN
STUDIO: Universal. RELEASE DATE: November 13, 1933. RUNNING TIME: 71 minutes. PRODUCER: Carl Laemmle, Jr. DIRECTOR: James Whale. SCREENPLAY: R. C. Sherriff, based on the novel by H. G. Wells. DIRECTOR OF PHOTOGRAPHY: Arthur Edeson, ASC. SPECIAL EFFECTS: John P. Fulton. ART DIRECTOR: Charles D. Hall. EDITOR: Ted Kent.

CAST: *Jack Griffin, The Invisible One* Claude Rains; *Flora Cranley* Gloria Stuart; *Dr. Kemp* William Harrigan; *Dr. Cranley* Henry Travers; *Mrs. Hall* Una O'Connor; *Mr. Hall* Forrester Harvey; *Chief of Police* Holmes Herbert; *Constable Jaffers* E. E. Clive; *Chief of Detectives* Dudley Digges; *Inspector Bird* Harry Stubbs; *Inspector Lane* Donald Stuart; *Milly* Merle Tottenham; *Reporter* Dwight Frye; *Informer* John Carradine; *Doctor* Jameson Thomas; *Boy* John Merivale; *Man with Bicycle* Walter Brennan.

REVIEWS: "No actor has ever made his first appearance on the screen under quite as peculiar circumstances as Claude Rains does." (Mordaunt Hall, *New York Times*, November 18, 1933) "Although Rains' face is never seen, he performs his part cleverly, his voice carrying a sinister note that is very effective." (Kate Cameron, *New York Daily News*, November 18, 1933)

1934

CRIME WITHOUT PASSION
STUDIO: Paramount. RELEASE DATE: August 17, 1934. RUNNING TIME: 70 minutes. PRODUCERS/DIRECTORS: Ben Hecht and Charles MacArthur. SCREENPLAY: Ben Hecht and Charles MacArthur, based on the story "Caballero of the Law" by Ben Hecht. DIRECTOR OF PHOTOGRAPHY: Lee Garmes. SPECIAL EFFECTS: Slavko Vorkapich. MUSIC: Frank Tours. FILM EDITOR: Arthur Ellis.

CAST: *Lee Gentry* Claude Rains; *Carmen Brown* Margo; *Katy Costello* Whitney Bourne; *Eddie White* Stanley Ridges; *State's Attorney O'Brien* Leslie Adams; *Della* Greta Granstedt; *Miss Keely* Esther Dale; *Lieutenant Norton* Charles Kennedy; *Judge* Fuller Melish; *Buster Malloy* Paula Trueman; *Furies* Betty Sundmark, Fraye Gilbert, Dorothy Bradshaw; *Reporters* Ben Hecht, Charles MacArthur; cameos by Helen Hayes, Fanny Brice, Mickey King, Alice Anthon, and the Bobby Duncan Troupe.

REVIEW: "Mr. Rains handles his role in a masterly fashion. He gets full effect out of the cleverly written speeches and gives an extraordinarily clear characterization." (Mordaunt Hall, *New York Times*, January 9, 1935)

1935

THE MAN WHO RECLAIMED HIS HEAD
STUDIO: Universal. RELEASE DATE: January 8, 1935. RUNNING TIME: 82 minutes. PRODUCER: Carl Laemmle, Jr. DIRECTOR: Edward Ludwig. SCREENPLAY: Jean Bart and Samuel Ornitz, based on Bart's play. DIRECTOR OF PHOTOGRAPHY: Merritt Gerstad. ART DIRECTOR: Albert S. D'Agostino. FILM EDITOR: Murray Seldeen.

CAST: *Paul Verin* Claude Rains; *Adele Verin* Joan Bennett; *Henri Dumont* Lionel Atwill; *Linette Verin* Baby Jane Quigley; *Fernand DeMarnay* Henry O'Neill; *Laurent* Henry Armetta; *Curly* Wallace Ford; *Marchand* Lawrence Grant; *Baron* Ferdinand Gottschalk; *Charlus* William B. Davidson; *His Excellency* Gilbert Emery; *Danglas* Hugh O'Connell; *Jean* Rollo Lloyd; *Louise* Bessie Barriscale; *Pierre* G. P. Hunley; *Mimi* Valerie Hobson; *LuLu* Doris Lloyd; *Chon-Chon* Noel Francis; *Dignitaries* Walter Walker, Edward Martindel, Crauford Kent, C. Montague Shaw; *Munitions Board Directors* Edward Van Sloan, Purnell Pratt, Jameson Thomas; *Margot* Judith Wood; *Andre* Lloyd Hughes; *Antoine* Bryant Washburne, Jr.; *Petty Officer* Boyd Irwin.

REVIEWS: "This cautious reporter is not prepared to admit that Mr. Rains' portrait of applied hysteria is the brilliant piece of acting that some of his disciples appear to believe. But it is certainly arresting, and it is dosed with the kind of virtuoso terrorism that makes it difficult for you to breathe when he is on the screen." (Andre Sennwald, *New York Times*, January 9, 1935) "The tempo of the film is slow and deliberate, but Mr. Claude Rains is there to carry it along." (*The Times* [London], June 10, 1935) "With his performance in *Crime without Passion* still sharply etched in the minds of serious moviegoers, Claude Rains comes to the Rialto Theatre again to put himself over in the grandest manner." (Wanda Hale, *New York Daily News*, January 9, 1935)

MYSTERY OF EDWIN DROOD
STUDIO: Universal. RELEASE DATE: February 4, 1935. RUNNING TIME: 87 minutes. PRODUCER: Carl Laemmle, Jr. DIRECTOR: Stuart Walker. SCREENPLAY: John L. Balderston and Gladys Unger, based on the novel *The Mystery of Edwin Drood* by Charles Dickens; adaptation by Bradley King and Leopold Atlas. DIRECTOR OF PHOTOGRAPHY: George Robinson. ART DIRECTOR: Albert S. D'Agostino. MUSIC: Edward Ward. FILM EDITOR: Edward Curtiss.

CAST: *John Jasper* Claude Rains; *Neville Landless/Mr. Datchery* Douglass Montgomery; *Rosa Bud* Heather Angel; *Helena Landless* Valerie Hobson; *Edwin Drood* David Manners; *Crisparkle* Francis L. Sullivan; *Opium Den Woman* Zeffie Tilbury; *Mrs. Twinkleton* Ethel Griffies; *Thomas Sapsea* E. E. Clive; *Mr. Grewgious* Walter Kingsford; *Durdles* Forrester Harvey; *Mrs. Tope* Vera Buckland; *Mrs. Tisher* Elsa Buchanan; *Deputy* George Ernest; *Chief Verger Tope* J. M. Kerrigan; *Mrs. Crisparkle* Louise Carter; *Opium Fiends* Harry Cording, D'Arcy Corrigan; *Crisparkle Maid* Anne O'Neal; *Villager* Will Geer.

REVIEW: "Mr. Rains, who has become the devil's own brother during his brief and hair-raising screen career, is brilliantly repellant. His searching eyes and malignantly arched brows are tainted with mania. In the opium den after the murder, when he wrestles with his conscience during his drugged stupor, Mr. Rains makes your flesh crawl." (Andre Sennwald, *New York Times*, March 21, 1935)

THE CLAIRVOYANT
STUDIO: Gainsborough/Gaumont-British. RELEASE DATE (USA): June 7, 1935. RUNNING TIME: 81 minutes. PRODUCER: Michael Balcon. DIRECTOR: Maurice Elvey. SCREENPLAY: Charles Bennett, Bryan Edgar Wallace, and Robert Evans, based on the novel by Ernst Lothar as translated by B. Ryan. DIRECTOR OF PHOTOGRAPHY: G. MacWilliams. MUSICAL DIRECTOR: Louis Levy. MUSIC: Arthur Benjamin. SET DECORATION: Joe Strasser. FILM EDITOR: Paul Capon.

CAST: *Maximus* Claude Rains; *Rene* Fay Wray; *Topsy* Mary Clare; *Simon* Ben Field; *Christine* Jane Baxter; *Lord Southwood* Athole Stewart; *James J. Bimeter* C. Denier Warren; *MacGregor* Frank Cellier; *Derelict* Donald Cathrop; *Counsel* Felix Aylmer; *Customs Official* Jack Raine; *Page* Graham Moffat; *Guard* George Merritt; *Man* Eliot Markeham; *Showman* Percy Parsons; *Lodging Housekeeper* Margaret Davidge.

REVIEW: "A rather meandering melodrama which would be utterly unimportant except for Mr. Rains' presence. His vigorous and sensitive performance is about all that holds a faulty story structure together." (Frank S. Nugent, *New York Times*, June 8, 1935)

THE LAST OUTPOST
STUDIO: Paramount. RELEASE DATE: October 11, 1935. RUNNING TIME: 75 minutes. EXECUTIVE PRODUCER: Henry Herzbrun. PRODUCER: E. Lloyd Sheldon. DIRECTORS: Louis Gasnier and Charles Barton. SCREENPLAY: Philip MacDonald, based on the story "The Drum" by F. Britten Austin;

adaptation by Frank Partos and Charles Brackett, with Marguerite Roberts, Arthur Phillips, Eugene Walter, and Max Marcin. DIRECTOR OF PHOTOGRAPHY: Theodor Sparkuhl. ART DIRECTORS: Hans Dreier and Earl Hedrick. FILM EDITOR: Jack Dennis.

CAST: *Michael Andrews* Cary Grant; *John Stevenson* Claude Rains; *Rosemary Hayden* Gertrude Michael; *Ilya* Kathleen Burke; *Nurse Rowland* Margaret Swope; *Cullen* Jameson Thomas; *Haidar* Nick Shaid; *Lieutenant Prescott* Colin Tapely; *Private Foster* Billy Bevan; *General* Claude King; *Mirov* Akim Tamiroff; *Turkish Major* Georges Revenant; *Amrak* Harry Semels; *Head Nurse* Elspeth Dudgeon; *Sergeant* Robert Adair; *Armenian Patriarch* Meyer Ouhayoun; *Doctor* Olaf Hytten; *Colonel* Frank Elliott.

1936

HEARTS DIVIDED
STUDIO: Warner Bros./Cosmopolitan/First National. RELEASE DATE: June 20, 1936. RUNNING TIME: 70 minutes. EXECUTIVE PRODUCERS: Jack L. Warner and Hal B. Wallis. PRODUCER/DIRECTOR: Frank Borzage. SCREENPLAY: Laird Doyle and Casey Robinson, based on the play *Glorious Betsy* by Rida Johnson Young. DIRECTOR OF PHOTOGRAPHY: George Folsey. ART DIRECTOR: Robert Haas. MUSIC: Erich Wolfgang Korngold, with original music and songs by Harry Warren and Al Dubin. FILM EDITOR: William Holmes.

CAST: *Betsy Patterson* Marion Davies; *Jerome Bonaparte* Dick Powell; *Henry* Charles Ruggles; *Napoleon Bonaparte* Claude Rains; *John* Edward Everett Horton; *Sir Henry* Arthur Treacher; *Charles Patterson* Henry Stephenson; *Aunt Helen* Clara Blandick; *Isham* John Larkin; *Pichon* Walter Kingsford; *Du Fresne* Etienne Giradot; *Cambaceres* Halliwell Hobbes; *Thomas Jefferson* George Irving; *Madame Letizia Bonaparte* Beulah Bondi; *Gabriel* Freddie Archibald; *Mammy* Hattie McDaniel; *Servant* Sam McDaniel; *Pippin* Philip Hurlic; *Innkeeper* Hobart Cavanaugh; *Livingston* Granville Bates; *James Monroe* John Elliot; *Black Man* Clinton Rosemond; *Footman* Wilfrid Lucas; with the Hall Johnson Choir.

REVIEW: "The year's most disappointing picture . . . saved from utter downfall by innumerable devices of direction and by the performances of the supporting people. Claude Rains is a capricious yet superbly ruthless Napoleon." (John T. McManus, *New York Times*, June 13, 1936)

ANTHONY ADVERSE
STUDIO: Warner Bros. RELEASE DATE: August 29, 1936. RUNNING TIME:

139 minutes. EXECUTIVE PRODUCERS: Hal Wallis and Jack L. Warner. DI-
RECTOR: Mervyn LeRoy (with Michael Curtiz, uncredited). SCREENPLAY:
Sheridan Gibney, based on the novel by Hervey Allen. DIRECTOR OF PHO-
TOGRAPHY: Tony Gaudio. ART DIRECTOR: Anton Grot. MUSIC: Erich
Wolfgang Korngold. FILM EDITOR: Ralph Dawson.

CAST: *Anthony Adverse* Fredric March; *Angela Giuseppi* Olivia de Havilland;
Vincent Nolte Donald Wood; *Maria* Anita Louise; *John Bonnyfeather* Edmund
Gwenn; *Don Luis* Claude Rains; *Denis Moore* Louis Hayward; *Faith Paleologus*
Gale Sondergaard; *Neleta* Steffi Duna; *Carlo Cibo* Akim Tamiroff; *Debrulle* Ralph
Morgan; *Ouvrard* Fritz Leiber; *Tony Giuseppi* Luis Alberni; *Anthony, age 10* Billy
Mauch; *Father Xavier* Henry O'Neill; *Brother Francois* Pedro de Cordoba; *Cap-
tain Jorham* Joseph Crehan; *Signora Bovino* Rafaela Ottiano; *Napoleon Bonaparte*
Rollo Lloyd; *Mother Superior* Eily Malyon; *Mrs. Jorham* Clara Blandick; *Anthony's
Son, Anthony* Scott Beckett; *Major Doumet* J. Carroll Naish; *Coach Driver* Frank
Reicher; *Angela, as a Child* Ann Howard; *De Bourriene* Leonard Mudie; *Captain
Matanaza* Addison Richards; *Innkeeper* Egon Brecher.

1937

STOLEN HOLIDAY
STUDIO: Warner Bros. RELEASE DATE: February 6, 1937. RUNNING
TIME: 76 minutes. EXECUTIVE PRODUCER: Hal B. Wallis. DIRECTOR:
Michael Curtiz. SCREENPLAY: Casey Robinson; original story by Warren Duff
and Virginia Kellogg. DIRECTOR OF PHOTOGRAPHY: Sid Hickox. ART
DIRECTOR: Anton Grot. MUSICAL DIRECTOR: Leo F. Forbstein. FILM
EDITOR: Terry Morse.

CAST: *Nicole Picot* Kay Francis; *Stefan Orloff* Claude Rains; *Anthony Wayne* Ian
Hunter; *Suzanne* Alison Skipworth; *Leon* Alexander D'Arcy; *Helen Tuttle* Betty
Lawford; *Francis Chalon* Walter Kingsford; *LeGrande* Charles Halton; *Charles Ra-
nier* Frank Reicher; *Dupont* Frank Conroy; *Deputy Bergery* Egon Brecher; *Prefect
of Police* Robert Strange; *Madame Delphine* Kathleen Howard; *Borel* Wedgewood
Nowell.

REVIEW: "Rains gives the swindler-romancer a high polish." (*Variety*, February
3, 1937)

THE PRINCE AND THE PAUPER
STUDIO: Warner Bros. RELEASE DATE: May 8, 1937. RUNNING TIME:
118 minutes. EXECUTIVE PRODUCERS: Jack L. Warner and Hal B. Wallis.
DIRECTOR: William Keighley (and William Dieterle, uncredited). SCREEN-

PLAY: Laird Doyle, based on the novel by Mark Twain and dramatic adaptation by Catherine Chisholm Cushing. DIRECTORS OF PHOTOGRAPHY: Sol Polito and George Barnes. ART DIRECTOR: Robert Haas. MUSICAL DIRECTOR: Leo F. Forbstein. FILM EDITOR: Ralph Dawson.

CAST: *Miles Hendon* Errol Flynn; *Earl of Hertford* Claude Rains; *Duke of Norfolk* Henry Stephenson; *John Canty* Barton MacLane; *Tom Canty* Billy Mauch; *Prince Edward* Bobby Mauch; *Captain of the Guard* Alan Hale; *First Lord* Eric Portman; *Second Lord* Lionel Pape; *Archbishop of Canterbury* Halliwell Hobbes; *Barmaid* Phyllis Barry; *Clemens* Ivan Simpson; *Henry VIII* Montagu Love; *Father Andrew* Fritz Leiber; *Grandmother Canty* Elspeth Dudgeon; *Mrs. Canty* Mary Field; *Lady Jane Seymour* Helen Valkis; *St. John* Lester Matthews; *First Guard* Robert Adair; *Second Guard* Harry Cording; *Ruffler* Lionel Braham; *Innkeeper* Lionel Belmore; *The Watch* Harry Beresford.

THEY WON'T FORGET
STUDIO: Warner Bros. RELEASE DATE: October 9, 1937. RUNNING TIME: 92 minutes. EXECUTIVE PRODUCER: Jack L. Warner. DIRECTOR: Mervyn LeRoy. SCREENPLAY: Robert Rossen and Aben Kandel, based on the novel *Death in the Deep South* by Ward Greene. DIRECTOR OF PHOTOGRAPHY: Arthur Edeson, ASC. ART DIRECTOR: Robert Haas. MUSICAL DIRECTOR: Leo F. Forbstein. MUSIC AND ARRANGEMENTS: Adolph Deutsch. FILM EDITOR: Thomas Richards.

CAST: *Andy Griffin* Claude Rains; *Sybil Hale* Gloria Dickson; *Robert Hale* Edward Norris; *Michael Gleason* Otto Kruger; *Bill Brock* Allyn Joslyn; *Mary Clay* Lana Turner; *Imogene Mayfield* Linda Perry; *Joe Turner* Elisha Cook, Jr.; *Detective Laneart* Cy Kendall; *Tump Redwine* Clinton Rosemund; *Carlisle P. Buxton* E. Alyn (Fred) Warren; *Mrs. Hale* Sybil Harris; *Jim Timberlake* Clifford Soubier; *Detective Pindar* Granville Bates; *Mrs. Mountford* Ann Shoemaker; *Governor Mountford* Paul Everton; *Harmon Drake* Donald Briggs; *Ransom Clay* Wilmer Hines; *Shattuck Clay* Trevor Bardette; *Luther Clay* Elliott Sullivan; *Soda Jerk* Eddie Acuff; *Reporter* Frank Faylen; *Judge Moore* Leonard Mudie; *Confederate Soldiers* Henry Davenport, Harry Beresford, Edward McWade.

REVIEW: "Credit must go to Mr. LeRoy for his remarkably skillful direction—there are a few touches as fine as anything the screen has done; to Aben Kandel and Robert Rossen for their excellent script; and to all the cast, but notably to Mr. Rains, for his savage characterization of the ambitious prosecutor." (Frank S. Nugent, *New York Times*, July 15, 1937)

1938

GOLD IS WHERE YOU FIND IT

STUDIO: Warner Bros./Cosmopolitan/First National. RELEASE DATE: February 12, 1938. RUNNING TIME: 91 minutes. EXECUTIVE PRODUCERS: Jack B. Warner and Hal Wallis. DIRECTOR: Michael Curtiz. SCREENPLAY: Warren Duff and Robert Buckner, based on the novel by Clements Ripley. DIRECTOR OF PHOTOGRAPHY: Sol Polito. TECHNICOLOR CONSULTANT: Natalie Kalmus. ART DIRECTOR: Ted Smith. COSTUMES: Milo Anderson. MUSIC: Max Steiner.

CAST: *Jared Whitney* George Brent; *Serena Ferris* Olivia de Havilland; *Colonel Chris Ferris* Claude Rains; *Roseanne Ferris McCooey* Margaret Lindsay; *Ralph Ferris* John Litel; *Molly Featherstone* Marcia Ralston; *Slag Minton* Barton MacLane; *Lance Ferris* Tim Holt; *Harrison McCooey* Sidney Toler; *Judge* Henry O'Neill; *Joshua* Willie Best; *Mr. Crouch* Robert McWade; *Enoch Howitt* George "Gabby" Hayes; *Dr. Parsons* Harry Davenport; *McKenzie* Russell Simpson; *Senator Walsh* Clarence Kolb; *Senator Hearst* Moroni Olsen; *Nixon* Granville Bates; *Grogan* Robert Homans; *Deputy* Eddie Chandler.

THE ADVENTURES OF ROBIN HOOD

STUDIO: Warner Bros. RELEASE DATE: May 14, 1938. RUNNING TIME: 102 minutes. EXECUTIVE PRODUCERS: Jack L. Warner and Hal B. Wallis. DIRECTORS: William Keighley and Michael Curtiz. DIALOGUE DIRECTOR: Irving Rapper. SCREENPLAY: Norman Reilly Raine and Seton I. Miller. DIRECTORS OF PHOTOGRAPHY: Tony Gaudio and Sol Polito. TECHNICOLOR PHOTOGRAPHY: Al M. Greene. TECHNICOLOR CONSULTANT: Natalie Kalmus. FILM EDITOR: Ralph Dawson. COSTUMES: Milo Anderson. MUSIC: Erich Wolfgang Korngold.

CAST: *Robin Hood* Errol Flynn; *Maid Marian* Olivia de Havilland; *Sir Guy of Gisbourne* Basil Rathbone; *Prince John* Claude Rains; *Little John* Alan Hale; *Will Scarlett* Patric Knowles; *Richard the Lion-Heart* Ian Hunter; *Friar Tuck* Eugene Pallette; *Sheriff of Nottingham* Melville Cooper; *Bess* Una O'Connor; *Much* Herbert Mundin; *Bishop of the Black Canons* Montagu Love; *Sir Essex* Leonard Wiley; *Sir Mortimer* Kenneth Hunter; *Sir Geoffrey* Robert Warwick; *Sir Baldwin* Colin Kenny; *Sir Ivor* Lester Matthews; *Dickon Malbete* Harry Cording; *Captain of Archers* Howard Hill; *Tavern Proprietor* Ivan Simpson; *Sir Rafe* Robert Noble; *Crippen* Charles McNaughton; *Humility Prin* Lionel Belmore; *Sir Nigel* Austin Fairman; *Sir Norbert* Crauford Kent; *Archery Official* Wilfred Lucas; *Archery Referee* Holmes Herbert; *Additional cast* Halliwell Hobbes, Olaf Hytten, John Sutton.

REVIEW: "On the side of villainy, we have such foil sports as Basil Rathbone as Guy of Gisbourne, Claude Rains as the treacherous Prince John, Melville Cooper as the blustery High Sheriff, Montagu Love as the evil Bishop of Black Canon. Deep-dyed they are, and how the children's matinees will hiss them!" (Frank S. Nugent, *New York Times*, May 13, 1938)

WHITE BANNERS
STUDIO: Warner Bros./Cosmopolitan. RELEASE DATE: June 25, 1938. RUNNING TIME: 88 minutes. EXECUTIVE PRODUCERS: Jack L. Warner and Hal B. Wallis. DIRECTOR: Edmund Goulding. SCREENPLAY: Lenore Coffe, Cameron Rogers, and Abem Finkle, based on the novel by Lloyd C. Douglas. DIRECTOR OF PHOTOGRAPHY: Charles Rosher. ART DIRECTOR: John Hughes. COSTUMES: Milo Anderson. FILM EDITOR: Thomas Richards. MUSIC: Max Steiner.

CAST: *Paul Ward* Claude Rains; *Hannah Parmalee* Fay Bainter; *Peter Trimble* Jackie Cooper; *Sally Ward* Bonita Granville; *Sam Trimble* Henry O'Neill; *Marcia Ward* Kay Johnson; *Thomas Bradford* James Stephenson; *Dr. Thompson* J. Farrell McDonald; *Joe Ellis* William Pawley; *Bill Ellis* Edward Pawley; *Charles Ellis* John Ridgely; *Hester* Mary Field; *Sloan* Edward McWade.

FOUR DAUGHTERS
STUDIO: Warner Bros./First National. RELEASE DATE: September 24, 1938. RUNNING TIME: 90 minutes. EXECUTIVE PRODUCERS: Jack L. Warner and Hal B. Wallis. DIRECTOR: Michael Curtiz. DIALOGUE DIRECTOR: Irving Rapper. SCREENPLAY: Julius J. Epstein and Lenore Coffee, based on the short story "Sister Act" by Fannie Hurst. DIRECTOR OF PHOTOGRAPHY: Ernest Haller. ART DIRECTOR: John Hughes. GOWNS: Orry-Kelly. FILM EDITOR: Ralph Dawson. MUSICAL DIRECTOR: Leo F. Forbstein. MUSIC: Max Steiner, with Max Rubinowitsch.

CAST: *Adam Lemp* Claude Rains; *Felix Deitz* Jeffrey Lynn; *Mickey Borden* John Garfield; *Ben Crowley* Frank McHugh; *Aunt Etta* May Robson; *Emma Lemp* Gale Page; *Ann Lemp* Priscilla Lane; *Thea Lemp* Lola Lane; *Kay Lemp* Rosemary Lane; *Ernest Talbot* Dick Foran; *Mrs. Ridgefield* Vera Lewis; *Jake* Tom Dugan; *Sam* Eddie Acuff; *Earl* Donald Kerr; *Doctor* Wilfred Lucas.

REVIEW: "Claude Rains is irresistibly persuasive and attractive as the father." (*Variety*, August 17, 1938)

Appendix

1939

THEY MADE ME A CRIMINAL

STUDIO: Warner Bros. RELEASE DATE: January 28, 1939. RUNNING TIME: 92 minutes. EXECUTIVE PRODUCER: Hal B. Wallis. DIRECTOR: Busby Berkeley. ASSISTANT DIRECTOR: Russ Saunders. SCREENPLAY: Sig Herzig, based on the play *Sucker* by Bertram Millhauser and Beulah Marie Dix. DIRECTOR OF PHOTOGRAPHY: James Wong Howe. ART DIRECTOR: Anton Grot. FILM EDITOR: Jack Killifer. GOWNS: Milo Anderson. MUSIC: Max Steiner. MUSICAL DIRECTOR: Leo. F. Forbstein.

CAST: *Johnnie Bradfield* John Garfield; *Detective Phelan* Claude Rains; *Peggy* Gloria Dickson; *Grandma* May Robson; *Tommy* Billy Halop; *Angel* Bobby Jordan; *Spit* Leo Gorcey; *Dippy* Huntz Hall; *T. B.* Gabriel Dell; *Goldie* Ann Sheridan; *Doc Ward* Robert Gleckler; *Charles Magee* John Ridgely; *Budgie* Barbara Pepper; *Ennis* William Davidson; *Lenihan* Ward Bond; *Malvin* Robert Strange; *Smith* Louis Jean Heydt; *Gaspar Rutchek* Frank Riggi; *Manager* Cliff Clark; *Collucci* Dick Wessel; *Milt* Bernard Punsley; *Speed* Irving Bacon; *Fight Announcer* Sam Hayes.

SONS OF LIBERTY

STUDIO: Warner Bros. RELEASE DATE: April 1939. RUNNING TIME: 21 minutes. EXECUTIVE PRODUCER: Jack L. Warner. DIRECTOR: Michael Curtiz. SCREENPLAY: Crane Wilbur. DIRECTORS OF PHOTOGRAPHY: Sol Polito and Ray Rennahan. COSTUMES: Milo Anderson. MAKEUP: Perc Westmore. MUSICAL DIRECTOR: Leo F. Forbstein.

CAST: *Haym Salomon* Claude Rains; *Rachel Salomon* Gale Sondergaard; *Alexander MacDougal* Donald Crisp; *George Washington* Montagu Love; *Madison* Henry O'Neill; *Colonel Tilgham* James Stephenson; *Nathan Hale* Larry Williams; *Robert Morris* Moroni Olsen; *Jacob* Vladimir Sokoloff.

JUAREZ

STUDIO: Warner Bros. RELEASE DATE: June 10, 1939. RUNNING TIME: 125 minutes. PRODUCER: Hal B. Wallis. DIRECTOR: William Dieterle. DIALOGUE DIRECTOR: Irving Rapper. SCREENPLAY: John Huston, Wolfgang Reinhardt, and Aeneas MacKenzie, based on *Juarez and Maximilian* by Franz Werfel and *The Phantom Crown* by Bertita Harding. DIRECTOR OF PHOTOGRAPHY: Tony Gaudio. ART DIRECTOR: Anton Grot. GOWNS: Orry-Kelly. MAKEUP: Perc Westmore. MUSIC: Erich Wolfgang Korngold. MUSICAL DIRECTOR: Leo F. Forbstein.

CAST: *Carlotta* Bette Davis; *Benito Juarez* Paul Muni; *Maximillian von Hapsburg* Brian Aherne; *Napoleon III* Claude Rains; *Porfirio Diaz* John Garfield; *Marechal Bazaine* Donald Crisp; *Alejandro Uradi* Joseph Calleia; *Eugenie* Gale Sondergaard; *Col. Miguel López* Gilbert Roland; *Miguel Miramón* Henry O'Neill; *José de Montares* Montagu Love; *Dr. Basch* Harry Davenport; *Achille Fould* Walter Fenner; *Drouyn de Lhuys* Alexander Leftwich; *Countess Battenberg* Georgia Caine; *Señor de Leon* Gennaro Curci; *Tomas Mejia* Bill Wilkerson; *Mariano Escobedo* John Miljan; *John Bigelow* Hugh Sothern; *Carbajal* Irving Pichel; *Duc de Morny* Frank Reicher; *Prince Metternich* Walter Kingsford; *Marshal Randon* Holmes Herbert; *LeMarc* Louis Calhern; *Pepe* Manuel Diaz.

DAUGHTERS COURAGEOUS
STUDIO: Warner Bros. RELEASE DATE: July 22, 1939. RUNNING TIME: 100 minutes. EXECUTIVE PRODUCER: Hal B. Wallis. DIRECTOR: Michael Curtiz. SCREENPLAY: Julius J. Epstein and Philip G. Epstein, based on the play *Fly Away Home* by Dorothy Bennett and Irving White. DIRECTORS OF PHOTOGRAPHY: James Wong Howe and Ernest Haller. ART DIRECTOR: John Hughes. GOWNS: Howard Shoup. MUSIC: Max Steiner. MUSICAL DIRECTOR: Leo F. Forbstein. MAKEUP: Perc Westmore.

CAST: *Gabriel López* John Garfield; *Jim Masters* Claude Rains; *Johnny Heming* Jeffrey Lynn; *Nan Masters* Fay Bainter; *Sam Sloan* Donald Crisp; *Penny* May Robson; *George* Frank McHugh; *Eddie Moore* Dick Foran; *Manuel López* George Humbert; *Judge Hornsby* Berton Churchill; *Buff Masters* Priscilla Lane; *Tinka Masters* Rosemary Lane; *Linda Masters* Lola Lane; *Cora Masters* Gale Page; *Joe* Tom Dugan; *Rich Sucker* Howard Cavanagh; *Conductors* Wilfred Lewis and Jack Mower; *Court Clerk* Nat Carr; *Bar Owner* George Cheseboro; *Tim* Jack Gardner.

REVIEW: "Claude Rains makes the glib, fascinating husband very attractive. His irresistible charm makes it easy to understand why his four daughters love him even after an absence of 20 years during which he has been 'keeping a rendezvous with the universe.'" (Louella O. Parsons, *Los Angeles Examiner*, July 21, 1939)

MR. SMITH GOES TO WASHINGTON
STUDIO: Columbia. RELEASE DATE: October 19, 1939. RUNNING TIME: 126 minutes. PRODUCER/DIRECTOR: Frank Capra. SCREENPLAY: Sidney Buchman, based on the story "The Man from Montana" By Lewis R. Foster. DIRECTOR OF PHOTOGRAPHY: Joseph Walker. ART DIRECTOR: Lionel Banks. GOWNS: Kolloch. FILM EDITORS: Gene Havlik and Al Clark. MUSIC: Dimitri Tiomkin. MUSICAL DIRECTOR: M. W. Stoloff.

Appendix

CAST: *Jefferson Smith* James Stewart; *Saunders* Jean Arthur; *Senator Joseph Paine* Claude Rains; *Jim Taylor* Edward Arnold; *Governor Hopper* Guy Kibbee; *Diz Moore* Thomas Mitchell; *Chick McGann* Eugene Palette; *Ma Smith* Beulah Bondi; *Senate Majority Leader* H. B. Warner; *Senate President* Harry Carey; *Susan Paine* Astrid Allwyn; *Mrs. Hopper* Ruth Donnelly; *Senator MacPherson* Grant Mitchell; *Senator Monroe* Porter Hall; *Senate Minority Leader* Pierre Watkin; *Nosey* Charles Lane; *Carl Cook* Dick Elliott; *Sweeney* Jack Carson; *Ragner* Allan Cavan; *Schultz* Lloyd Whitlock; *Diggs* Maurice Costello; *The Hopper Boys* Billy, Delmar, Gary, Harry Watson, and John Russell; with Baby Dumpling and H. V. Kaltenberg.

REVIEW: "Claude Rains in his many years as a screen actor has never bettered his performance as 'The Silver Knight,' the veteran senator who has had to compromise with the powerful state boss so that he might hold his position and be assured of reelection. He is not in any sense a villain, but a man driven to do the will of his master." (Louella O. Parsons, *Los Angeles Examiner*, October 25, 1939)

NOTE: *Mr. Smith Goes to Washington* marked Rains's first Academy Award nomination for Best Actor in a Supporting Role. His competition included Brian Aherne in *Juarez*, Harry Carey in *Mr. Smith Goes to Washington*, Brian Donlevy in *Beau Geste*, but the award went to Thomas Mitchell in *Stagecoach*.

FOUR WIVES
STUDIO: Warner Bros./First National. RELEASE DATE: December 25, 1939. RUNNING TIME: 110 minutes. EXECUTIVE PRODUCER: Hal B. Wallis. DIRECTOR: Michael Curtiz. DIALOGUE DIRECTOR: Jo Graham. SCREENPLAY: Julius J. Epstein, Philip G. Epstein, and Maurice Hanline, based on the story "Sister Act" by Fannie Hurst. DIRECTOR OF PHOTOGRAPHY: Sol Polito. ART DIRECTOR: John Hughes. GOWNS: Howard Shoup. MAKEUP: Perc Westmore. FILM EDITOR: Ralph Dawson; MUSIC: Max Steiner. MUSICAL DIRECTOR: Leo F. Forbstein.

CAST: *Adam Lemp* Claude Rains; *Felix Deitz* Jeffrey Lynn; *Dr. Clinton Forrest, Jr.* Eddie Albert; *Aunt Etta* May Robson; *Ben Crowley* Frank McHugh; *Ernest Talbot* Dick Foran; *Dr. Clinton Forrest* Henry O'Neill; *Mrs. Ridgefield* Vera Lewis; *Frank* John Qualen; *Mickey Borden* John Garfield; *Joe* Olin Howland; *Charlie* Pat West; *Mathilde* Ruth Tobey; *Boy Soprano* Dennie Jackson; *Conductor* Wilfred Lucas; *Lab Technician* George Reeves.

1940

SATURDAY'S CHILDREN
STUDIO: Warner Bros. RELEASE DATE: May 4, 1940. RUNNING TIME: 97

minutes. EXECUTIVE PRODUCER: Hal B. Wallis. ASSOCIATE PRODUC-
ER: Henry Blanke. DIRECTOR: Vincent Sherman. SCREENPLAY: Julius J.
Epstein and Philip G. Epstein, based on the play by Maxwell Anderson. DIA-
LOGUE DIRECTOR: Irving Rapper. ASSISTANT DIRECTOR: Elmer Deck-
er. DIRECTOR OF PHOTOGRAPHY: James Wong Howe. ART DIRECTOR:
Hugh Reticker. SPECIAL EFFECTS: Robert Burks. GOWNS: Milo Anderson.
MUSICAL DIRECTOR: Leo F. Forbstein. SOUND: H. G. Riggs.

CAST: *Rims Rosson* John Garfield; *Bobby Halevy* Anne Shirley; *Henry Halevy*
Claude Rains; *Florrie Sands* Lee Patrick; *Herbie Smith* George Tobias; *Willie Sands*
Roscoe Karns; *Gertrude Mills* Dennie Moore; *Mrs. Halevy* Elizabeth Risdon; *Mr.
Norman* Berton Churchill; *Cab Driver* Frank Faylen; *Mr. MacReady* John Ridgely;
Mrs. MacReady Margot Stevenson; *Mac* Jack Mower; *Carpenters* John Qualen,
Tom Dugan; *Mailman* Creighton Hale; *Nurses* Maris Wrixon, Lucille Fairbanks.

REVIEW: "Claude Rains is strong in the support as girl's plodding and sympathetically understanding father." (*Variety*, April 10, 1940)

THE SEA HAWK
STUDIO: Warner Bros. RELEASE DATE: August 31, 1940. RUNNING TIME:
126 minutes. EXECUTIVE PRODUCER: Hal B. Wallis. ASSOCIATE PRO-
DUCER: Henry Blanke. DIRECTOR: Michael Curtiz. DIALOGUE DIREC-
TOR: Jo Graham. ASSISTANT DIRECTOR: Jack Sullivan. SCREENPLAY:
Howard Koch and Seton I. Miller. DIRECTOR OF PHOTOGRAPHY: Sol
Polito. FILM EDITOR: George Amy. ART DIRECTOR: Anton Grot. COS-
TUMES: Orry-Kelly. MAKEUP: Perc Westmore. MUSIC: Erich Wolfgang Korn-
gold. MUSICAL DIRECTOR: Leo F. Forbstein. ORCHESTRATIONS: Hugo
Friedhofer, Milan Roder, Ray Heindorf, and Simon Bucharoff. A First National
Picture.

CAST: *Captain Geoffrey Thorpe* Errol Flynn; *Doña Maria* Brenda Marshall; *Don
José Alvarez de Córdoba* Claude Rains; *Elizabeth I* Flora Robson; *Carl Pitt* Alan
Hale; *Lord Wolfingham* Henry Daniell; *Miss Latham* Una O'Connor; *Abbott* James
Stephenson; *Captain López* Gilbert Roland; *Danny Logan* William Lundigan; *Oli-
ver Scott* Julien Mitchell; *Philip II* Montagu Love; *Eli Matson* J.M. Kerrigan; *Martin
Burke* David Bruce; *William Tuttle* Clifford Brooke; *Walter Boggs* Clyde Cook; *In-
quisitor* Fritz Leiber; *Monty Preston* Ellis Irving; *Kroner* Francis McDonald; *Captain
Mendoza* Pedro de Cordoba; *Peralta* Ian Keith.

REVIEW: "Little credit can be extended to the overwritten script, with long
passages of dry and uninteresting dialogue, or to the slow-paced, uninspiring

direction of Michael Curtiz. . . . Of the extended supporting cast, Claude Rains, Donald Crisp, Alan Hale and Henry Daniell, as most prominent." (*Variety*, July 21, 1940)

LADY WITH RED HAIR
STUDIO: Warner Bros./First National. RELEASE DATE: November 30, 1940. RUNNING TIME: 78 minutes. EXECUTIVE PRODUCERS: Jack L Warner and Bryan Foy. ASSOCIATE PRODUCER: Edmund Grainger. DIRECTOR: Kurt Bernhardt. DIALOGUE DIRECTOR: Hugh Cummings. ASSISTANT DIRECTOR: Art Lucker. SCREENPLAY: Charles Kenyon and Milton Krims; story by N. Brewster Morse and Norbert Faulkner, based on the memoirs of Mrs. Leslie Carter. DIRECTOR OF PHOTOGRAPHY: Arthur Edeson. FILM EDITOR: James Gibbon. ART DIRECTOR: Max Parker. GOWNS: Milo Anderson. MAKEUP: Perc Westmore. MUSIC: H. Roemheld. MUSICAL DIRECTOR: Leo Forbstein. SOUND: Oliver S. Garretson. TECHNICAL ADVISOR: Lou Payne.

CAST: *Mrs. Leslie Carter* Miriam Hopkins; *David Belasco* Claude Rains; *Lou Payne* Richard Ainley; *Mrs. Dudley* Laura Hope Crews; *Mrs. Frazier* Helen Westley; *Charles Bryant* John Litel; *Mrs. Brooks* Mona Barrie; *Mr. Clifton* Victor Jory; *Mr. Chapman* Cecil Kellaway; *Mr. Williams* Cornel Wilde; *Mr. Foster* Fritz Leiber; *Dudley Carter* Johnnie Russell; *Henry DeMille* Selmer Jackson.

REVIEW: "Claude Rains provides a standout characterization as David Belasco, and his work, coupled with that of Miriam Hopkins as Mrs. Carter, does much to maintain interest in the proceedings." (*Variety*, November 13, 1940)

1941

FOUR MOTHERS
STUDIO: Warner Bros. RELEASE DATE: January 4, 1941. RUNNING TIME: 81 minutes. EXECUTIVE PRODUCER: Hal B. Wallis. ASSOCIATE PRODUCER: Henry Blanke. DIRECTOR: William Keighley. SCREENPLAY: Steven Morehouse Avery, suggested by the story "Sister Act" by Fannie Hurst. DIRECTOR OF PHOTOGRAPHY: Charles Rosher. FILM EDITOR: Ralph Dawson. SOUND: Charles Lang. MUSICAL DIRECTOR: Leo F. Forbstein. MUSIC: Heinz Roemheld, with Jack Scholl. ART DIRECTOR: Robert Haas. GOWNS: Howard Shoup. MAKEUP: Perc Westmore.

CAST: *Adam Lemp* Claude Rains; *Felix Deitz* Jeffrey Lynn; *Clint Forrest* Eddie Albert; *Ben Crowley* Frank McHugh; *Aunt Etta* May Robson; *Emma Lemp Talbot* Gale Page; *Ernest Talbot* Dick Foran; *Mrs. Ridgefield* Vera Lewis; *Ann Lemp Deitz*

Priscilla Lane; *Kay Lemp Forrest* Rosemary Lane; *Thea Lemp Crowley* Lola Lane; *Mr. Davis* Thurston Hall.

HERE COMES MR. JORDAN
STUDIO: Columbia. RELEASE DATE: August 21, 1941. RUNNING TIME: 93 minutes. PRODUCER: Everett Riskin. DIRECTOR: Alexander Hall. SCREEN-PLAY: Sidney Buchman and Seton I. Miller, based on the play *Heaven Can Wait* by Harry Segall. DIRECTOR OF PHOTOGRAPHY: Joseph Walker. FILM ED-ITOR: Viola Lawrence. ASSISTANT DIRECTOR: William Mull. ART DIREC-TOR: Lionel Banks. MUSIC: Frederick Hollander. MUSICAL DIRECTOR: M. W. Stoloff. GOWNS: Edith Head.

CAST: *Joe Pendleton* Robert Montgomery; *Bette Logan* Evelyn Keyes; *Mr. Jordan* Claude Rains; *Julia Farnsworth* Rita Johnson; *Messenger 7013* Edward Everett Horton; *Max Corkle* James Gleason; *Tony Abbott* John Emery; *Inspector Williams* Donald MacBride; *Lefty* Don Costello; *Sisk* Halliwell Hobbs; *Bugs* Benny Rubin.

REVIEW: "Plenty of laughs geared for widest audience appeal. . . . Rains and Gleason click effectively with standout performances." (*Variety*, July 30, 1941)

THE WOLF MAN
STUDIO: Universal. RELEASE DATE: December 20, 1941. RUNNING TIME: 71 minutes. PRODUCER/DIRECTOR: George Waggner. ASSISTANT DI-RECTOR: Vernon Keays. SCREENPLAY: Curt Siodmak. DIRECTOR OF PHOTOGRAPHY: Joseph Valentine. FILM EDITOR: Ted Kent. ART DI-RECTOR: Jack Otterson. ASSOCIATE ART DIRECTOR: Robert Boyle. SET DECORATOR: Russell A. Gausman. MUSIC: Charles Previn, Hans J. Salter, and Frank Skinner. MUSICAL DIRECTOR: Charles Previn. SOUND: Bernard B. Brown. PHOTOGRAPHIC EFFECTS: John P. Fulton. MAKEUP: Jack P. Pierce. GOWNS: Vera West.

CAST: *Sir John Talbot* Claude Rains; *Dr. Lloyd* Warren William; *Paul Montford* Ralph Bellamy; *Frank Andrews* Patric Knowles; *Bela, the Gypsy* Bela Lugosi; *Lawrence Talbot* Lon Chaney; *Gwen Conliffe* Evelyn Ankers; *Maleva* Maria Ouspenskaya; *Jenny Williams* Fay Helm; *Charles Conliffe* J. M. Kerrigan; *Mr. Twiddle* Forrester Harvey; *Kendall* Leyland Hodgson; *Mrs. Williams* Doris Lloyd; *Reverend Norman* Harry Stubbs; *Richardson* Tom Stevenson; *Villagers* Olaf Hytten and Gibson Gowland; *Talbot Chauffeur* Eric Wilton; *Mrs. Bally* Ottola Nesmith; *Mrs. Wykes* Connie Leon; *Gypsy Woman* Jesse Arnold; *Phillips* Ernie Stanton.

REVIEW: "Embellished by a cast of well-known players and having a fairly dressy

Appendix

production, it is one of the more successful of this type of film." (*New York Herald-Tribune*, undated clipping, December 1941)

1942

KINGS ROW
STUDIO: Warner Bros./First National. RELEASE DATE: April 18, 1942. RUNNING TIME: 127 minutes. EXECUTIVE PRODUCER: Hal B. Wallis. ASSOCIATE PRODUCER: David Lewis. DIRECTOR: Sam Wood. SCREENPLAY: Casey Robinson, based on the novel by Henry Bellamann. DIRECTOR OF PHOTOGRAPHY: James Wong Howe. FILM EDITOR: Ralph Dawson. ART DIRECTOR: Carl Jules Weyl. PRODUCTION DESIGNER: William Cameron Menzies. MUSICAL SCORE: Erich Wolfgang Korngold. ORCHESTRAL ARRANGEMENTS: Hugo Friedhofer. MUSICAL DIRECTOR: Leo F. Forbstein. SPECIAL EFFECTS: Robert Burks. SOUND: Robert B. Lee. GOWNS: Orry-Kelly. MAKEUP: Perc Westmore.

CAST: *Randy Monaghan* Ann Sheridan; *Parris Mitchell* Robert Cummings; *Drake McHugh* Ronald Reagan; *Cassandra Tower* Betty Field; *Dr. Henry Gordon* Charles Coburn; *Dr. Alexander Q. Tower* Claude Rains; *Mrs. Harriet Gordon* Judith Anderson; *Louise Gordon* Nancy Coleman; *Elise Sandor* Kaaren Verne; *Col. Skeffington* Henry Davenport; *Mme. Van Eln* Maria Ouspenskaya; *Pa Monaghan* Ernest Cossart; *Tod Monaghan* Pat Moriarty; *Anna* Ilka Gruning; *Sam Winters* Minor Watson; *Dr. Berdoff* Lugwig Stossel; *Mr. Sandor* Erwin Kalser; *Dr. Candell* Egon Brecher; *Randy as a Child* Ann Todd; *Drake as a Child* Douglas Croft; *Parris as a Child* Scotty Beckett; *Cassandra as a Child* Mary Thomas; *Louise as a Child* Joan Duval; *Mrs. Tower* Eden Gray; *Benny Singer* Danny Jackson; *Willie* Henry Blair; *Aunt Mamie* Leah Baird; *Poppy Ross* Julie Warren; *Ginny Ross* Mary Scott.

REVIEW: "Claude Rains gives a fine, intelligent performance as Dr. Tower and I must say the movie reason for his treatment of his daughter [schizophrenia instead of incest] is infinitely better than the reason given in the book." (Louella O. Parsons, *Los Angeles Examiner*, April 2, 1942)

MOONTIDE
STUDIO: Twentieth Century-Fox. RELEASE DATE: May 29, 1942. RUNNING TIME: 94 minutes. PRODUCER: Mark Hellinger. DIRECTOR: Archie Mayo. SCREENPLAY: John O'Hara, based on the novel by Willard Robertson. DIRECTOR OF PHOTOGRAPHY: Charles Clarke. FILM EDITOR: William Reynolds. SOUND: Eugene Grossman and Roger Heman. MUSIC: Cyril J. Mockridge and David Buttolph. ART DIRECTORS: James Basevi and Rich-

235

ard Day. SET DECORATOR: Thomas Little. COSTUMES: Gwen Wakeling. MAKEUP: Guy Pearce.

CAST: *Bobo* Jean Gabin; *Anna* Ida Lupino; *Tiny* Thomas Mitchell; *Nutsy* Claude Rains; *Dr. Brothers* Jerome Cowan; *Woman on Boat* Helene Reynolds; *Reverend Price* Ralph Byrd; *Bartender* William Halligan; *Takeo* Victor Sen Yung; *Hirota* Chester Gan; *Mildred* Robin Raymond; *Pop Kelly* Arthur Aylesworth; *Hotel Clerk* Arthur Hohl; *Mac* John Kelly; *Mr. Simpson* Tully Marshall; *Policeman* Ralph Dunn; *First Waiter* Tom Dugan.

NOW, VOYAGER
STUDIO: Warner Bros. RELEASE DATE: October 31, 1942. RUNNING TIME: 117 minutes. PRODUCER: Hal B. Wallis. DIRECTOR: Irving Rapper. DIALOGUE DIRECTOR: Edward Blatt. SCREENPLAY: Casey Robinson, based on the novel by Olive Higgins Prouty. DIRECTOR OF PHOTOGRAPHY: Sol Polito. FILM EDITOR: Warren Low. MONTAGES: Don Siegel. SPECIAL EFFECTS: Willard Van Enger. ART DIRECTOR: Robert Haas. SET DECORATOR: Fred M. MacLean. SOUND: Robert B. Lee. MUSIC: Max Steiner. MUSICAL DIRECTOR: Leo F. Forbstein. ORCHESTRAL ARRANGEMENTS: Hugo Friedhofer. GOWNS: Orry-Kelly. MAKEUP: Perc Westmore.

CAST: *Charlotte Vale* Bette Davis; *Jerry Durrance* Paul Henreid; *Dr. Jaquith* Claude Rains; *Mrs. Henry Windle Vale* Gladys Cooper; *June Vale* Bonita Granville; *Lisa Vale* Ilka Chase; *Elliot Livingston* John Loder; *Deb McIntyre* Lee Patrick; *Mr. Thompson* Franklin Pangborn; *Miss Trask* Katherine Alexander; *Frank McIntyre* James Rennie; *Dora Pickford* Mary Wickes; *Tina* Janis Wilson; *Tod Andrews* Michael Ames; *Leslie Trotter* Charles Drake; *Giuseppe* Frank Puglia; *William* David Clyde; *Captain* Lester Matthews; *Lloyd* Ian Wolfe; *Hilda* Claire du Brey.

REVIEW: "Those first scenes . . . show Miss Davis as dowdy, plump and possessed of a phobia that probably cries out for the ministrations of a psychiatrist. . . . Treatment by the doctor, played by Claude Rains, transforms the patient into a glamorous, modish, attractive woman. . . . As the curer of Miss Davis' mental ills, Claude Rains gives his usual restrained, above-par performance." (*Variety*, August 19, 1942)

1943

CASABLANCA
STUDIO: Warner Bros. RELEASE DATE: January 23, 1943. RUNNING TIME: 102 minutes. PRODUCER: Hal B. Wallis. DIRECTOR: Michael Curtiz. SCREENPLAY: Julius Epstein, Philip Epstein, and Howard Koch, based on the

unproduced play *Everybody Comes to Rick's* by Murray Burnett and Joan Alison. DIRECTOR OF PHOTOGRAPHY: Arthur Edeson. FILM EDITOR: Owen Marks. SPECIAL EFFECTS: Lawrence Butler and Willard Van Enger. ART DIRECTOR: Carl Jules Weyl. MONTAGES: Don Siegel and James Leicester. MUSIC: Max Steiner; songs "Knock on Wood," "Muse's Call," and "That's What Noah Done," M. K. Jerome and Jack Scholl; song "As Time Goes By," Herman Hupfield. ORCHESTRAL ARRANGEMENTS: Hugo Friedhofer. MUSICAL DIRECTOR: Leo Forbstein. DIALOGUE DIRECTOR: Hugh MacMullan. SOUND: Francis J. Sheid. SET DECORATOR: George James Hopkins. MAKEUP: Perc Westmore. WARDROBE: Orry-Kelly.

CAST: *Rick Blaine* Humphrey Bogart; *Ilsa Lund* Ingrid Bergman; *Victor Laszlo* Paul Henreid; *Captain Louis Renault* Claude Rains; *Major Heinrich Strasser* Conrad Veidt; *Ugarte* Peter Lorre; *Signor Ferrari* Sydney Greenstreet; *Carl* S. Z. Sakall; *Sam* Dooley Wilson; *Yvonne* Madeleine Le Beau; *Berger* John Qualen; *Annina Brandel* Joy Page; *Jan Brandel* Helmut Dantine; *Croupier* Marcel Dalio; *Sascha* Leonid Kinskey; *Singer* Corinna Mura; *Herr Leuchtag* Ludwig Stossel; *Frau Leuchtag* Ilka Gruning; *Arab Vendor* Frank Puglia; *Abdul* Dan Seymour; *Heinz* Richard Ryan; *German Banker* Gregory Gay; *Pickpocket* Curt Bois.

REVIEW: *Casablanca* provided Rains with one of his most iconic screen roles, second only to *The Invisible Man*, and yet critics of the time gave him mostly perfunctory notice. Even Louella Parsons, usually a great Rains booster, noted only that "Claude Rains, as the French prefect of police, is delightful." (*Los Angeles Examiner*, January 30, 1943)

NOTE: *Casablanca* earned Rains his second Academy Award nomination for Best Actor in a Supporting Role. Also nominated were Charles Bickford in *The Song of Bernadette*, J. Carrol Naish in *Sahara*, Akim Tamiroff in *For Whom the Bell Tolls*, with the award going to Charles Coburn in *The More the Merrier*.

FOREVER AND A DAY
STUDIO: RKO. RELEASE DATE: March 26, 1943. RUNNING TIME: 104 minutes. PRODUCERS/DIRECTORS: Rene Clair, Edmund Goulding, Cedric Hardwicke, Frank Lloyd, Victor Saville, Robert Stevenson, and Herbert Wilcox. SCREENPLAY: Contributed to by Charles Bennett, C. S. Forrester, Lawrence Hazard, Michael Hogan, W. P. Lipscomb, Alice Duer Miller, John Van Druten, Alan Campbell, Peter Godfrey, S. M. Herzig, Christopher Isherwood, Gene Lockhart, R. C. Sherriff, Claudine West, Norman Corwin, Jack Hartfield, James Hilton, Emmet Lavery, Frederick Lonsdale, Donald Ogden Stewart, and Keith Winter. DIRECTORS OF PHOTOGRAPHY: Robert De Grasse, Lee

Garmes, Russell Metty, Nicholas Musuraca. FILM EDITORS: Elmo J. Williams
and George Crone.

CAST: Brian Aherne, Ida Lupino, Merle Oberon, C. Aubrey Smith, Robert
Cummings, Ruth Warrick, Kent Smith, Roland Young, Gladys Cooper, Ray Mil-
land, Anna Neagle, Claude Rains, Charles Laughton, Dame May Whitty, Una
O'Connor, Edward Everett Horton, Cedric Hardwicke, Buster Keaton, Jessie
Matthews, Herbert Marshall, Robert Coote, Ian Hunter, Nigel Bruce, Reginald
Gardiner, Arthur Treacher, Edmund Gwenn, Halliwell Hobbes, Patric Knowles,
Montagu Love, Victor McLaglen, Richard Haydn, Clyde Cook, Elsa Lanchester,
Gene Lockhart, Reginald Owen, Donald Crisp, George Kirby, Billy Bevan, Au-
brey Mather, Walter Kingsford, Ivan Simpson, Eric Blore, Wendy Barrie, Ethel
Griffies, June Lockhart, and Lumsden Hare.

REVIEW: "Claude Rains . . . does not impress as the menace." (*Variety*, January
20, 1943)

PHANTOM OF THE OPERA
STUDIO: Universal. RELEASE DATE: August 27, 1943. RUNNING TIME:
92 minutes. PRODUCER: George Waggner. EXECUTIVE PRODUCER: Jack
Gross. DIRECTOR: Arthur Lubin. SCREENPLAY: Eric Taylor and Samuel
Hoffenstein, based on the novel *The Phantom of the Opera* by Gaston Leroux, ad-
aptation by John Jacoby. DIRECTORS OF PHOTOGRAPHY: Hal Mohr and
W. Howard Greene. FILM EDITOR: Russell Schoengarth. ART DIRECTORS:
John B. Goodman and Alexander Golitzen. TECHNICOLOR CONSUL-
TANT: Natalie Kalmus. ASSISTANT DIRECTOR: Charles Gould. SET DEC-
ORATORS: Russell A. Gausman and Ira S. Webb. DIALOGUE DIRECTOR:
Joan Hathaway. SOUND DIRECTOR: Bernard B. Brown. SOUND TECH-
NICIAN: Joe Lapis. MUSICAL SCORE AND DIRECTION: Edward Ward.
OPERA SEQUENCES: William Von Wymetal and Lester Horton. CHORAL
DIRECTOR: William Tyroler. ORCHESTRATIONS: Harold Zweifel and Ar-
thur Schutt. MAKEUP: Jack P. Pierce. COSTUMES: Vera West.

CAST: *Anatole Garron* Nelson Eddy; *Christine DuBois* Susanna Foster; *Erique
Claudin* Claude Rains; *Raoul Daubert* Edgar Barrier; *Signor Ferretti* Leo Carillo;
Mme. Biancarolli Jane Farrar; *Lecours* Fritz Feld; *Amiot* J. Edward Bromberg;
Vercheres Steven Geray; *Villeneuve* Frank Puglia; *Gerard* Hume Cronyn; *Christine's
Aunt* Barbara Everest; *Franz Liszt* Fritz Leiber; *Mme. Lorenzi* Nicki Andre; *Jeanne*
Gladys Blake; *Yvette* Elvira Curci; *Marcel* Hans Herbert; *Landlady* Kate Lawson;
Pleyel Miles Mander; *Celeste* Rosina Galli; *Le Fort* Walter Stahl; *Desjardines* Paul
Marion; *Nurse* Beatrice Roberts; *Reporters* Muni Seroff, Dick Bartell, Jim Mitch-

ell, and Wheaton Chambers; *Ferretti's Maid* Belle Mitchell; *Office Manager* Ernest Golm; *Georgette* Renee Carson; *Gendarmes* Lane Chandler and Stanley Blystone; *Office Boy* John Walsh; *Policeman* Alphonse Martell; *Usher* Edward Clark; *Stagehands* William Desmond and Hank Mann.

REVIEWS: "Claude Rains intelligently assumes the character of the mad violinist whose homicidal tendency is unleashed when he believes his concerto has been stolen by a music publisher, and imparts a haunting performance, by turns tender and terrifying." (*Variety*, August 13, 1943) "Rains gives the performance his expected, assured performance that joins with the screenplay to lift the hooey horror characterization to a motivated, unfortunate human being." (*Box Office Digest*, August 23, 1943) "The script never tells us that Claudin, the broken-down violinist, is Christine's father. But the sensitive performance by Rains leaves no other conclusion possible." (*Hollywood Reporter*, August 13, 1943)

1944

PASSAGE TO MARSEILLES
STUDIO: Warner Bros. RELEASE DATE: March 11, 1944. RUNNING TIME: 110 minutes. PRODUCER: Hal B. Wallis. DIRECTOR: Michael Curtiz. SCREENPLAY: Casey Robinson and Jack Moffitt, based on a novel by Charles Nordhoff and James N. Hall. DIRECTOR OF PHOTOGRAPHY: James Wong Howe. SPECIAL EFFECTS: Jack R. Cosgrove (director) and Edwin DuPar. FILM EDITOR: Owen Marks. DIALOGUE DIRECTOR: Herschel Daugherty. ART DIRECTOR: Carl Jules Weyl. SET DECORATOR: George James Hopkins. MONTAGE: James Leicester. MUSIC: Max Steiner. ORCHESTRAL ARRANGEMENTS: Leonid Raab. MUSICAL DIRECTOR: Leo F. Forbstein. TECHNICAL ADVISOR: Sylvain Robert. SOUND: Everett A. Brown. ASSISTANT DIRECTOR: Frank Heath. GOWNS: Leah Rhodes. MAKEUP: Perc Westmore.

CAST: *Jean Matrac* Humphrey Bogart; *Captain Freycinet* Claude Rains; *Paula* Michele Morgan; *Major Duval* Sydney Greenstreet; *Renault* Philip Dorn; *Garou* Helmut Dantine; *Marius* Peter Lorre; *Petit* George Tobias; *Manning* John Loder; *Grandpere* Vladimir Sokoloff; *Chief Engineer* Eduardo Cianelli; *Captain Malo* Victor Francen; *First Mate* Konstantin Shayne; *Second Engineer* Louis Mercier; *Second Mate* Monte Blue; *Lieutenant Hastings* Stephen Richards; *Jourdain* Hans Conreid; *Bijou* Frederick Brunn; *Mess Boy* Billy Roy; *Lieutenant Lenoir* Charles LaTorre.

REVIEW: "Not only does [Rains] have the biggest part in the picture, but he practically captures all the acting honors in a film filled with good acting." (*Variety*, February 16, 1944)

MR. SKEFFINGTON
STUDIO: Warner Bros. RELEASE DATE: August 12, 1944. RUNNING TIME: 146 minutes. PRODUCERS: Julius J. Epstein and Philip G. Epstein. DIRECTOR: Vincent Sherman. SCREENWRITERS: Julius J. and Philip G. Epstein, based on the novel *Mr. Skeffington* by "Elizabeth." DIRECTOR OF PHOTOGRAPHY: Ernest Haller. FILM EDITOR: Ralph Dawson. MUSIC: Franz Waxman. ORCHESTRAL ARRANGEMENTS: Leonid Raab. MUSICAL DIRECTOR: Leo F. Forbstein. ART DIRECTOR: Robert Haas. SET DECORATOR: Fred M. McLean. SOUND: Robert B. Lee. MONTAGE: James Leicester. GOWNS: Orry-Kelly. MAKEUP: Perc Westmore.

CAST: *Fanny Trellis* Bette Davis; *Job Skeffington* Claude Rains; *George Trellis* Walter Abel; *"Trippy" Trellis* Richard Waring; *Dr. Byles* George Coulouris; *Young Fanny* Marjorie Riordan; *MacMahon* Robert Shayne; *Jim Conderley* John Alexander; *Edward Morrison* Jerome Cowan; *Johnny Mitchell* Charles Drake; *Chester Forbish* Peter Whitney; *Manby* Dorothy Peterson; *Thatcher* Bill Kennedy; *Rev. Hyslup* Tom Stevenson; *Dr. Melton* Walter Kingsford; *Soames* Halliwell Hobbes; *Fanny at age two* Gigi Perreau; *Fanny at age five* Bunny Sunshine; *Fanny at age ten* Sylvia Arslan; *Singer* Dolores Gray; *Marie* Ann Doran; *Dr. Fawcette* Erskine Sanford; *Miss Morris* Molly Lamont; *Clinton* William Forrest; *Perry Lanks* Cyril Ring; *Mrs. Thatcher* Bess Flowers.

REVIEW: "Claude Rains plays with honor and dignity in the plainly subordinate title role, but it is hard to conceive why he never gives his wife a light chip on the jaw." (Bosley Crowther, *New York Times*, May 26, 1944)

NOTE: For *Mr. Skeffington* Rains earned his third Academy Award nomination for Best Actor in a Supporting Role. He competed with Hume Cronyn in *The Seventh Cross*, Clifton Webb in *Laura*, Monty Woolley in *Since You Went Away*, and Barry Fitzgerald, who won the prize for *Going My Way*.

1945

STRANGE HOLIDAY
STUDIO: Elite Pictures Corporation. RELEASE DATE: October 19, 1945 (rerelease: September 2, 1946). RUNNING TIME: 61 minutes. PRODUCERS: A. W. Hackel, Edward Finney, and Max King. DIRECTOR/SCREENWRITER: Arch Oboler. DIRECTOR OF PHOTOGRAPHY: Robert Surtees. FILM EDITOR: Fred Feitshans. MUSIC: Gordon Jenkins. ART DIRECTOR: Bernard Herzbrun. SPECIAL EFFECTS: Howard Anderson and Ray Mercer. ASSISTANT DIRECTOR: Sam Nelson. SOUND: W. H. Wilmarth.

CAST: *John Stevenson* Claude Rains; *John, Jr.* Bobbie Stebbins; *Peggy Lee* Barbara Bates; *Woodrow, Jr.* Paul Hilton; *Jean Stevenson* Gloria Holden; *Sam Morgan* Milton Kibbee; *Farmer* Walter White, Jr.; *Truck Driver* Wally Maher; *Examiner* Martin Kosleck; *Betty* Priscilla Lyons; *Boyfriend* David Bradford; *Newsboy* Tommy Cook; *Regan* Griff Barnett; *First Detective* Ed Max; *Miss Simms, Secretary* Helen Mack; *Guard* Charles McAvoy.

NOTE: *Strange Holiday* was re-released by Producers Releasing Corporation (PRC) on September 2, 1946, in a revised version, running 55 minutes.

THIS LOVE OF OURS
STUDIO: Universal. RELEASE DATE: November 2, 1945. RUNNING TIME: 90 minutes. PRODUCER: Howard Benedict. DIRECTOR: William Dieterle. SCREENPLAY: Bruce Manning, John Klorer, and Leonard Lee, based on the play *Come Prima Meglio de Prima* ("Like Before Better than Before") by Luigi Pirandello. (Working title: *As It Was Before!*) DIRECTOR OF PHOTOGRAPHY: Lucien Ballard. FILM EDITOR: Frank Gross. MUSIC: Hans J. Salter. ART DIRECTORS: John B. Goodman, Robert Clatworthy, and Eugene Lourie. SET DECORATORS: Russell A. Gausman and Oliver Emert. GOWNS: Vera West. MERLE OBERSON'S COSTUMES: Travis Banton. DIRECTOR OF SOUND: Bernard B. Brown. SOUND TECHNICIAN: Charles Carroll. ASSISTANT DIRECTOR: Fred Frank. HAIR STYLIST: Carmen Dirigo. DIALOGUE DIRECTOR: Victor Stoloff. ASSOCIATE PRODUCER: Edward Dodds. MAKEUP: Jack Pierce.

CAST: *Karin Touzac* Merle Oberon; *Joseph Targel* Claude Rains; *Michel Touzac* Charles Korvin; *Uncle Bob* Carl Esmond; *Susette Touzac* Sue England; *Chadwick* Jess Barker; *Dr. Jerry Wilkerson* Harry Davenport; *Dr. Lane* Ralph Morgan; *Dr. Bailey* Fritz Lieber.

1946

CAESAR AND CLEOPATRA
STUDIO: The Rank Organization. RELEASE DATE: January 1946. Released in Great Britain by Eagle Lion, and in the United States by United Artists. RUNNING TIME: 138 minutes. PRODUCER/DIRECTOR: Gabriel Pascal. SCENARIO AND DIALOGUE: George Bernard Shaw. GENERAL MANAGER OF PRODUCTION: Tom White. SCRIPT EDITOR: Marjorie Deans. DÉCOR AND COSTUMES: Oliver Messel. ART DIRECTOR: John Bryan (courtesy Gainsborough Pictures Ltd.). MUSIC: George Auric. CONDUCTOR: Muir Matheson, with the National Symphony Orchestra. DIRECTOR OF PHOTOGRAPHY: F. A. Young, with Jack Hildyard, Robert Krasker, and

Jack Cardiff. CAMERA OPERATOR: Ted Scaife. FILM EDITOR: Frederick Wilson. SOUND: John Dennis. DUBBING: Desmond Dew. MATTE SHOTS: Percy Day. CHIEF OF COLOR CONTROL DEPARTMENT: Natalie Kalmus. COLOR ASSISTANT: Joan Bridge.

CAST: *Julius Caesar* Claude Rains; *Cleopatra* Vivien Leigh (courtesy of David O. Selznick); *Apollodorus* Stewart Granger; *Ftatateeta* Flora Robson; *Pothinus* Francis L. Sullivan; *Rufio* Basil Sydney; *Theodotus* Ernest Thesiger; *Lucius Septimus* Raymond Lovell; *Achillas* Anthony Eustral; *Ptolemy* Anthony Harvey; *Nubian Slave* Robert Adams; *First Centurion* Michael Rennie; *Second Centurion* James McKechnie; *Cleopatra's Lady Attendants* Olga Edwards and Harda Swanhilde; *Major Domo* Esme Percy; *Belzanor* Stanley Holloway; *Bel Affris* Leo Genn; *Persian* Alan Wheatley; *Boatman* Anthony Holles; *First Porter* Charles Victor; *Second Porter* Ronald Shiner; *Sentinel* John Bryning; *Auxiliary Sentinels* John Laurie and Charles Rolfe; *Noblemen* Felix Aylmer and Ivor Bernard; *Guardsmen* Valentine Dyall and Charles Deane; *Harpist* Jean Simmons.

REVIEW: "Mr. Rains is delightful as Caesar, manifesting with arch and polished grace all the humor and tolerance and understanding that Mr. Shaw saw in the man. . . . Mr. Rains also handles with sympathy and moving delicacy the fleeting intimations of a middle-aged man's yearn toward youth." (Bosley Crowther, *New York Times*, September 6, 1946)

NOTORIOUS
STUDIO: RKO Radio Pictures. RELEASE DATE: September 6, 1946. RUNNING TIME: 101 minutes. PRODUCER/DIRECTOR: Alfred Hitchcock. ASSISTANT PRODUCER: Barbara Keon. FIRST ASSISTANT DIRECTOR: William Dortman. SCREENPLAY: Ben Hecht, based on an original story by Alfred Hitchcock. DIRECTOR OF PHOTOGRAPHY: Ted Tetzlaff. FILM EDITOR: Theron Warth. SPECIAL EFFECTS: Vernon L. Walker and Paul Eagler. MUSIC: Roy Webb. MUSICAL DIRECTOR: C. Bakaleinikoff. SOUND: John E. Tribby and Terry Kellum. SET DECORATORS: Darrell Silvera and Claude Carpenter. ART DIRECTORS: Albert S. D'Agostino and Carroll Clark. COSTUMES: Edith Head.

CAST: *Devlin* Cary Grant; *Alicia Huberman* Ingrid Bergman; *Alexander Sebastian* Claude Rains; *Paul Prescott* Louis Calhern; *Madame Sebastian* Leopoldine Konstantin; *Dr. Anderson* Reinhold Schunzel; *Walter Beardsley* Moroni Olsen; *Eric Mathis* Ivan Triesault; *Joseph* Alex Minotis; *Mr. Hopkins* Wally Brown; *Ernest Weylin* Gavin Gordon; *Commodore* Charles Mendl; *Dr. Barbosa* Ricardo Costa; *Hupka* Eberhard Krumschmidt; *Ethel* Fay Baker; *Señor Ortiza* Antonio Moreno; *Knerr*

Appendix

Frederick Ledebor; *Dr. Silva* Luis Serrano; *Adams* William Gordon; *Judge* Charles D. Brown; *Rossner* Peter Von Zerneck; *Huberman* Fred Nurney.

REVIEW: "Mr. Grant, who is exceptionally solid, is matched for acting honors in the cast by Claude Rains as the Nazi big-wig. . . . Mr. Rains' shrewd and tense performance of this invidious character is responsible for much of the anguish that the siuation creates." (Bosley Crowther, *New York Times*, August 19, 1946)

NOTE: The role of Sebastian Alexander was Rains's final, and unsuccessful, Academy Award nomination for Best Actor in a Supporting Role. He lost to Harold Russell, the maimed returning soldier in *The Best Years of Our Lives*. Also in competition were Charles Coburn in *The Green Years*, William Demarest in *The Jolson Story*, and Clifton Webb in *The Razor's Edge*.

ANGEL ON MY SHOULDER
STUDIO: United Artists. RELEASE DATE: September 20, 1946. RUNNING TIME: 95 minutes. PRODUCER: Charles B. Rogers. DIRECTOR: Archie Mayo. SCREENPLAY: Harry Segall and Roland Kibbee, based on an original story by Harry Segall. DIRECTOR OF PHOTOGRAPHY: James Van Trees. FILM EDITOR: Asa Clark. EDITING SUPERVISOR: George Arthur. MUSIC: Dmitri Tiomkin. ART DIRECTOR: Bernard Herzbrun. SPECIAL EFFECTS: Harry Redmond, Jr. PRODUCTION MANAGERS: David Sussman and William J. Fender. ASSOCIATE PRODUCER: David W. Siegel. SET DRESSER: Edward G. Boyle. SOUND: Frank Webster. GOWNS: Maria Donovan. MEN'S WARDROBE: Robert Marten. PHOTOGRAPHIC EFFECTS: Howard Anderson. MAKEUP: Ern Westmore.

CAST: *Eddie Kagle* Paul Muni; *Barbara Foster* Anne Baxter; *Nick* Claude Rains; *Dr. Higgins* Onslow Stevens; *Albert* George Cleveland; *Smiley Williams* Hardie Albright; *Bellamy* James Flavin; *Minister* Erskine Sanford; *Rosie* Marion Martin; *Chairman* Jonathan Hale; *Jim* Murray Alper; *Brazen Girl* Joan Blair; *Scientist* Fritz Leiber; *Warden* Kurt Katch; *Agatha* Sarah Padden; *Big Harry* Addison Richards; *Shaggsy* Ben Welden; *Mr. Bentley* George Meeker; *Bailiff* Lee Shumway; *Intern* Russ Whiteman; *Gangsters* James Dundee, Mike Lally, Saul Gores, and Duke Taylor; *Kramer* Chester Clute; *Prison Yard Captain* Edward Keane.

REVIEW: "Rains shines as the Devil, shading the character with a likeable puckishness good for both sympathy and chuckles." (*Variety*, September 18, 1946)

DECEPTION
STUDIO: Warner Bros. RELEASE DATE: October 26, 1946. RUNNING

TIME: 111 minutes. PRODUCER: Henry Blanke. DIRECTOR: Irving Rapper. SCREENPLAY: John Collier and Joseph Than, based on the play *Jealousy* by Louis Verneuil. DIRECTOR OF PHOTOGRAPHY: Ernest Haller. FILM EDITOR: Alan Crosland, Jr. MUSIC: Erich Wolfgang Korngold. MUSIC DIRECTOR: Leo F. Forbstein. SOUND: Dolph Thomas. DIALOGUE DIRECTOR: Jack Daniels. WARDROBE: Bernard Newman. SPECIAL EFFECTS: William McGann (director) and Edwin DuPar. MAKEUP: Perc Westmore.

CAST: *Christine Radcliffe* Bette Davis; *Karel Novak* Paul Henreid; *Alexander Hollenius* Claude Rains; *Bertram Gribble* John Abbott; *Jimmy, the Manservant* Benson Fong; *Norma* Louise Austin; *Manager* Kenneth Hunter; *Andre* Jean DeBriac; *Wedding Guests* Philo McCullough, Gertrude Carr, and Bess Flowers.

REVIEWS: "In the play, the man who is bumped off never appears on the stage. Miss Davis might have wished that in the film, too, he were kept more discreetly concealed. For the mephistophelian performance of Claude Rains in this villanous role makes her look completely childish and, from the viewpoint of logic, absurd. As a famous and worldly composer with some vicious attachment to a dame, he fills out a fascinating portrait of a titanic egoist." (Bosley Crowther, *New York Times*, October 19, 1946) "What a performance Claude Rains gives as that composer! Suave, haughty, playing with his mistress the way a cat plays with a mouse. . . . I have seen Rains in many a picture, but 'Deception' is his top performance. His cruelty to the girl, his pretense of helping her husband . . . are all done with typical Rains finesse." (Louella O. Parsons, *Los Angeles Examiner*, November 20, 1946)

1947

THE UNSUSPECTED
STUDIO: Warner Bros. RELEASE DATE: October 11, 1947. RUNNING TIME: 103 minutes. PRODUCER: Charles Hoffman. DIRECTOR: Michael Curtiz. SCREENPLAY: Bess Meredyth and Ranald MacDougall, based on the novel by Charlotte Armstrong. DIRECTOR OF PHOTOGRAPHY: Elwood Bredell. FILM EDITOR: Frederick Richards. MUSIC: Franz Waxman. MUSICAL DIRECTOR: Leo F. Forbstein. SPECIAL EFFECTS PHOTOGRAPHY: Robert Burks. SPECIAL EFFECTS: David C. Kertesz and Harry Barndollar. ART DIRECTOR: Anton Grot. SET DECORATOR: Howard Winterbottom. COSTUMES: Milo Anderson. MAKEUP: Perc Westmore.

CAST: *Matilda Frazier* Joan Caulfield; *Victor Grandison* Claude Rains; *Althea Keane* Audrey Totter; *Jane Moynihan* Constance Bennett; *Oliver Keane* Hurd Hatfield; *Steven Francis* Howard Michael North; *Richard Donovan* Fred Clark; *Press*

Appendix

Jack Lambert; *Max* Harry Lewis; *Donovan's Assistant* Ray Walker; *Mrs. White* Nana Bryant; *Justice of the Peace* Walter Baldwin; *Roslyn* Barbara Woodell; *Bill* Douglas Kennedy; *Irving* Ross Ford; *Announcer* Art Gilmore; *Dr. Edelman* David Leonard.

REVIEW: "Rains is intriguing as the fashionable radio ghoul . . ." (Bosley Crowther, *New York Times*, October 4, 1947)

1949

THE PASSIONATE FRIENDS
STUDIO: Pinewood/Cineguild. RELEASE DATE: January 20, 1949. RUN-NING TIME: 91 minutes. PRODUCER: Ronald Neame. DIRECTOR: David Lean. SCREENPLAY: Eric Ambler, adapted by David Lean and Stanley Haynes; based on the novel by H. G. Wells. DIRECTOR OF PHOTOGRAPHY: Guy Green. CAMERA OPERATOR: Oswald Morris. FILM EDITOR: Geoffrey Foot. SET DESIGNER: John Bryan. COSTUMES: Margaret Furse. ASSISTANT DIRECTOR: George Pollock. ASSOCIATE PRODUCER: Norman Spencer. SOUND: Stanley Lambourne and Gordon K. McCallum. DUBBING EDITOR: Winston Ryder. CONTINUITY: Margaret Sibley. HAIR DRESSER: Biddy Chrystal. MUSIC: Richard Addinsell, performed by the Philharmonica Orchestra of London, conducted by Muir Matheson.

CAST: *Mary Justin* Ann Todd; *Howard Justin* Claude Rains; *Steven Stratton* Trevor Howard; *Pat* Isabel Dean; *Miss Layton* Betty Ann Davies; *Servant* Arthur Howard; *Hotel Manager* Guido Lorraine; *Hall Porter* Marcel Poncin; *Solicitor* Wilfrid Hyde-White; *Chambermaid* Natasha Sokolova; *Flowerwoman* Helen Burls; *Charwoman* Frances Waring; *Bridge Guest* Wanda Rogerson; *Emigration Official* Jean Serrett.

REVIEW: "Polished acting, masterly direction and an excellent script put 'The Passionate Friends' in the top Rank of British productions. . . . Claude Rains, in the role of the banker husband, as a model of competence . . ." (*Variety*, February 2, 1949)

NOTE: *The Passionate Friends* was retitled *One Woman's Story* for American release.

ROPE OF SAND
STUDIO: Paramount. RELEASE DATE: September 23, 1949. RUNNING TIME: 104 minutes. PRODUCER: Hal B. Wallis. DIRECTOR: William Diet-erle. SCREENPLAY AND ORIGINAL STORY: Walter Doniger. ADDITION-AL DIALOGUE: John Paxton. DIRECTOR OF PHOTOGRAPHY: Charles B. Lang. PROCESS PHOTOGRAPHY: Farciot Eduoart. SPECIAL EFFECTS:

Gordon Jennings. EDITORIAL SUPERVISOR: Warren Low. SOUND: Harold Lewis and Walter Oberst. MUSIC: Franz Waxman, with music and lyrics to "The Zulu Warrior" and "The Crickets" by Josef Marais. ART DIRECTORS: Hans Dreier and Franz Bachelin. SET DECORATORS: Sam Comer and Grace Gregory. ASSISTANT DIRECTOR: Richard McWhorter. COSTUMES: Edith Head. MAKEUP: Wally Westmore.

CAST: *Mike Davis* Burt Lancaster; *Paul Vogel* Paul Henreid; *Arthur Martingale* Claude Rains; *Suzanne Renaud* Corinne Calvet; *Toady* Peter Lorre; *Dr. Francis Hunter* Sam Jaffe; *Thompson* John Bromfield; *Pierson* Mike Mazurki; *John* Kenny Washington; *Chairman* Edmund Breon; *Ingram* Hayden Rorke; *Waiter* David Hoffman; *Jacques, the Headwaiter* Georges Renavent; *Henry, the Bartender* David Thursby; *Clerk* James R. Scott; *Specialty Singers* Josef Marais and Miranda.

REVIEW: "Among the characters moving through the piece [is] Claude Rains doing a nifty performance of the effete head of the syndicate." (*Variety*, June 29, 1949)

SONG OF SURRENDER
STUDIO: Paramount. RELEASE DATE: October 28, 1949. RUNNING TIME: 93 minutes. PRODUCER: Richard Maibaum. DIRECTOR: Mitchell Leisen. SCREENPLAY: Richard Maibaum, based on a story by Ruth McKenney and Richard Bransten. DIRECTOR OF PHOTOGRAPHY: Daniel L. Fapp. SPECIAL PHOTOGRAPHIC EFFECTS: Gordon Jennings. PROCESS PHOTOGRAPHY: Farciot Eduoart. MAKEUP SUPERVISOR: Wally Westmore. SOUND: John McCay and John Cope. FILM EDITOR: Alma Macrorie. ART DIRECTORS: Hans Dreier and Henry Bumstead. DIALOGUE DIRECTOR: Phyllis Loughton. ASSISTANT DIRECTOR: John Coonan. MUSIC: "Song of Surrender": music, Victor Young; lyrics, Jay Livingston and Ray Evans, sung by Buddy Clark. "Serenade" by Franz Schubert, sung by Richard Tucker. "Una Furtiva Lagrima," "O Sole Mio," "O Paradiso," and "La Donna é Mobile" from Enrico Caruso's RCA Victor recordings. COSTUMES: Mary Kay Dodson. MAKEUP SUPERVISOR: Wally Westmore.

CAST: *Abigail Hunt* Wanda Hendrix; *Elisha Hunt* Claude Rains; *Bruce Eldridge* Macdonald Carey; *Phyllis Cantwell* Andrea King; *Deacon Parry* Henry Hull; *Mrs. Beecham* Elizabeth Patterson; *Mr. Willis* Art Smith; *Countess Marina* Eva Gabor; *Dubois* John Beal; *Clyde Atherton* Dan Tobin; *General Seckle* Nicholas Joy; *Simon Beecham* Peter Miles; *Auctioneer* Ray Walker; *Faith Beecham* Gigi Perreau; *Mr. Beecham* Ray Bennett; *Mr. Torrance* Clancy Cooper; *Mrs Parry* Georgia Backus.

NOTE: Also known as *Abigail, Dear Heart; Now and Forever;* and *The Sin of Abby Hunt.*

1950

THE WHITE TOWER
STUDIO: RKO. RELEASE DATE: June 24, 1950. RUNNING TIME: 98 minutes. PRODUCER: Sid Rogell. DIRECTOR: Ted Tetzlaff. SCREENPLAY: Paul Jarrico, based on the novel by James Ramsay Ullman. DIRECTOR OF PHOTOGRAPHY: Ray Rennahan. ASSOCIATE PHOTOGRAPHER: Tony Braun. TECHNICOLOR CONSULTANT: Morgan Padelford. SPECIAL EFFECTS: Harold Wellman. FILM EDITOR: Samuel E. Beetley. MUSIC: Roy Webb. MUSICAL DIRECTOR: Constantine Bakaleinikoff. SOUND: Roland Van Hessen and Clem Portman. ART DIRECTORS: Albert S. D'Agostino and Ralph Berger. SET DECORATORS: Darrell Silvera and Harley Miller. HAIR STYLES: Larry Germain.

CAST: *Martin Ordway* Glenn Ford; *Carla Alton* Alida Valli; *Paul Delambre* Claude Rains; *Andreas* Oscar Homolka; *Nicholas Radcliffe* Cedric Hardwicke; *Hein* Lloyd Bridges; *Astrid Delambre* June Clayworth; *Frau Andreas* Lotte Stein; *Knubel* Fred Essler; *Frau Knubel* Edit Angold.

REVIEW: "Claude Rains, as a garrulous weakling, is something of a bore . . ." (Bosley Crowther, *New York Times*, July 3, 1950)

WHERE DANGER LIVES
STUDIO: RKO. RELEASE DATE: July 8, 1950. RUNNING TIME: 82 minutes. PRODUCER: Irving Cummings, Jr. DIRECTOR: John Farrow. SCREENPLAY: Charles Bennett, based on the story "White Rose for Julie" by Leo Rosten. DIRECTOR OF PHOTOGRAPHY: Nicholas Musuraca. FILM EDITOR: Eda Warren. MUSIC: Roy Webb. MUSICAL DIRECTOR: Constantine Bakaleinikoff. ART DIRECTORS: Albert S. D'Agostino and Ralph Berger. SET DECORATORS: Darrell Silvera and John Sturtevant. COSTUMES: Michael Woulfe. MAKEUP: Mel Burns.

CAST: *Dr. Jeff Cameron* Robert Mitchum; *Margo Lannington* Faith Domergue; *Frederick Lannington* Claude Rains; *Julie* Maureen O'Sullivan; *Police Chief* Charles Kemper; *Klauber* Ralph Dumke; *Mr. Bogardus* Billy House; *Dr. Maynard* Harry Shannon; *Milo DeLong* Philip Van Zandt; *Dr. Mullenbach* Jack Kelly; *Mrs. Bogardus* Lillian West; *Nurse Collins* Ruth Lewis; *Nurse Seymour* Julia Faye; *Nurse Clark* Dorothy Abbott; *Assistant Police Chief* Lester Dorr; *Intern* Art Depuis.

CLAUDE RAINS

REVIEW: "Story is a highly contrived, never credible chase melodrama. Other than Mitchum and Domergue . . . footage gives little length to the supporting players and Rains has only one sequence at the start of the action." (*Variety*, June 21, 1950).

1951

SEALED CARGO

STUDIO: RKO. RELEASE DATE: May 19, 1951. RUNNING TIME: 90 minutes. EXECUTIVE PRODUCER: Samuel Bischoff. PRODUCER: William Duff. DIRECTOR: Alfred Werker. SCREENPLAY: Dale Van Every, Oliver H. P. Garrett, and Roy Huggins, based on the novel *The Gaunt Woman* by Edmund Gilligan. DIRECTOR OF PHOTOGRAPHY: George Diskant. FILM EDITOR: Ralph Dawson. MUSIC DIRECTOR: C. Bakaleinikoff. ART DIRECTOR: Albert S. D'Agostino.

CAST: *Pat Bannon* Dana Andrews; *Margaret McLean* Carla Balenda; *Captain Skalder* Claude Rains; *Conrad* Philip Dorn; *McLean* Onslow Stevens; *Steve* Skip Homeier; *Holger* Eric Feldary; *Skipper Ben* J. M. Kerrigan; *Dolan* Arthur Shields; *Caleb* Morgan Farley; *Ambrose* Dave Thursby; *Anderson* Henry Rowland; *Smitty* Charles A. Browne; *Owen* Don Dillaway; *Tom* Al Hill; *Lt. Cameron* Lee McGregor; *Holtz* William Andrews; *Second Mate* Richard Norris; *Schuster* Whit Bissell; *Villagers* Kathleen Ellis, Karen Norris, and Harry Mancke.

REVIEW: "Claude Rains clicks in his characterization of the German officer, getting across his menacing aspect underneath his quiet, cultured front." (*Variety*, April 25, 1951)

1953

THE MAN WHO WATCHED THE TRAINS GO BY

STUDIO: Eros. RELEASE DATE: Europe: February 1953. USA: June 5, 1953 (under the title *The Paris Express*). RUNNING TIME: 82 minutes. PRODUCERS: Raymond Stross and Josef Shaftel. DIRECTOR: Harold French. SCREENPLAY: Paul Jarrico and Harold French, based on the novel by Georges Simenon. CINEMATOGRAPHER: Otto Heller. FILM EDITOR: Vera Campbell. ASSEMBLING EDITOR: Peter Hunt. ART DIRECTOR: Paul Sherrif. MUSIC: Benjamin Frankel (also conductor). PRODUCTION MANAGER: Ernest Holding. ASSISTANT DIRECTOR: Adrian Pryce-Jones. CAMERA OPERATOR: Gus Drisse. LOCATION MANAGER: Teddy Joseph. SOUND EDITOR: Leo Trumm. SOUND RECORDING: W. Lindop. MAKEUP: Stuart Freeborn. TECHNICOLOR CONSULTANT: Joan Bridge. ASSOCIATE PRODUCER: David Berman.

Appendix

CAST: *Kees Popinga* Claude Rains; *Michelle* Marta Toren; *Inspector Lucas* Marius Goring; *Jeanne* Anouk Aimee; *Julius De Koster* Herbert Lom; *Mrs. Popinga* Lucie Mannheim; *Merkemans* Felix Aylmer; *Louis* Ferdy Mayne; *Goin* Eric Pohlman; *De Koster* Gibb McLaughlin; *Mrs. Lucas* Mary Mackenzie; *Karl Popinga* Robin Alaouf; *Frida Popinga* Joan St. Clair; *Train Conductor* Michael Alain.

REVIEW: "The picture lacks quality, character, sympathy and suspense–and when [Rains] goes mad at the finish, he's not the only one in the house." (Bosley Crowther, *New York Times*, June 6, 1952)

1956

LISBON
STUDIO: Republic. RELEASE DATE: August 17, 1956. RUNNING TIME: 90 minutes. PRODUCER/DIRECTOR: Ray Milland. SCREENPLAY: John Tucker Battle, based on a story by Martin Racklin. DIRECTOR OF PHOTOGRAPHY: Jack Marta. FILM EDITOR: Richard L. Van Enger. MUSIC: Nelson Riddle.

CAST: *Captain Robert John Evans* Ray Milland; *Sylvia Merrill* Maureen O'Hara; *Aristides Mavros* Claude Rains; *Maria Magdalena Masanet* Yvonne Furneaux; *Serafim* Francis Lederer; *Lloyd Merrill* Percy Marmont; *Inspector Joao Casimiro Fonseca* Jay Novello; *Edgar Selwyn* Edward Chapman; *Philip Norworth* Harold Jamison; *Tio Rabio* Humberto Madeira.

REVIEW: "As a production, the picture is rich in pictorial effects, but it could have used a little sharper overseeing of story material, particularly that opening sequence in which sadistic Claude Rains, international crook, smashes a song bird with his tennis racquet so his hungry cat can have some breakfast." (*Variety*, August 1, 1956)

NOTE: *Lisbon* was shot in a widescreen process called "Naturama" in "Trucolor."

1959

THIS EARTH IS MINE
STUDIO: Universal-International. RELEASE DATE: June 26, 1959. RUNNING TIME: 126 minutes. EXECUTIVE PRODUCER: Edward Muhl. PRODUCERS: Casey Robinson and Claude Heilman. DIRECTOR: Henry King. SCREENPLAY: Casey Robinson, based on the novel *The Cup and the Sword* by Alice Tisdale Hobart. DIRECTORS OF PHOTOGRAPHY: Winton C. Hoch and Russell Metty. FILM EDITOR: Ted Kent. ART DIRECTORS: Alexander Golitzen, George W. Davis, and Eric Orbom. SET DECORATORS: Russell

249

A. Gausman, Ruby R. Levitt, and Oliver Emert. SOUND: Leslie I. Carey and Vernon W. Kramer. GOWNS: Bill Thomas. HAIR STYLIST: Larry Germain. MAKEUP: Bud Westmore. In Technicolor and CinemaScope.

CAST: *John Rambeau* Rock Hudson; *Elizabeth Rambeau* Jean Simmons; *Martha Fairon* Dorothy McGuire; *Phillipe Rambeau* Claude Rains; *Francis Fairon* Kent Smith; *Charlotte Rambeau* Anna Lee; *Buz* Cindy Robbins; *Luigi Griffanti* Ken Scott; *Andre Swann* Francis Bethancourt; *Monica* Stacey Graham; *Mama Griffanti* Augusta Merighi; *Chu* Peter Chong; *Derek* Jack Mather; *Yakowitz* Ben Astar; *Petucci* Alberto Morin; *Mrs. Petucci* Penny Santon; *Berke* Emory Parnell; *Nate Forster* Lionel Ames; *Judge Gruber* Dan White; *Maria* Geraldine Wall; *David* Lawrence Ung.

REVIEW: "Claude Rains fares best. His role is not explored in any depth, but it has the merit of being easily recognizable and consistent." (*Variety*, April 17, 1959)

1960

THE LOST WORLD
STUDIO: Twentieth Century-Fox. RELEASE DATE: June 27, 1960. RUNNING TIME: 97 minutes. PRODUCER/DIRECTOR: Irwin Allen. SCREENPLAY: Irwin Allen and Charles Bennett, based on the novel by Sir Arthur Conan Doyle. DIRECTOR OF PHOTOGRAPHY: Winton Hoch, ACE. SPECIAL EFFECTS PHOTOGRAPHY: L. B. Abbott, Emil Kosa, and James B. Gordon. EFFECTS TECHNICIAN: Willis O'Brien. FILM EDITOR: Hugh S. Fowler. ART DIRECTORS: Duncan Cramer, Walter M. Simonds, and Ad Schaumer. SET DECORATORS: Walter M. Scott, Joseph Kish, and John Sturtevant. MUSIC: Bert Shefter and Paul Sawtell. ORCHESTRATIONS: Howard Jackson and Sid Cutner. SOUND: E. Clinton Ward and Harry M. Leonard. PRODUCTION ILLUSTRATOR: Maurice Zuberano. COSTUME DESIGNER: Pal Zastupnevich. MAKEUP: Ben Nye. HAIR STYLIST: Helen Turpin.

CAST: *Lord John Roxton* Michael Rennie; *Jennifer Holmes* Jill St. John; *Ed Malone* David Hedison; *Professor George Edward Challenger* Claude Rains; *Manuel Gomez* Fernando Lamas; *Professor Summerlee* Richard Haydn; *David Holmes* Ray Stricklyn; *Costa* Jay Novello; *Native Girl* Vitina Marcus; *Burton White* Ian Wolfe; *Stuart Holmes* John Graham; *Professor Waldron* Colin Campbell.

REVIEW: "Claude Rains, transformed by a somewhat pinkish hairdo and beard, is a caricature of the dedicated, belligerent zoologist." (*New York Times*, July 14, 1960)

Appendix

1960 [1963]

BATTLE OF THE WORLDS

STUDIO: Ultra Films/Sicilia Cinematographica. RELEASE DATE: Italy, 1960; USA, 1963 (a Topaz Films release). RUNNING TIME: 83 minutes. DIRECTOR: Anthony Dawson (Antonio Margheriti). WRITER/DIRECTOR, ENGLISH VERSION: George Higgins III. SCREENPLAY: Vassily Petron. DIRECTOR OF PHOTOGRAPHY: Raffaello Masciocchi. FILM EDITOR: Jorge Serrallonga. PRODUCTION SUPERVISOR: Tommaso Sagone. PRODUCTION ASSISTANTS: Averoe Stefani, Nino Masini, and Cosmo Dies. SOUND: Giovanni Rossi. CAMERA OPERATOR: Cesare Allione. CAMERA ASSISTANT: Danilo Desidero. MUSIC: Mario Migliardi. ASSISTANT DIRECTOR: Renzo Ragazzi. SCRIPT GIRL: Tersicore Koloson.

CAST: *Professor Benjamin Benson* Claude Rains; *Fred Steel* Bill Carter; *Eva Barnett* Maya Brent; *Commander Bob Cole* Umberto Orsini; *Cathy Cole* Jacqueline Derval; *General Varrick* Renzo Palmer; *Mrs. Collins* Carol Danell; with Maria Mustari, Giuliano Gemma, Jim Dolen, John Stacey, Massimo Righi, Joseph Pollini, and Aldo D'Ambrosio.

1962

LAWRENCE OF ARABIA

STUDIO: Columbia. RELEASE DATE: December 16, 1962. RUNNING TIME: 222 minutes. PRODUCERS: Sam Spiegel and David Lean. DIRECTOR: David Lean. ASSISTANT DIRECTOR: Roy Stevens. SECOND UNIT DIRECTORS: Andre Smagghe and Noel Howard. SCREENPLAY: Robert Bolt and Michael Wilson (uncredited). DIRECTOR OF PHOTOGRAPHY: F. A. Young. SECOND UNIT PHOTOGRAPHY: Skeets Kelly, Nicholas Roeg, and Peter Newbrook. FILM EDITOR: Anne V. Coates. ART DIRECTOR: John Stoll. ASSISTANT ART DIRECTORS: Roy Rossotti, George Richardson. PRODUCTION DESIGNER: John Box. MUSIC: Maurice Jarre. MUSICAL ARRANGEMENTS: Gerard Schurmann. MUSICAL COORDINATOR: Morris Stoloff. MUSICAL PERFORMANCE: London Philharmonic Orchestra, conducted by Adrian Boult. SOUND: Winston Ryder and John Cox. SOUND RECORDING: Paddy Cunningham. ASSISTANT DIRECTOR: Roy Stevens. PRODUCTION MANAGER: John Palmer. CONTINUITY: Barbara Cole. WARDROBE: John Wilson Apperson. MAKEUP: Charles Parker. HAIR STYLIST: A. G. Scott.

CAST: *T. E. Lawrence* Peter O'Toole; *Prince Faisal* Alec Guinness; *Auda Abu Tayi* Anthony Quinn; *General Allenby* Jack Hawkins; *Turkish Bey* José Ferrer; *Col Brighton* Anthony Quayle; *Mr. Dryden* Claude Rains; *Jackson Bentley* Arthur Kennedy;

General Murray Donald Wolfit; *Sherif Ali* Omar Sharif; *Gasim* I. S. Johar; *Majid* Gamil Ratib; *Farraj* Michel Ray; *Tafas* Zia Mohyeddin; *Daud* John Dimech; *Medical Officer* Howard Marion Crawford; *Club Secretary* Jack Gwillam; *R.A.M.C. Colonel* Hugh Miller; *Allenby's Aide* Kenneth Fortescue; *Harith Elder* John Ruddock; *Reciter* Henry Oscar; *Turkish Sergeant* Fernando Sancho; *Regimental Sergeant-Major* Stuart Saunders.

REVIEW: "Playing a diplomat, Claude Rains, always fine and now a vintage actor, is simply not on the screen long enough to suit us." (Stanley Kauffmann, *The New Republic*, January 12, 1963)

1963

TWILIGHT OF HONOR
STUDIO: Metro-Goldwyn-Mayer. RELEASE DATE: October 16, 1963. RUNNING TIME: 104 minutes. PRODUCERS: William Perlberg and George Seaton. DIRECTOR: Boris Sagal. SCREENPLAY: Henry Denker, based on the novel by Al Dewlen. DIRECTOR OF PHOTOGRAPHY: Philip Lathrop. CAMERA OPERATOR: Joe Jackman. FILM EDITOR: Hugh S. Fowler. ART DIRECTORS: George W. Davis and Paul Groesse. SET DECORATORS: Henry Grace and Hugh Hunt. MUSIC: John Green (also conductor). RECORDING SUPERVISOR: Franklin Milton. MIXER: Larry Jost. ASSISTANT DIRECTORS: Donald Roberts, Al Shenberg, and Richard Lang. MAKEUP SUPERVISOR: William Tuttle. MAKEUP: Ron Berkeley and Agnes Flanagan. HAIR STYLIST: Mary Keats.

CAST: *David Mitchell* Richard Chamberlain; *Laura Mae Brown* Joey Heatherton; *Ben Brown* Nick Adams; *Art Harper* Claude Rains; *Susan Harper* Joan Blackman; *Norris Bixby* James Gregory; *Cole Clinton* Pat Buttram; *Amy Clinton* Jeanette Nolan; *Judge James Tucker* Edgar Stehli; *Charles Crispin* James Bell; *Paul Farish* George Mitchell; *Judd Elliot* Donald Barry; *Sheriff* Buck Wheeler; *Therese Braden* Robin Raymond; *Vera Driscoll* June Dayton; *Ballentine* Vaughn Taylor; *Alice Clinton* Linda Evans; *McWade* Arch Johnson; with Burt Mustin.

REVIEW: "Rains comes through with his customary brilliance." (*Variety*, September 13, 1963)

1965

THE GREATEST STORY EVER TOLD
STUDIO: United Artists. RELEASE DATE: January 9, 1965. RUNNING TIME: 225 minutes. PRODUCER/DIRECTOR: George Stevens. DIRECTOR, PROLOGUE SEQUENCE (uncredited): David Lean. SCREENPLAY: George

Stevens and James Lee Barrett. EXECUTIVE PRODUCER: Frank I. Davis. AS-
SOCIATE PRODUCERS: George Stevens, Jr., and Antonio Vellani. DIREC-
TORS OF PHOTOGRAPHY: William C. Mellor and Loyal Griggs. FILM EDI-
TORS: Harold F. Kress, Argyle Nelson, and Frank O'Neill. SOUND: Franklin
Milton, William Steinkamp, and Charles Wallace. SET DESIGN: David Hall.
ART DIRECTORS: Richard Day and William Creber. COSTUMES: Vittorio
Nino Novarese and Marjorie Best. SECOND UNIT DIRECTORS: Richard
Talmadge and William Hale. CHORAL SUPERVISOR: Ken Darby. SPECIAL
VISUAL EFFECTS: J. McMillan Johnson, Clarence Slifen, A. Arnold Gillespie,
and Robert R. Hoag. MUSIC: Alfred Newman (also conductor).

CAST: *Jesus* Max Von Sydow; *Mary* Dorothy McGuire; *Joseph* Robert Loggia;
Herod the Great Claude Rains; *Herod Antipas* José Ferrer; *Herodias* Marian Seldes;
Aben John Abbott; *Captain of Lancers* Rodolfo Acosta; *Chuza* Philip Coolidge;
Herod's Commander Michael Ansara; *Archelaus* Joe Perry; *John the Baptist* Charlton
Heston; *The Dark Hermit* Donald Pleasence; *Judas Iscariot* David McCallum; *Mat-
thew* Roddy McDowall; *James the Younger* Michael Anderson, Jr.; *James the Elder*
David Sheiner; *Peter* Gary Raymond; *Simon the Zealot* Robert Blake; *Andrew* Burt
Brinckerhoff; *John* John Considine; *Thaddeus* Jamie Farr; *Philip* David Hedison;
Nathaniel Peter Mann; *Thomas* Tom Reese; *Pilate* Telly Savalas; *Claudia* Angela
Lansbury; *Questor* Paul Stewart; *General Varus* Harold J. Stone; *Melchior* Cyril
Delevanti; *Balthazar* Mark Lenard; *Caspar* Frank Silvera; *Mary Magdalene* Joanna
Dunham; *Mary of Bethany* Ina Balin; *Man at Tomb* Pat Boone; *Lazarus* Michael
Tolan; *Veronica* Carroll Baker; *Uriah* Sal Mineo; *Bar Amand* Van Heflin; *Old
Aram* Ed Wynn; *Woman with No Name* Shelley Winters; *Theophilus* Chet Stratton;
Annas Ron Whelan; *Joseph of Arimathaea* Abraham Sofaer; *Speaker of Capernaum*
John Lupton; *Scribe* Russell Johnson; *Caiaphas* Martin Landau; *Shemiah* Nehemi-
ah Persoff; *Nicodemus* Joseph Schildkraut; *Soark* Victor Buono; *Emmissary* Robert
Busch; *Alexander* John Crawford; *Roman Captain* John Wayne; *Simon of Cyrene*
Sidney Poitier; *Dumah* Joseph Sirola; *Barabbas* Richard Conte.

REVIEW: "There are two exceptions to the generally bad acting. One is Claude
Rains as the sick old Herod who slaughters the innocents. The other is Max Von
Sydow." (Stanley Kauffmann, *The New Republic*, March 6, 1965)

NOTE: Produced "in creative association with Carl Sandburg" and shot in Ultra
Panavision 70 and Technicolor.

Radio and Recording Work

The following are checklists only; for more details, see John Soister's fine work *Claude Rains: A Comprehensive Illustrated Reference* (Jefferson, N.C.: McFarland & Co., 1999).

1932
THE GOOD EARTH (NBC, September 13)

1933
A BILL OF DIVORCEMENT (*The Fleischmann Hour*, NBC, February 2)

1934
THE FLEISCHMANN HOUR (NBC, March 17)

1935
THE GREEN GODDESS (*Lux Radio Theatre*, NBC, January 6)
THE TELL-TALE HEART (*The Fleischmann Hour*, NBC, April 4)
THE LAST OUTPOST (*Hollywood Hotel*, CBS, July 5)

1936
ANTHONY ADVERSE (*Hollywood Hotel*, CBS, July 17 and 24)
MADAME SANS-GENE (*Lux Radio Theatre*, CBS, December 14)

1937
THE GAME OF CHESS (*The Royal Gelatin Hour*, NBC, April 29)
JULIUS CAESAR (*1937 Shakespeare Festival*, CBS, June–July)
GIFT OF THE GODS (*The Royal Gelatin Hour*, NBC, July 1)
THE CASK OF AMONTILLADO (*Sunday Night Party*, NBC, July 18)
KRAFT MUSIC HALL (NBC, August 12)

1938
PARK AVENUE PENNERS (CBS, January 2)
THEY WON'T FORGET (*Warner Brothers Academy Theater*, NBC, spring)
KRAFT MUSIC HALL (NBC, June 9)
WHITE BANNERS (*Hollywood Hotel*, CBS, June 10)
JULIUS CAESAR (*Great Plays*, NBC, November 20)
CONFESSION (*The Lux Radio Theatre*, CBS, November 21)

1939
THERE'S ALWAYS JOE WINTERS (*The Royal Gelatin Hour*, NBC, January 5)

THE EIGERWUND (*The Royal Gelatin Hour*, NBC, March 30)
KIND LADY (*Texaco Star Theatre*, CBS, October 11)
KRAFT MUSIC HALL (NBC, December 28)

1940

THE STORY OF BENEDICT ARNOLD (*Cavalcade of America*, NBC, April 2)
THE LITTLEST REBEL (*Lux Radio Theatre*, CBS, October 14)

1941

AS A MAN THINKETH (*Cavalcade of America*, NBC, January 15)
THE LINCOLN HIGHWAY (NBC, February 22)
CALLING AMERICA (Mutual Network, July 11)
YOUR HAPPY BIRTHDAY (NBC, July 12)
THE HOBO WITH A HARVARD ACCENT (*The Lincoln Highway*, NBC, July 12)
CALLING AMERICA (NBC, July 25)
BLIND ALLEY (*Great Moments from Great Plays*, NBC, August 1)
A MAN TO REMEMBER (*Philip Morris Playhouse*, CBS, September 26)
THE HAUNTING FACE (*Inner Sanctum Mysteries*, ABC, September 28)
MILLIONS FOR DEFENSE (CBS, October 14)
CAPTAIN PAUL (*Cavalcade of America*, NBC, October 27)

1942

HERE COMES MR. JORDAN (*Lux Radio Theatre*, NBC, January 26)
KEEP 'EM ROLLING (Mutual Network, February 2)
CRIMINAL CODE (*Philip Morris Playhouse*, CBS, March 20)
YOU'RE ON YOUR OWN (*This Is War*, CBS, NBC, ABC, and the Mutual Network, March 21)
THE LINCOLN HIGHWAY (NBC, return appearance)
IN THIS CRISIS (*Calvalcade of America*, NBC, April 20)
BACK WHERE YOU CAME FROM (*Plays for Americans*, NBC, June 7)
SOLDIER OF A FREE PRESS (*Calvalcade of America*, NBC, September 7)
UNDERGROUND (*Philip Morris Playhouse*, CBS, September 18)
THE MAN WHO PLAYED WITH DEATH (*Inner Sanctum Mysteries*, ABC, September 27)
THE KING OF DARKNESS (*Inner Sanctum Mysteries*, ABC, October 11)
THE MISSIONARY AND THE GANGSTER (*Radio Reader's Digest*, CBS, October 25)
THE LAUGHING MURDERER (*Inner Sanctum Mysteries*, ABC, November 8)

1943

THE FRENCH UNDERGROUND (*Radio Reader's Digest*, CBS, January 24)
THE TEXACO STAR THEATRE (CBS, February 7)

1945

STAGE DOOR CANTEEN (CBS, March 2)
PHILCO RADIO HALL OF FAME (NBC, March 18)
THE CITADEL (*Theatre of Romance*, CBS, March 20)
PRESIDENT FRANKLIN D. ROOSEVELT: DEATH AND FUNERAL (*A Legacy for America*, CBS, May 15)
DR. CHRISTIAN: DIAGNOSIS AFTER DEATH; JERE TO LIEBE; THE LADY AND THE WOLF (CBS, June 6, 13, 20)

1946

MURDER IN THE BIG BAND (*Radio Reader's Digest*, November 7)
THE FRED ALLEN SHOW (NBC, December 8)

1947

THE WAXWORK (*Suspense*, CBS, March 20)
THE KRAFT MUSIC HALL (NBC, May 8)
MANY MOONS (*Radio Reader's Digest*, CBS, May 9)
FREEDOM PLEDGE (Philadelphia broadcast, September 16)
A PIECE OF STRING (*Radio Reader's Digest*, CBS, October 30)

1948

TOPAZE (*Studio One*, CBS, July 6)
VALLEY FORGE (*Theatre Guild of the Air/U.S. Steel Hour*, ABC, November 14)
THE HANDS OF MR. OTTORMOLE (*Suspense*, CBS, December 2)

1949

THE GAME OF LOVE AND DEATH (*Theatre Guild of the Air/U.S. Steel Hour*, ABC, January 2)
JACK HAS A MUSIC LESSON (*Jack Benny Program*, CBS, February 27)
THE HORN BLOWS AT MIDNIGHT (*Ford Theatre*, CBS, March 4)
BANQUO'S CHAIR (*Philip Morris Playhouse*, CBS, March 25)
THE GOAL IS FREEDOM (CBS, April 4)
EXPERIMENT IN TERROR (Armed Forces Radio Network, May 8)
CRIME WITHOUT PASSION (*Ford Theatre*, CBS, May 20)
MADAME BOVARY (*Ford Theatre*, CBS, October 8)

1950

MR. PEALE AND THE DINOSAUR (*Cavalcade of America*, NBC, March 7)

1952

MIDNIGHT BLUE (*The Big Show*, NBC, January 6)
THE CATBIRD SEAT (*The Big Show*, NBC; February 10)
THREE WORDS (*Cavalcade of America*, NBC, February 19)
THE JEFFERSONIAN HERITAGE (National Association of Broadcasters, fall series)

1953

OUR HIDDEN WEALTH (*Medicine, USA*, NBC, March 28)
THE LIVING DECLARATION (*Kaleidoscope*, NBC, July 4)
PHILADELPHIA ORCHESTRA CONCERT (WFIL Radio, Philadelphia, December 17)

1954

THE CONFIDENTIAL CLERK (excerpts; *Stage Struck: A Review of the 1953–54 Theatrical Season*, CBS, May 21)
THE CROSS EXAMINATION (*First Came the Word*)

1955

BUILDERS OF AMERICA (NBC, May 26)

1956

TITANIC (NBC, March 28)

Television Work

1951

TOAST OF THE TOWN (CBS, April 8)

1953

OMNIBUS (CBS)
"The Bentons at Home" (January 25)
MEDALLION THEATRE (CBS)
"The Man Who Liked Dickens" (August 1)
"The Archer Case" (October 3)
PHILADELPHIA ORCHESTRA CONCERT (WFIL-TV, Philadelphia, December 17)

1954

OMNIBUS (CBS)
The Confidential Clerk (February 14)

1956

ALFRED HITCHCOCK PRESENTS (CBS)
"And So Died Riabouchinska" (February 12)
KRAFT TELEVISION THEATRE (NBC)
"A Night to Remember" (March 28)
THE ALCOA HOUR (NBC)
"President" (May 13)
KAISER ALUMINUM HOUR (NBC)
Antigone (September 11)
GENERAL MOTORS
"Aim to Live" (undated commerical, headlight alignment campaign)

1957

ALFRED HITCHCOCK PRESENTS (CBS)
"The Cream of the Jest" (March 10)
HALLMARK HALL OF FAME
On Borrowed Time (November 17)
THE PIED PIPER OF HAMELIN (NBC, November 26)

1959

ALFRED HITCHOCK PRESENTS (CBS)
"The Diamond Necklace" (February 22)
PLAYHOUSE 90 (CBS)
Judgment at Nuremberg (April 16)
ONCE UPON A CHRISTMAS TIME (CBS, December 9)

1960

NAKED CITY (ABC)
"To Walk in Silence" (September 11)
HALLMARK HALL OF FAME (NBC)
Shangri-La (October 24)

1961

ALFRED HITCHCOCK PRESENTS (NBC)
"The Horseplayer" (March 14)

Appendix

1962

ALFRED HITCHCOCK PRESENTS (NBC)
"The Door without a Key" (January 16)
RAWHIDE (CBS)
"Incident of Judgment Day" (February 8)
WAGON TRAIN (NBC)
"The Daniel Clay Story" (February 21)
DUPONT SHOW OF THE WEEK (NBC)
"The Outpost" (September 16)
SAM BENEDICT (NBC)
"Nor Practice Makes Perfect" (September 29)

1963

BOB HOPE PRESENTS THE CHRYSLER THEATRE (NBC)
"Something About Lee Wiley" (October 11)
DUPONT SHOW OF THE WEEK (NBC)
"The Takers" (October 13)

1964

DR. KILDARE (NBC)
"Why Won't Anybody Listen?" (February 27)
THE REPORTER (CBS)
"A Time to Be Silent" (December 4)

1965

BOB HOPE PRESENTS THE CHRYSLER THEATRE (CBS)
"Cops and Robbers" (February 19)

Recordings

1940s (exact year unknown)

THE CHRISTMAS TREE (Mercury Childcraft Records)

1948

BIBLE STORIES FOR CHILDREN (Capitol Records)

1949

VALLEY FORGE (Fort Orange Radio Distributing Company)

1952

AN EVENING WITH WILL SHAKESPEARE (Theatre Masterworks)

1953

LITERARY READINGS IN THE COOLIDGE AUDITORIUM (The Archive of Recorded Poetry and Literature, Library of Congress)

1957

THE SONG OF SONGS AND THE LETTERS OF HELOISE AND ABE-LARD (Caedmon Records)

1959

BUILDERS OF AMERICA: WASHINGTON AND LINCOLN (Columbia Masterworks)

1960

REMEMBER THE ALAMO (Noble Records)
THE JEFFERSONIAN HERITAGE (National Association of Educational Broadcasters)

1961

ENOCH ARDEN (CBS Records)

Notes and Sources

Claude Rains had an extraordinary facility for memorization, a gift that aided him exceedingly well in learning his roles and that enabled him to vividly recall a multitude of conversations and encounters from his early childhood onward. Unless otherwise noted below, all quotations and memories attributed to Rains in this book are taken from approximately thirty hours of undated audiotape interviews conducted by San Francisco journalist Jonathan Root in the mid-1960s for a biographical project on Rains cut short by the actor's final illness and Root's own premature death. The tapes were eventually purchased by the Rains estate, along with Root's fragmentary chapter drafts and many preliminary notes. The original analog tapes are now part of the Claude Rains Collection at the Howard Gotlieb Archival Research Center at Boston University. (This book utilized Jessica Rains's professionally enhanced digital copies of the originals.) Although Rains's recollections may seem, as presented, so detailed as to suggest some degree of fictionalization, in fact the interviews have been only lightly edited for clarity and grammar. Rains had a near-photographic memory, which served him well as a prompter and stage manager in his early years.

Another major resource was a pair of scrapbooks, lovingly maintained by Audrey Homan, an adoring Rains fan in Britain, covering the actor's stage work in the 1920s and early film work of the 1930s. She made a gift of them to Rains on the occasion of his daughter's birth, fearing for their safety during the looming war. The scrapbooks, unfortunately, largely lack source information (the clippings are taken from dozens of London periodicals, many of them now untraceable), but they nonetheless provide rich and informative documentation. (Sources have been identified wherever possible.) Unsourced, undated, or partial clippings are cited simply in these notes as "Rains scrapbook" unless additional information is available.

All quotes and anecdotes attributed to Jessica Rains are taken from several taped interviews and voluminous personal conversations and e-mail correspondence between the summer of 2000 and the summer of 2005; Jessica provided extensive additional information throughout the book while the manuscript was taking shape. All specific tax information is taken from copies of Rains's tax returns at the Gotlieb Center. Reviews, scrapbook clippings, and ephemera are cited below; full citations for books and major articles are included in the Bibliography.

Introduction

1 HE WAS PERFECT: Roddy McDowall, videotaped interview by Jessica Rains and Aljean Harmetz, 1999.

2 PRIMARY AND MOST INSPIRING: John Gielgud, videotaped interview by Jessica Rains, 1996.

3 I WAS LOST FOR MANY YEARS: Unsourced, undated clipping, Rains scrapbook.

3 I CAN IMAGINE AN AMERICAN FILMGOER: Priestley, *Particular Pleasures*, p. 136.

4 MIXTURE OF DECORUM AND WILDNESS: Thomson, *A Biographical Dictionary of Film*, p. 611.

1. Bloody Idiots Who Couldn't Learn Their Lines

6 1945 OBITUARY: "Fred Rains," *New York Times*, December 4, 1945.

15 THE SON OF A LONDON GRAIN MERCHANT: Useful general background information on Tree's life was found in Pearson, *Beerbohm Tree*, and Cran, *Herbert Beerbohm Tree*.

22 WINKLES: Clyde Fitch, typescript of *The Last of the Dandies* (1901); Billy Rose Theatre Collection, New York Public Library for the Performing Arts.

24 TREE MANAGED THE FIRST LINE OR TWO: Walter Havers, "Call-Boy to Star: The Career of a Great Actor," *London Magazine*, undated clipping, Rains scrapbook.

2. Marriages and Mustard Gas

27 AT VARIOUS TIMES: Claude Rains, carbon copy of unpaginated affidavit, circa 1935, filed in connection with divorce proceedings. Jessica Rains collection.

28 A LARGE "SEVERANCE PAYMENT": Personal communication from Nelson family.

31 FALSE PRIDE AND HIS APPALLING SENSITIVENESS: Walter Havers, "Call-Boy to Star: The Career of a Great Actor," *London Magazine*, undated clipping, Rains scrapbook.

32 HIS BEARING WHEN HE ENTERS: Shaw, *You Never Can Tell*, in *Plays Pleasant*, p. 297.

33 BOUNCED A GOOD DEAL: Unsigned review of *Iphigenia in Taurus*, *New York Times*, May 16, 1915, unpaginated clipping, Jessica Rains collection.

34 A SOLDIER IS A MAN HUNTER: "History of the Regiment," http.//www.londonscottishregt.org/history.cfm.

37 I ONCE ASKED HER HOW SHE GOT ON WITH CLAUDE: John Gielgud, video-taped interview with Jessica Rains, 1996.

37 AFTER THE DIVORCE: Isabel Jeans would later work extensively in film, including three pictures for Alfred Hitchcock: *Downhill* (1926), *Easy Virtue* (1927), and *Suspicion* (1941). She specialized in courtly, grand dame roles and is probably best remembered as Aunt Alicia in *Gigi* (1958). In Rains's estimation, "She became a very mannered actress."

37 I WAS DEMOBILIZED: Rains affidavit.

40 A LITTLE TOO VIGOROUS: Rains scrapbook.

41 A GREAT FAILURE: Gielgud interview.

44 A HAUNTING THING: *Times* (London), Rains scrapbook.

45 NEXT WAS THE ROLE: Immediately after *Daniel*, Rains may have performed in Clemence Dane's *A Bill of Divorcement* at St. Martin's Theatre, though most sources credit the pivotal role of Hilary Fairfield, a shell-shocked soldier divorced by his wife while confined in an asylum, to Malcolm Keen; and Keen did play the role in a silent film version the following year. But the role appears in several published checklists of Rains's stage credits. It is possible that he acted as an unbilled understudy or replacement; but it seems more likely that these sources are confusing the 1921 stage production with Rains's later performance of the role on American radio.

45 THE PRINCIPAL METHOD OF TUITION: Hardwicke, *Let's Pretend*, p. 34.

46 FORMIDABLE INSTRUCTOR: The volatile Elsie Chester is memorably described by Jonathan Croall in *Gielgud: A Theatrical Life*, p. 41; and in Sheri-

dan Morley's *John G: The Authorized Biography of John Gielgud*, in which she is called bluntly "a disabled old bat" (p. 31).

46   I'D HAD ONE PROFESSIONAL JOB: Gielgud interview.

47   I WORKED AS HARD AS I COULD: Gielgud, *Early Stages*, p. 62.

48   HE HAD BEEN HELPING HIS MOTHER: Gielgud interview.

49   A SUCCESSION OF PARABLES: Rains scrapbook.

49   I PLAYED A SMALL PART: Gielgud interview.

50   A "FIRST RATE" ACTOR: Rains scrapbook.

50   MR. CLAUDE RAINS AS DICK DUDGEON: Rains scrapbook.

51   MUST YOU BE SO VERY C-H-A-R-M-I-N-G: Quoted in Soister, *Claude Rains*, p. 211.

51   IT IS TO MR. RAINS'S CREDIT: Rains scrapbook.

52   THE NOTICES WERE ALMOST THE BEST: MacDermott, *Everymania*, pp. 70–71.

53   WAS OMITTED FROM THE PROGRAMME: Rains scrapbook.

54   VILE LITTLE RESTAURANT IN HONG KONG: Ibid.

54   SCOWLED AND DEEPENED; MUCH CLEVERNESS IN THE FIRST TWO ACTS: Ibid.

54   THERE IS SOME BRILLIANT ACTING: Ibid.

56   VERY ATTACHED TO HER "LODGER": Lanchester, *Elsa Lanchester Herself*, p. 85.

56   I'VE BEEN ALL DAY ON THE ROAD: Kaiser, *From Morn to Midnight*, pp. 506–507.

57   WE OBSTINATELY DECLINE: Rains scrapbook.

57   HIS TOUCH IS LIGHT AND SURE: Rains scrapbook.

57   THERE MUST BE SOMETHING RADICALLY WRONG: Rains scrapbook.

3. An Actor Abroad

59   WHY DO YOU WANT TO GO TO AMERICA? John Gielgud, videotaped interview by Jessica Rains, 1996.

60 A FLORID, SHOWY IMPERSONATION: J. Brooks Atkinson, *New York Times*, February 9, 1927.

60 BEATRIX "SUPERB" AND RAINS "EQUALLY SPLENDID": Undated *Philadelphia Ledger* clipping, Rains scrapbook.

61 MY WIFE HAD BEEN INACTIVE: Claude Rains, carbon copy of unpaginated, undated affidavit, circa 1935, filed in connection with divorce proceedings, Jessica Rains collection.

62 HE WAS VERY QUIET: Vincent Sherman, videotaped interview by Jessica Rains, June 1999.

63 BEATRIX REMAINED IN NEW YORK: Rains affidavit.

63 AND IS SHE VERY PROPER? Rains scrapbook.

63 IN NOVEMBER: Rains affidavit.

64 EARLY IN DECEMBER: Ibid.

64 CLAUDE RAINS MAKES A CAPITAL FIGURE: J. Brooks Atkinson, *New York Times*, April 16, 1929.

64 I WENT BACK TO ENGLAND: Rains affadavit.

66 EVERY YEAR OUR FOREMOST DRAMA ORGANIZATION OPENS: Brooks Atkinson, *New York Times*, October 18, 1932.

67 CLAUDE RAINS, WHO IS ONE OF THE BEST ACTORS: Brooks Atkinson, *New York Times*, September 9, 1932.

67 AN ABANDONED COMBINATION: Rains scrapbook.

68 ACCENTUATED HIS DEFORMITIES: *Catholic World*, October 1932.

4. Invisibility and After

71 FILM RIGHTS TO *THE INVISIBLE MAN*: Undated, unpaginated entry for *The Invisible Man*, Universal Pictures, *Catalog of Literary Properties* (Universal Pictures Catalog of Literary Properties, Library of Congress, Washington, DC).

71 $6,000 WAS PAID: Ibid.

72 OH THOU WHO ART INVISIBLE: Gattis, *James Whale: A Biography*, p. 175.

73 OUR MEAL OF HORROR IS NOT COMPLETE: Ibid, p. 177.

74 DIDN'T EVEN POSSESS A REFERENCE COPY: Curtis, *James Whale*, pp. 199–200, for Weld.

74 INVISIBLE LUNATIC: Haining, ed., *H. G. Wells Scrapbook*, p. 124.

75 TERMS OF THE CONTRACT: Rains's personal copy of the *Invisible Man* contract has not survived, but for point of comparison, Karloff had found a salary of $750 a week unacceptable.

76 WE USED A COMPLETELY BLACK SET: John P. Fulton, "How We Made *The Invisible Man*," *American Cinematographer*, September 1931.

76 WE PHOTOGRAPHED THOUSANDS OF FEET OF FILM: Ibid.

77 FIRST, THERE WAS THE SHOT OF THE WALL AND THE MIRROR: Ibid. A visual reconstruction of the complicated matte process is included in my documentary *Now You See Him: The Invisible Man Revealed*, included on Universal Home Video's DVD edition of *The Invisible Man*, hosted and narrated by film historian Rudy Behlmer.

77 ON AT LEAST ONE OCCASION: Ibid.

78 THE OPTICAL WORK PROVED FAR MORE EXPENSIVE: *Invisible Man* production file memorandum, Universal collection, University of Southern California Film and Television Archive, Los Angeles, California.

78 A BIT "POTSCHKE": Gloria Stuart, videotaped interview by the author, August 1997.

78 UNANTICIPATED TREATMENT: Although Gloria Stuart has recounted this now-legendary anecdote, with some slight variations, to numerous interviewers, a close viewing of the film raises questions about the story. Stuart and Rains have only one scene together (in the film's final moments she plays to Rains's voice, which emanates from an empty bed), and they appear together in only a handful of static camera setups, none of which offers Rains the opportunity to back anyone into the camera. The shot in which he greets her shows the performers meeting face-on behind a low piece of furniture; Rains, appearing taller than Stuart, is obviously standing on a fixed-position platform or box; there would be no way he could perform an upstaging maneuver. Two subsequent shots, showing Jack Griffin leading Stuart to a window seat and later to the door, appear to employ a double for Rains, because Stuart, wearing high heels (not acting in stocking feet as claimed), is almost exactly the same height as the Invisible Man. The rest of the sequence consists of the actors seated, Rains standing once, with several static close-ups intercut. Stuart's account may

describe some preliminary rehearsal, but almost certainly not the scene as it was actually filmed.

78   AN "ACTOR'S ACTOR": Milano, *Monsters*, pp. 118–119.

79   WELL, WELL, YOUR FIRST TRIP TO CALIFORNIA: Vincent Sherman, video-taped interview by Jessica Rains, June 1999.

79   WITH RED WIRE WHEELS: Ibid.

80   EVERYBODY WORRIED: Gordon, *My Side*, p. 298.

81   WHEN THE SCRIPT WAS FINISHED: Rains scrapbook.

81   A MOST FORCEFUL CONVERSATIONALIST: Ibid.

81   AND THAT'S MY IDEA: Ibid.

81   BELIEVE IT OR NOT: Ibid.

81   CHARLIE AND BEN LOOKED AT ONE ANOTHER: Ibid.

82   MARGO'S CASTING: Margo eventually was given a five-year contract with RKO and later married the actor Eddie Albert.

82   TRICKY DOUBLE-EXPOSURE SEQUENCE: Rains quoted in *Film Weekly*, Rains scrapbook.

84   EXTRAORDINARILY CLEAR CHARACTERIZATION: Mordaunt Hall, review of *Crime without Passion*, *New York Times*, January 9, 1935.

84   I WAS PRETTY SURE: Review of *Crime without Passion*, *Family Circle*, Rains scrapbook.

84   NOT A PICTURE FOR THE PEOPLE: Louella O. Parsons, review of *Crime without Passion*, *Los Angeles Examiner*, January 9, 1935.

85   LOWELL SHERMAN WAS MENTIONED . . . STUDIO GOT A BARGAIN: Universal Pictures interoffice memoranda (1935) on *The Man Who Reclaimed His Head*, University of Southern California Film and Television Library, Los Angeles. Despite receiving top billing, Rains still wasn't quite able to command top pay. For *The Man Who Reclaimed His Head*, Joan Bennett, in the part of Verin's wife, Adele, received a flat fee of $12,500; Lionel Atwill, another celebrated émigré from the New York theatre, received $2,000 a week.

85   HAS THE OVERWROUGHT AND UNDERDONE LOOK: Andre Sennwald, review of *The Man Who Reclaimed His Head*, *New York Times*, January 9, 1935.

85   TWO OF THE CHOICEST MAD SCIENTIST ROLES: The parts eventually went

to Peter Lorre, making his American screen debut in *Mad Love*; and Ernest Thesiger, who made the part of Dr. Pretorious his own in *Bride of Frankenstein*.

86   RAINS IMPARTS A WEALTH OF WEIRDNESS: Review of *Mystery of Edwin Drood*, *Variety*, March 27, 1935.

88   IT HAD MORE SUBSTANCE: Fay Wray, audiotaped interview by Terry Pace, 2004; transcript courtesy of Mr. Pace.

89   SEEMED TO ME ALL THE WHILE TO REFLECT: Wray, "Claude Rains as I Know Him," *Film Weekly*, August 9, 1935, Rains scrapbook.

89   CLAUDE RAINS DOMINATES: Review of *The Clairvoyant*, *Film Weekly*, Rains scrapbook.

5. Mr. Rains Goes to Burbank

91   HERE IS A REAL-LIFE DRAMA: "'Am I Married?' Asks Actress," *Daily Sketch*, undated clipping, Rains scrapbook.

92   THE SCRIPT I WAS PRESENTED WITH: Rains, letter to Freedman, 1935, Lucy Chase Williams collection.

93   MR. RAINS' LOW HUSKY VOICE: Graham Greene, review of *The Last Outpost*, *The Spectator*, October 1935.

93   IMPRESSIVE LONG-TERM CONTRACT: Claude Rains contract file, 1936–1946, Warner Bros. collection, University of Southern California, Los Angeles.

94   THE ARTIST AGREES TO CONDUCT HIMSELF: Ibid.

95   IN ADDITION TO BEING A TENDER ROMANCE: Louella Parsons, review of *Hearts Divided*, *Los Angeles Examiner*, June 12, 1936.

96   IN THE HANDS OF AN ACTOR: W. H. Mooring, review of *Anthony Adverse*, *Film Weekly*, undated clipping, Rains scrapbook.

96   IF THE PICTURE IS AT ALL DISTINGUISHED: Review of *Stolen Holiday*, *New York Times*, February 1, 1937.

97   FOR ITS PERFECTION, CHIEF CREDIT MUST GO TO MR. LEROY: Frank Nugent, review of *They Won't Forget*, *New York Times*, July 15, 1937.

98   ANXIOUS TO START A FAMILY: Vincent Sherman, videotaped interview by Jessica Rains, June 1999.

98   A STORY OF UGLINESS: Frank Nugent, review of *Gold Is Where You Find It*, *New York Times*, February 14, 1938.

99   A DAUGHTER THEY NAMED JENNIFER: Later known as Jessica, she would be Rains's only child.

100   DEAR JACK: Behlmer, ed., *Inside Warner Bros.*, p. 82.

100   UNDER OUR CONTRACT WITH CLAUDE RAINS: Rains contract file.

101   HIS PERFORMANCE WAS SO REAL: Davis quoted in Etheridge, "Bette Davis and Claude Rains."

101   EVERY NOW AND THEN: Ibid.

101   IT HAS COME TO MY ATTENTION: Rains contract file.

103   I DO NOT BELIEVE THAT MR. ENFIELD: Rains contract file.

103   WE LEAFED AND LEAFED: Capra, *The Name above the Title*, pp. 261–262.

104   HAWKS'S AND RAINS'S ATTITUDE: Rains contract file. Trilling noted also that Warners wanted Rains for the part of Sir Francis Bacon in their upcoming production *The Knight and the Lady*, but that he believed that Rains would do the Capra film instead. The Warners movie, eventually retitled *The Private Lives of Elizabeth and Essex* and starring Bette Davis and Errol Flynn, featured Donald Crisp as Bacon.

104   LISTEN, JEFF: Sidney Buchman, *Mr. Smith Goes to Washington* (screenplay), in Gassner and Nichols, eds., *Twenty Best Film Plays*, p. 627. The final cut of the film trimmed the speech somewhat.

105   BUCHMAN HATED THE SUICIDE ATTEMPT: McBride, *Frank Capra*, p. 416.

106   GROTESQUE DISTORTION: Quoted in Capra, *The Name above the Title*, p. 287.

106   JOSEPH P. KENNEDY WIRED: Ibid., p. 289.

106   THOSE WEREN'T BUTTERFLIES IN HER STOMACH: Capra quoted in Oller, *Jean Arthur*, p. 3.

107   RAINS BEGAN RENEGOTIATING: Rains contract file.

109   I TARGETED THE SCREENPLAY: Curt Siodmak, introduction to Riley, ed., *MagicImage Film Books Presents The Wolf Man*.

109   HOW ANYBODY COULD POSSIBLY CLEAN UP "KINGS ROW": Ted Le Berthon, undated clipping, *Los Angeles Daily News* opinion piece on *Kings Row*, Mo-

tion Picture Producers and Directors Association censor's file on *Kings Row*, Margaret Herrick Library, Academy of Motion Picture Arts and Sciences, Beverly Hills, California.

110 DEFINITELY UNACCEPTABLE: Ibid.

110 DECLINED INSTANTLY: Wallis and Higham, *Starmaker*, p. 101.

110 BETTE DAVIS WANTED THE PART: Ibid.: "Bette Davis wanted to play it, but we all felt the picture would be thrown off balance because of her fame and talent."

6. Now, Contract Player

114 TURNED DOWN THE PART: Wallis and Higham, *Starmaker*, pp. 105–106.

114 FREUDIAN CLICHÉS: They weren't quite clichés at the time, and novelist Prouty herself had benefited from psychiatric treatment following a breakdown. *Now, Voyager*, as both novel and film, did much to demystify psychiatry for a lay audience; in particular, the character of Dr. Jaquith, played so sympathetically by Rains, portrayed psychiatry as especially user-friendly to women. Prouty is today perhaps best known as the academic and psychiatric benefactor of Sylvia Plath.

115 POLISHED AND EVEN-TEMPERED: Review of *Now, Voyager*, *New York Times*, October 23, 1942.

116 YOU CANNOT SELL ME: Ingrid Bergman, interview in Anobile, ed., *Film Classics Library: Casablanca*, p. 5.

116 KOCH RECALLED: Koch, *Casablanca: Script and Legend*, p. 22.

116 I DIDN'T KNOW FROM ONE DAY TO THE OTHER: Bergman, interview in Anobile, *Film Classics Library*, p. 6.

117 BREEN OFFICE INSISTED: Behlmer, ed. *Inside Warner Bros.*, pp. 212–213.

117 BOGART DRANK: For detailed observations of Bogart's chronic alcohol dependence, see Sperber and Lax, *Bogart*.

118 ACTOR LEONID KINSKEY: Mank, *The Hollywood Hissables*, p. 324.

118 PETER LORRE . . . RECALLED RAINS'S PERFECTIONISM: Mank, ibid.

118 MR. RAINS IS PROPERLY SLIPPERY: Review of *Casablanca*, *New York Times*, January 10, 1943.

119 THEY WANTED A TREMENDOUS LONG VIEW: Bergman, interview in Anobi-le, *Film Classics Library*, p. 7.

119 CLAUDE RAINS INADVERTENTLY SAVED THE ENDING: Aljean Harmetz, videotaped interview by Jessica Rains, 1996.

119 RAINS IS IN PENNSYLVANIA: Behlmer, ed., *Inside Warner Bros.*, p. 217.

119 WE NEEDED A GOOD PUNCH LINE: Wallis and Higham, *Starmaker*, p. 91.

120 CLAUDE RAINS . . . DOES NOT IMPRESS: *Variety*, review of *Forever and a Day*, January 20, 1943.

121 ARTHUR LUBIN REMEMBERED: MacQueen, "'43 *Phantom* Found New Formula for Classic Tale."

121 TOLD FILM HISTORIAN SCOTT MACQUEEN: Ibid.

123 HER HUSBAND HAD BEEN ATTACKED: Higham outlines the theory in his Davis biography *Bette*.

123 BECAUSE BETTE DAVIS IS A SLOW DIRECTOR: Freedland, *The Warner Brothers*, p. 163.

124 HE FORGOT HIS CHARACTER: Davis quoted in Etheridge, "Bette Davis and Claude Rains."

125 RAINS HAD GREAT CONCENTRATION: Vincent Sherman, videotaped interview by Jessica Rains, June 1999.

125 DEMONSTRATES THE HORRORS OF EGOCENTRICITY: James Agee, review of *Mr. Skeffington*, *Nation*, June 3, 1944, p. 661.

126 IS ALTOGETHER DELIGHTFUL: Bosley Crowther, *New York Times*, November 1, 1945.

132 THIS PRESS FOOLISHNESS: Dukore, ed., *Bernard Shaw and Gabriel Pascal*, p. 167.

132 UNTIL HE DESCENDED ON ME: George Bernard Shaw, foreword to Deans, *Meeting at the Sphinx*, p. vii.

133 HE SHOCKS ME BY HIS UTTER INDIFFERENCE: Ibid.

133 I PITY POOR RANK: Shaw quoted in Dukore, ed., *Bernard Shaw and Gabriel Pascal*, p. 169.

134 OLD AND STRINGY: Walker, *Vivien*, p. 168.

134 SHOULD NOT HAVE A DIRECTOR: Robson quoted in Dukore, ed., *Collected Screenplays*, p. 134.

134 THE FIRST AUTHORITY I LOOKED UP: Rains scrapbook.

135 HAD NO COUNTERPART IN EGYPT: Pascal, *The Disciple and His Devil*, p. 109.

135 THE SUN WAS SHINING: Ibid.

135 PROFESSIONALLY HE IS NOT AN EASY MAN: Deans, *Meeting at the Sphinx*, pp. 72–73.

136 HADN'T MADE A FILM IN EIGHT YEARS: Ainley's last film role was as the exiled duke in *As You Like It* (1936), starring Laurence Olivier.

7. MacGuffins, Deceptions, Domestic Recriminations

141 IT IS DIFFICULT NOT TO FIND: D. Mosdell, undated review of *Notorious* in *The Canadian Forum*, cited in Deschner, *The Films of Cary Grant*, p. 186.

142 WHAT SEEMED TO BE A JINX: Lawrence, *Actor: The Life and Times of Paul Muni*, pp. 289–290.

142 THAT'S QUITE A PART YOU'VE GOT THERE, CLAUDIE: Davis quoted in Etheridge, "Bette Davis and Claude Rains."

142 THE CENSORS RUINED IT: Ibid.

143 SHOULD HAVE CONCLUDED AS A COMEDY: Rapper quoted in Higham and Greenberg, *The Celluloid Muse*, p. 203.

143 IT IS THE CHARACTER OF HOLLENIUS: Review of *Deception*, *Newsweek*, October 28, 1946, p. 93.

143 A FRIEND OF STOKOWSKI: Rains scrapbook.

143 CLAUDE RAINS RIGHTFULLY STOLE THE PICTURE: Davis quoted in Etheridge, "Bette Davis and Claude Rains."

144 IN VIEW OF THE FACT: Letter from Mike Levee to Jack Warner, 1946 contract file, Warner Bros. Collection, University of Southern California, Los Angeles.

144 THE FILM WAS A FINANCIAL . . . SUCCESS: According to Soister (*Claude Rains*, p. 162), *The Unsuspected* earned $875,000 above its costs.

146 DAVID LEAN LIKED CLAUDE: Ronald Neame, videotaped interview by Jessica Rains, 1999.

146 I SAID I WAS GOING TO STOP THE PICTURE: Quoted in Brownlow, *David Lean*, p. 253.

147   CLAUDE ALWAYS AMUSED ME: Ibid.

147   I KNEW HE WAS A HEAVY DRINKER: Neame interview.

149   CLAUDE RAINS . . . IS SOMETHING OF A BORE: Bosley Crowther, review of *The White Tower, New York Times*, July 3, 1950.

150   MURMURING MY WAY THROUGH THE MOVIES: "Gratified Old Revolutionary," *New Yorker*, February 15, 1951, p. 25.

151   I SEARCHED MY SOUL: Robinson, *All My Yesterdays*, p. 257.

151   LIES: Kingsley, *Sidney Kingsley: Five Prizewinning Plays*, ed. Nina Couch, p. 335.

151   WARM FRIENDS: Ibid., p 335.

151   CLAUDE HAD A DOUBLE PROBLEM: Ibid.

152   NO "JACK" OR "CLAUDE": Seff, *Supporting Player*, p. 56.

152   HE'D ALWAYS PUT SIDNEY OFF: Hunter quoted in Soister, *Claude Rains*, p. 249.

153   FUCK SIDNEY KINGSLEY: Ibid.

153   I FIND IT QUITE A JOB: "Gratified Old Revolutionary."

153   CLAUDE USED TO GATHER US: Richard Seff, correspondence to the author, February 16, 2008.

153   UNFORTUNATELY, DICKIE: Seff, *Supporting Player*, p. 61.

154   SORT OF DRIBBLED TO AN END: Seff correspondence.

154   THIS WAS AN ERA: Seff, *Supporting Player*, p. 61.

154   MARY MARTIN: Ibid., p. 60.

155   IT SEEMED TO ME: Robinson, *All My Yesterdays*, p. 267.

156   UNHAPPILY SQUANDERED: *Time*, December 17, 1956.

157   WHENEVER I CAME TO NEW YORK: Neame interview.

158   THEY FOUND HIM NEAR THE CAR: Untitled, undated clipping fragment, *West Chester Citizen*, Rains scrapbook. This was not Rains's first traffic mishap. He recalled that he originally learned to drive after only four lessons, and then promptly bumped into a policeman.

159   BRADBURY HIMSELF WAS IN AWE: Ray Bradbury, conversation with author, August 2006.

160 WHEN THE PLAY CLOSED: *New York World Telegram and Sun*, undated clippings, Rains scrapbook.

8. New Stages and Final Curtains

162 STUDIO PUBLICIST BOB RAINS: Bob Rains, *Beneath the Hollywood Tinsel*, pp. 115–17.

168 SARCASTIC AND DISMISSIVE REVIEWS: Reviews of *The Lost World*: *Time*, July 18, 1960; *New York Times*, July 14, 1960.

169 IT WAS LIKE HAVING MR. SKEFFINGTON: Ariane Ulmer, in conversation with the author, August 2007.

170 THEY SET TO WORK WITH MUTUAL SUSPICION: Chapin, *Musical Chairs*, p. 145.

170 PLAYING A DIPLOMAT: Stanley Kauffmann, review of *Lawrence of Arabia*, *The New Republic*, January 12, 1963, p. 28.

171 LEAN "WAS ON ANOTHER PLANET POLITICALLY": Kevin Brownlow, correspondence to the author, May 2008.

174 DEAR MR. RAINS: Undated 1964 fan mail, Claude Rains Collection, Howard Gotlieb Archival Research Center, Boston University.

175 THE TWO MEN WERE WAITING TO SEE: Jonathan Root, undated notes (circa 1965) for proposed biography, *The Love Habit*, Jessica Rains collection.

176 HE WAS FLYING DOWN: Ibid.

179 CLAUDE, DEAR: Bette Davis, handwritten note to Claude Rains, circa August 1965, Claude Rains Collection, Howard Gotlieb Archival Research Center, Boston University.

179 THE COMPANY REVERED RAINS: Joanna Miles, telephone interview with the author, February 2008.

179 IT IS TORPID THEATRE: Review of *So Much of Earth, So Much of Heaven*, *Variety*, September 8, 1963.

180 I REGRET TO TELL YOU: Letter from Nochem S. Winnet to Jonathan Root, September 10, 1965, Jessica Rains collection.

181 ALL THINGS ONCE ARE THINGS FOREVER: Richard Monckton Milnes, Lord Houghton, excerpt from "Ghazeles" in Nicholson and Lee, eds., *The Oxford Book of English Mystical Verse*, pp. 156–157:

All things once are things forever;
Soul, once living, lives forever;
Blame not what is only once,
When that once endures forever;
Love, once felt, though soon forgot,
Moulds the heart to good for ever;
Once betrayed from childly faith,
Man is conscious man forever;
Once the void of life revealed,
It must deepen on forever,
Unless God fill up the heart
With himself for once and ever;
Once made God and man at once,
God and man are one forever.

183 HE WAS AN IMMACULATE ACTOR: Vincent Sherman, videotaped interview by Jessica Rains, June 1999.

183 I FEEL LIKE CLAUDE: De Marinis, *A Lovely Monster*, p. 163.

Bibliography

Anobile, Richard J., ed. *Film Classics Library: Casablanca*. London: Picador, 1974.

Beerbohm, Max. *Herbert Beerbohm Tree: Some Memories of Him and of His Art*. London: Hutchinson & Co. [1919?]

Behlmer, Rudy, ed. *Inside Warner Bros., 1935–1951*. New York: Viking Penguin, 1985.

Brownlow, Kevin. *David Lean: A Biography*. New York: St. Martin's Press, 1996.

Capra, Frank. *The Name above the Title: An Autobiography*. New York: Macmillan, 1971.

Capua, Michelangelo. *Vivien Leigh: A Biography*. Jefferson, N.C.: McFarland and Co., 2003.

Chapin, Schuyler. *Musical Chairs: A Life in the Arts*. New York: G. P. Putnam's Sons, 1977.

Chapman, John, ed. *The Best Plays of 1950–1951 and the Yearbook of the Drama in America*. New York: Dodd, Mead and Co., 1951.

Cran, Mrs. George. *Herbert Beerbohm Tree*. London: John Lane, the Bodley Head, 1909.

Croall, Jonathan. *Gielgud: A Theatrical Life*. London: Methuen, 2001.

Curtis, James. *James Whale: A New World of Gods and Monsters*. London: Faber and Faber, 1998.

Deans, Marjorie. *Meeting at the Sphinx: Gabriel Pascal's Production of Bernard Shaw's Caesar and Cleopatra*. London: MacDonald & Co., 1946.

De Marinis, Rick. *A Lovely Monster: The Adventures of Claude Rains and Dr. Tellenbeck*. New York: Simon and Schuster, 1975.

Deschner, Donald. *The Films of Cary Grant*. Secaucus, N.J.: Citadel Press, 1973.

Dukore, Bernard F., ed. *Bernard Shaw and Gabriel Pascal*. Toronto: University of Toronto Press, 1996.

——, ed. *The Collected Screenplays of Bernard Shaw*. Athens: University of Georgia Press, 1980.

Edwards, Anne. *Vivien Leigh: A Biography*. New York: Simon & Schuster, 1977.

Etheridge, Ann. "Bette Davis and Claude Rains: Two Opposites that Attracted." *American Classic Screen* 5, no. 2: 9–13.

Freedland, Michael. *The Warner Brothers*. New York, St. Martin's Press, 1983.

Gassner, John, and Dudley Nichols, eds. *Twenty Best Film Plays*. New York: Crown Publishers, 1943.

Gattis, Mark. *James Whale: A Biography*. London: Cassell, 1995.

Gielgud, John. *Backward Glances*. London: Hodder & Stoughton, 1989.

———. *Early Stages: 1921–1936*. New York: Taplinger Publishing Co., 1976.

Gordon, Ruth. *My Side: The Autobiography of Ruth Gordon*. New York: Harper & Row, 1976.

Haining, Peter, ed. *The H. G. Wells Scrapbook*. New York: Clarkson N. Potter, 1978.

Hardwicke, Cedric. *Let's Pretend*. London: Grayson & Grayson, 1932.

Harmetz, Aljean. *Round Up the Usual Suspects: The Making of Casablanca–Bogart, Bergman, and World War II*. New York: Hyperion, 1992.

Higham, Charles. *Bette: The Life of Bette Davis*. New York: Macmillan Publishing Co., 1969.

Higham, Charles, and Joel Greenberg. *The Celluloid Muse: Hollywood Directors Speak*. London: Angus and Robertson, 1969.

Kael, Pauline, *5001 Nights at the Movies*. New York: Holt, Rinehart and Winston, 1982.

Kaiser, Georg. *From Morn to Midnight*. In Haskell M. Block and Robert G. Shedd, eds., *Masters of Modern Drama*. New York: Random House, 1962.

Kingsley, Sidney. *Darkness at Noon: A Play Based on the Novel by Arthur Koestler*. New York: Random House, 1951.

———. *Sidney Kingsley: Five Prizewinning Plays*. Ed. Nina Couch. Columbus: Ohio State University Press, 1995.

Koch, Howard. *Casablanca: Script and Legend*. Woodstock, N.Y.: Overlook Press, 1973.

Lanchester, Elsa. *Elsa Lanchester Herself*. New York: St. Martin's Press, 1983.

Lawrence, Jerome. *Actor: The Life and Times of Paul Muni*. New York: G. P. Putnam's Sons, 1974.

MacDermott, Norman. *Everymania: The History of the Everyman Theatre*. London: Society for Theatre Research, 1975.

MacQueen, Scott. "'43 *Phantom* Found New Formula for Classic Tale," *American Cinematographer*, September 1993, pp. 80–85.

Mank, Gregory William. *The Hollywood Hissables*. Metuchen, N.J.: Scarecrow Press, 1989.

Mantle, Burns. *The Best Plays of 1919–1920 and the Year Book of the Drama in America*. (Reprint.) New York: Dodd, Mead & Co., 1962.

McBride, Joseph. *Frank Capra: The Catastrophe of Success*. New York: Simon and Schuster, 1992.

McDowall, Roddy. *Double Exposure: Take Two*. New York: William Morrow and Co., 1989.

Bibliography

Milano, Ray. *Monsters: A Celebration of the Classics from Universal Studios*. Ed. Jennifer Osborne. New York: Del Rey Books, 2006.

Mooring, W. H. "He Hates Humbug," *Film Weekly*, April 2, 1935, p. 11.

Morley, Sheridan. *John G: The Authorized Biography of John Gielgud*. London: Hodder & Stoughton, 2001.

Nadel, Norman. *A Pictorial History of the Theatre Guild*. New York: Crown Publishers, 1969.

Nicholson, D. H. S., and A. H. E. Lee, eds. *The Oxford Book of English Mystical Verse*. Oxford: Clarendon Press, 1917.

Oller, John. *Jean Arthur: The Actress Nobody Knew*. New York: Limelight Editions, 1997.

Ostwald, Peter. *Vaslav Nijinsky: A Leap into Madness*. New York: Carroll Publishing Group, 1991.

Pascal, Valerie. *The Disciple and His Devil*. New York: McGraw-Hill Book Co., 1970.

Pearson, Hesketh. *Beerbohm Tree: His Life and Laughter*. London: Methuen and Co., 1956.

Porter, Katherine. "The Plow and the Star." *Collier's*, November 19, 1938.

Priestley, J. B. *Particular Pleasures*. London: Heinemann, 1975.

Rains, Bob. *Beneath the Hollywood Tinsel: The Human Side of Hollywood Stars*. Prospect, Conn.: Biographical Publishing Co., 2001.

Riley, Philip J., ed. *MagicImage Film Books Presents The Wolf Man: The Original 1941 Shooting Script*. Abescon, N.J.: MagicImage Filmbooks, 1993.

Roberts, Katherine. "The Plow and the Star." *Collier's*, November 19, 1938, p. 13.

Robinson, Edward G., with Leonard Spigelgass. *All My Yesterdays: An Autobiography*. New York: Hawthorn Books, 1973.

Salmon, Eric, ed. *Granville Barker and His Correspondents*. Detroit: Wayne State University Press, 1986.

Seff, Richard. *Supporting Player: My Life upon the Wicked Stage*. Philadelphia: Xlibris Corp., 2006.

Shaw, George Bernard. *Plays Pleasant*. (Reprint of 1898 ed.) London: Penguin Books, 2003.

——. *Selected Correspondence of Bernard Shaw, vol. 3: Bernard Shaw and Gabriel Pascal*, ed. Bernard F. Dukore. Toronto: University of Toronto Press, 1996.

Silke, James R. *Here's Looking at You, Kid: Fifty Years of Fighting, Working, and Dreaming at Warner Bros*. Boston: Little, Brown and Co., 1976.

Soister, John T., with Joanna Wioskowski. *Claude Rains: A Comprehensive Illustrated Reference*. Jefferson, N.C.: McFarland & Co., 1999.

Sperber, A. M., and Eric Lax. *Bogart*. New York: William Morrow and Co., 1997.

Spoto, Donald. *The Dark Side of Genius: The Life of Alfred Hitchcock*. Boston: Little, Brown and Co., 1983.

Stine, Whitney. *Mother Goddam: The Story of the Career of Bette Davis*. New York: Hawthorn Books, 1974.

Thomson, David. *A Biographical Dictionary of Film*. 3rd ed. New York: Alfred A Knopf, 1994.

Truffaut, François. *Hitchcock*. New York: Touchstone/Simon and Schuster, 1967.

Universal Studios. *Monsters: A Celebration of Universal's Classics*.

Waldau, Roy S. *Vintage Years of the Theatre Guild: 1928–1939*. Cleveland: The Press of Case Western Reserve University, 1972.

Walker, Alexander. *Vivien: The Life of Vivien Leigh*. New York: Weidenfeld and Nicolson, 1987.

Wallis, Hal, and Charles Higham. *Starmaker: The Autobiography of Hal Wallis*. New York: Macmillan, 1980.

Waring, J. P. *The London Stage: A Calendar of Plays and Players, 1900–1929*. 3 vols. Metuchen, N.J.: Scarecrow Press, 1981–1983.

Weaver, Tom, Michael Brunas, and John Brunas. *Universal Horrors: The Studio's Classic Films, 1931–1946*. 2nd ed. Jefferson, N.C.: McFarland & Co., 2007.

Wray, Fay. "Claude Rains as I Know Him." *Film Weekly*, August 9, 1935.

Index

Index

Index

Index